Marriages And Deaths From Lynchburg, Virginia Newspapers 1794-1836

Compiled by
Lucy Harrison Miller Baber
Louise Ann Blunt
Marion Armistead Lewis Collins

CLEARFIELD COMPANY

Reprinted for Clearfield Company, Inc.
by Genealogical Publishing Company Inc.
Baltimore, Maryland
1993

Copyright © 1980
Genealogical Publishing Co., Inc.
Baltimore, Maryland
All Rights Reserved
Library of Congress Catalogue Card Number 79-55836
International Standard Book Number 0-8063-0874-5
Made in the United States of America

Sponsored by
RANDALL HOLT CHAPTER
National Society Daughters of the American Colonists

Associates in Research

Caroline Davies Wise Baber
Mary Stuart Carmichael
Ellis Nowlin Cosby
Esther Draughon Dotson
Mary Rebecca Foster
Martha B. Hancock
Beatrice Jameson Hehl
Elizabeth Spencer Hopkins
Wilda Vehlow Menagh
Carletta Sterling Mixer
Ada McDaniel Nolan
Elizabeth Bailey Norman
Katherine Wingfield Perrow
Elizabeth Hudson Rorabaugh

Preface

HIS BOOK is the result of a two-year project of the Randall Holt Chapter, NSDAC, in which seventeen members participated. The project was begun under Carletta Sterling Mixer, Regent, and concluded under Louise Ann Blunt, Regent.

This project was an attempt to abstract and compile all facts as to marriages and deaths found in extant copies of Lynchburg newspapers published from 1794 through 1836. Such an undertaking was made possible, and its usefulness immeasurably increased, by having had access to the carefully preserved file of early Lynchburg newspapers held by the Jones Memorial Library in Lynchburg. Their treasured file is remarkably complete, despite the fact that some issues are understandably missing. We are indebted to Josephine B. Wingfield, then Librarian, for granting us the privilege of examining fragile originals when photocopies or microfilm copies were illegible. We also appreciate the courteous assistance provided us by the Library staff, especially Delores Swanson and Eric Frank.

Originally planned as two separate volumes, one on marriages the other on deaths, the material was reworked for this publication into one book with two parts. Part I, the section on marriages, consists of a single alphabetical listing which includes all brides and grooms. The amount of detail in the paid notices or the news accounts varied considerably but generally included the date and place of marriage, name of bride's parents and name of the officiating minister or official.

The deaths, which constitute Part II, are also alphabetically arranged. Information includes date and place of death, age at death and in many instances, the place of birth and former place of residence of the deceased. Reference is frequently made to civil or military service. Interestingly, there are more than seventy references to Revolutionary War service. The paper usually referred to the cause of death, but it has been included here only if the circumstances were unusual, or if insight was provided into medical knowledge and problems of the times. The infant mortality rate reflected is astounding.

Throughout the book references are made to specific pages and columns of a newspaper. In recording place-references, the name of a state follows that of a city or county only if it is other than the State of Virginia.

We are grateful to John Frederick Dorman, F.A.S.G., for writing the *Introduction* providing background information and an appraisal of the book's genealogical usefulness.

We appreciate Kathleen Shaner Eubank's painstaking typing of the manuscript; and Jacquelin Ambler Nicholas Harvey's invaluable help in finalizing the manuscript for publication.

The inclusion of a few 1837 entries was not intended. We have tried to be accurate and regret any transcribing errors.

Introduction

S THE LARGEST TOWN in the upper James River Valley, Lynchburg has long been a commercial and cultural center in central Virginia. *The Union Gazette,* established in 1793 by Robert Mosby Bransford and the next year titled *Lynchburg and Farmer's Gazette,* continued only to 1796, but other newspapers were founded within the next few years. *The Lynchburg Press* was first published on 6 May 1809, with Fleming Grantland as printer and Samuel K. Jennings as editor. After several changes of ownership and an expansion of the title to *Lynchburg Press and Public Advertiser,* it was in 1820 published by John Hampden Pleasants, who after 1822 continued as editor of the *Lynchburg Virginian* until his removal to Richmond two years later to begin his distinguished career as editor of the *Whig.* Throughout the nineteenth century, until its demise in 1893, the *Lynchburg Virginian* was the principal newspaper in the city.

The Lynchburg newspapers served the inhabitants of a wide area, and the marriage and obituary notices printed in them provide vital statistics relating to many Virginians. Of particular importance are the many references to residents of Buckingham County, since the records of that county have been destroyed. Even for the other nearby counties which still have their court records, however, these marriage and obituary notices are of great value since the court orders relating to probate of wills or granting of administrations seldom, if ever, specify the exact date of death, and when the minister's return of a marriage has not been preserved, the marriage bond (usually given a few days before the ceremony) can provide only an approximate date of marriage.

Although the majority of persons mentioned herein resided within fifty miles of Lynchburg, others lived elsewhere in the state and many of the marriages and obituaries from out of state are important in showing patterns of migration to the south and west, particularly to Alabama, Kentucky, Mississippi and Tennessee. The obituaries as well sometimes mention birthplaces in England, Scotland and Ireland.

The information presented in this volume is taken not only from the columns of paid notices but also from news items, and includes mention of international personalities of interest to the readers, such as Gen. Lafayette's father-in-law.

Erroneous reports of the deaths of national figures sometimes were published widely, only to be corrected in subsequent issues. The Kentucky newspapers several times noted the death of Daniel Boone while he was still living, and *The Lynchburg Virginian* in 1826 also erred in reporting the demise of John Randolph of Roanoke.

The history of the Lynchburg area is much enriched by the publication of these data.

John Frederick Dorman

Washington, D.C.
27 May 1979

Marriages from Lynchburg, Virginia Newspapers

ABBITT, MR. GEO. married on Feb. 13, 1824 to Miss Jane Webb, dau. of Mr. William Webb of Buckingham, by The Rev. R. R. Smith. Groom of Buckingham.
The Lynchburg Virginian, March 2, 1824, p. 3.

ABBOTT, JOSIAH B., ESQ. married on 7th inst. in Richmond, Virginia to Miss Catherine C. Randolph, dau. of the late Harry Randolph. Groom was Junior editor of Richmond WHIG.
The Lynchburg Virginian, August 16, 1832, p. 3, c. 5.

ACRE, MISS ELIZABETH - See entry for Mr. John Bradley.

ACREE, THOMAS O. married on the 12th inst. to Paulina P. Steen, dau. of William Steen, Esq. of Bedford, by The Rev. John Early.
The Lynchburg Virginian, April 17, 1826, p. 3, c.4.

ADAMS, MISS ELIZA M. - See entry for William Ward.

ADAMS, GEORGE married on 14th Oct. last to Miss Justinia Watkins, dau. of Joel Watkins, Esq. of Buckingham Co., by The Rev. Samuel Armistead. Groom of Pittsylvania Co.
The Lynchburg Virginian, November 23, 1829, p. 3, c. 5.

ADAMS, ISAAC, ESQ. married on Tuesday, the 21st of June to Mrs. Orney Foster by Elder Stephen Hubbard. Bride and Groom are both of Patrick Co.
The Lynchburg Virginian, July 5, 1832, p. 3, c. 4.

ADAMS, ISAAC married on Tuesday evening the 12th inst. to Miss Susan E. Duval, dau. of Major William Duval of Buckingham, by The Rev. Thos. Burge. Groom is of Lynchburg.
The Lynchburg Virginian, June 18, 1832, p. 3, c. 3.

ADAMS, JOHN married on 25th to Miss Malinda Burnett.
The Lynchburg Virginian, January 12, 1826, p. 3, c. 4.

ADAMS, JOHN married on Dec. 16th, 1830 to Miss Elizabeth Davison, all of this place, by The Rev. John S. Lee.
The Lynchburg Virginian, December 20, 1830, p. 3, c. 2.

ADAMS, MISS JULIAN - See entry for Hezikiah R. Foote.

ADAMS, MISS MARY - See entry for Jefferson Taylor.

ADAMS, MISS MARY ANN- See entry for Mr. Armistead Ayers.

ADAMS, MISS NANCY - See entry for John T. Hunt.

ADAMS, RICHARD married on the 29th ult. to Miss Elizabeth Wills, dau. of Justinian Wills, by The Rev. Mosby Arnold. All of Bedford.
The Lynchburg Virginian, October 6, 1836, p. 3, c. 3.

ADDINGTON, MISS VIRGINIA - See entry for The Rev. Leroy M. Lee.

AGNEW, MISS NANCY JANE - See entry for George Young.

AISTROP, LORENZA D. married on Thursday, 14th inst. to Miss Sarah Woody, dau. of Thos. Woody, by The Rev. Isaac Paul. All of Nelson Co.
The Lynchburg Virginian, February 21, 1828, p. 3, c. 5.

ALCOCK, MISS POLLY - See entry for Mr. William Gilbert.

ALDRIDGE, MISS EMILY - See entry for Anthony H. Davies.

ALDRIDGE, THOMAS, ESQ. married on Tuesday last to Jeanette Scott, dau. of late Robert Scott of Campbell Co., by The Rev. Wm. S. Reid. Groom of Tuscumbia, Alabama. Married in this place (Lynchburg).
The Lynchburg Virginian, December 6, 1827, p. 3, c. 4.

ALEXANDER, MISS CAROLINE D. - See entry for Capt. Nathaniel Strange.

ALEXANDER, MISS CATHARINE A. - See entry for Dr. Hector Harris.

ALEXANDER, MISS HENRIETTA - See entry for Henry B. Ely, Esq.

ALEXANDER, MR. JAMES married on 13 inst. at "Rose Hill" Albemarle to Miss Rebecca Ann, youngest dau. of Mr. Thomas Wills of Albemarle, by The Rev. Mr. Boyd. Groom was Editor of The Abington Republican.
The Lynchburg Virginian, December 31, 1832, p. 3, c. 2.

ALLCOCK, IRA R. married on Oct. 23, 1823 to Mrs. Phoebe Johnson, relict of the late Mr. Thomas Johnson of Amherst, by The Rev. Mr. Hales. Groom of Amherst Co.
The Lynchburg Virginian, October 31, 1823, p. 3.

ALLEN, MISS BETSY - See entry for Wm. T. Hazelewood.

ALLEN, MISS ELIZA - See entry for Nathan Speece.

ALLEN, MISS ELIZA H. - See entry for The Hon. Samuel Houston.

ALLEN, MISS GRACY ANN - See entry for Capt. John D. Bowling.

ALLEN, JAMES S. married on Dec. 17, 1818 to Miss Elizabeth Byars, dau. of Mr. John Byars of Lynchburg. Groom of Botetourt.
The Lynchburg Press and Public Advertiser, Dec., 21, 1818, p. 3.

ALLEN, MISS NANCY - See entry for Capt. Edward Carter.

ALLEN, MISS SARAH P. - See entry for Capt. John I. Oglesby.

ALMOND, EDWARD O. married on 2nd inst. to Miss Judith Cheadle by The Rev. Sam'l. Armistead.
The Lynchburg Virginian, June 1, 1827, p. 3, c. 3.

AMBLER, JOHN JACQUELIN married on Friday, 15th inst. to Miss Elizabeth
Barbour, dau. of Hon. P. P. Barbour of Va., by The Rev. Mr. Hawley
at home of Hon. James Barbour, in Washington City. All of Va.
The Lynchburg Virginian, February 21, 1828, p. 3, c. 5.

AMYX, MISS FLEANOR - See entry for Mr. Joseph M. Walker.

ANDERSON, MISS HARRIET - See entry for James W. Fitzgerald.

ANDERSON, JAMES married to Miss Anne Bread from Black Lake, L. I.
The Lynchburg Virginian, February 19, 1828, p. 3, c. 4.

ANDERSON, JEREMIAH E., ESQ. married on the 3rd inst. to Miss Elizabeth
A. Brooks, dau. of The Rev. James Brooks of Campbell Co., by The
Rev. James Kelly. Groom is from Pittsylvania Co.
The Lynchburg Virginian, November 5, 1829, p. 3, c. 5.

ANDERSON, JOHN married on July 22nd to Miss Dolly Martin by The Rev.
Sam'l. Armistead. All of Campbell Co.
The Lynchburg Virginian, August 12, 1830, p. 3, c. 4.

ANDERSON, MISS LOUISA - See entry for Mr. Robert W. Thurman.

ANDERSON, MISS SARAH ANN - See entry for Lorenza Stewart, Esq.

ANDERSON, WILLIAM, ESQ. married Wednesday evening the 17th inst. to
Miss Lucy C. Clark by The Rev. John Watson at Mr. Henry Moorman's.
Bride and groom from Campbell Co.
The Lynchburg Virginian, December 25, 1834, p. 3, c. 4.

ANDREWS, H. M. married on Jan. 26, 1825 to Miss Clarissa King, dau.
of Jacob King deceased, by The Rev. Isaac H. Judah. Groom
merchant of Lynchburg and late of Philadelphia.
The Lynchburg Virginian, January 28, 1825, p. 3, c. 5.

ANDREWS, JOHN married on Feb. 13, 1823 to Miss Martha Arnold of Campbell
Co. by The Rev. _____ Ally. Groom of Bedford Co.
The Lynchburg Virginian, February 21, 1823, p. 3.

ANDREWS, ROBERT married on 15th inst. to Miss Martha White by The Rev.
Samuel Armistead. Bride of Charlotte Co.
The Lynchburg Virginian, June 1, 1827, p. 3, c. 3.

ANDREWS, ROBERT S. married on Dec. 24, 1817 to Miss Elenor Thompson,
dau. of Mr. David Thompson of Lynchburg, by The Rev. William S.
Reid. Groom of Lynchburg.
The Lynchburg Press, December 26, 1817, p. 3.

ANTHONY, REV. ABNER married on 18th inst. to Miss Elmira Arthur, dau.
of Capt. Lewis C. Arthur, by The Rev. Mr. Witt. All of Bedford.
The Lynchburg Virginian, February 25, 1836, p. 3, c. 5.

ANTHONY, MR. ABNER, JR. married on 24th inst. to Miss Jane, dau. of Mr.
James Brown of Campbell Co., by The Rev. Wm. Leftwich (Whitehead).
The Lynchburg Virginian, March 3, 1836, p. 3, c. 2.

ANTHONY, DR. JOHN married on 24th ult. to Miss Louisa M. Peatross, dau.
of Capt. Wm. L. Peatross, by S. S. Bryant. All of Pittsylvania Co.
The Lynchburg Virginian, July 2, 1835, p. 3, c. 6.

ANTHONY, MISS MARY ANN - See entry for George W. Cabell.

ANTHONY, MISS SARAH ELIZA - See entry for B. H. Randolph.

ARINGTON, JESSE R. married on 4th inst. 1827 to Sarah B. Good by The
Rev. Isaac Cockreign at house of Mr. Robert Elliott. All of this
county (Campbell). Both bride and groom from Lynchburg.
The Lynchburg Virginian, June 28, 1827, p. 3, c. 4.

ARMISTEAD, ADDISON married on Dec. 11, 1828 to Miss Nancy Stuart.
Bride of Charlotte Co.
The Lynchburg Virginian, January 5, 1829, p. 3, c. 5.

ARMISTEAD, ANDERSON H., ESQ. married on Thursday evening to Miss
Elizabeth A., dau. of Col. Maurice H. Langhorne, Jr., by The Rev.
Wm. S. Reid. All of this place.
The Lynchburg Virginian, March 16, 1835, p. 3, c. 3.

ARMISTEAD, HENRY M. married on Feb. 21, 1833 to Miss Angelina W. Brown
by The Rev. Hugh Carlisle. Both of Charlotte Co. Groom son of
The Rev. Samuel Armistead.
The Lynchburg Virginian, March 11, 1833, p. 3, c. 4.

ARMISTEAD, DR. JOHN O. married Jan. 13, 1830 to Miss Elizabeth B.
Jennings in Prince Edward Co. by The Rev. Mr. Witt of Cumberland Co.
The Lynchburg Virginian, February 1, 1830, p. 3, c. 4.

ARMISTEAD, MISS MARTHA ANN - See entry for Capt. Daniel W. Williamson.

ARMISTEAD, MISS MARY ANN - See entry for Daniel Nunnelly.

ARMISTEAD, SAMUEL M. married on Thursday, Nov. 24th to Miss Frances M.
Cobbs by The Rev. Mr. Pollard. All of Campbell County.
The Lynchburg Virginian, December 8, 1831, p. 3, c. 5.

ARNOLD, MISS ELIZA ANN - See entry for Dr. Daniel H. Brown.

ARNOLD, MISS MARTHA - See entry for John Andrews.

ARNOLD, HON. THOMAS D. married on 27th ult. in Tazewell, Tennessee
to Miss Luritta Rose by The Rev. Chas. McAnally.
The Lynchburg Virginian, August 9, 1832, p. 3, c. 4.

ARNOLD, WILLIAM married to Mrs. S. Thornton from England at St. Mary's Church, Lancaster, England.
The Lynchburg Virginian, January 24, 1823, p. 1, c. 6.

ARTHUR, MISS ELMIRA A. - See entry for The Rev. Abner Anthony.

ASHLEY, GEN. WILLIAM R. married to Mrs. Wilcox, dau. of James W. Moss, Esq., in Columbia, Missouri recently. Groom is Representative from Congress from that place.
The Lynchburg Virginian, November 19, 1832, p. 3, c.4.

ATKINSON, _____ - See entry for Cleveland, _____.

ATKISSON, HECTOR married on Tuesday, 19th inst. to Sarah Franklin of Lynchburg by The Rev. William Duncan. Both of this place (Lynchburg).
The Lynchburg Virginian, November 22, 1822, p. 3, c.4.

AUNSPAUGH, DANIEL married on April 26, 1825 to Miss Mary Stone, dau. of Mr. Godleib Stone of Bedford, by The Rev. Samuel Phillips. Groom of Bedford.
The Lynchburg Virginian, May 5, 1825, p. 3.

AUSTIN, DANIEL married on 12th inst. to Mary Hawkins, dau. of Wm. Hawkins, by The Rev. Orson Martin. All of Henry Co.
The Lynchburg Virginian, January 14, 1827, p. 3.

AUSTIN, MISS ESTHER - See entry for John C. Reid.

AUSTIN, DR. JOHN married on the 13th ultimo to Miss Sarah Baller, dau. of Maj. John Baller of Bath Co., by The Rev. Samuel Brown. Groom is of New London.
The Lynchburg Virginian, September 3, 1835, p. 3, c.4.

AUSTIN, MR. JOHN married on the 4th inst. to Miss Sarah E. Callaway, eldest dau. of Capt. Thomas Callaway of Campbell Co., by The Rev. Miles Foy. Groom of Bedford.
The Lynchburg Virginian, October 11, 1832, p. 3, c. 4.

AYERS, MR. ARMISTEAD married on Tuesday last to Miss Mary Ann Adams by The Rev. D. S. Doggett. All of this place.
The Lynchburg Virginian, October 18, 1832, p. 3, c. 5.

AYRES, WILLIAM married on the 15th inst. to Miss Julia A. Henderson of Caswell Co., North Carolina by The Rev. Jas. McAden. Groom of Danville.
The Lynchburg Virginian, October 23, 1834, p. 3, c. 4.

BABCOCK, CHRISTOPHER married on July 18, 1833 to Miss Julia E. Hendrick, dau. of Bernard G. Hendrick, Esq. of Franklin Co. Groom of Richmond.
The Lynchburg Virginian, July 22, 1833, p. 3, c. 6

BAGBY, MRS. - See entry for Tarlton Jones.

BAGBY, MISS AMANDA MELVINA - See entry for William B. Watson.

BAGWELL, JOHN W., ESQ. married on 29th inst. to Miss Sarah Ann Barksdale, dau. of Capt. Grief Barksdale of Charlotte Co., by The Rev. Wm. S. Reid.
The Lynchburg Virginian, December 6, 1832, p. 3, c. 3.

BAILY, MRS. ELIZABETH - See entry for David Hodge.

BAILEY, MISS ELIZABETH - See entry for Robert Orr; also entry for David Hodge.

BAILEY, MISS FRANCES - See entry for Watkins Mason.

BAILEY, MISS JEMIMA - See entry for Henry Moon.

BAILEY, MRS. MARTHA J. - See entry for The Rev. Henry B. North.

BAILEY, SAMUEL married on Tuesday evening, the 23rd ult. to Miss Martha Townley, dau. of John Townley, Esq., by The Rev. Robert B. Thompson. All of Lynchburg.
The Lynchburg Virginian, January 1, 1835, p. 3, c. 3.

BAILEY, MISS SARAH - See entry for Edmund Pate.

BAILEY, WILLIAM married on Feb. 26, 1824 to Miss Elizabeth Walton at house of Elisha Betts, Esq. in the Co. of Botetourt. Groom of Lynchburg.
The Lynchburg Virginian, March 12, 1824, p. 3.

BAILEY, WILLIAM married on Thursday, 24 inst. to Miss Henrietta D. Scott, dau. of Mrs. Sarah B. Scott, by The Rev. Wm. S. Reid at the Seven Islands, Halifax Co. Groom of Lynchburg.
The Lynchburg Virginian, October 5, 1835, p. 2, c. 1.

BAILEY, YANCEY married on Jan. 9, 1833 to Miss Mary M. Marshall by The Rev. Samuel Armistead. Both bride and groom of Campbell Co.
The Lynchburg Virginian, January 21, 1833, p. 3, c. 4.

BAKER, DR. _____ married on 17th inst. to Mary Ann Richardina Gilliam at Oxford, N. C.
The Lynchburg Virginian, February 16, 1827, p. 3, c. 3.

BALLENTINE, MISS Ann - See entry for George Valentine.

BALLER, MISS SARAH - See entry for Dr. John Austin.

BALDWIN, MISS FRANCES PEYTON - See entry for Alexander H. H. Stuart.

BALLINGER, MISS SUSAN - See entry for Mace Pendleton.

BANAGH, JAMES married on May 1, 1823 to Miss Elizabeth Richardson, late of Goochland, at Mr. Ed. Winston's in Amherst Co., by The Rev. John S. Lee. Groom of Lynchburg.
The Lynchburg Virginian, May 2, 1823, p. 3, c. 5.

BARBOUR, MISS ELIZABETH - See entry for John Jacqueline Ambler.

BARCLAY, HUGH married on Nov. 15, 1821 to Miss Mary Woods, dau. of Michael Woods, Esq. of Nelson Co., by The Rev. William H. Foot. Groom of Rockbridge Co.
The Lynchburg Press, Dec. 7, 1821, p. 3.

BARGE, CATHERINE - See entry for James Porter.

BARGER, MISS MARY - See entry for Nathaniel W. Wooding.

BARKER, JOHN P. married to Miss Ellen Bellows of N.H. Married at Charlestown, N.H.
The Lynchburg Virginian, January 24, 1823, p. 1, c. 6.

BARKER, MISS MAHALA S. - See entry for John Sale.

BARKSDALE, ELISHA, JR. married on Oct. 22nd. to Miss Judith Barksdale, dau. of Armistead Barksdale, Esq. of Halifax, by The Rev. Charles Dresser. Groom a merchant of Halifax Court House.
The Lynchburg Virginian, November 5, 1835, p. 3, c. 3.

BARKSDALE, MISS JUDITH - See entry for Elisha   Barksdale, Jr.

BARKSDALE, MISS SARAH ANN - See entry for John W. Bagwell.

BARNES, MISS ABIGIAL C. - See entry for Joseph D. Evans.

BARNES, MISS ANGELINA L. - See entry for Henry B. Richards.

BARNET, MISS ESTHER - See entry for George Davis.

BARNETT, ROBERT J. married on Wednesday last to Miss Mary A., dau. of Mr. Arch. Brown of Lynchburg, by The Rev. Edward Cannon. Groom of Rockbridge.
The Lynchburg Virginian, July 11, 1831, p. 3, c. 4.

BARTON, MISS MARY - See entry for Robert H. Miller.

BARTON, THOMAS PENNANT married on April 28, 1833 at Washington City to Miss Cora Livingston, dau. of the Sec. of State, by The Rev. Mr. Hawley. Groom of Pennsylvania.
The Lynchburg Virginian, May 6, 1833, p. 3, c. 4.

BASS, MISS NANCY H. - See entry for Joseph B. Buckley.

BATES, HIX married on Thurs., 21st May to Miss Mary Jane, dau of Thomas
    J. Marshall, by The Rev. S. Anderson. Bride and groom of Halifax.
    The Lynchburg Virginian, June 25, 1829, p. 3, c. 4.

BATES, JOHN N. married on Feb. 25, 1833 to Miss Martha Ann Irvine by
    The Rev. William S. Reid. Bride and groom of Lynchburg.
    The Lynchburg Virginian, March 4, 1833, p. 3, c. 5.

BAUGHN, MISS ELIZABETH - See entry for Thomas Hatcher.

BAXTER, SIDNEY S. married on the 8th inst. to Miss Anna B. Nickolls,
    dau. of Mrs. Selina Nickolls, all of Rockbridge Co.
    The Lynchburg Virginian, October 19, 1829, p. 3, c. 4.

BEALE, MISS CATHARINE C. - See entry for John S. Hurt.

BEAVERS, EDWIN R. married on January 29th to Miss Elizabeth Carter,
    eldest dau. of Col. Jonathan Carter, by The Rev. John H. Watson.
    All of Pittsylvania Co., Virginia.
    The Lynchburg Virginian, February 19, 1829, p. 3, c. 5.

BECK, MISS GEORGIANNA - See entry for John T. Hill.

BECK, JAMES C. married on the 10th inst. to Miss Minerva R. A. Edwards
    by The Rev. William A. Smith. Married at Dr. Gustavus A. Edwards.
    Bride and groom of Amherst town.
    The Lynchburg Virginian, February 19, 1829, p. 3, c. 5.

BECKHAM, MISS FRANCES - See entry for Samuel Young.

BECKHAM, MISS MARY ANN - See entry for John W. Drean.

BECKHAM, WILLIAM married on June 14, 1825 to Miss Elizabeth Pugh, dau.
    of Mr. John Pugh of Amherst, by The Rev. Daniel Day. Groom of
    Amherst.
    The Lynchburg Virginian, June 23, 1825, p. 3.

BEKIN, MISS ELIZA JANE - See entry for The Rev. Lewis F. Cosby.

BECKHAM, MISS ELIZABETH - See entry for Thomas A. Drean.

BELL, MRS. CATHARINE - See entry for Benjamin Hawkins.

BELL, HON. JOHN married on the 20th ult. to Mrs. Jane Yeatman by The
    Rev. Dr. Edgar. All of Nashville, Tenn. Groom late speaker of
    the House of Representatives.
    The Lynchburg Virginian, November 12, 1835, p. 3, c. 3.

BELL, MISS LUCY R. S. - See entry for O. F. Reynolds.

BELL, MISS MARY MILLER NORTHANA - See entry for James M. Smith, Esq.

BELL, MISS SARAH - See entry for John P. Shelton.

BELL, MR. WILLIAM L. married on Jan. 27, 1824 to Miss Elizabeth Leftwich, dau. of The Rev. Wm. Leftwich of Bedford Co., by The Rev. William Harris. Groom of Lynchburg.
The Lynchburg Virginian, February 3, 1824, p. 3.

BELLOWS, MISS ELLEN - See entry for John P. Barker.

BENNETT, COLEMAN D. ESQ. married on 16th inst. to Miss Sarah S. Jones, eldest dau. of Richard Jones, Esq. of Pittsylvania Co., by The Rev. Charles Dresser of Halifax. Groom from Pittsylvania Co.
The Lynchburg Virginian, Dec. 25, 1834, p. 3, c. 4.

BENNETT, WILLIAM A. married on Thursday, last to Miss Eliza J. Morton by The Rev. Dr. Leech. Both of Lynchburg.
The Lynchburg Virginian, November 6, 1826, p. 3.

BENSON, MR. HENRY married on Tuesday evening the 28th inst. to Miss Elizabeth Clara, dau. of Mr. Edward Brown of Richmond, formerly of Lynchburg, by The Rev. Phillip Courtney. Groom of Charlottesville, Virginia.
The Lynchburg Virginian, July 4, 1836, p. 3, c. 4.

BERGER, MISS ELIZABETH - See entry for David W. Nowlin.

BERNARD, MISS ELIZABETH R. - See entry for James S. Jones.

BERNARD, MISS MARTHA ANN - See entry for Joshua R. Holmes.

BERNARD, MISS MARY P. - See entry for John Hancock.

BEVERLEY, HENRY S. married on March 14, 1822 to Susan Doswell, dau. of Maj. John Doswell, of Nottoway Co., by The Rev. Mr. Wherrey. Groom of Fredericksburg.
The Lynchburg Press, March 22, 1822, p. 3.

BIBB, MISS EVELINE D. - See entry for Barnett C. Ray.

BIBB, MARTIN T. married on 1st of March to Miss Sarah Duncan, dau. of late Fleming Duncan, by The Rev. John Davis. All of Amherst Co.
The Lynchburg Virginian, March 3, 1831, p. 3, c. 5.

BIBB, WILLIAM H. married on 17th in Amherst Co. to Miss Jane Pryor, dau. of William Pryor, Esq., by The Rev. John Davis. All of Amherst Co.
The Lynchburg Virginian, March 3, 1831, p. 3, c. 5.

BIGBIE, WILLIAM married on Dec. 11, 1822 to Miss Frances W. Sharp, dau. of Mrs. Daniel Oglesby of Bedford County, by The Rev. Frederick Kabler. Groom of Buckingham Co.
The Lynchburg Virginian, December 17, 1822, p. 3.

BIGGERS, ABRAM F. married on Sept. 26, 1821 to Miss Matilda Roberts of
Lynchburg by The Rev. George W. Charlton. Groom of Lynchburg.
The Lynchburg Press, September 28, 1821, p. 3.

BILBRO, MISS ANN - See entry for The Rev. James Leftwich.

BINGHAM, MISS JULIA - See entry for Garland Poindexter.

BINGHAM, MISS MARTHA M. - See entry for William Shands.

BLACKBURN, JONATHAN married on Nov. 10, 1797 to Miss Prudence Burford
at home of her father, Henry Burford in Bedford. Bride of Bedford;
groom of Kentucky.
The Lynchburg and Farmers Gazette, Nov. 13, 1797, p. 3, c. 1.

BLAIN, WILLIAM married on Sept. 29, 1817 to Miss Elizabeth Hoop, age 19
of Lynchburg, by The Rev. Bartlet Martin. Groom of Lynchburg.
The Lynchburg Press, Oct. 10, 1817, p. 3.

BLAIR, JOHN S. married on Nov. 27, 1827 to Ann S. Phillips, dau. of
Moses Phillips, by The Rev. J. Boyd. Bride of Amherst; groom of
Lynchburg.
The Lynchburg Virginian, Nov. 29, 1827, p. 3.

BLAIR, WILLIAM H. married on Tues. 12th inst. to Miss Clara Lewis Sale,
dau. of Capt. Wm. Sale, by The Rev. J. Boyd. Bride and groom of
Amherst.
The Lynchburg Virginian, Feb. 14, 1828, p. 3, c. 5.

BLAIR, WINSTON S. married on Jan. 8, 1829 to Mrs. Ann Lane by The Rev.
Wm. Wright. Bride and groom of Amherst Co.
The Lynchburg Virginian, Jan. 22, 1829, p. 3, c. 5.

BLANKINSHIP, MISS SUSAN - See entry for Alexander S. Dandridge.

BLINCOE, MISS MARY - See entry for The Rev. Wm. N. Ward.

BLOUNT, MISS SUSAN - See entry for Robert Hunter, Jr.

BOAS, MISS ANGELINA T. - See entry for Robert Isbell.

BOAZ, DAVID P. married on Tues. the 24th inst. to Miss Winifred Ann
Eliza Plunkett, dau. of Mr. Ambrose Plunkett of Campbell, by The
Rev. Thomas Burge. The groom of Buckingham.
The Lynchburg Virginian, Feb. 28, 1831, p. 3, c. 4.

BOBOCK, MISS MARTHA - See entry for Wilson Hix.

BOLLING, EDWARD, JR. married on the 6th inst. to Miss Elizabeth Clark,
dau. of Mr. _____ Clark of this county, by The Rev. Sam'l.
Davidson. Bride of Lynchburg, groom of Buckingham. Groom son of
Edward Bolling of Buckingham.
The Lynchburg Virginian, May 18, 1826, p. 3, c. 5.

BOLLING, LEWIS L. married on 19th ult. to Frances Ann Penn by The Rev.
Lewis Dawson. Bride and groom both of Amherst.
The Lynchburg Virginian, Aug. 2, 1827, p. 3, c. 3.

BOON, MISS ELIZABETH - See entry for William Martin.

BOOKER, MISS MARY B. - See entry for Dolphin Drew.

BOOTH, JOHN married on Wed. evening the 7th inst. to Miss Elizabeth
Craghead, dau of Mr. John Craghead, by The Rev. John Ayres. All
of Franklin Co.
The Lynchburg Virginian, March 19, 1832, p. 3, c. 3.

BOOTH, STEPHEN married on the 21st inst. to Miss Mary Conway, only dau.
of Dr. Edward Conway, by The Rev. John Farris. Both bride and
groom of Franklin Co.
The Lynchburg Virginian, Sept. 28, 1826, p. 3, c. 4.

BOOTH, THOMAS married on Tuesday last at Florence, Ala. to Miss Frances
Cox. Mr. Booth and wife lodged at Lagrance in Franklin Co. The
bridegroom awoke and found his wife a lifeless corpse.
The Lynchburg Virginian, Jan. 9, 1832, p. 3, c. 1.

BOOTH, WILLIAM married on Wed. 7 inst. to Miss Mary Smith, dau. of Mr.
Henry Smith by The Rev. Abner Anthony. All of Franklin Co.
The Lynchburg Virginian, March 19, 1832, p. 3, c. 3.

BOSWELL, WALTER B. married on Dec. 17, 1822 to Miss Sarah Ann Woodroof
of Amherst by The Rev. William S. Reid. Groom of Lynchburg.
The Lynchburg Virginian, Dec. 20, 1822, p. 3.

BOUDAR, MISS MERCIE H. - See entry for Mr. George H. Carter.

BOULDIN, JAMES E. ESQ. married on May 3, 1825 to Miss Melinda L. Saunders,
dau. of Col. David Saunders of Bedford, by The Rev. William S. Reid.
The Lynchburg Virginian, May 12, 1825, p. 3.

BOULDIN, MISS MARTHA - See entry for John Breckenridge Cabell, Esq.

BOUSEMAN, GEORGE married on June 25, 1833 to Miss Rebecca Dillon, dau.
of William Dillon, by The Rev. Stephen Wood. All of Franklin Co.
The Lynchburg Virginian, July 15, 1833, p. 3, c. 6.

BOWEN, FORDICE F. married on Nov. 19, 1823 to Miss Hannah Ann Mitchell
of Lynchburg by The Rev. William S. Reid. Groom of Lynchburg.
The Lynchburg Virginian, Nov. 21, 1823, p. 3.

BOWEN, MISS SARAH M. - See entry for Woodville Latham.

BOWERS, LEONARD married Sept. 9, 1830 to Martha Dickerson of Lynchburg
by The Rev. Edward Cannon.
The Lynchburg Virginian, Sept. 13, 1830, p. 3, c. 3.

BOWLS   MISS MALINDA - See entry for George Feaganes.

BOWLING, JAMES married on Nov. 11, 1819 to Miss _____ Davis of Amherst.
  Groom of Amherst.
  The Lynchburg Press and Public Advertiser, Nov. 19, 1819, p. 3.

BOWLING, CAPT. JOHN D. married on the 11th inst. to Miss Gracy Ann
  Allen, dau. of Robert Allen, deceased, by The Rev. Wm. Duncan.
  All of Amherst.
  The Lynchburg Virginian, Nov. 23, 1829, p. 3, c. 5.

BOWLING, WILLIAM M. married on Nov. 2, 1817 to Miss Jerusha Wingfield,
  dau. of John Wingfield of Franklin Co., by The Rev. M. Pedigo.
  Groom of Amherst Co., son of James Bowling.
  The Lynchburg Press, Nov. 7, 1817, p. 3.

BOYD, FRANCES - See entry for Fielding L. Williams.

BOYD, JOHN married to Harriet Henderson of Lynchburg and Fluvanna Co.
  The Lynchburg Virginian, Feb. 21, 1828, p. 3.

BOYD, MISS LUCY ANN S.— See entry for Robert C. Hendrice.

BRADFUTE, MISS MARIA CHAMPE - See entry for William Henry Lucas, Esq.

BRADLEY, HEZEKIAH married on May 29th to Miss Isabella H. S. Earl, late
  of this place.
  The Lynchburg Virginian, July 4, 1831, p. 3, c. 4.

BRADLEY, MR. JOHN married on Wed. last, 7th inst. to Miss Elizabeth
  Acres by The Rev. Edward Cannon. All of this place.
  The Lynchburg Virginian, Dec. 12, 1831, p. 3, c. 4.

BRADLEY, MISS LUCY ANN - See entry for Josiah H. Whitlow.

BRADLEY, WILLIS married on April 3, 1833 to Miss Eliza H. Townley, dau.
  of John Townley, by The Rev. Wm. S. Reid. All of this place.
  The Lynchburg Virginian, April 11, 1833, p. 3, c. 4.

BRAFFORD, MISS POLLY - See entry for David Moore.

BRANCH, MISS MARGARET - See entry for Gen. Daniel Donelson.

BRANCH, MISS REBECCA - See entry for Colonel R. W. Williams.

BRANCH, ROBERT G. married on 15th inst. to Miss Agnes W. Wood, dau. of
  James D. Wood, Esq. of Prince Edward. Groom: Professor Languages
  in Hampden-Sydney College.
  The Lynchburg Virginian, April 30, 1835, p. 3, c. 5.

BRAND, MISS FRANCES A. - See entry for Jesse Burton Harrison, Esq.

BRANSFORD, MISS ANN P. - See entry for John H. Tyree.

BRANSFORD, MISS ELIZA - See entry for Addison Ford.

BRANSFORD, MISS JUDITH A. - See entry for Mr. Charles C. Hudson.

BRENT, MISS MARY - See entry for Tipton B. Harrison.

BRIANT, MISS ELIZABETH - See entry for Mr. John Langhorne.

BRIDGELAND, MISS MARY ANN - See entry for Richard Ligon.

BRIDGES, CAPT. DAVID married on Tues. evening 8th inst. to Miss Martha
Lousa McKinney, only dau. of Wm. McKinney, Esq. of this place by
The Rev. Jacob Mitchell. The groom is of Richmond.
The Lynchburg Virginian, March 10, 1831, p. 3, c. 5.

BRIDGES, JAMES R. married on 23rd inst. in Manchester to Miss Nancy
Elizabeth Trent, dau. of Wm. Callaway, Esq. of Franklin Co., by
The Rev. Wm. J. Armstrong.
The Lynchburg Virginian, Dec. 6, 1830, p. 3, c. 4.

BRIGGS, MR. ROBERT M. married on 11 ult. to Miss Ann E. Jones formerly
of Lynchburg, by The Rev. Ezra Styles Ely. Groom of that place.
The Lynchburg Virginian, August 11, 1836, p. 3, c. 2.

BROOKS, MISS ELIZABETH A. - See entry for Jeremiah E. Anderson, Esq.

BROOKS, MISS MARTHA - See entry for John Farmer.

BROOKS, PLEASANT D. married on April 25, 1833 to Miss Frances N.
Gilbert, dau. of Mr. Kemuel C. Gilbert, Sen., by Elder M. Greer.
Both bride and groom of Franklin Co.
The Lynchburg Virginian, May 6, 1833, p. 3, c. 4.

BROWDER, MR. _____ married on 13th inst. to Miss Nancy Irby, dau.
of The Rev. Samuel Irby, all of Halifax. Married by The Rev.
John A. Mills.
The Lynchburg Virginian, Nov. 17, 1834, p. 3, c. 4.

BROWN, ALEXANDER married on April 27, 1819 to Miss Lucy S. Rives, dau.
of Robert Rives, Esq. of Nelson, by The Rev. James Boyd. Groom
of Lynchburg.
The Lynchburg Press and Public Advertiser, May 3, 1819, p. 3.

BROWN, MISS ANGELINA W. - See entry for Henry M. Armistead.

BROWN, MISS ANOFLINA M. - See entry for John B. Otey.

BROWN, DANIEL married on Aug. 31, 1824 to Miss Lucy Ann Moon, of Bedford.
by The Rev. Mr. Leftwich. Groom of Lynchburg.
The Lynchburg Virginian, Sept. 3, 1824, p. 3.

BROWN, MR. DANIEL H. married on Wed. the 1st inst. to Miss Eliza Ann,
dau. of The Rev. Mosby Arnold of Bedford County. Married by The
Rev. Robert J. Carson. Groom from Campbell County.
The Lynchburg Virginian, Oct. 26, 1835, p. 3, c. 5.

BROWN, EDWIN M. of Greenbrier, formerly of Lynchburg, married on Jan.
13, 1830 to Miss Anne Eliza Norvell, dau. of Capt. Reuben Norvell
of Amherst, by The Rev. William S. Reid.
The Lynchburg Virginian, Jan. 14, 1830, p. 3, c. 6.

BROWN, MISS ELIZABETH CLARA - See entry for Mr. Henry Benson.

BROWN, MISS FRANCES - See entry for Edwin Robinson.

BROWN, HENRY J. ESQ. married on last Thurs. evening to Miss Lucy
Claiborne, eldest dau. of Philip Duval, Esq. of Buckingham, by
The Rev. Thos. Burge. Groom attorney-at-law.
The Lynchburg Virginian, July 30, 1829, p. 3, c. 4.

BROWN, MISS ISABELLA - See entry for John A. Wharton.

BROWN, MISS JANE - See entry for Mr. Abner Anthony, Jr.

BROWN, MISS JANE C. - See entry for William E. Coleman.

BROWN, JAMES E. ESQ. married on Jan. 7, 1829 to Mrs. Ann D. McDowell
of Staunton. Married at residence of Chiswell Dabney by The
Rev. W. S. Reid.
The Lynchburg Virginian, Jan. 15, 1829, p. 3, c. 5.

BROWN, MR. JOHN S. married last evening to Miss Lucinda Moorman, youngest dau. of Mr. James C. Moorman of Lynchburg. Married in Lynchburg by The Rev. John Earley.
The Lynchburg Virginian, Dec. 15, 1831, p. 3, c. 3.

BROWN, JOHN THOMPSON, ESQ. married on Thurs., the 6th inst. to Miss
Mary E. Wilcox, dau. of John V. Wilcox of Petersburg, by The Rev.
Mr. Syme. Groom of Harrison Co., formerly of Lynchburg.
The Lynchburg Virginian, May 17, 1830, p. 3, c. 5.

BROWN, MISS MARTHA A. - See entry for Capt. Archibald Hailet.

BROWN, MISS MARY A. - See entry for Robert J. Barnett.

BROWN, MISS MARY ANN - See entry for Abner Snow.

BROWN, MISS MARY RANDOLPH - See entry for Thomas Matthews.

BROWN, MISS MARY S. - See entry for The Rev. Andrew Hart.

BROWN, MILDRED WARNER - See entry for Adolphus Peticolus.

BROWN, MISS SARAH - See entry for James W. Dibrell.

BROWN, MISS SARAH ANN - See entry for William Rock.

BROWN, MISS SARAH F. - See entry for A. Robertson.

BROWN, SPOTSWOOD married on the 18th inst. to Miss Elizabeth Ewing by
The Rev. Samuel Phillips. All of Bedford.
The Lynchburg Virginian, Nov. 30, 1835, p. 3, c. 4.

BROWN, MISS SUSAN F. - See entry for Arthur B. Davies.

BROWN, TARLTON married on the 20th inst. to Miss Lucy Moorman, eldest
dau. of Thomas Moorman of Campbell Co., by The Rev. John Early.
Groom of Franklin Co.
The Lynchburg Virginian, April 27, 1826, p. 3, c. 3.

BROWN, THOMAS R., ESQ. married on July 30, 1833 to Miss Mary Ann
Coleman, dau. of late Mr. Henry Coleman of Caroline Co., by The
Rev. James B. Taylor. Groom of Amherst Co.
The Lynchburg Virginian, Aug. 8, 1833, p. 3, c. 4.

BRYANT, MISS NANCY - See entry for Wm. W. Dinwiddie.

BUCKLEY, JOSEPH B. married on 15 inst. to Nancy H. Bass, dau. of Capt.
Francis Bass, by The Rev. James McDonald. All of Campbell Co.
The Lynchburg Virginian, May 22, 1828, p. 3, c. 5.

BURFORD, MISS PRUDENCE - See entry for Jonathan Blackburn.

BULLOCK, MISS MARTHA ANN - See entry for Major John Smith.

BULLOCK, MISS MARY JANE - See entry for F. H. Farrar.

BURCH, SAMUEL married on Nov. 3, 1824 to Miss Mahala Puryear, of
Lynchburg, by The Rev. John S. Lee. Groom of Lynchburg.
The Lynchburg Virginian, Nov. 20, 1824, p. 3.

BURCH, THOMAS married Sept. 16, 1830 to Mrs. Susan Hall of Amherst by
The Rev. John Davies.
The Lynchburg Virginian, Sept. 20, 1830, p. 3, c. 4.

BURCHETT, MISS SALLY - See entry for Reuben Kingston.

BURCKS, MISS MARTHA ANN ELIZABETH - See entry for Mr. John M. Feazel.

BURD, MISS AMANDA M. F. - See entry for William Patteson.

BURD, MISS ANN - See entry for Mr. John G. Shelton.

BURD, MISS ELIZABETH M. - See entry for Alfred Rucker.

BURD, MISS EVALINE - See entry for Richard S. Tilden.

BURD, MISS MARY W. - See entry for John G. Shelton.

BURFORD, DR. GEORGE H. married on Feb. 11, 1819 to Miss Mary Hansard, dau. of John Hansard of Amherst, by The Rev. Mr. Dawson. Groom of Amherst.
The Lynchburg Press & Public Advertiser, Feb. 15, 1819, p. 3.

BURFORD, MR. GEORGE W. married on 10th ult. to Miss Susan Taylor by The Rev. Thomas Jones. Bride and groom both of Amherst.
The Lynchburg Virginian, Dec. 18, 1834, p. 3, c. 4.

BURFORD, MISS JULIA ANN - See entry for Archibald Cox.

BURFORD, MISS MARTHA ANN - See entry for John H. Freeman.

BURFORD, MISS MATILDA W. - See entry for John T. Tinsley.

BURFORD, SYLVESTER L. married on Thurs. Dec. 9th to Miss Susan C. Cox, dau. of Reuben Cox, Esq. of Amherst, by The Rev. Dr. Wm. J. Holcombe.
The Lynchburg Virginian, Nov. 13, 1830, p. 3, c. 4.

BURFORD, MISS THERMUTHIUS T. - See entry for Garland Freeman.

BURGESS, JOHN married on the 11 inst. to Mrs. _____ Driskill by The Rev. Samuel Armistead. All of Campbell Co.
The Lynchburg Virginian, June 16, 1836, p. 3, c. 4.

BURKS, MISS ELIZABETH JANE - See entry for Hugh R. Scott.

BURKS, MISS FRANCES ANN - See entry for Charles M. Christian.

BURKS, MISS MARGARET P. - See entry for Thomas H. Scott.

BURKS, RICHARD H. married on Nov. 11, 1819 to Miss Eliza Shelton of Amherst by The Rev. Wm. Duncan.
The Lynchburg Press & Public Advertiser, Nov. 19, 1819, p. 3, c. 3.

BURKS, ROWLAND P. married on Aug. 7, 1817 to Miss Ann M. Tinsley, dau. of Mr. George Tinsley of Amherst Co. Groom of Amherst Co.
The Lynchburg Press, Aug. 15, 1817, p. 3.

BURNETT, MISS ELIZABETH - See entry for The Rev. Benjamin Hewitt.

BURNETT, MISS MALINDA - See card for John Adams.

BURNETT, MR. WILLIAMSON married on 19th inst. at Bedford to Miss Celia Ann Nance, dau. of Mr. John Nance, by The Rev. Wm. Leftwich. Both of Bedford.
The Lynchburg Virginian, Nov. 27, 1834, p. 3, c. 5.

BURR, COL. AARON married on July 1, 1833 at Harlem Heights, N.Y. to Mrs. Eliza James by Dr. Bogart.
The Lynchburg Virginian, July 11, 1833, p. 3, c. 4.

BURRUSS, RICHARD married on Jan. 5, 1819 (married on Tues. last) to Miss
Jane V. Hansford of Amherst by The Rev. Pleasant Thurman. Groom of
Amherst.
The Lynchburg Press & Public Advertiser, Jan. 11, 1819, p. 3, c. 4.

BURTON, MR. JESSE A. married on the 3rd inst. to Miss Damarias Cobbs,
dau. of John L. Cobbs, Esq. of Bedford, by The Rev. Charles H. Page.
The Lynchburg Virginian, Sept. 8, 1834, p. 3, c. 4.

BURTON, MR. JONES W. married on 30th Oct. to Miss Pamelia H. Watson by
The Rev. David B. Nicholson. All of Pittsylvania Co.
The Lynchburg Virginian, Nov. 10, 1834, p. 3.

BURTON, PATRICK P., ESQ. married on 18th inst. in Rockbridge to Mary
Shields, dau. of Alexander Shields, Esq. Groom of Bedford, bride
of Rockbridge. Married by _____.
The Lynchburg Virginian, Nov. 1, 1827, p. 3, c. 4.

BURTON, WILLIAM C. married on Dec. 13, 1832 to Miss Sarah J. Cocke, dau.
of the late George Cocke, of Campbell Co. by The Rev. Livingston
Walker. Groom son of Jesse Burton of Campbell Co.
The Lynchburg Virginian, Dec. 20, 1832, p. 3, c. 5.

BURWELL, LOUIS PHILLIP, ESQ. married on 25th ult. in Winchester, Va. to
Miss Susan Ann, dau. of the late Daniel Lee, Esq. of the former
place. Groom resident of "The Grove" on James River.
The Lynchburg Virginian, Feb. 15, 1836, p. 3, c. 4.

BURWELL, MISS MARY - See entry for Landon C. Garland, Esq.

BUTLER, WILLIAM married on 20th inst. to Miss Doshea Callaway by The
Rev. Abner Early. All of Campbell Co.
The Lynchburg Virginian, Jan. 2, 1832, p. 3, c. 5.

BUTTS, DANIEL married on March 2, 1819 to Miss Elizabeth Matoon age 11,
of Vienna, New York by The Rev. E. Stebbins. Groom, age 15 of
Augusta, Ga.
The Lynchburg Press & Public Advertiser, Mar. 18, 1819, p. 3, c. 4.

BYARS, MISS ELIZABETH - See entry for James S. Allen.

BYARS, MISS MARTHA - See entry for Socrates Mitchell.

BYRD, MISS EVELYN - See entry for Quarles Tomplins, Esq.

C

CABANISS, MISS LUCY R. - See entry for Micajah Davies.

CABELL, EDWARD A., ESQ. married on Mar. 13, 1823 to Mary R. Garland,
dau. of David S. Garland, Esq. of New Glasgow, Amherst Co. by The
Rev. Wm. S. Reid. Groom of Nelson Co.
The Lynchburg Virginian, March 18, 1823, p. 3.

CABELL, MISS EMELINE S. - See entry for Benjamin E. Scruggs.

CABELL, MISS FRANCES - See entry for Thomas P. Friend.

CABELL, GEORGE K., ESQ. married on Wed. evening last at New Glasgow to
    Miss Eliza V. Garland, dau. of D. S. Garland, Esq. by Dr. Waller.
    The groom is of Lynchburg.
    The Lynchburg Virginian, Sept. 14, 1829, p. 3, c. 4.

CABELL, GEORGE W., ESQ. married last evening to Miss Mary Ann Anthony,
    dau. of C. Anthony, Esq. by The Rev. F. G. Smith. All of this place.
    The Lynchburg Virginian, Feb. 19, 1829, p. 3, c. 5.

CABELL, JOHN BRECKENRIDGE, ESQ. married on 24th inst. to Miss Martha
    Bouldin, dau. of Judge Bouldin of Charlotte Co., Va.
    The Lynchburg Virginian, Jan. 26, 1826, p. 3, c. 4.

CABELL, JOHN N. married last evening to Miss Maria A. Hanna by The Rev.
    F. G. Smith. All of the theatre. Playing at the theatre in Lybg.
    The Lynchburg Virginian, Apr. 13, 1829, p. 3, c. 4.

CABELL, MISS JUDITH SCOTT - See entry for Richard K. Cralle.

CABELL, LANDON R., ESQ. married on Jan. 15, 1829 to Miss Marian Fontaine
    Cabell by The Rev. F. G. Smith at residence of A. S. Henry, Esq. in
    Campbell Co.
    The Lynchburg Virginian, Jan. 19, 1829, p. 3, c. 4.

CABELL, MISS LOUISE - See entry for Henry Carrington.

CABELL, MISS MARION FONTAINE - See entry for Landon R. Cabell, Esq.

CABELL, MAYO married on Dec. 8, 1825 to Miss Mary Cornelia Daniel, dau.
    of Judge William Daniel of Lynchburg, by The Rev. Wm. S. Reid.
    Groom of Nelson Co.
    The Lynchburg Virginian, Dec. 15, 1825, p. 3.

CABELL, PATRICK HENRY, ESQ. married on the 15th inst. to Elizabeth Lee,
    dau. of Daniel Lee of Winchester, by The Rev. J. E. Jackson. Groom
    of Lynchburg.
    The Lynchburg Virginian, Feb. 27, 1826, p. 3, c. 5.

CABELL, DR. PAUL C. married on June 12, 1823 to Miss Mary Irvine, dau.
    of Capt. Wm. Irvine of Bedford, by The Rev. Wm. S. Reid. Groom
    of Halifax.
    The Lynchburg Virginian, June 20, 1823, p. 3.

CABELL, MISS SARAH - See entry for Henry Ward, Esq.

CABELL, MISS SARAH J. - See entry for Dr. Thomas Massie.

CABELL, WILLIAM L. married on Thurs. night last to Miss Eliza Daniel,
    dau. of Judge Wm. Daniel of Lynchburg, by The Rev. W. S. Reid.
    All of this place (Lynchburg).
    The Lynchburg Virginian, Jan. 7, 1828, p. 3, c. 3.

CABILL, MISS MARIA - See entry for Columbus Iding.

CABILL, MISS POLLY - See entry for George Iding.

CAIRNS, MISS POLLY - See entry for Philip Shuster.

CALHOUN, A. P. married on Jan. 3, 1833 at Columbia, S. C. to Miss
   Eugenia Chappell, eldest dau. of Col. J. J. Chappell, by The
   Rev. Mr. Henry. Groom eldest son of The Hon. J. C. Calhoun.
   The Lynchburg Virginian, Jan. 28, 1833, p. 3, c. 4.

CALHOUN, ANDREW P., ESQ. married on the 5th inst. to Miss Margaret
   Green, dau. of Duff Green of Washington, by The Rev. Mr. Hawley.
   Groom of South Carolina.
   The Lynchburg Virginian, May 16, 1836, p. 3, c. 3.

CALL, MISS E. - See entry for Zachariah Turner.

CALLAHAN, MISS CATHERINE - See entry for Joseph Robinson.

CALLAHAN, MRS. PHEBE - See entry for Capt. John Rice.

CALLAND, MISS ANN B. - See entry for Thomas Jones.

CALLAND, MRS. ELIZA - See entry for William Leftwich.

CALLAND, MISS ELIZABETH S. - See entry for Achilles H. Moorman.

CALLAND, MISS LETITIA - See entry for Dr. T. C. Shelton.

CALLAWAY, MISS AMANDA - See entry for Tazewell Taliaferro.

CALLAWAY, MISS DOSHEA - See entry for William Butler.

CALLAWAY, MISS ELIZABETH - See entry for Samuel Read.

CALLAWAY, MISS MATILDA ANN - See entry for John Smith, Jr.

CALLAWAY, ROBERT married on 18th ult. to Elizabeth Ann Whitlow, dau. of
   Stratford Whitlow, Esq., by The Rev. Mr. Roach. All of Campbell.
   The Lynchburg Virginian, June 16, 1836, p. 3, c. 4.

CALLAWAY, MISS SARAH E. - See entry for Mr. John Austin.

CALLAWAY, MISS ANN - See entry for Abraham Clements.

CALWELL, DR. HENRY B. married on 31st ult. at Philadelphia to Miss Mary
   Jane Orsmby, dau. of E. Churehouan, Esq. of Baltimore, by The Mayor
   of Philadelphia. Groom of White Sulphur Springs, Va.
   The Lynchburg Virginian, Nov. 14, 1836, p. 3, c. 3.

CAMDEN, MISS ANN BELL - See entry for Peter G. Camden.

CAMDEN, PETER G., ESQ. married to Miss Ann Bell Camden, only dau. of the
   late Marshall Camden formerly of Amherst Co., by The Rev. Samuel
   Findly at Frankfort, Ky.
   The Lynchburg Virginian, Mar. 11, 1830, p. 3, c. 3.

CAMM, MISS ELIZABETH - See entry for David B. Patterson.

CAMM, MARY - See entry for William Saunders.

CAMM, MISS SARAH - See entry for Benjamin A. Donald, Esq.

CAMPBELL, THE REV. ALEXANDER W. married on Sept. 4, to Miss Mary
Mosely, dau. of late Dr. Bennet Mosely of Bedford Co., by The
Rev. James Mitchell. Groom of Lexington, Kentucky.
The Lynchburg Virginian, Sept. 6, 1832, p. 3, c. 4.

CAMPBELL, GUSTAUS married on Thursday, Dec. 24, 1829 to Francis Baker
Pettit of Amherst County, Virginia.
The Lynchburg Virginian, Jan. 7, 1830, p. 3, c. 6.

CAMPBELL, MR. GUSTAVUS married on Thurs. 4 inst. to Miss Mary Horton,
dau. of late Craven Horton of Campbell Co., by The Rev. Mr. Carson.
Groom of Campbell Co.
The Lynchburg Virginian, June 15, 1835, p. 3, c. 3.

CAMPBELL, COL. JAMES married on May 23, 1821 to Sophia W. Spencer, dau.
of Samuel T. Spencer of Charlotte Co., Va., by The Rev. Mr. Lyle.
Groom of Leaksville, N.C.
The Lynchburg Press, June 1, 1821, p. 3.

CAMPBELL, JAMES married on the 16th inst. to Catharine C. Hare by The
Rev. Dr. Samuel Philips. Groom is of Bedford. Bride is of this
place.
The Lynchburg Virginian, June 21, 1830, p. 3, c. 3.

CAMPBELL, JOHN K., ESQ. married on Sept. 9, 1832 to Miss Elisabeth P.
Duval, dau. of Philip Duval, Esq. of Campbell Co., Va., by The
Rev. Mr. Doggett. Groom of Florida.
The Lynchburg Virginian, Sept. 13, 1832, p. 3, c. 4.

CAMPBELL, MISS LUCINDA ANN - See entry for John F. Hawkins.

CAMPBELL, MISS MARY J. - See entry for Joseph Wilson.

CAMPBELL, MISS MARY M. - See entry for Lloyd Dorsey.

CAMPBELL, WILLIAM married on 14th inst. to Miss Martha Ingram, eldest
dau. of Mr. Alexander Ingram, by The Rev. Stephen Hubbard. All
of Franklin Co.
The Lynchburg Virginian, Jan. 25, 1827, p. 3, c. 5.

CAMPBELL, WILLIAM T. married on the 15th inst. to Miss Ann Henry Terry,
dau. of Wm. Terry, Esq., by The Rev. N. H. Cobbs. All of Liberty,
Virginia.
The Lynchburg Virginian, June 23, 1836, p. 3, c. 5.

CANNEFAX, MISS ANN T. - See entry for Thomas W. Nowlin.

CANNIFAX, MISS RHODA - See entry for George Wheeler.

CARDWELL, MISS ELMIRA J. - See entry for James F. Martin.

CARLTON, MR. AMBROSE married to Miss Ann Dow Gardner, dau. of the late Dr. James Gardner of Lyon, Mass. Married in Lyon, Mass. Groom of Richmond, Va.
The Lynchburg Virginian, Sept. 17, 1832, p. 3, c. 5.

CARNAHAN, MISS HANNAH - See entry for W. K. McDonald.

CARPER, MAJ. MOSES G. married on 27th ult. to Miss Catharine Tate, dau. of late Col. Edmund Tate, by Elder Moses Greer. All of Franklin Co.
The Lynchburg Virginian, Dec. 15, 1834, p. 3, c. 4.

CARR, MISS JANE C. - See entry for Peyton Harrison.

CARRINGTON, HENRY married on May 22, 1820 to Louisa Cabell, dau. of William Cabell of Buckingham. Groom of Charlotte.
The Lynchburg Press & Public Advertiser, May 30, 1820, p. 3.

CARRINGTON, MISS NANCY - See entry for Job Blair McPhail.

CARRINGTON, MISS SOPHONISBA ANN - See entry for Dr. Nathaniel R. Powell.

CARROLL, SAMUEL married on 5th inst. at Fort Lewis, Botetourt, Va. to Miss Jane G. R. White by The Rev. Mr. Fulton.
The Lynchburg Virginian, Jan. 12, 1832, p. 3, c. 5.

CARTER, MISS ANN P. - See entry for Henry B. Ely.

CARTER, CHAMPE married on Oct. 10, 1832 at Red Hill to Miss Mary W. E. Montgomery by The Rev. Wm. S. Reid. Both of Amherst Co.
The Lynchburg Virginian, Oct. 25, 1832, p. 3, c. 4.

CARTER, CAPT. EDWARD married on 10th ult. to Nancy Allen of Henry by The Rev. James Matterson. Groom of Pittsylvania Co.
The Lynchburg Press, June 2, 1814, p. 3, c. 2.

CARTER, MISS ELIZABETH - See entry for Edwin R. Beaver.

CARTER, MISS ELIZABETH C. - See entry for Mr. Charles B. Taliaferro.

CARTER, MR. GEORGE H. married on 7th inst. in Richmond to Miss Mercie H. Boudar, all of that city, the latter formerly of Lynchburg. Married by The Rev. T. O'Brien.
The Lynchburg Virginian, July 18, 1836, p. 3, c. 3.

CARTER, MISS LAURA B. - See entry for Beverley Davies.

CARTER, MISS NANCY - See entry for Thomas Phelps.

CARTER, DOCT. WILLIAM married on Wed. 30th of March to Miss Sarah A. Morris, dau. of Benjamin S. Morris, Esq. of Henry County, by The Rev. Joseph Pedigo.
The Lynchburg Virginian, April 25, 1831, p. 3, c. 2.

CARVALLO, DON MANUEL married on 5th of Nov. to Miss Mary E. Causten, second dau. of James H. Causten, Esq. of that city. Married in Washington by The Rev. Dr. Mulledy.
The Lynchburg Virginian, Nov. 13, 1834, p. 3, c. 4.

CARVER, REUBEN married on Sunday last to Miss Ann B. Turner, dau. of Major Henry Turner, by The Rev. Dan'l. Day. Bride and groom of Amherst Co.
The Lynchburg Virginian, Oct. 5, 1826, p. 3, c. 3.

CARWILE, MISS _____ - See entry for Richard McCraw.

CARWILES, MISS MARY - See entry for Mr. James Trent.

CARY, MISS ELIZA - See entry for Benjamin Hunt.

CARY, JOHN, ESQ. married to Miss Susan Lambeth, dau. of Geo. K. Lambeth, Esq., all of this place on Thursday last by The Rev. Mr. Parks.
The Lynchburg Virginian, Jan. 17, 1831, p. 3, c. 4.

CARY, MISS SARAH S. - See entry for Peter C. Nelson.

CASKIE, JOHN married on July 10, 1817 to Miss Martha Jane Norvell, dau. of Capt. Reuben Norvell of Amherst Co., by The Rev. Wm. S. Reid. Groom of Lynchburg.
The Lynchburg Press, July 18, 1817, p. 3.

CAUSTEN, MISS MARY E. - See entry for Don Manuel Carvallo.

CAULDWELL, WATSON married on the 6th inst. to Miss Mary A. Winfrey by The Rev. Gabriel Walker. Bride and groom of Buckingham Co.
The Lynchburg Virginian, April 20, 1826, p. 3, c. 4.

CAWTHON, MISS ANN Y. - See entry for Jonathon Rucker.

CAWTHORN, MISS JANE M. - See entry for Ferdenand M. Wiley.

CAWTHORNE, MISS LOUISE - See entry for Daniel W. Floed.

CAWTHON, MRS. MARY - See entry for Capt. Wm. Weaver.

CHANDLER, MISS ELIZABETH H. - See entry for William Phaup.

CHANEY, MISS LOUISA - See entry for Western Willis.

CHAPLIN, MISS ELIZABETH F. - See entry for John R. McDaniel.

CHAPLIN, WILLIAM R. married on Dec. 17, 1818 to Miss Elizabeth Jones of Campbell Co. by The Rev. Wm. S. Reid. Groom of Lynchburg.
The Lynchburg Press & Public Advertiser, Dec. 21, 1818, p. 3.

CHAPMAN, JOHN BIDDLE, ESQ. married on 22nd inst. in Richmond, Va. to
Mary Gabriella Randolph, adopted dau. of Dr. John Brockenbrough,
by The Rev. Bishop Moore. Groom of Philadelphia.
The Lynchburg Virginian, May 30, 1833, p. 3, c. 4.

CHAPPELL, MISS EUGENIA - See entry for A. P. Calhoun.

CHARLTON, THE REV. GEO. W. married on evening of 11th inst. to Martha
R. Wright of West Hoy, Greensville Co., Va. by The Rev. Hez G.
Leigh. Groom of Richmond.
The Lynchburg Virginian, Aug. 24, 1829, p. 3, c. 5.

CHEADLE, MISS JUDITH W. - See entry for Edward O. Almond.

CHEATHAM, MR. BEAZLY married on the 5th inst. to Miss Catharine Harris,
dau. of Henry T. Harris of this county, by The Rev. Sam'l Armistead.
The Lynchburg Virginian, Nov. 20, 1828, p. 3, c. 5.

CHEATHAM, MISS MARTHA W. - See entry for Dade M. Fisher.

CHEATHAM, MISS SARAH - See entry for William Thompson, Jr.

CHEATHAM, THOMAS O. married on the 24th Sept. last to Miss Elizabeth
Ann Rosser, dau. of Wm. Rosser, Esq., by The Rev. John S. Lee.
All of Campbell.
The Lynchburg Virginian, Oct. 16, 1834, p. 3, c. 4.

CHEETWOOD, MISS ANNELIZA - See entry for Albert A. Sherman.

CHEWNING, ALBERT G. married on Jan. 6, 1833 to Miss Nicy H. Digges, dau.
of Major William H. Digges, by The Rev. Henry S. Payton. Bride of
Nelson Co., groom of Louisa Co.
The Lynchburg Virginian, Feb. 14, 1833, p. 3, c. 4.

CHEWNING, MISS SARAH - See entry for John Hubbard.

CHICK, CAPT. RICHARD W. married on Dec. 23, 1823 to Miss Elizabeth C.
Lee, dau. of Mr. Guy Lee of Buckingham Co., by The Rev. Poindexter
P. Smith. Groom of Buckingham Co.
The Lynchburg Virginian, Jan. 2, 1824, p. 3.

CHILDRESS, LEONARD H. married on Thursday last to Miss Caroline Talliaferro,
dau. of Capt. Benj. Talliaferro, by The Rev. Wm. Duncan. All of
Amherst.
The Lynchburg Virginian, Sept. 18, 1828, p. 3, c. 6.

CHILTON, MISS ANN - See entry for Edward P. Johnston, Esq.

CHILTON, MISS ANN S. - See entry for Charles H. Moorman.

CHILTON, MISS CATHERINE L. K. - See entry for Robert S. Chilton.

CHILTON, ROBERT S. married on Thursday 28th ult. to Miss Catharine L. K.
Chilton, dau. of Raleigh Chilton, Esq. of Campbell Co., Va., by The
Rev. Samuel Davidson.
The Lynchburg Virginian, Aug. 4, 1836, p. 3, c. 4.

CHRISTIAN, CHARLES B. married on Thursday 27th ult. to Miss Matilda Page,
eldest dau. of Francis Page of Amherst, by The Rev. John Alcock.
Groom of Surry Co., N.C.
The Lynchburg Virginian, Jan. 7, 1828, p. 3, c. 3.

CHRISTIAN, CHARLES M. married on 15th inst. to Frances Ann Burks, eldest
dau. of Joseph Burks, Esq. of Campbell Co., by The Rev. P. P. Smith.
Groom of Amherst.
The Lynchburg Virginian, Dec. 22, 1825, p. 3, c. 3.

CHRISTIAN, MISS MARTHA PHILADELPHIA - See entry for Dr. Jeffrey Palmer.

CHRISTIAN, DR. WM. H. B. married on Sept. 13, 1821 to Miss Saluda Baker
Fuqua, dau. of the late Capt. Samuel Fuqua of Charlotte Co., by The
Rev. Richard Dabbs. Groom of Campbell Co.
The Lynchburg Press, Sept. 21, 1821, p. 3.

CLAIBORNE, CAPT. LEONARD married on Dec. 24, 1818 to Miss Letitia W.
Clarke, dau of Col. William Clarke of Pittsylvania, by The Rev.
Robert Hurt. Groom of Halifax.
The Lynchburg Press and Public Advertiser, Jan. 7, 1819, p. 3.

CLARK, MISS ANN ELIZABETH W. - See entry for Capt. Augustine Leftwich.

CLARK, MISS CATHARINE C. - See entry for William Smith.

CLARK, MAJOR DAVID H. married on Tues. 25th ultimo to Martha Maria Clark,
dau. of S. B. Clark of Prince Edward, by The Rev. Daniel Will. Groom
of Pittsylvania.
The Lynchburg Virginian, April 21, 1828, p. 3, c. 6.

CLARK, MISS ELIZABETH - See entry for Edward Bolling, Jr.

CLARK, MISS ELIZABETH - See entry for James Hendrick, Esq.

CLARK, HENRY married on Wed. evening, June 27, 1821 to Judith Moorman,
dau. of James C. Moorman, Esq. (vicinity of Lynchburg) by The Rev.
Wm. S. Reid.
The Lynchburg Press, June 29, 1821, p. 3, c. 3.

CLARK, MR. JEFFERSON married on 18th July to Miss Catherine Matilda
Spencer of Charlottesville, Va. Married at Charlottesville.
The Lynchburg Virginian, Aug. 20, 1829, p. 3, c. 6.

CLARK, JOHN A. married on Sept. 3rd. to Miss Elizabeth Foults, dau. of
the late Mr. Jennings Foults of Prince Edward, by The Rev. Wm.
Montgomerie. Groom of Pittsylvania.
The Lynchburg Virginian, Sept. 18, 1818, p. 3, c. 6.

CLARK, MISS LUCY C. - See entry for William Anderson, Esq.

CLARK, SAMUEL CHRISTOPHER married on 5th inst. to Miss Elmira Williams, dau. of Mr. John Williams, by The Rev. Samuel Armstead. All of Campbell County.
The Lynchburg Virginian, Dec. 18, 1834, p. 3, c. 4.

CLARK, MISS MARTHA MARIA- See entry for Major David Clark.

CLARK, MICAJAH married on Tues. the 21st ult. to Miss Eliza Mason by The Rev. Samuel Armistead. All of Charlotte.
The Lynchburg Virginian, Jan. 3, 1831, p. 1, c. 3.

CLARK, MISS SARAH U. - See entry for William Massie, Esq.

CLARKE, MISS LETITIA W. - See entry for Capt. Leonard Claiborne.

CLARKE, MISS LUCINDA - See entry for Hillary G. Richardson.

CLARKSON, M. P. married on Thurs. 15 Jan. to Miss Zelinda S. Herndon, eldest dau. of David Herndon, Esq. of Campbell, by The Rev. Jesse Witt. Groom of Kentucky.
The Lynchburg Virginian, Feb. 16, 1835, p. 3, c. 5.

CLARKSON, MISS JULIA ANN - See entry for Capt. Thomas Dixon.

CLAY, HENRY, JR. Married on Oct. 10, 1832 to Miss Maria Julia Prather, dau. of late Thomas Prather, Esq. of Louisville, by The Rev. G.W. Ashbridge. Groom son of Henry Clay, Esq. of Kentucky.
The Lynchburg Virginian, Oct. 25, 1832, p. 3, c. 4.

CLAY, JOHN RANDOLPH, ESQ. married on 2nd of April last in chapel of British Factory at St. Petersburg, Russia to Frances Ann Sophia Gibbs, dau. of Harry Leake Gibbs of St. Petersburg, by The Rev. Edward Low.
The Lynchburg Virginian, June 8, 1835, p. 3, c. 4.

CLAY, ODEN G. married on Oct. 9, 1822 to Ann Davies, dau. of Mr. Samuel B. Davies of Bedford, by The Rev. Wm. S. Reid. Groom of Bedford.
The Lynchburg Virginian, Oct. 29, 1822, p. 3.

CLAYTOR, JAMES L. married on March 9, 1825 to Miss Paulina Smith, dau. of Mr. Samuel Smith of Bedford, by The Rev. John V. Kelly. Groom of Lynchburg.
The Lynchburg Virginian, Mar. 15, 1825, p. 3.

CLAYTOR, John P. married on Feb. 7, 1833 to Miss Mary E. R. Toomer, youngest dau. of Mr. Charles Toomer, by The Rev. M. Jenny. Groom merchant of Lower Alton, Ill., formerly of Bedford. Bride of same place, formerly of Leakesville, N. C.
The Lynchburg Virginian, Mar. 7, 1833, p. 3, c. 3.

CLAYTOR, SAMUEL married on Jan. 22, 1822 to Miss Rosanna E. Murrell, dau. of Mr. John Murrell, Sr. of Lynchburg, by The Rev. Wm. S. Reid. Groom of Bedford.
The Lynchburg Press, Jan. 25, 1822, p. 3.

CLEAVLAND, _____ married on Nov. 9, 1819 to Miss _____ Atkinson
of Amherst, by The Rev. William Duncan. Groom of Amherst.
The Lynchburg Press & Public Advertiser, Nov. 19, 1819, p. 3.

CLEMENTS, ABRAHAM, ESQ. married on Wed. evening 23rd inst. to Miss Ann
Callaway by The Rev. Charles Callaway. All of Pittsylvania Co.
The Lynchburg Virginian, Oct. 5, 1829, p. 3, c. 3.

CLOCKE, MRS. MARTHA W. - See entry for James M. Smith.

CLOPTON, MISS ELIZA - See entry for Dr. Wm. Holcombe.

COBBS, MISS ADALINE - See entry for Henry L. Davies.

COBBS, MRS. ANN - See entry for Jacob Feazle.

COBBS, CHARLES married on Thurs. the 16th inst. to Miss Ann Scott, dau.
of Wm. Scott deceased. All of Campbell Co.
The Lynchburg Press, Aug. 17, 1821, p. 3, c. 4.

COBBS, CHARLES married on Jan. 23, 1830 to Miss Lucy Walker in Charlotte
Co. by The Rev. Samuel Armistead.
The Lynchburg Virginian, Feb. 1, 1830, p. 3, c. 4.

COBBS, MISS DAMARIAS - See entry for Mr. Jesse A. Burton.

COBBS, MISS EVALINA P. - See entry for William Salmons.

COBBS, MISS FRANCES M. - See entry for Samuel M. Armistead.

COBBS, MISS MARTHA - See entry for Micajah Davis, Esq.

COCKE, MISS HARRIET - See entry for Chas. Reynolds.

COCKE, MISS MARY - See entry for Capt. John Rosser.

COCKE, MISS SARAH J. - See entry for William Christopher Burton.

COFER, MISS CAROLINE L. - See entry for John W. Skenk.

COLE, ELIZA - See entry for Bright Pickett.

COLE, DR. JOHN L. married on Dec. 25, 1828 to Casandra Caroline White,
dau. of Capt. John White of Pittsylvania Co., by The Rev. Griffith
Dickerson. Groom of Stokes Co., N.C.
The Lynchburg Virginian, Jan. 1, 1829, p. 3, c. 4.

COLE, THE REV. JOSIAL married on the 5th inst. to Miss Susanna Wallace by
The Rev. Dr. Leach. Bride and groom both of Lynchburg.
The Lynchburg Virginian, Dec. 14, 1826, p. 3, c. 3.

COLEMAN, MRS. CAROLINE MATILDA - See entry for Arthur Tominson.

COLEMAN, DAVID married on the 30th ult. to Eliza Moses, dau. of Peter
Moses of Buckingham, by The Rev. Sam'l. Davidson.
The Lynchburg Virginian, April, 14, 1825, p. 3, c. 4.

COLEMAN, GEORGE W. married on Wed. the 3rd inst. to Miss Sarah W. Hunt, dau. of Capt. John Hunt, by The Rev. Charles Dresser. All of Pittsylvania.
The Lynchburg Virginian, Sept. 25, 1834, p. 3, c. 5.

COLEMAN, JOSEPH married on the 26th inst. to Miss Catharine Pinkard of Franklin by The Rev. Matthew Jackson. Groom of Amherst.
The Lynchburg Virginian, Sept. 3, 1835, p. 3, c. 4.

COLEMAN, CAPT. LINDSEY married on Thurs. inst. to Mrs. Isabella Read of Bedford Co. by The Rev. Mr. Russell.
The Lynchburg Virginian, June 3, 1830, p. 3, c. 6.

COLEMAN, MISS MARY ANN - See entry for Thomas R. Brown.

COLEMAN, MRS. MILDRED - See entry for John Duncan.

COLEMAN, STEPHEN married to Nancy P. Harrison, dau. of Capt. Ainsworth Harrison of Wilson Co., Tenn., formerly of Pittsylvania Co., Va. Groom of Madison Co., Ala.
The Lynchburg Virginian, Sept. 22, 1825, p. 3.

COLEMAN, MISS SUSAN H. - See entry for James A. Luck.

COLEMAN, WILLIAM E. married on the 2nd inst. to Miss Jane C. Brown, youngest dau. of Benjamin Brown, Esq., by The Rev. Wm. S. Reid. All of Amherst.
The Lynchburg Virginian, Mar. 24, 1836, p. 3, c. 4.

COLES, MISS MILDRED C. - See entry for John R. Edmunds.

CONWAY, MISS MARY - See entry for Stephen Booth.

COOK, MAJ. ROBERT married on the 8th inst. to Miss Susan Martin, dau. of Col. Joseph Martin of Henry Co., groom of Pittsylvania Co. Married by The Rev. Arnold Walker.
The Lynchburg Virginian, Oct. 20, 1828, p. 3, c. 5.

CORBIN, MR. OCTAVIOUS N. married on the 24th ult. in Wilmington, N. C. to Miss Sarah Jane Lillington, dau. of John A. Lillington, Esq. Groom formerly of Lynchburg.
The Lynchburg Virginian, Jan. 20, 1831, p. 3, c. 5.

CORNEAL, MISS MARTHA ELIZABETH - See entry for Roger Martin.

COSBY, THE REV. LEWIS F. married on Jan. 13, 1833 at Abingdon, Va. to Miss Eliza Jane Belkin by The Rev. D. R. Preston. Bride of Abingdon, Va. Groom formerly of Lynchburg.
The Lynchburg Virginian, Jan. 24, 1833, p. 3, c. 6.

COUSINS, FRANCIS M. married on Thurs. evening, the 27th ult. to Miss
    Lucinda Norman, dau. of Mr. William Norman of Henry Co., by The
    Rev. William Wray. Groom of Pittsylvania Co.
    The Lynchburg Press, Mar. 22, 1822, p. 3.

COWHERD, MISS SUSAN ANN - See entry for William Henry Dickerson.

COWLES, THE REV. HENRY B. married on Thurs. last to Miss Juliet, dau.
    of Wm. Irvine, Esq. deceased of Bedford, by The Rev. John Early.
    Groom of the Virginia Conference.
    The Lynchburg Virginian, Mar. 21, 1836, p. 3, c. 2.

COX, MISS ADELAIDE MATILDA - See entry for Landon Cabell Read.

COX, MISS ANN - See entry for Isaac R. Reynolds.

COX, ARCHIBALD married on Feb. 21, 1833 to Miss Julia Ann Burford by
    The Rev. W. I. Holcombe. Bride and groom of Amherst Co.
    The Lynchburg Virginian, Feb. 25, 1833, p. 3, c. 5.

COX, MISS EMILY - See entry for Amasa Holmes.

COX, MISS FRANCES - See entry for Thomas Booth.

COX, MISS MARTHA ANN L. STAPLES - See entry for William A. Staples.

COX, MISS SUSAN C. - See entry for Sylvester Burford.

CRAGHEAD, CHARLES P. married on Tues. evening the 6th inst. to Miss
    Elvira Saunders, eldest dau. of Littleberry Saunders of Bedford
    Co., by The Rev. John Ayres. Groom of Franklin.
    The Lynchburg Virginian, Mar. 19, 1832, p. 3, c. 3.

CRAGHEAD, MISS ELIZABETH - See entry for John Booth.

CRAGHEAD, JOHN married on Tues. 21st inst. to Miss Julia Smith, dau. of
    Mr. Wm. Smith, by The Rev. Abner Anthony. All of Franklin Co.
    The Lynchburg Virginian, Jan 6, 1831, p. 3, c. 4.

CRAIG, MR. WILLIAM married on 27th ult. to Miss Elizabeth Jameison, dau.
    of Samuel Jameison, Esq., by Elder Joseph Pedigo. All of Franklin
    Co.
    The Lynchburg Virginian, Dec. 15, 1834, p. 3, c. 4.

CRALLE, MISS MARIA - See entry for Albert G. Long.

CRALLE, RICHARD K., ESQ. married on Thurs. last to Miss Judith Scott
    Cabell, dau. of Dr. John J. Cabell, by The Rev. Wm. S. Reid. Groom
    attorney-at-law of Nottoway.
    The Lynchburg Virginian, Feb. 9, 1829, p. 3, c. 4.

CRANK, ALEXANDER married on Oct. 30, 1832 to Miss Julia Ann Hatcher, dau.
    of Julius Hatcher, by The Rev. Wm. Harris. All of Bedford.
    The Lynchburg Virginian, Nov. 12, 1832, p. 3, c. 5.

CRAWFORD, BENNET A., ESQ. married June 19, 1823 in Lexington to Hannah Hare, dau. of late Dr. Hare of Nelson Co. Groom attorney-at-law of Amherst.
The Lynchburg Virginian, June 20, 1823, p. 3.

CRAWFORD, DAVID married on June 21st at Laurel Furnace, Dickson Co., Tenn. to Mrs. Elizabeth D. Fulcher, late of Amherst Co., Va.
The Lynchburg Virginian, Aug. 6, 1829, p. 3, c. 5.

CRAWFORD, MISS ELIZABETH H. - See entry for Alden B. Spooner.

CRAWFORD, GABRIELLA SOPHIA - See entry for The Rev. Chas. H. Page.

CRAWFORD, VAN TROMP, ESQ. married June 19, 1828 at Liberty to Miss Maria M. Dunn, dau. of Maj. Sylvester Dunn. All of Amite Co., Miss.
The Lynchburg Virginian, July 21, 1828, p. 3, c. 5.

CRAWFORD, W. S., ESQ. married last Thurs. at the Glebe in Amherst Co., Va. to Miss A. F. D. Penn by The Rev. Charles Page.
The Lynchburg Virginian, May 15, 1827, p. 3, c. 4.

CRAWLEY, MISS NANCY - See entry for Peter Fore.

CREASEY, LITTLETON V. married on 30th ult. to Miss Ann Sophia, dau. of Mr. Wm. Thurman of Lynchburg, by The Rev. H.B. Cowles. Groom of Fincastle, Va.
The Lynchburg Virginian, July 2, 1835, p. 3, c. 6.

CRENSHAW, CAPT, JOHN married Nov. 15, 1825 to Miss Lucy McDaniel, dau. of Maj. Arch McDaniel, by The Rev. Samuel Phillips. All of Bedford Co.
The Lynchburg Virginian, Nov. 24, 1825, p. 3, c. 4.

CRENSHAW, MISS MARY W. - See entry for Wm. Mead.

CREWS, JOHN married Oct. 18th to Sarah Anne Taliaferro, dau. of Roderick Taliaferro, by The Rev. James Boyd. All of Nelson Co., Va.
The Lynchburg Virginian, Nov. 1, 1827, p. 3, c. 4.

CREWS, MISS VIRGINIA - See entry for Ebenezer F. Gardner.

CRIDER, MR. JACOB married on 19th inst. to Miss Nancy Rorar by The Rev. Joel T. Adams. All of Pittsylvania Co., Va.
The Lynchburg Virginian, Dec. 31, 1832, p. 3, c. 2.

CRITZ, ARCHILESS married on 18th inst. to Miss Luvenia S. Penn by The Rev. John C. Traylor. All of Patrick Co.
The Lynchburg Virginian, June 6, 1831, p. 3, c. 4.

CROW, MR. SAMUEL married to Miss Amanda Gouldman, dau. of Edward Gouldman of Buckingham Co., by The Rev. Wm. Cornell.
The Lynchburg Virginian, May 10, 1837, p. 3, c. 3.

CRUMP, MR. BEVERLY married Jan. 28th to Miss Frances M. Gray, dau. of Mr. Birkell Gray, by The Rev. Vinal Smith. All of Bedford Co., Va.
The Lynchburg Virginian, Feb. 5, 1835, p. 3.

CRUMPECKER, JOHN married Dec. 22, 1831 to Elizabeth, dau. of Mr. Isham Royalty of this place. Groom of Bedford.
The Lynchburg Virginian, Dec. 26, 1831, p. 3, c. 4.

CUMPTON, JOAB married Dec. 30, 1828 to Miss Emily Ramsey, dau. of James Ramsey, by The Rev. John Ayres. All of Bedford.
The Lynchburg Virginian, Jan. 8, 1829, p. 3, c. 4.

CUNNINGHAM, MISS MARY - See entry for Redmund McClure.

CURD, JOHN E. married on 3rd inst. to Miss Susan F. Luster, dau. of John
Luster, by The Rev. A. C. Dempry. All of Botetourt Co., Va.
The Lynchburg Virginian, Aug. 14, 1837, p. 3, c. 4.

CURL, MISS ELIZABETH - See entry for Jesse Perry.

CURL, JAMES married to Miss Eliza Fuqua, dau. of Moses Fuqua of Bedford,
by The Rev. Jessie Witt. Groom of Lunenburg.
The Lynchburg Virginian, Oct. 24, 1836, p. 3, c. 3.

CURTIS, MISS ANN JANE - See entry for Lucian Goggin.

CYRUS, NICHOLAS married May 7, 1819 to Mrs. Jane Davidson by The Rev.
Obidiah Edge. Bride and groom of Lynchburg.
The Lynchburg Press & Public Advertiser, May 27, 1819, p. 3, c. 5.

D

DABNEY, MISS CATHERINE M. - See entry for The Hon. Sceaton Grantland.

DABNEY, GEORGE EDWARD married to Miss Martha Cornelia Price, dau. of
Joseph F. Price of Hanover Co., by The Rev. James Taylor. Groom
of Campbell Co., Va.
The Lynchburg Virginian, May 20, 1833, p. 3, c. 5.

DABNEY, JOHN BLAIR married Oct. 4, 1821 to Elizabeth L. Towles, dau. of
Major Oliver Towles, Jr. of this Corporation, by The Rev. Wm. S.
Reid. Groom of Campbell Co., an attorney-at-law.
The Lynchburg Press, Oct. 5, 1821, p. 3.

DANDRIDGE, ALEXANDER S. married on 6th inst. to Miss Susan Blankenship,dau.
of Jos. Blankenship, by The Rev. Mr. Kabler. All of Campbell Co.
The Lynchburg Virginian, Sept. 10, 1827, p. 3, c. 5.

DANIEL, MISS MARY C. - See entry for Mayo Cabell.

DANIEL, JUDGE WILLIAM married to Miss Paulina J. Cabell.
The Lynchburg Virginian, Feb. 2, 1826, p. 3.

DAVENPORT, _____ married on the 7th inst. to Miss Martha Jones, dau.
of Mr. Tarlton Jones, by The Rev. Samuel Armistead.
The Lynchburg Virginian, Feb. 23, 1829, p. 3, c. 5.

DAVENPORT, MISS DOROTHY D. - See entry for William Edwards.

DAVENPORT, MISS ELIZA L. - See entry for Robert Tinsley.

DAVENPORT, MISS NANCY C. - See entry for John C. Shackleford.

DAVENPORT, RICHARD G. married on Dec. 14, 1831 inst. at Milton, N.C. to
Miss Mary Hubbard by The Rev. Mr. Penick. Both of Halifax, Va.
The Lynchburg Virginian, Dec. 26, 1831, p. 3, c. 4.

DAVENPORT, MISS SUSAN - See entry for Dr. Wm. L. Lambeth.

DAVIDSON, MISS DELANA - See entry for Murry Webb.

DAVIDSON, MRS. JANE - See entry for Nicholas Cyrus.

DAVIES, MISS ANN - See entry for Oden G. Clay.

DAVIES, ANTHONY H., ESQ. married on Thurs. 23rd inst. to Miss Emily Aldridge, dau. of Col. Tho's Aldridge of Tuscumbia, formerly of Amherst., by The Rev. Mr. Wall of Florence. Groom merchant in Tuscumbia.
The Lynchburg Virginian, Sept. 20, 1827, p. 3, c. 2.

DAVIES, ARTHUR B. married on Dec. 17, 1822 to Miss Susan F. Brown, dau. of Mr. Benjamin Brown of Amherst, by The Rev. Wm. S. Reid. Groom of Amherst Co.
The Lynchburg Virginian, Dec. 20, 1822, p. 3.

DAVIES, MR. BEVERLY married on Thurs. the 3rd inst. at Woodlawn to Miss Laura B., dau. of the late Capt. Edward Carter, by The Rev. Wm. S. Reid. All of Amherst.
The Lynchburg Virginian, Nov. 7, 1836, p. 3, c. 4.

DAVIES, MISS EDITHA - See entry for Dr. Wm. B. Davies.

DAVIES, MISS ELIZABETH - See entry for Mr. Lodowick Moorman.

DAVIES, MISS ELIZABETH JANE - See entry for Barnett L. Parrish.

DAVIES, HENRY L. married on the 16th inst. to Adaline Cobbs, dau. of Mr. Edmund Cobbs, by The Rev. Nicholas H. Cobbs. All of Bedford.
The Lynchburg Virginian, June 21, 1830, p. 3, c. 3.

DAVIES, DR. HOWELL married on Tues. evening, the 1st inst. to Mrs. Abby Jackson by The Rev. Wm. S. Reid. All of this place.
The Lynchburg Virginian, Oct. 8, 1822, p. 3, c. 6.

DAVIES, MACAJAH married on the 16th inst. to Miss Lucy R. Cabaniss of Pittsylvania Co. by Elder Edwin G. Cabaniss.
The Lynchburg Virginian, Nov. 1, 1827, p. 3, c. 4.

DAVIES, SAMUEL R., ESQ. married on Wed. evening last at Montpeliea near Amherst Court House to Miss Sarah Franklin, dau. of late Maj. Jas. Franklin, by The Rev. Charles Page.
The Lynchburg Virginian, Sept. 24, 1829, p. 3, c. 3.

DAVIES, WHITING married on the 1st inst. to Miss Sarah Ann S. Parks by The Rev. Chas. H. Page. All of Amherst.
The Lynchburg Virginian, Dec. 15th, 1836, p. 3, c. 4.

DAVIES, DR. WM. B. married on the 14th inst. to Miss Editha Davies by The Rev. Charles H. Page. Bride of Amherst Co. Groom of Bedford.
The Lynchburg Virginian, Apr. 16, 1829, p. 3, c. 4.

DAVIS, MISS _____ - See entry for James Bowling.

DAVIS, ADDISON married on Tuesday the 7th ult. to Miss Lucy M. dau. of
Mr. Benjamin Schoolfield of this place.
The Lynchburg Virginian, May 16, 1833, p. 3, c. 5.

DAVIS, ALLEN married on the 7th ult. in Washington, N.C. to Mrs. Milly
Davis, his former wife, by John R. Davis, Esq.
The Lynchburg Virginian, Mar. 5, 1835, p. 3, c. 4.

DAVIS, MISS EMILY DAVIS - See entry for Martin D. Tinsley.

DAVIS, MISS FRANCES - See entry for Michael Hart.

DAVIS, GEORGE married on the 11 inst. at Philadelphia, Pa. to Miss
Esther Barnet, niece of Mr. Simpson Morris, Esq. of Philadelphia,
by The Rev. Isaac Leeser. Bride of London. Groom of Philadelphia
and of the firm Hart & Davis.
The Lynchburg Virginian, Nov. 19, 1829, p. 3, c. 4.

DAVIS, JAMES, ESQ. married on the 16th of Feb. to Miss Mary H. Morris,
dau. of late Thomas Morris of Amherst Co., by The Rev. John Davis.
The Lynchburg Virginian, March 3, 1831, p. 3, c. 5.

DAVIS, MR. JOHN F. married on the 7th inst. to Miss Delight Thomas of
Richmond by The Rev. James B. Taylor.
The Lynchburg Virginian, Oct. 19, 1835, p. 3, c. 4.

DAVIS, JOSEPH married on 7th inst. to Miss Sophia, dau. of Mr. Wm. C.
Moon of Charlotte, by The Rev. Samuel Armistead.
The Lynchburg Virginian, Dec. 22, 1931, p. 3, c. 5.

DAVIS, MRS. LUCY M. DAVIS - See entry for Henry Lewis.

DAVIS, MISS MARTHA ANN - See entry for Thomas W. Spurlock.

DAVIS, MISS MARY A. - See entry for Robinson Stabler.

DAVIS, MISS MARY MATILDA - See entry for Hobson Johns.

DAVIS, MICAJAH, ESQ. married on Thurs. last at residence of John Alexander,
Esq. to Miss Martha, dau. of Mr. Waddy Cobbs of Bedford, by The Rev.
Nicholos H. Cobbs.
The Lynchburg Virginian, July 11, 1831, p. 3, c. 4.

DAVIS, MRS. MILLY - See entry for Allen Davis.

DAVIS, MISS NANCY B. - See entry for Elliott Wortham.

DAVIS, MISS POLLY - See entry for Cornelius W. Pierce.

DAVIS, CAPT. RICHARD married on Aug. 24, 1819 to Miss Sophia
Wharton, dau. of John Wharton of Bedford Co., by The Rev. Samuel
Phillips. Groom of Bedford Co.
The Lynchburg Press & Public Advertiser, Aug. 31, 1819, p. 3, c. 5.

DAVIS, MISS SARAH ANN - See entry for Wm. W. Smith.

DAVIS, MISS SUSAN G. - See entry for George W. Morris.

DAVIS, THOMAS married on Nov. 1, 1832 to Miss Sarah B. Schoolfield, dau. of Mr. Benjamin Schoolfield, by The Rev. D. S. Doggett. All of Lynchburg. Groom formerly of Washington City.
The Lynchburg Virginian, Nov. 5, 1832, p. 3, c. 5.

DAVISON, MISS ELIZABETH - See entry for John Adams.

DAWSON, MISS ANN G. - See entry for James L. Lamkin.

DAWSON, MISS ELIZABETH - See entry for Dr. Robert P. Phelps.

DAWSON, MISS JANE - See entry for Willis Reynolds.

DAWSON, LUDWELL L. married on the 7th inst. to Miss Jane M. Watt, dau. of Col. James Watt of Buckingham, by The Rev. James Saunders. Groom of Amherst.
The Lynchburg Virginian, Nov. 16, 1826, p. 3, c. 4.

DAWSON, RODERICK married on the 11th inst. to Miss Lucy Majors, dau. of Mr. John Majors, by The Rev. Dr. Wm. I. Waller. Bride and groom of Bedford.
The Lynchburg Virginian, Nov. 16, 1829, p. 3, c. 6.

DAWSON, WILLIAM R., ESQ. married on Thurs. the 3rd inst. to Miss Eliza Pointer, dau. of Mr. John Pointer of St. Louis, formerly a resident of Lynchburg, Va., by The Rev. Mr. Edmonson. Groom of St. Charles, Missouri, formerly resident of Buckingham, Va.
The Lynchburg Virginian, May 30, 1831, p. 3, c. 3.

DAY, HENRY T. married on Jan. 29, 1824 to Miss Elizabeth Penn, dau. of George Penn of Amherst, by The Rev. Daniel Day.
The Lynchburg Virginian, Feb. 3, 1824, p. 3.

DAY, MISS SARAH - See entry for Jonathan Martin.

DENNIS, MISS ELIZABETH J. - See entry for Nathaniel I. Venable.

DENNIS, ISAAC H. married on the 18th ult. to Miss Mary A. Price by The Rev. H. P. Goodrich. All of Prince Edward.
The Lynchburg Virginian, May 19, 1835, p. 3, c. 5.

DIBRELL, CHARLES L. married on May 14, 1823 to Mary Jane Lambeth of Campbell Co., dau. of Meridith Lambeth, by The Rev. Wm. S. Reid. Groom of Lynchburg.
The Lynchburg Virginian, May 16, 1823, p. 3.

DIBRELL, MISS CATHERINE M. - See entry for Thomas Mieure.

DIBRELL, MISS FRANCES - See entry for The Rev. Wm. W. Hendricks.

DIBRELL, MISS JUDY ANN - See entry for Nelson J. Hatcher.

DIBRELL, JAMES W. married on May 26, 1824 to Miss Sarah Brown, dau. of
Benjamin Brown of Amherst, by The Rev. Wm. S. Reid. Groom of Lynchburg.
The Lynchburg Virginian, May 28, 1824, p. 3.

DIBRELL, MISS LEANNA LEE - See entry for George W. Staples.

DIBRELL, MISS MARTHA R. - See entry for Dr. Ezekiel Gilbert.

DIBRELL, DOCT. MATTHEW W. married July 20th to Miss Martha Louisa Hill,
dau. of Col. William Hill, by The Rev. H. W. Pasley at Athens,
Monroe Co., Miss. Groom formerly of Va.
The Lynchburg Virginian, Aug. 10, 1837, p. 3, c. 3.

DIBRELL, MISS WILMOUTH W. - See entry for James Garry.

DICKEN, SAMUEL W. married on 9th inst. to Miss Eliza W. Talbot by The
Rev. Archibald Smith. Groom of Lewisburg, birde of this place.
The Lynchburg Virginian, Nov. 19, 1835, p. 3, c. 3.

DICKERSON, MISS MARTHA - See entry for Leonard Bowers.

DICKERSON, WILLIAM married Nov. 10, 1825 to Miss Mary Gray, dau. of Col.
John P. Gray of Bedford, by The Rev. Samuel Phillips. Groom of
Bedford.
The Lynchburg Virginian, Nov. 24, 1825, p. 3.

DICKERSON, WM. HENRY married on 14th ult. to Miss Susan Ann, dau. of the
late Reuben Cowhers, by The Rev. Raymond Minor. All of Louisa Co.
The Lynchburg Virginian, July 11, 1831, p. 3, c. 4.

DICKERSON, WM. W. married on Thurs. last to Sarah Liggan by The Rev.
Edward Cannon. Bride and groom both of Lynchburg.
The Lynchburg Virginian, Jan. 16, 1826, p. 3, c. 4.

DICKEY, MISS NANCY - See entry for Mr. Robert C. Martin.

DICKINSON, MR. WILLIAM married on Thurs. 10th inst. to Miss Mary Gray,
dau. of Col. John P. Gray, by The Rev. Sam'l. Phillips. All of
Bedford.
The Lynchburg Virginian, Nov. 24, 1825, p. 3, c. 4.

DICKY, JAMES married on 12th ult. to Miss Margaret Evans, eldest dau.
of Mr. Sampson Evans. All of Campbell.
The Lynchburg Virginian, Feb. 3, 1831, p. 3, c. 4.

DIDLAKE, MISS MARY M. - See entry for Samuel Shelton.

DIESON, MISS PAULINE - See entry for Thomas Hoye.

DIGGES, MISS NICY H. - See entry for Albert G. Chewning.

DILLARD, MISS MARTHA ANN - See entry for Mr. Charles Ward.

DILLARD, HENRY married on July 7, 1833 to Miss Mary Jane Taliaferro, dau.
of Dr. R. M. Taliaferro of Rocky Mount, Franklin Co., Va. by The
Rev. N. J. Cobbs.
The Lynchburg Virginian, July 15, 1833, p. 3, c. 6.

DILLARD, MR. JAMES A. married on 21st inst. to Miss Sarah L. dau. of
the late Capt. Mickleberry Montague of Powhatan by The Rev. Edward
Baptist. Groom of Amherst.
The Lynchburg Virginian, May 30, 1833, p. 3, c. 4.

DILLARD, JAMES M. married on 22nd inst. to Miss Mary Mundy, dau. of
Charles Mundy by The Rev. Archibald B. Smith. All of Amherst.
The Lynchburg Virginian, Sept. 26, 1836, p. 3, c. 3.

DILLARD, JOHN (DR.) married on June 27th, 1826 to Miss Nancy Winston,
dau. of Col. Anthony Winston. Married in Franklin Co., Ala.
Groom of Tuscumbia, Ala. but both formerly of Va.
The Lynchburg Virginian, July 20, 1826, p. 3, c. 5.

DILLON, MISS ANN W. - See entry for Thomas J. Stratton.

DILLON, MISS REBECCA - See entry for George Booseman.

DINWIDDIE, MISS JULIAN - See entry for R. H. Walthall.

DINWIDDIE, WM. W. married on Wed., 5th inst. to Miss Nancy Bryant, dau.
of late John Bryant, by The Rev. Isaac Cochran. Bride and groom
both of Campbell County.
The Lynchburg Virginian, Dec. 13, 1827, p. 3, c. 4.

DIVERS, MISS ANN - See entry for Landon Taliaferro.

DIVERS, OTEY married on March 13, 1823 to Miss Theresse Ferguson by The
Rev. Moses Greer. Bride and groom both of Franklin Co.
The Lynchburg Virginian, March 28, 1823, p. 3.

DIX, MISS MARTHA - See entry for Dr. Fayette Winston.

DIXON, JAMES married on Thurs. evening last to Miss Mary A. dau. of The
Rev. Thomas Jones of this place, by The Rev. Henry B. Cowles.
Groom of Campbell Co.
The Lynchburg Virginian, Feb. 26, 1835, p. 3, c. 5.

DIXON, MISS SARAH ANN - See entry for Mr. Robert G. Johnson.

DIXON, CAPT. THOMAS. married on Thurs. last to Miss Julia Ann Clarkson,
dau. of John Clarkson, by The Rev. John D. Ewing. All of Rockbridge.
The Lynchburg Virginian, June 9, 1836, p. 3, c. 4.

DOALSBEAR, MISS LUCY - See entry for The Rev. Lorenza Dow.

DODD, JOSEPH married on April 2, 1818 to Miss Elizabeth Hattan. Bride
and groom of Amherst.
The Lynchburg Press, April 17, 1818.

DODSON, GEORGE C. married on Wed., Dec. 1, 1830 to Miss Lucinda P.
Foster by The Rev. Jno. Washburn. All of Patrick.
The Lynchburg Virginian, Dec. 16, 1830, p. 3, c. 2.

DODSON, MR. MILTON R. married on April 21 to Miss Jane Philpott by
The Rev. Mr. Lowe. All of Patrick.
The Lynchburg Virginian, May 2, 1831, p. 3, c. 3.

DOE, BENJAMIN, ESQ. married to Nancy Moore. Groom of Canterbury, N.H.
The Lynchburg Virginian, June 9, 1825, p. 3, c. 3.

DONALD, BENJAMIN A., ESQ. married on March 31, 1824 to Miss Sarah Camm,
dau. of the late John Camm of Lynchburg, by The Rev. Wm. S. Reid.
Groom of Bedford.
The Lynchburg Virginian, April 2, 1824, p. 3.

DONELSON, GEN. DANIEL S. married on the 18th inst. to Miss Margaret
Branch, dau. of The Hon. John Branch, Secretary of the Navy.
Married in Washington. Groom is of Tennessee.
The Lynchburg Virginian, Oct. 28, 1830, p. 3, c. 4.

DONNELL, MISS ARIANNA - See entry for James Holmes.

DOOLEY, MISS EMELINE - See entry for James M. Jeter.

DORSEY, LLOYD married on Jan. 8, 1829 to Miss Mary M. Campbell, dau. of
Capt. James Campbell of Bedford, by The Rev. Samuel Phillips.
Groom of Lynchburg.
The Lynchburg Virginian, Jan. 15, 1829, p. 3, c. 5.

DOSWELL, MISS SUSAN - See entry for Henry S. Beverley.

DOUGLAS, JOHN L. married on Oct. 29, 1823, to Sarah Terrill, dau. of
Chas. Terrill, deceased, at Robert Ward's house in Pittsylvania,
by The Rev. Dickerson. Groom of Campbell.
The Lynchburg Virginian, Nov. 7, 1823, p. 3.

DOUTHAT, MISS ELIZABETH - See entry for Dr. John T. W. Reid.

DOW, THE REV. LORENZO married to Miss Lucy Doalsbear of Montville.
Married at Hebron.
The Lynchburg Press & Public Advertiser, Apr. 18, 1820.

DOYLE, MISS ELIZABETH - See entry for Lindsey Shoemaker.

DRAKE, SAMUEL married on April 11, 1824 to Miss Ann Fisher, dau. of
Palmer Fisher of the Baltimore and Washington Theatres at Georgetown, D.C.
The Lynchburg Virginian, Apr. 30, 1824, p. 3.

DREAN, JOHN W. married on Wed. evening last to Miss Mary Ann, dau. of
Mrs. Mary Ann Beckham, by The Rev. Edward Cannon. All of this place.
The Lynchburg Virginian, June 6, 1831, p. 3, c. 4.

DREAN, THOMAS A. married on Wed. evening, 5th ult. to Miss Elizabeth
　Beckham by The Rev. Martin P. Parks. Both bride and groom are
　of this town.
　The Lynchburg Virginian, Oct. 10, 1831, p. 3, c. 4.

DREW, DOLPHIN married on Feb. 3, 1825 to Miss Mary B. Booker, dau. of
　Mr. Peter E. Booker, by The Rev. John Early. All of this place.
　The Lynchburg Virginian, Feb. 11, 1825, p. 3.

DRISKILL, MRS. _____ See entry for John Burgess.

DUDLEY, MISS ANNA F. - See entry for John W. Schoolfield.

DUDLEY, JOHN WILLIAM married on 29th of October to Miss Audalusia
　Fourqureen by The Rev. Charles Dresser. Bride of Halifax.
　Groom of Lynchburg.
　The Lynchburg Virginian, Nov. 5, 1835, p. 3, c. 3.

DUFFEL, HENRY L. married on Wed. evening the 1st inst. to Mrs. Mary R.
　West by The Rev. Henry B. Cowles. All of this place.
　The Lynchburg Virginian, Oct. 9, 1834.

DUFFEL, MATILDA - See entry for Benjamin Wilks.

DUFFAL, MISS REBECCA S. - See entry for Arthur H. Moon.

DUNCAN, MISS JANE - See entry for John Russel.

DUNCAN, JOHN married on Nov. 12, 1819 to Mrs. Mildred Coleman of
　Amherst. Groom of Amherst. Married by Wm. Duncan.
　The Lynchburg Press & Public Advertiser, Nov. 19, 1819, p. 3, c. 3.

DUNCAN, MISS SARAH - See entry for Martin T. Bibb.

DUNN, MISS MARIA M. - See entry for Van Tromp Crawford.

DUNNINGTON, MISS MARY ANN - See entry for Joseph E. Venable.

DUPUY, MISS JANE G. - See entry for Capt. Thomas McKinney.

DUPUY, LINNEUS married on Thurs. evening the 28th ult. to Miss Seline
　Tate of this place by The Rev. F. G. Smith.
　The Lynchburg Virginian, May 2, 1831, p. 3, c. 3.

DUVAL, MRS. ELIZABETH - See entry for John Rucker.

DUVAL, MISS ELIZABETH P. - See entry for John K. Campbell.

DUVAL, MISS LUCY CLAIBORNE - See entry for Henry J. Brown.

DUVAL, MISS MARY ANN FRANCES - See entry for Richard H. Toler.

DUVAL, MISS SUSAN - See entry for Isaac Adams.

DUVAL, THOMAS J. married last evening to Elizabeth Stevens by The Rev.
Wm. S. Reid. Bride and groom both of Lynchburg.
The Lynchburg Virginian, Jan. 18, 1827, p. 3, c. 4.

DWIGHT, TIMOTHY, married to Miss Arietta Lincoln at Gardiner, Ky.
The Lynchburg Virginian, July 1, 1830.

E

EARL, MISS ISABELLA H. S. - See entry for Hezekiah Bradley.

EARLY, MISS SARAH - See entry for Claiborn Porter.

EARLY, CAPT. TUBAL married on Nov. 8, 1825 to Mrs. Charlotte Scruggs of
Bedford by The Rev. Samuel Phillips. Groom of Bedford.
The Lynchburg Virginian, Nov. 10, 1825, p. 3, c. 3.

EAST, MISS FRANCES - See entry for Samuel Worsham.

EASTIN, MISS MARY A. - See entry for Lucius J. Polk, Esq.

ECHOLS, JOSEPH married on June 11, 1814 to Elizabeth Lambeth, dau. of
Meredith Lambeth of Campbell, by The Rev. Wm. R. Martin. Groom
of Lynchburg.
The Lynchburg Press, June 23, 1814, p. 3.

ECHOLS, OBADIAH married on Thursday last to Mrs. Mildred Vawter of
this place by The Rev. Robert Ryland. Groom of Pittsylvania.
The Lynchburg Virginian, Aug. 8, 1831, p. 3, c. 4.

EDGAR, ALFRED married on the 11th inst. in Liberty to Miss Elizabeth
Mathews by The Rev. Samuel Philips.
The Lynchburg Virginian, July 19, 1832, p. 3, c. 3.

EDGAR, MISS TABITHA P. - See entry for John S. Ewing.

EDLEY, DAVID R., ESQ. Attorney, married last evening to Miss Missouri
Morriss by The Rev. F. G. Smith. All of this place.
The Lynchburg Virginian, Sept. 18, 1828, p. 3, c. 6.

EDMONDS, MISS E. - See entry for Dr. John Stricklan.

EDMONDSON, MISS ALICE - See entry for Joseph A. Logan.

EDMUNDS, MISS ELIZABETH - See entry for Robert G. Jennings.

EDMUNDS, JOHN R. married on 13th of Jan. in Charlotte Co. to Miss
Mildred C., dau. of Isaac Coles, deceased, by The Rev. Clement
Read. Groom of Halifax.
The Lynchburg Virginian, Feb. 11, 1836, p. 3, c. 5.

EDWARDS, MISS MINERVA R. A. - See entry for James C. Beck.

EDMUNDS, CAPT. PIZARRO married on July 25th to Miss Ann Eppes Howard,
dau. of Benjamin Howard, deceased, of Cumberland Co., by The Rev.
Mr. Curtis. Groom of Lovingston, Nelson Co., Va.
The Lynchburg Virginian, Aug. 15, 1833, p. 3, c. 4.

EDWARDS, WILLIAM married on Jan. 5th last to Miss Dorothy D. Davenport,
dau. of Ballard Davenport of Todd Co., Ky., by The Rev. Aaron
Trabue. Groom of Logan Co., formerly of Cumberland Co., Va.
The Lynchburg Virginian, May 26, 1836, p. 3, c. 3.

EFFINGER, MISS MARIA C. - See entry for W. M. Massie, Esq.

ELAM, MISS FRANCES - See entry for Wm. Elam.

ELAM, WILLIAM married on the 27th inst. at Charlotte to Miss Frances
Elam, eldest dau. of Mrs. Elam of Charlotte, by The Rev. Fowler.
The Lynchburg Virginian, July 8, 1830, p. 3, c. 5.

ELDER, ALFRED married on Feb. 20th to Miss Eliza Jones of Campbell by
The Rev. Samuel Armistead.
The Lynchburg Virginian, Feb. 7, 1831, p. 3, c. 4.

ELLIOTT, MISS ANN E. - See entry for Hill McCraw.

ELLIOTT, MISS ELIZABETH - See entry for George A. Wyllie.

ELLIOTT, MISS LAVINIA M. A. - See entry for James Staples.

ELLIOTT, PETER married on April 10, 1824 to Miss Mary Godfrey formerly
of Richmond, by The Rev. John Early. Groom of Lynchburg.
The Lynchburg Virginian, April 16, 1824, p. 3.

ELLIOTT, ROBERT married on the 5th inst. to Miss Jemima, dau. of Mr.
John Finch of Campbell court-house, by The Rev. Mr. Angel of
Pittsylvania. Groom of Bedford.
The Lynchburg Virginian, Mar. 16, 1835, p. 3, c. 3.

ELLIOT, WILLIAM married on Jan. 14, 1830 to Miss Theadosha Gibbs, dau.
of Mr. Wm. Gibbs, by The Rev. Wm. Harris. All of Bedford Co.
The Lynchburg Virginian, Jan. 21, 1830, p. 3, c. 4.

ELLIS, THE HON. POWHATAN married on Monday evening 28th ult. at Washington City to Eliza Winn, dau. of Timothy Winn, Esq. of Washington.
Groom was Senator in Congress from state of Mississippi.
The Lynchburg Virginian, March 10, 1831, p. 3, c. 5.

ELY, HENRY B., ESQ. married on 2nd inst. to Ann P. Carter at Mr. Layne's
near New London by The Rev. F. G. Smith.
The Lynchburg Virginian, May 8, 1826, p. 3, c. 4.

ELY, HENRY B., ESQ. Attorney-at-law, married Thurs. evening, Aug. 28th,
to Miss Henrietta Alexander, dau. of Col. Gerard Alexander, by The
Rev. Nicholas H. Cobbs at "Otter View" near New London. All of
Campbell Co.
The Lynchburg Virginian, Sept. 11, 1834, p. 3, c. 4.

EMMERSON, MISS ELIZABETH - See entry for Onslon G. Murrell.

EMMONS, MISS ELIZABETH - See entry for Dixon C. Morgan.

ENGELIKEN, MISS REBECCA MARIA - See entry for Jacob Peters.

EPPERSON, MISS POLLY - See entry for Richardson Puckett.

EPPERSON, WILLIAM - married on July 22, to Miss Elizabeth Foster by The Rev. Sam'l Armistead. All of Halifax.
The Lynchburg Virginian, Aug. 12, 1830, p. 3, c. 4.

EPPERSON, WM. R. married on the 16th inst. to Miss Eliza Anne W. Forrest, dau. of James Forrest, Esq. of Halifax, by The Rev. Samuel Armistead. Groom formerly of this place, but now of Brookneal.
The Lynchburg Virginian, June 24, 1830, p. 3, c. 5.

ESSEX, MISS ELIZABETH - See entry for Medad Lyman.

ESTES, ELISHA B. married on Thurs. 10th inst. to Miss Matilda Caroline Rice, dau. of Capt. Hudson M. Garland, by The Rev. James Boyd. All of New Glasgow.
The Lynchburg Virginian, Jan. 17, 1828, p. 3, c. 4.

EUBANK, MISS LUCY - See entry for Capt. James Ware.

EUBANK, MISS MARY JANE - See entry for Dr. George N. Rose.

EVANS, JOSEPH D. married on 28th ult. to Miss Abigail C. Barnes, dau. of Doct. Asa Barnes of Lunenburg Co., by The Rev. Wm. B. Rouzit.
The Lynchburg Virginian, Aug. 6, 1835, p. 3, c. 5.

EVANS, MISS MARGARET - See entry for James Dickey.

EVANS, THOMAS D. married on the 23rd inst. to Miss Jane B. Ross, dau. of Wm. Ross, Esq., by The Rev. E. Wadsworth. All of Lynchburg.
The Lynchburg Virginian, March 24, 1836, p. 3, c. 4.

EWING, MISS ELIZABETH - See entry for Spotswood Brown.

EWING, JOHN S. married on Nov. 19, 1822 to Miss Tabitha P. Edgar, dau. of Capt. Thomas Edgar of Bedford, by The Rev. Mr. Hunter. Groom of Prince Edward.
The Lynchburg Virginian, Nov. 29, 1822, p. 3.

F

FARMER, JOHN married on Tues. Evening, Dec. 23rd. to Miss Martha Brooks by The Rev. Josiah Cole. All of this place.
The Lynchburg Virginian, Dec. 25, 1834, p. 3, c. 4.

FARNSWORTH, ANN D. - See entry for Alfred Tinsley.

FARRAR, MR. F. H. married on the 3rd ult. to Miss Mary Jane Bullock, dau.
of Mr. James Bullock of Lynchburg, by The Rev. Mr. Page. Married
at Natchez. Groom from Concordea Parish, La.
The Lynchburg Virginian, Dec. 8th, 1836, p. 3, c. 5.

FARRIS, HEZEKIAH married on the 14th inst. to Miss Sarah Young, dau. of
The Rev. John Young of Amherst Co., by The Rev. John Doors. Groom
of Tenn.
The Lynchburg Virginian, Feb. 23, 1826, p. 3, c. 4.

FARRIS, JOSIAH married on 27th inst. at Patrick C. H. to Mary Penn, dau.
of Gabriel Penn, Esq., by The Rev. Mr. Lowe. Groom of Tennessee.
The Lynchburg Virginian, Nov. 24, 1825, p. 3, c. 4.

FEAGANES, GEORGE married on Feb. 19, 1824 to Miss Malinda Bowls, dau.
of Charles Bowls of Amherst, by The Rev. Mr. William Duncan. Groom
of Amherst.
The Lynchburg Virginian, Mar. 2, 1824, p. 3.

FEAR, MISS MARY - See entry for George W. Kent.

FEAR, MISS SARAH - See entry for Silas Vawter.

FEAZEL, MR. JOHN M. married on Nov. 1st. to Miss Martha Ann Elizabeth
Burcks of St. Louis. Groom of Clariton, Missouri.
The Lynchburg, Virginian, Nov. 24, 1834, p. 3, c. 4.

FEAZEL, MISS MARY M. - See entry for William F. Wolls.

FEAZLE, MISS ANN A. - See entry for Mr. James F. Martin.

FEAZLE, MR. JACOB married on Thurs. evening last to Mrs. Ann Cobbs by
The Rev. W. S. Reid. All of this place.
The Lynchburg Virginian, Oct. 5, 1829, p. 3, c. 3.

FERGUSON, MISS CYNTHIA - See entry for Henry F. Walker.

FERGUSON, DUGALD married on July 9, 1823 to Miss Evalina Freeland, dau.
of Col. Wm. I. Freeland of Bent Creek, Buckingham Co., by The Rev.
Mr. Burge. Groom of Bent Creek, Buckingham, Co.
The Lynchburg Virginian, July 18, 1823, p. 3.

FERGUSON, MISS THERESSE - See entry for Otey Divers.

FIELDS, MISS MARGARET - See entry for John C. Scott.

FINCH, MISS JEMIMA - See entry for Robert Elliott.

FINNY, MISS LOUISE W. - See entry for Mr. Charles C. Lee.

FISHER, MISS ANN - See card of Samuel Drake.

FISHER, DADE M. married on the 11th inst. to Miss Martha W. Cheatham, youngest dau. of Robert Cheatham of Campbell, by The Rev. Thomas Burge.
The Lynchburg Virginian, Sept. 25, 1828, p. 3, c. 5.

FISHER, DR. GABRIEL S. married on Mon. 16th inst. to Editha White, dau. of Capt. Jacob White of Bedford, by The Rev. Charles Price. Groom of Danville, Ky.
The Lynchburg Virginian, July 26, 1827, p. 3, c. 3.

FISHER, MISS MARY ANN AMBLER - See entry for Nicholas C. Kinney, Esq.

FITZGERALD, JAMES W. married Jan. 13, 1830 to Miss Harriet Anderson, dau. of The Rev. Nathan Anderson, by The Rev. James Reid. All of Pittsylvania Co.
The Lynchburg Virginian, Jan. 25, 1830, p. 3, c. 4.

FLOED, MR. DANIEL W. married on 12 inst. to Miss Louisa Cawthorne by The Rev. John Davies. All of Amherst Co.
The Lynchburg Virginian, Aug. 17, 1829, p. 3, c. 4.

FLOOD, MISS ELIZA BOLLING - See entry for Wm. A. Poore.

FLOOD, MR. JOHN married on Tues., 29th inst. to Miss Frances H. Russel, dau. of Thomas Russel of Buckingham, by The Rev. Wm. Hendrick. Groom late of Tenn.
The Lynchburg Virginian, Oct. 5, 1829, p. 3, c. 3.

FLOYD, SAMUEL married on July 21, 1833 at West Castle, Caswell Co., N.C. to Miss Pamelia F. Sale by Benjamin C. West, Esq.
The Lynchburg Virginian, Aug. 1, 1833, p. 3, c. 5.

FLOYD, WM. H. married on Sept. 12, 1832 to Miss Mary Jane Oglesby of this place by The Rev. D. S. Dogget. Groom formerly of Petersburg.
The Lynchburg Virginian, Sept. 13, 1832, p. 3, c. 4.

FONTAIN, MISS ANDASIA E.-See entry for Abner O. Nash, Esq.

FOOT, MR. MICAJAH R. married on 18th inst. to Miss Maria L. Smith, dau. of Wm. Smith, Esq. of Pittsylvania, by The Rev. Chas. Dresser. Groom of Halifax Co.
The Lynchburg Virginian, Dec. 31, 1832, p. 3, c. 2.

FOOTE, MR. HEZEKIAH R. married on the 23rd ult. to Miss Julian Adams, age 10 yrs., 1 month, & 19 days in Decatur, Dekalb Co., Ga.
The Lynchburg Virginian, May 27, 1830, p. 3, c. 6.

FORD, ADDISON married on Wed. last to Miss Eliza Bransford by The Rev. John Early. Groom is of Buckingham.
The Lynchburg Virginian, Mar. 5, 1835, p. 3, c. 4.

FORD, CALVIN married on Jan. 29, 1833 to Miss Olivia Jones, dau. of Mr. James S. Jones, by The Rev. Samuel Armistead.
The Lynchburg Virginian, Feb. 11, 1833, p. 3, c. 3.

FORE, PETER married on Jan. 29, 1833 to Miss Nancy Crawley by The Rev. Samuel Armistead.
The Lynchburg Virginian, Feb. 11, 1833, p. 3, c. 3.

FORREST, MISS ELIZA ANN W. - See entry for Wm. R. Epperson.

FORTUNE, JOHN B. married on Jan. 7, 1833 to Miss Salina N. C. Hargrave, dau. of Capt. John Hargrave of Nelson, by The Rev. Henry S. Peyton.
The Lynchburg Virginian, Feb. 14, 1833, p. 3, c. 4.

FORTUNE, RICHARD C. married on June 7, 1825 to Miss Mary M. Vaughan, dau. of Capt. George Vaughan of Nelson, by The Rev. James Boyd. Groom of Nelson Co.
The Lynchburg Virginian, June 9, 1825, p. 3.

FOSDICK, WILLIAM married on Jan. 5, 1833 to Miss Mary Johnston, dau. of Mr. James Johnston, by The Rev. Henry Brown. All of Campbell Co. Bride 25 years old, groom 75 years old.
The Lynchburg Virginian, Jan. 21, 1833, p. 3, c. 4.

FOSTER, MISS ELIZABETH - See entry for Wm. Epperson.

FOSTER, MRS. FLORA B. - See entry for Capt. Benjamin Norvell.

FOSTER, MISS LUCINDA P. - See entry for Geo. C. Dodson.

FOSTER, MRS. ORNEY - See entry for Isaac Adams, Esq.

FOSTER, MISS RUTH S. - See entry for Edward Tatum.

FOULTS, MISS ELIZABETH - See entry for John A. Clark.

FOURQUREAN, MISS ANDALUSIA - See entry for John Wm. Dudley.

FOURQUREAN, THOMAS A. married on Tues. evening last to Miss Julia Ann Pulling, dau. of Thos. Pulling deceased of Richmond, by The Rev. Wm. S. Reid. Groom of this place.
The Lynchburg Virginian, Oct. 8, 1835, p. 3, c. 3.

FOWLER, MISS ANN G. - See entry for Edward C. Lankford.

FOWLER, JOHN married on Jan. 29, 1833 to Miss Ann G. Martin by The Rev. William I. Holcombe. Both bride and groom of this place, Lynchburg.
The Lynchburg Virginian, Feb. 8, 1833, p. 3, c. 5.

FOWLER, MISS JUDA G. - See card of Fountain G. Hurt.

FOX, ELIZABETH K. - See entry for John Stagg.

FOX, FOUNTAIN T. married in Frankfort, Ky. to Miss Eliza Jane Hunton, dau. of Maj. Thos. Hunton deceased, formerly of Albemarle Co., by The Rev. Samuel Findly.
The Lynchburg Virginian, Mar. 11, 1830, p. 3, c. 3.

FOX, W. H. married on the 4th ult. to Miss Louisa O. Tait by The Rev.
   Mr. Potts. Bride formerly of Lynchburg, Va. Groom of Natchez, Miss.
   The Lynchburg Virginian, Oct. 9, 1834, p. 3, c. 3.

FRANKLIN, CAMPBELL married on Jan. 5, 1819 to Miss Catharine Guthrie of
   Amherst. Groom of Lynchburg.
   The Lynchburg Press & Public Advertiser, Jan. 11, 1819, p. 3, c. 4.

FRANKLIN, MISS ELIZABETH - See entry for James R. Mitchell.

FRANKLIN, MISS SARAH - See entry for Samuel R. Davies.

FRANKLIN, MISS SARAH - See entry for Hector Atkisson.

FRAZER, MISS CAROLINA GEORGIANA - See entry for Prince Lucian Murat.

FRAZIER, ABEL married on the 14th inst. at Bedford Co. to Miss Cath
   J. Orange, dau. of Wm. S. Orange, Esq., by The Rev. Vinol Smith.
   The Lynchburg Virginian, Oct. 20, 1834, p. 3, c. 4.

FRAZIER, MISS MILDRED - See entry for Peter Webber.

FREELAND, MISS EVALINA - See entry for Dugald Ferguson.

FREEMAN, GARLAND married on the 10th inst. to Miss Thermuthius T., dau.
   of Mr. Ambrose Burford of Amherst, by the Rev. Wm. I. Holcombe.
   The Lynchburg Virginian, Dec. 17, 1835, p. 3, c. 3.

FREEMAN, JOHN H. married on 17th inst. to Miss Martha Ann Burford by
   The Rev. T. Jones. Bride of Amherst Co. Groom of Bedford.
   The Lynchburg Virginian, Feb. 22, 1836 p. 3, c. 4.

FRIEND, THOMAS R. married on Nov. 1, 1832 to Miss Frances Cabell, dau.
   of Dr. John G. Cabell, by The Rev. F. G. Smith. Groom of Charlotte.
   Bride of this place.
   The Lynchburg Virginian, Nov. 5, 1832, p. 3, c. 5.

FULCHER, MISS ELIZABETH D. - See entry for David Crawford.

FUQUA, ABNER married on Tues. last to Miss Nancy Fuqua, eldest dau. of
   Capt. Moses Fuqua, by The Rev. Jessie Witt. All of Bedford Co.
   near Otter Bridge.
   The Lynchburg Virginian, Mar. 5, 1829, p. 3, c. 2.

FUQUA, MISS ELIZA - See entry for James Curl.

FUQUA, GILES married on Dec. 18, 1832 to Eliza N. Saunders, dau. of
   Fracis[sic] Saunders, Esq. of Buckingham Co. Groom of Charlotte.
   Married by The Rev. Samuel Armistead. Carried also in press of
   Jan. 21, 1833, p. 3, c. 4.
   The Lynchburg Virginian, Dec. 24, 1832, p. 3, c. 2.

FUQUA, MISS JUDITH - See entry for Bird S. Leftwich.

FUQUA, MISS NANCY - See entry for Abner Fuqua.

FUQUA, MISS RACHEL - See entry for James T. Hunt.

FUQUA, MISS SARAH - See entry for Armistead Hamlet.

FUQUA, MISS SALUDA BAKER - See entry for Dr. H. B. Christian.

FURBUSH, MISS MARY ANN - See entry for Samuel O. Wheeler.

FURLONG, MISS LUCY - See entry for William Isbell.

G

GABBERT, THOMAS M. married on April 23, 1833 to Miss Mary Savage, dau. of James Savage of Union District, S.C.. Groom formerly of Va.
The Lynchburg Virginian, May 9, 1833, p. 3, c. 5.

GADD, EDNA - See entry for Cajah T. Johnson.

GAINS, GEORGE W. married to Eliza Norvell, dau. of Henry Holdcroft Norvell. Both bride and groom of Lynchburg.
The Lynchburg Virginian, March 27, 1827, p. 3.

GANAWAY, WARNER married on June 3, 1819 to Miss Elizabeth Snead, dau. of William Snead of Lynchburg, by The Rev. John S. Gee. Groom of Lynchburg.
The Lynchburg Press and Public Advertiser, June 7, 1819, p. 3.

GARDIN, DR. THOMAS J. married to Robina Scott, dau. of Capt. Robert Scott of Campbell. Groom of Charlotte Co.
The Lynchburg Virginian, Jan. 30, 1826, p. 3, c. 5.

GARDNER, MISS ANN DOW - See entry for Mr. Ambrose Carlton.

GARDNER, EBENZER F. married on Tuesday evening last to Miss Virginia Crews, dau. of Thomas Crews of Amherst, by The Rev. Wm. S. Reid. Married in Amherst Co. Groom, merchant of Pattonsburg.
The Lynchburg Virginian, March 9, 1827, p. 3, c. 2.

GARLAND, MISS CAROLINE - See entry for Maurice H. Garland.

GARLAND, MISS ELIZA V. - See entry for George K. Cabell, Esq.

GARLAND, MR. HUDSON M. married on Oct. 14th to Miss Letitia B. Pendleton, dau. of Micajah Pendleton, Esq. of Nelson Co.,by The Rev. James Boyd. Groom of Amherst Co.
The Lynchburg Virginian, Nov. 6, 1828, p. 3, c. 5.

GARLAND, LANDON C., ESQ. married last Thursday evening to Miss Mary
Burwell, dau. of Col. Armistead Burwell of Mecklenburg, by The Rev.
Mr. Steele. Groom is Professor of Chemistry in Washington College.
The Lynchburg Virginian, Nov. 3, 1831, p. 3, c. 3.

GARLAND, PROF. LANDON C. married on Tuesday evening last to Miss
Louisa F. Garland, dau. of David S. Garland, Esq. of Amherst Co.,
by The Rev. James Boyd. Groom of Randolph-Macon College.
The Lynchburg Virginian, Jan. 4, 1836, p. 3, c. 4.

GARLAND, MISS LOUISA F. - See entry for Prof. Landon C. Garland

GARLAND, MISS MARY ANN - See entry for Preston H. Garland.

GARLAND, MISS M. CAROLINA RICE - See entry for Elisha B. Estes.

GARLAND, MISS MARY R. - See entry for Edward A. Cabell, Esq.

GARLAND, MAURICE H., ESQ. Attorney-at-law, married to Miss Caroline
Garland, dau. of Spottswood Garland, Esq. of Nelson Co., by The
Rev. James Boyd.
The Lynchburg Virginian, March 15, 1830, p. 3, c. 3.

GARLAND, NICHOLAS A., ESQ. married on 10th inst. 1827 to Mary C. M.
Philips, dau. of Doct. Samuel Philips, by The Rev. Nicholas Cobbs.
The Lynchburg Virginian, July 19, 1827, p. 3, c. 5.

GARLAND, PRESTON H. married to Mary Ann Garland, dau. of James P.
Garland. Both bride and groom of Amherst Co.
The Lynchburg Virginian, Nov. 23, 1826, p. 3.

GARLAND, SAMUEL M., ESQ. married on Wednesday last to Miss Mildred
Powell, dau. of Dr. James Powell, by The Rev. Charles H. Page.
Married at Amherst Court House.
The Lynchburg Virginian, July 15, 1830, p. 3, c. 6.

GARLAND, MISS SARAH A. - See entry for William M. Waller, Esq.

GARRY, JAMES married Oct. 5, 1830 to Wilmouth W. Dibrell, dau. of C. L.
Dibrell, by The Rev. Wm. W. Hendrick. Married at Flat Creek - her
father's home.
The Lynchburg Virginian, Oct. 7, 1830, p. 3, c. 3.

GARTH, JOHN, ESQ. married on the 30th ult. to Miss Emily Houston, dau.
of Mathew Houston, Esq. of Rockbridge, by The Rev. Samuel Houston.
Groom of Buchanan.
The Lynchburg Virginian, May 12, 1836, p. 3, c. 4.

GAVAN, MISS ANN - See entry for George R. Richardson.

GIBBS, FRANCES ANN SOPHIA - See entry for John Randolph Clay, Esq.

GIBBS, JOHN D. married on Oct. 5th to Miss Lucy Jane Moorman, dau. of
Mr. John H. Moorman, by The Rev. Nicholas H. Cobbs. All of Bedford.
The Lynchburg Virginian, Dec. 5, 1836, p. 3, c. 3.

GIBBS, THEADOSHA - See entry for William Elliot.

GIGAN, MISS SARAH - See entry for William W. Dickerson.

GILBERT, MISS ANN ELIZABETH - See entry for Mr. Edmund W. Rosser.

GILBERT, DR. EZEKIEL B. married to Martha R. Dibrell. Bride of Campbell.
Groom of Amherst.
The Lynchburg Virginian, Nov. 6, 1826, p. 3.

GILBERT, MISS FRANCES N. - See entry for Pleasant D. Brooks.

GILBERT, MR. WILLIAM married on Wednesday to Miss Polly Alcock. Bride
and groom both of Amherst.
The Lynchburg Virginian, Dec. 1, 1834, p. 3, c. 5.

GILES, WILLIAM B. married to Ann Payne, dau. of Giles Payne of Pittsylvania Co.
The Lynchburg Virginian, Feb. 11, 1828, p. 3.

GILLIAM, DR. G. married on Dec. 24, 1828 to Miss Eliza B. Jones, dau.
of James Jones of Campbell Co., by The Rev. Samuel Armistead.
Groom of Buckingham Co.
The Lynchburg Virginian, Jan. 5, 1829, p. 3, c. 5.

GILLIAM, MISS MARY ANN RICHARDINA - See entry for Dr. Baker.

GLANCY, JESSE married on Aug. 21, 1832 to Mrs. Dolly Trace of Vermont
by T. Atkinson, Esq. Groom of Salsbury.
The Lynchburg Virginian, Aug. 27, 1832, p. 3, c. 5.

GODDARD, MISS CATHERINE - See entry for Henry Leuba.

GODFREY, MISS MARY - See entry for Peter Elliott.

GOGGIN, MISS EMILY MILDRED - See entry for Edwin M. Matthews.

GOGGIN, LUCIEN married on Thurs. evening, April 29, 1830 to Miss Ann
Jane Curtis, dau. of George Curtis, Esq. of Mason Co. Kentucky,
by The Rev. Dr. Wm. J. Holcombe. Married in this place. Groom
is of Lynchburg.
The Lynchburg Virginian, May 3, 1830, p. 3, c. 4.

GOLDIN, MISS MARY - See entry for Edwin H. Woodson.

GOOD, MISS SARAH B. - See entry for Jesse B. Arington.

GOODE, MISS ELIZABETH H. - See entry for William W. Mosby.

GOODE, JOHN married on March 5, 1823 to Ann Maria Leftwich, dau. of Capt.
Jack Leftwich of Bedford, by The Rev. William Leftwich. Groom of
Bedford.
The Lynchburg Virginian, March 18, 1823.

GOODE, MISS MARTHA A. W. - See entry for Marshall L. Harris.

GOODE, WM. O., ESQ. married on Thurs. 10th inst. to Miss Sarah Massie,
dau. of Dr. Massie of Nelson, by The Rev. Charles Page. The Groom
is attorney at law, of Mecklenburg.
The Lynchburg Virginian, Sept. 14, 1829, p. 3, c. 4.

GOODMAN, ACHILLES M. married to Mary King, dau. of William King. Bride
and groom of Amherst.
The Lynchburg Virginian, April 10, 1826, p. 3.

GOODWIN, MISS VIRGINIA - See entry for Hezekiah Jones.

GORDON, MISS ANN B. J. - See entry for Mr. Hugh White, Jr.

GORDON, MISS MARIA LOUISA - See entry for Elias Ogden.

GOUGH, WILLIAM married on 8th inst. 1825 to Miss Sarah Holcombe, dau.
of late John Holcombe of Campbell, by The Rev. Wm. S. Reid. Groom
is of Campbell.
The Lynchburg Virginian, Sept. 15, 1825, p. 3, c. 4.

GOULDER, HENRY R. married on Aug. 18, 1819 to Miss Lucinda S. Rohr of
Lynchburg by The Rev. William S. Reid. Groom of Lynchburg.
The Lynchburg Press & Public Advertiser, Aug. 20, 1819, p. 3.

GOULDMAN, MISS AMANDA - See entry for Mr. Samuel Crow.

GOUMER, MISS MARY E. R. - See entry for John P. Claytor.

GOVEN, ARCHIBALD married on 6th inst. at Forest Hall (or Hill) Amherst
Co. to Miss Lucy Ann Waller, dau. of Mr. Wm. J. Waller, by The
Rev. Mr. Page. Groom of Hanover Co.
The Lynchburg Virginian, Feb. 16, 1835, p. 3, c. 5.

GRACE, MRS. DOLLY - See entry for Jesse Glancy.

GRAHAM, MISS MARTHA - See entry for Mr. George Sampson.

GRANT, MISS MINERVA B. - See entry for The Rev. Amos Treadway.

GRANTLAND, THE HON. SEATON married on Tues., 21st inst. at the residence
of Mr. Wm. Pollard to Miss Catherine M. Dabney, dau. of the late
Capt. George Dabney of Hanover, by The Rev. Geo. Woodbridge. Groom
member of Congress from Georgia.
The Lynchburg Virginian, Oct. 29, 1835, p. 3, c. 6.

GRAY, MRS. CATHERINE DANGERFIELD - See entry for Achilles Murat.

GRAY, MISS FRANCES M. - See entry for Beverly Crump.

GRAY, M. D., ESQ. married on the 21st inst. to Miss Ann Jordan, dau. of
Jubal Jordan, Esq., by The Rev. Samuel Phillips. All of Bedford Co.
The Lynchburg Virginian, July 25, 1836, p. 3, c. 4.

GRAY, MISS MARY - See entry for Wm. Dickinson.

GRAY, ROBERT H. married on Dec. 17, 1822 to Miss Jane Jordan, dau. of
Mr. Jacob Jordan of Lynchburg, by The Rev. Joseph Carson. Groom
of Lynchburg.
The Lynchburg Virginian, Dec. 20, 1822, p. 3, c. 4.

GREEN, MISS ANN LAURA - See entry for Isaac Shelby Reed, Esq.

GREEN, GETTY K. - See entry for William Thompson.

GREEN, JOHN married on Wed. evening, April 28, 1830 to Miss Mary Ann
Griffey, dau. of Mrs. Nancy Griffey, by The Rev. Edward Cannon.
All of this place.
The Lynchburg Virginian, April 29, 1830, p. 3, c. 5.

GREEN, MISS MARGARET - See entry for Andrew P. Calhoun.

GREEN, MISS MARY MOSLEY - See entry for Wm. T. McGhee.

GREEN, THOMAS, ESQ. married on May 30, 1833 to Miss Mary Roane Ritchie,
second dau. of Thomas Ritchie, Esq., by The Rev. Bishop Moore.
All of Richmond.
The Lynchburg Virginian, June 6, 1833, p. 3, c. 5.

GREENALL, MISS SARAH VIRGINIA - See entry for Capt. Ammon Hancock.

GREENTREE, MATILDA - See entry for Phillip M. Price.

GREGORY, MISS ELIZABETH L. - See entry for Joseph E. Storey.

GREGORY, JOHN T. married on the 11th inst. to Miss Sophia Kyle, dau. of
Mr. David Kyle of Buckingham, by The Rev. Thomas Burge. Groom of
this place.
The Lynchburg Virginian, Dec. 18, 1828, p. 3, c. 4.

GRIFFEY, MISS MARY ANN - See entry for John Green.

GRIFFIN, MISS ELIZABETH - See entry for Harvey Mitchell.

GRIFFIN, DR. JOHN H. married on 18th inst. to Miss Sarah Jane McClanahan,
dau. of John McClanahan, Esq., by The Rev. Nicholas H. Cobbs. All
of Botetourt Co.
The Lynchburg Virginian, Sept. 27, 1832, p. 3, c. 4.

GRIFFITH, MISS BELINDA - See entry for Richard Powell.

GRIGGS, GEORGE married on the 20th inst. to Miss Frances Wills, dau. of
    Thomas Wills, by The Rev. Joseph Pedigo. All of Henry Co.
    The Lynchburg Virginian, July 25, 1836, p. 3, c. 4.

GUTHRIE, MISS CATHARINE - See entry for Franklin Campbell.

GWATHMEY, MRS. ANN. - See entry for Wm. Morgan.

GWATKINS, CHARLES B. married on the 22nd ult. to Miss Charlotte Ann
    Tinsley, by The Rev. Dr. Samuel Philips. All of Bedford Co.
    The Lynchburg Virginian, Oct. 6, 1836, p. 3, c. 3.

GWATKINS, MISS ELIZA ANN - See entry for Edward Hunter.

GWATKYNS, MISS ELIZABETH - See entry for Joseph Edwin Royall.

H

HADEN, MISS JANE - See entry for Samuel Tardy.

HAGGARD, MR. HENRY W. married on Thurs. night, the 4th inst. to Matilda
    Ann W. London, dau. of Mr. Larkin London, deceased, by The Rev.
    Daniel Day. The groom late of Kentucky.
    The Lynchburg Virginian, Aug. 18, 1836, p. 2, c. 5.

HAGOOD, MISS ANN - See entry for Wm. Mitchell.

HAILET, CAPT. ARCHIBALD married on the 22nd to Miss Martha A. Brown,
    dau. of Mrs. Elizabeth N. Brown, by The Rev. Mosby Arnold. All
    of this County.
    The Lynchburg Virginian, Oct. 26, 1835, p. 3, c. 5.

HAIRSTON, MISS ANN - See entry for Marshall Hairston, Esq.

HAIRSTON, MARSHALL, ESQ. married on the 12th inst. to Miss Ann Hairston,
    dau. of Col. Samuel Hairston of Franklin Co., by The Rev. Mr. Pedigo.
    Groom of Henry Co.
    The Lynchburg Virginian, March 30, 1829, p. 3, c. 4.

HALE, MISS ABIGAIL P. - See entry for John Jones.

HALE, MR. GILES W. B. married to Miss Rosina Lucke, eldest dau. of Mr.
    Gustavus Lucke, deceased, by The Rev. Mr. Pekin. Married in
    Richmond; groom of Franklin.
    The Lynchburg Virginian, Nov. 8, 1834, p. 3, c. 5.

HALL, LAWRENCE H. married on the 14th inst. in Todd Co. Kentucky to Miss
    Mary A. M. Terry, youngest dau. of Col. Nathaniel Terry, late of
    Halifax Co., Va., by The Rev. George P. Giddings. Groom was for-
    merly of Petersburg, Va.
    The Lynchburg Virginian, July 12, 1832, p. 3, c. 5.

HALL, MISS LYDIA - See entry for W. Holt.

HALL, MRS. SUSAN - See entry for Thomas Burch.

HALSEY, MISS ELIZA - See entry for Christopher McIver.

HALSEY, SETH married on Thursday evening, 15th inst. to Miss Julia D.B. Peters, dau. of Elisha Peters, Esq. of Bedford, by The Rev. Nicholas H. Cobbs. Groom from Lynchburg, Va.
The Lynchburg Virginian, July 19, 1830, p. 3, c. 4.

HAMBLET, ARMISTEAD married on Nov. 1, 1822 to Miss Sarah Fuqua, dau. of Capt. Samuel Fuqua, by The Rev. Samuel Armistead.
The Lynchburg Virginian, Nov. 15, 1822, p. 3.

HAMBLET, THOMAS married on March 14, 1822 to Miss Sarah Hancock, dau. of Mr. Martin Hancock of Charlotte Co., by The Rev. Samuel Armistead.
The Lynchburg Press, March 15, 1822, p. 3.

HAMLET, MR. SEATON married on Tues. the 6th inst. to Miss Elizabeth W. Sandidge, dau. of Mr. Alexander Sandidge of Amherst, by The Rev. John Davis. Groom of Nelson.
The Lynchburg Virginian, Nov. 15, 1832, p. 3, c. 4.

HAMLIN, PETER married on the 12th inst. to Miss Virginia A. Michaux, dau. of Maj. Richard Michaux of Pittsylvania, by The Rev. Jno. Rankin. Groom of Rockingham, N. C.
The Lynchburg Virginian, June 21, 1832, p. 3, c. 4.

HANCOCK, CAPT. AMMON married on Thursday last to Miss Sarah Virginia Greenhall by The Rev. Wm. S. Reid. All of this place.
The Lynchburg Virginian, Nov. 26, 1832, p. 3, c. 4.

HANCOCK, MR. CLEMENT married on Thursday evening last to Miss Martha A.M. Harvey, youngest dau. of Nathan Harvey, Esq. of Charlotte Co.
The Lynchburg Virginian, Nov. 24, 1831, p. 3, c. 4.

HANCOCK, JOHN married on Sept. 25, 1822 to Mary P. Bernard, of Lynchburg by The Rev. John Lee. Groom of Lynchburg.
The Lynchburg Virginian, Sept. 27, 1822, p. 3.

HANCOCK, N. H. married on Dec. 6, 1827 to Miss J. T. Atkins by The Rev. John Davidson. All of Charlotte Co.
The Lynchburg Virginian, Feb. 19, 1828, p. 3, c. 4.

HANCOCK, MR. NATHAN H. married on 8th inst. to Miss Paulina Catharine Rudd, dau. of Major Thomas Rudd of Lynchburg, by The Rev. Samuel Armstead.
The Lynchburg Virginian, Sept. 3, 1829, p. 3, c. 4.

HANCOCK, MISS SARAH - See entry for Thomas Hamlet.

HANCOCK, WILLIAM, ESQ. married on June 30, 1825 to Mrs. Nancy Hylton, widow of John Hylton, Esq. of Montgomery, by The Rev. Jesse Jones. Groom of Patrick.
The Lynchburg Virginian, July 28, 1825, p. 3, c. 5.

HANNA, MISS MARIA A. - See entry for John N. Cabell.

HANSFORD, MISS JANE V. - See entry for Richard Burruss.

HANSARD, MISS MARY - See entry for Dr. George H. Burford.

HARBOUR, MR. JAMES married May 26, 1819 to Miss Hannah Nowlin, dau. of
    Francis Nowlin of Patrick Co., by The Rev. Peter France. Groom
    youngest son of Mr. Moses Harbour. All of Patrick Co.
    The Lynchburg Press & Public Advertiser, June 10, 1819, p. 3, c. 5.

HARDWICK, MISS ELIZABETH - See entry for Robert S. Wilkins.

HARDWICK, JOHN V. married on April 11, 1833 in Richmond, Va. to Miss
    Sarah W. Walford of Richmond, by The Rev. Phillip Courtney. Groom
    formerly of Lynchburg.
    The Lynchburg Virginian, April 18, 1833, p. 3, c. 4.

HARDY, JOSEPH married on Oct. 16, 1832 to Miss Jane L. Wood, dau. of late
    Michael Wood, Esq. of Nelson Co., by The Rev. Mr. McClung. Groom of
    Missouri, formerly of Bedford Co.
    The Lynchburg Virginian, Oct. 29, 1832, p. 3, c. 3.

HARDY, MR. SAMUEL B. married on Wed. evening last to Miss Mary Jane
    Sparrow of this place, by The Rev. Wm. J. Holcombe. Groom of
    Botetourt.
    The Lynchburg Virginian, Dec. 31, 1832, p. 3, c. 3.

HARE, MISS CAROLINE ELIZABETH - See entry for Samuel M. Selden.

HARE, MISS CATHARINE C. - See entry for James Campbell.

HARE, MISS ELIZABETH - See entry for William S. Johnson.

HARE, MISS HANNAH - See entry for Bennet A. Crawford, Esq.

HARE, MISS MARY JANE - See entry for William A. Read.

HARGROVE, MRS. ELMIRA A. WILLIAMSON - See entry for Dr. B. F. Owens.

HARGRAVE, MISS SALINA N. L. - See entry for John B. Fortune.

HARKER, MISS ELIZABETH - See entry for Richard Reeves.

HARKER, MR. JOSEPH married on 3rd inst. to Miss Martha Packer by David
    D. Reamer, Esq. All of New Hanover, Burlington Co.
    The Lynchburg Virginian, Nov. 29, 1832, p. 3, c. 4.

HARLIN, MR. WILLIAM G. married on Thurs., 25th inst. to Miss Adeline, dau.
    of Mr. Richard Turner of Amherst Co., by The Rev. Thomas Burge.
    Groom of Buckingham.
    The Lynchburg Virginian, Nov. 29, 1830, p. 3, c. 4.

HARRIS, MISS - See entry for Jesse Harvey.

HARRIS, MISS CATHERINE - See entry for Mr. Beazly Cheatham.

HARRIS, MISS ELIZABETH - See entry for George W. Shelton.

HARRIS, DR. HECTOR married on the 18th inst. to Miss Catharine A. Alexander, dau. of Mrs. Elizabeth Alexander of New London, by The Rev. N. H. Cobbs. Groom is of Bedford.
The Lynchburg Virginian, Nov. 26, 1829, p. 3, c. 6.

HARRIS, MISS JANE ANN - See entry for Hardin Perkins.

HARRIS, MARSHALL L. married on the 19th inst. at Charlotte Court House to Miss Martha A. W. Goode, dau. of Hillery Goode, Esq. deceased, by The Rev. Mr. Clopton. Groom formerly of Hanover.
The Lynchburg Virginian, Nov. 26, 1829, p. 3, c. 6.

HARRIS, WILLIAM A. married on April 18, 1833 at Maysville, Kentucky to Miss Eleanor Wood, dau. of Mr. John Wood of Maysville, by The Rev. David Burnett. Groom formerly of Lynchburg.
The Lynchburg Virginian, May 6, 1833, p. 3, c. 4.

HARRISON, MISS ANN - See entry for Capt. Wm. Wiatt Norvell.

HARRISON, JESSE BURTON, ESQ. married on 11th inst. at New Orleans to Miss Frances A. Brand, eldest dau. of William Brand of New Orleans, by The Rev. Mr. Clapp. Groom formerly of Lynchburg.
The Lynchburg Virginian, July 30, 1835, p. 3, c. 5.

HARRISON, DR. JOHN P. married on Thurs., the 19th inst. to Miss Ann Tate, only daughter of John Poe, by The Rev. Stephen Taylor. All of Richmond.
The Lynchburg Virginian, May 30, 1831, p. 3, c. 3.

HARRISON, MISS LUCY - See entry for Lorenzo Norvell.

HARRISON, MISS MARGARET - See entry for James Metcalfe.

HARRISON, MISS MARTHA A. N. - See entry for James Penn.

HARRISON, MISS MARTHA J. - See entry for Robert Robinson.

HARRISON, MISS MARTHAL - See entry for Dr. David Moore.

HARRISON, MISS NANCY P. - See entry for Stephen Coleman.

HARRISON, PEYTON married on Jan. 6, 1825 to Miss Jane C. Carr, dau. of Mr. Dabney Carr, by The Rev. Bishop Moore. Groom formerly of Lynchburg.
The Lynchburg Virginian, Jan. 28, 1825, p. 3.

HARRISON, MISS SUSAN K. - See entry for Marcus C. Henderson.

HARRISON, TIPTON B. married on June 28, 1821 to Mary Brent, dau. of the
late Robert Brent, by The Rev. Wm. S. Reid. Groom attorney-at-law.
The Lynchburg Press, June 29, 1821, p. 3.

HARRISS, MISS ELIZABETH ANN - See entry for John G. Harriss.

HARRISS, JOHN G. married to Miss Elizabeth Ann Harriss, dau. of Mr.
John Harriss, by The Rev. John Watson. All of Campbell.
The Lynchburg Virginian, Nov. 13, 1834, p. 3, c. 4.

HARRISS, MARY M. - See entry for Clark Penn.

HART, THE REV. ANDREW married on Tues. evening inst. at New Glasgow,
Amherst Co. to Miss Mary S. Brown, dau. of the late Dr. James S.
Brown, by The Rev. W. S. Reid.
The Lynchburg Virginian, Oct. 15, 1829, p. 3, c. 4.

HART, MICHAEL married on the 28th inst. at Petersburg to Miss Frances
Davis, dau. of Mr. David Davis of Petersburg. Groom of this place.
The Lynchburg Virginian, March 29, 1832, p. 3, c. 5.

HARVEY, JESSE married on Dec. 20, 1827 to Miss Harris, of Charlotte Co.,
by The Rev. Samuel Armistead.
The Lynchburg Virginian, Jan. 3, 1828, p. 3, c. 2.

HARVEY, JOHN married on March 29, 1825 to Miss Mary Charlotte Mitchell,
dau. of Mr. Charles Mitchell of Richmond, by The Rev. Wm. S. Reid.
Groom of Botetourt.
The Lynchburg Virginian, April 8, 1825, p. 3.

HARVEY, MISS MARTHA A. M. - See entry for Mr. Clement Hancock.

HARVEY, MISS SOPHIA - See entry for John Powers.

HARVEY, MISS SUSAN - See entry for Washington Hunter.

HARVEY, MR. W. M., SR. married on 20th inst. to Miss Mary L. Massy of
Prince Edward Co. by The Rev. Samuel Armistead. Groom of Campbell
Co. and was 65 years old bride was 20 years.
The Lynchburg Virginian, Sept. 3, 1829, p. 3, c. 4.

HARVEY, WILLIAM married on 20th ult., 1832 to Miss Julia Ann White of
Charlotte Co. by The Rev. Samuel Armistead.
The Lynchburg Virginian, Dec. 13, 1832, p. 3, c. 5.

HARVEY, WILLIAM T. married on 4th inst., 1832 to Miss Susan Spencer by
The Rev. Samuel Armistead.
The Lynchburg Virginian, Dec. 13, 1832, p. 3, c. 5.

HATCHER, MR. CALEB H. married on the 8th inst. at Mr. Isaac Prestons in
Bedford Co. to Miss Florentine McDaniel Hurt by The Rev. James
Leftwich. Bride formerly of Salem, Botetourt Co., Va.
The Lynchburg Virginian, Dec. 15, 1836, p. 3, c. 4.

HATCHER, JONATHAN H. married to Ann M. Woodson, dau. of Anderson Woodson of Campbell; groom of Bedford Co.
The Lynchburg Virginian, March 2, 1826, p. 3.

HATCHER, MISS JULIA ANN - See entry for Alexander Crank.

HATCHER, NELSON J. married last evening to Miss Judy Ann Dibrell by The Rev. John Early. All of this place.
The Lynchburg Virginian, Jan. 27, 1831, p. 3, c. 5.

HATCHER, THOMAS married on Tues. the 29th ult. to Miss Elizabeth Baughn by The Rev. Wm. Leftwich. All of Bedford Co.
The Lynchburg Virginian, Oct. 12, 1835, p. 3, c. 4.

HATCHER, THOMAS F. married on Nov. 12, 1823 to Caroline Noell, dau. of Cornelius Noell of Bedford, by The Rev. William Harris. Groom of Bedford.
The Lynchburg Virginian, Nov. 21, 1823, p. 3.

HATTAN, MISS ELIZABETH - See entry for Joseph Dodd.

HAWKINS, MR. BENJAMIN married on June 3, 1824 to Miss Catharine Bell of Liberty, by The Rev. Dr. Samuel Phillips. Groom of Liberty.
The Lynchburg Virginian, June 11, 1824, p. 3.

HAWKINS, JOHN F. married on June 15, 1824, Tues. last, to Miss Lucinda Ann Campbell, dau. of Mr. Lewis Campbell of Bedford, by The Rev. F. Kabler. Groom of Bedford Co.
The Lynchburg Virginian, Friday, June 18, 1824, p. 3, c. 5.

HAWKINS, MISS MARY - See entry for Daniel Austin.

HAWKINS, MISS NANCY - See entry for J. Remiar Murphey.

HAWKINS, MR. SPOTSWOOD married on Tues. evening, 20th inst. to Miss Elizabeth M. Reese, dau. of Mr. John Reese, by The Rev. A. B. Smith. All of this place.
The Lynchburg Virginian, Oct. 26, 1835, p. 3, c. 5.

HAZLEWOOD, WM. T. married on 9th inst. to Miss Betsy Allen of Campbell Co. by The Rev. Frederick Kabler. Groom of Bedford.
The Lynchburg Virginian, Jan. 12, 1832, p. 3, c. 5.

HAZLWOOD, MISS SUSAN - See entry for Thomas Ramsey.

HAYTH, GILBERT married on Jan. 2, 1828 to Elizabeth Rucker, dau. of Reuben Rucker of Lynchburg, by The Rev. Edward Cannon.
The Lynchburg Virginian, Jan. 10, 1828, p. 3, c. 2.

HEATH, MISS MARTHA B. - See entry for Thomas B. Stevens.

HELMS, THOMAS married on the 4th inst. in Bedford to Miss Frances Saunders, age 18, dau. of Mr. Daniel Saunders of Bedford, by The Rev. Abner Anthony. Groom age 17 - of Franklin.
The Lynchburg Virginian, Oct. 24, 1836, p. 3, c. 4.

HENDERSON, HARRIET - See entry for John Boyd.

HENDERSON, JAMES P., ESQ. married on Tues., 3rd inst. at Oakridge, Nelson
Co. to Miss Margaret C. Pollard, dau. of Richard Pollard, Charge
d'Affaires, U.S. Govt. of Chili, by The Rev. Wm. S. Reid.
The Lynchburg Virginian, March 23, 1835, p. 3, c. 5.

HENDERSON, JOHN married to Miss Mary Henderson of Amherst Co., by The
Rev. Mr. Day. Groom of Amherst Co.
The Lynchburg Virginian, March 2, 1824, p. 3.

HENDERSON, MISS JULIA A. - See entry for William Ayres.

HENDERSON, MISS MARY - See entry for John Henderson.

HENDERSON, MARCUS C. married to Susan L. Harrison, dau. of Nicholas
Harrison. Bride of Lynchburg; groom of Alabama.
The Lynchburg Virginian, April 14, 1825, p. 3.

HENDERSON, WALTER, ESQ. married on 13th inst. to Miss Eliza Royall
Holcombe, dau. of Capt. Thomas A. Holcombe of this place, by The
Rev. J. D. Mitchell. Groom of Nelson Co.
The Lynchburg Virginian, Nov. 20, 1834, p. 3, c. 4.

HENDRICE, ROBERT C. married on Oct. 10, 1832 in Missouri to Miss Lucy
Ann Boyd, dau. of Mr. John Boyd of St. Louis, formerly of
Lynchburg, by The Rev. W. McAllister. Groom of Millersburg, Mo.
The Lynchburg Virginian, Nov. 8, 1832, p. 3, c. 5.

HENDRICK, MISS ANNE - See entry for Seth Ward, Jr.

HENDRICK, JAMES, ESQ. married on Dec. 24, 1822 to Elizabeth Clark, dau.
of Christopher Clark of New London, by The Rev. Wm. S. Reid. Groom
also of New London.
The Lynchburg Virginian, Jan. 3, 1823, p. 3.

HENDRICK, MR. JAMES S. married on 10th inst. to Miss Elizabeth Jones by
The Rev. David Fisher. Both of Campbell.
The Lynchburg Virginian, Dec. 15, 1831, p. 3, c. 3.

HENDRICK, MISS JULIA E. - See entry for Christopher Babcock.

HENDRICKS, MISS SUSAN - See entry for Thomas Morgan.

HENDRICKS, THE REV. WM. W. married on May 1, 1828 to Frances Dibrell by
The Rev. Wm. A. Smith. Broom of Buckingham Co. Bride of this
place.
The Lynchburg Virginian, May 5, 1828, p. 3, c. 4.

HENLEY, JULIAN R. married on the 25th inst. to Miss Julian Ann T. Steen,
youngest dau. of Wm. Steen, Esq. of Bedford, by The Rev. John Early.
Groom of this place.
The Lynchburg Virginian, March 26, 1829, p. 3, c. 5.

HENNEGER, H. married in Marion to Mrs. E. A. Peak. Groom age 104, bride age 74.
The Lynchburg Virginian, Nov. 30, 1835, p. 3, c. 4.

HERNDON, MISS ZELINDA S. - See entry for M. P. Clarkson.

HEWETT, THE REV. BENJAMIN married to Elizabeth Burnett of Bedford by The Rev. Scott.
The Lynchburg Virginian, Jan. 12, 1826, p. 3, c. 4.

HEWETT, MISS MILDRED - See entry for Jessee T. Hopkins.

HEWITT, MISS MARY ANN - See entry for Mr. Edwin Hoffman.

HEWSON, BETHUEL WASHBURN married on the 2nd inst. to Miss Emily Louisa Williams, eldest dau. of Nathaniel F. Williams, Esq., of Baltimore. Married in Baltimore. Groom is of Petersburg, formerly of Lynchburg.
The Lynchburg Virginian, Nov. 11, 1830, p. 3, c. 4.

HICKS, JOHN HAYWOOD of Tenn. married on Nov. 20, 1829 to Miss Sarah Clark Lynch, dau. of Capt. John Lynch, formerly a citizen of Lynchburg. Married in Jackson, Tenn. by The Rev. Edmund Jones, formerly of Petersburg, Va.
The Lynchburg Virginian, Jan. 14, 1830, p. 3, c. 6.

HIGGINBOTHAM, MISS CATHERINE - See entry for George Higginbotham.

HIGGINBOTHAM, GEORGE married on April 4, 1818 to Miss Catharine Higginbotham. Bride and groom of Amherst.
The Lynchburg Press, April 17, 1818, p. 3.

HIGHT, THOMAS married on 2nd inst. to Miss Martha Johnson, dau. of N. Johnson of Campbell, by The Rev. Samuel Armistead.
The Lynchburg Virginian, June 11, 1829, p. 3, c. 5.

HILL, MRS. ELIZA - See entry for The Rev. Robert Hurt.

HILL, MISS JANE W. - See entry for Moses H. Migann.

HILL, JEFFERSON L. married on Jan. 15, 1829 to Miss Frances W. Phillips, dau. of Moses Phillips, by The Rev. Wm. Duncan. All of Amherst.
The Lynchburg Virginian, Jan. 22, 1829, p. 3, c. 5.

HILL, JOHN T. married in Nashville, Tenn. to Georgianna Beck. Groom of Lynchburg and Nashville, Tenn.
The Lynchburg Virginian, Feb. 7, 1828, p. 3, c. 5.

HILL, MISS MARTHA LOUISA - See entry for Dr. Matthew W. Dibrell.

HILLHOUSE, FLEMING married to Elizabeth Philliman, dau. of Jacob Philliman of Franklin Co.
The Lynchburg Virginian, March 20, 1828, p. 3.

HITE, MADISON married on Jan. 12, 1815 to Miss Matilda Irvine of Lynchburg by The Rev. Wm. S. Reid. Groom of Winchester.
The Lynchburg Press, Jan. 26, 1815, p. 3, c. 2.

HIX, WILSON married on March 29th to Martha Bobock, second dau. of John Bobock, Esq. of Buckingham Co., by The Rev. Wm. W. Hendrick. All of Buckingham.
The Lynchburg Virginian, April 10, 1826, p. 3, c. 4.

HOBART, SAMUEL married on May 20th to Miss Margaret Jane Nixon by The Rev. John Ayres. All of Buckingham Co.
The Lynchburg Virginian, June 9, 1836, p. 3, c. 4.

HOBSON, COL. DARIUS of the U.S. Army married in Alabama to Miss Croe Pl Mackawis, or Jumping Rabbit, a belle of the Chickasaw tribe.
The Lynchburg Virginian, Dec. 21, 1829, p. 3, c. 5.

HOBSON, MISS LUCY - See entry for John R. Irvine.

HODGE, DAVID married on the 25th ult. to Mrs. Elizabeth Baily, age 40 years by John McGhee, Esq. Bride and groom were both of Columbia Co., Georgia. Groom was 102 years and 2 months of age. He was a Revolutionary soldier "at Braddocks defeat and served during the whole of the Revolutionary War".
The Lynchburg Press & Public Advertiser, Dec. 3, 1819, p. 2, c. 1.
See also: Lynchburg Virginian June 30, 1836, p. 3, c. 3 which gives bride's name as Miss Elizabeth Bailey.

HOFFMAN, DAVID married on Dec. 4, 1817 to Miss Mary Wiatt. Groom of Lynchburg and bride of Amherst.
The Lynchburg Press, Dec. 5, 1817, p. 3.

HOFFMAN, MR. EDWIN married on 16th inst. to Miss Mary Ann Hewitt, dau. of Mr. Stephen Hewitt, by The Rev. Samuel Phillips. All of Bedford.
The Lynchburg Virginian, Oct. 18, 1832, p. 3.

HOLCOMBE, MR. CHARLES A. married on 20th inst. to Miss Elizabeth A. Mosly by The Rev. David Fisher at the home of The Rev. Henry Brown. Both of Campbell.
The Lynchburg Virginian, Dec. 31, 1832, p. 3, c. 3.

HOLCOMBE, MISS ELIZA ROYALL - See entry for Walter Henderson, Esq.

HOLCOMBE, MISS MARTHA - See entry for Allen J. Wyllie.

HOLCOMBE, MISS SARAH - See entry for Wm. Gough.

HOLCOMBE, DR. WILLIAM married on Feb. 10, 1819 to Miss Eliza Clopton by The Rev. Wm. S. Reid. Bride and groom both of Lynchburg.
The Lynchburg Press & Public Advertiser, Feb. 15, 1819, p. 3.

HOLLAND, MISS SUSAN - See entry for Francis Johnson.

HOLMES, AMASA married to Emily Cox, dau. of James Cox of Bedford.
The Lynchburg Virginian, Nov. 12, 1826, p. 3.

HOLMES, JAMES married on Dec. 4, 1821 to Miss Arianna Donnell by The
Rev. Wm. S. Reid. Both bride and groom of Lynchburg.
The Lynchburg Press, Dec. 7, 1821, p. 3.

HOLMES, JOHN married on Feb. 17, 1824 to Miss Martha Steel by The Rev.
Mr. Ball. Bride from near New London.
The Lynchburg Virginian, March 5, 1824, p. 3.

HOLMES, JOSHUA R. married on Feb. 19, 1824 to Miss Martha Ann Bernard
by The Rev. Mr. Ball. Both of Lynchburg.
The Lynchburg Virginian, Feb. 20, 1824, p. 3.

HOLT, W. married on the 6th inst. to Miss Lydia Hall of this Co.
(Campbell) by The Rev. Sam'l Armistead.
The Lynchburg Virginian, Oct. 20, 1828, p. 3, c. 5.

HOOD, MISS SARAH - See entry for Mr. Benjamin Woodson.

HOOP, MISS ELIZABETH - See entry for William Blain.

HOPKINS, MISS ELIZABETH - See entry for Resin Lazenby.

HOPKINS, JAMES H. married on the 5th inst. to Miss Sarah J. Purcell, dau.
of Thomas Purcell, Esq. of Bedford, by The Rev. William Leftwich W.H.
(sic)
The Lynchburg Virginian, Oct. 20, 1836, p. 3, c. 3.

HOPKINS, JESSE T. married to Mildred Hewett, dau. of Col. John Hewett
of Bedford. Groom son of John Hopkins.
The Lynchburg Virginian, May 25, 1826, p. 3.

HORNER, JAMES E. married on Tues. last to Miss Anne Eliza Watson, dau.
of William Watson, Esq. of Amherst, by The Rev. Wm. S. Reid. Groom
is merchant of this place.
The Lynchburg Virginian, June 2, 1836, p. 3, c. 3.

HORTON, MISS MARY - See entry for Mr. Gustavus Campbell.

HOTCHKISS CARVER married on the 11th inst. to Miss Sally Scott by The
Rev. Mr. Bray. Married at Prospect. Groom is of Windsor, N.Y.
There is considerable detail about an alledged "breach of promise".
The Lynchburg Virginian, Oct. 28, 1830, p. 3, c. 4.

HOUSTON, MISS EMILY - See entry for John Garth, Esq.

HOUSTON, THE HON. SAMUEL married on Thurs. 22nd ult. to Miss Eliza H.
Allen, dau. of Col. Jno. Allen of Sumner Co., by The Rev. Wm.
Hume. Groom Governor of the state of Tennessee.
The Lynchburg Virginian, Feb. 12, 1829, p. 3, c. 4.

HOWARD, MISS ANN EPPES - See entry for Capt. Pizarro Edmunds.

HOWARD, COL. JOSEPH married on 9th inst. to Miss Mary Hylton, youngest
dau. of John Hylton, Esq. deceased, by The Rev. Michael Howery.
All of Floyd Co.
The Lynchburg Virginian, March 21, 1833, p. 3, c. 3.

HOWARD, JOSEPH (COL.) married on 5th inst. to Miss Jane, dau. of Daniel
Shelor, Esq., by The Rev. Michael Hawry. All of Floyd Co.
The Lynchburg Virginian, Jan. 21, 1836, p. 3, c. 4.

HOWE, THE REV. NORVAL D. married on the 5th inst. to Miss Susan Stevens,
dau. of Mr. John Stevens of Halifax, by The Rev. Sam'l Armistead.
The Lynchburg Virginian, Nov. 20, 1828, p. 3, c. 5.

HOYE, THOMAS married on Wed. 1st inst. to Miss Paulina Dieson, dau. of
the late Mr. Charles Dieson, by The Rev. Wm. S. Reid. All of
Lynchburg.
The Lynchburg Virginian, May 6, 1833, p. 3, c. 4.

HUBBARD, MISS DOLLY S. - See entry for George W. Matthews.

HUBBARD, JOHN married on Feb. 28, 1827 to Sarah Chewning, dau. of
Achilles Chewning, by The Rev. William Leftwich. Bride and groom
of Bedford.
The Lynchburg Virginian, March 9, 1827, p. 3, c. 2.

HUBBARD, MARGARET - See entry for Benjamin Williamson.

HUBBARD, MISS MARY - See entry for Richard G. Davenport.

HUDGINS, ELEANOR - See entry for James H. Simpson.

HUDSON, MR. CHARLES C. married on Tues. evening last to Miss Judith A.
Bransford, dau. of Samuel Bransford, Esq., by The Rev. D. S.
Doggett. All of this place.
The Lynchburg Virginian, Sept. 27, 1832, p. 3, c. 4.

HUDSON, EDWIN married on Thurs., 21st inst. to Miss Susan Kyle, dau. of
David Kyle of Buckingham Co., Va., by The Rev. Thomas Burge. Groom
of Charlottesville, Va.
The Lynchburg Virginian, Oct. 28, 1830, p. 3, c. 4.

HUDSON, JOHN married on March 30, 1824 to Miss Sophia Hudson, dau. of
Rush Hudson of Amherst, by The Rev. Wm. Duncan. Groom also of
Amherst Co.
The Lynchburg Virginian, April 2, 1824, p. 3.

HUDSON, MISS SOPHIA - See entry for John Hudson.

HUFF, MISS SARAH - See entry for Claiborne Manning.

HUNT, BENJAMIN married Tues. evening last, to Miss Eliza Cary, dau. of
Capt. Miles Cary of Campbell, by The Rev. Wm. I. Holcombe. Groom
formerly of Halifax.
The Lynchburg Virginian, Aug. 25, 1831, p. 3, c. 4.

HUNT, JAMES T. married on 28th inst. to Miss Rachel Fuqua of Charlotte, by The Rev. Samuel Armistead. Groom is of Campbell. Considerable detail about an alleged "breach of promise".
The Lynchburg Virginian, Nov. 4, 1830, p. 3, c. 5.

HUNT, JOHN T. married on Nov. 10, 1825 to Miss Mahala Sandidge, dau. of Capt. Benjamin Sandidge of Amherst, by The Rev. John Davis. Groom from Lynchburg.
The Lynchburg Virginian, Nov. 14, 1825, p. 3.

HUNT, JOHN T. married on the 26th ult. to Miss Nancy Adams, dau. of Thomas Adams, Esq. of Buckingham Co., by The Rev. Mr. Wingfield. Groom is of Lynchburg.
The Lynchburg Virginian, Nov. 4, 1830, p. 3, c. 5.

HUNT, MISS SARAH W. - See entry for George W. Coleman.

HUNTER, MISS CELINA W. - See entry for Allen Johnson.

HUNTER, EDWARD married on 17th inst. to Miss Eliza Ann Gwatkins, dau. of the late Col. Edward Gwatkins of Bedford, by The Rev. Thomas Jones of Lynchburg. Groom of Campbell Co.
The Lynchburg Virginian, May 26, 1836, p. 3, c. 3.

HUNTER, MISS JANE - See entry for Leonard Lipscomb.

HUNTER, ROBERT, JR. married on Nov. 10, 1825 to Miss Susan Blount, dau. of Charles Blount of Campbell Co., by The Rev. Isaac Cochrane. Groom of Campbell Co.
The Lynchburg Virginian, Dec. 1, 1825, p. 3.

HUNTER, WASHINGTON married on Nove. 17, 1825 to Miss Susan C. Harvey, dau. of Nathan Harvey of Charlotte Co., by The Rev. Samuel Armstead. Groom of Campbell Co.
The Lynchburg Virginian, Dec. 1, 1825, p. 3.

HUNTON, MISS ELIZA JANE - See entry for Fountain T. Fox.

HURT, MISS FLORENTINE MCDANIEL - See entry for Caleb H. Hatcher.

HURT, FOUNTAIN G. married on Wed. evening last to Miss Juda G. Fowler, dau. of John Fowler, by The Rev. Dr. Phillips. All of Bedford Co.
The Lynchburg Virginian, Nov. 2, 1835, p. 3, c. 4.

HURT, JOHN S. married on Dec. 30, 1823 to Miss Catharine C. Beale, dau. of Capt. James Beale, by The Rev. Mr. Burnett. Groom of Bedford.
The Lynchburg Virginian, Jan. 9, 1824, p. 3, c. 4.

HURT, THE REV. ROBERT married on Thurs. the 12th inst. to Mrs. Eliza Hill, dau. of John Morris, Esq. of Richmond, Va., by The Rev. Sam'l Armistead. Groom of the Western District of Tenn., late of Halifax, Va.
The Lynchburg Virginian, Nov. 30, 1835, p. 3, c. 4.

HUTTER, G. C., CAPT. married on Tues. evening the 6th of July, 1830, to Miss Harriet Risque, dau. of Maj. James B. Risque of Lynchburg, by The Rev. Mr. Harrell at the residence of Mr. James Kennerly (Jefferson Barracks).
The Lynchburg Virginian, July 29, 1830, p. 3, c. 4.

HYLTON, MISS MARY - See entry for Col. Joseph Howard.

HYLTON, MRS. NANCY - See entry for William Hancock.

I

IDING, COLUMBUS married on Sunday, 13th inst. to Miss Maria Cabill by Elder E. G. Cabiness. All of Henry Co.
The Lynchburg Virginian, Dec. 21, 1829, p. 3, c. 5.

IDING, GEORGE married on Sun. 13th inst. to Miss Polly Cabill by Elder Othniel Minter. All of Henry County.
The Lynchburg Virginian, Dec. 21, 1829, p. 3, c. 5.

INGRAM, MISS MARTHA - See entry for William Campbell.

INGRAM, PLEASANT married on the 14th ult. to Miss Nancy Welch, dau. of James Welch, by The Rev. Stephen Hubbard. All of Franklin Co.
The Lynchburg Virginian, Jan. 25, 1827, p. 3, c. 5.

IRBY, MISS NANCY - See entry for Mr. _____ Browder.

IRVIN, MISS ELIZA - See entry for James Webb, Esq.

IRVINE, MISS FRANCES - See entry for Dr. John H. Patteson.

IRVINE, JOHN R. married on Dec. 21, 1824 to Miss Lucy Hobson by The Rev. Wm. S. Reid. Bride of Bedford; groom of Lynchburg.
The Lynchburg Virginian, Dec. 24, 1824, p. 3.

IRVINE, MISS JULIET - See entry for The Rev. Henry B. Cowles.

IRVINE, MISS MARY - See entry for Dr. Paul C. Cabell.

IRVINE, MISS MATILDA - See entry for Madison Hite.

IRVINGS, MISS MARTHA ANN - See entry for John N. Bates.

ISBELL, MR. ROBERT married on Thurs. 17th inst. to Miss Angelina T. Boaz, dau. of Meshack Boaz, Esq., by The Rev. Thomas Burge. Bride of Buckingham, groom resident of Amherst.
The Lynchburg Virginian, Nov. 21, 1831, p. 3, c. 5.

ISBELL, WILLIAM married on Feb. 8, 1818 to Miss Lucy Furlong by The Rev. Pleasant Thurman. Both of Amherst.
The Lynchburg Press, Feb. 13, 1818, p. 3.

ISREAL, MISS NANCY - See entry for Dr. Williams.

J

JACKSON, MISS ABBY - See entry for Dr. Howell Davies.

JACKSON, MISS MARTHA - See entry for Samuel White.

JACKSON, PARMELIA F. - See entry for William Williamson.

JACKSON, MISS REBECCA - See entry for M. M. Noah.

JAMEISON, MISS ELIZABETH - See entry for Mr. William Craig.

JAMES, MISS ELIZA - See entry for Col. Aaron Burr.

JENNINGS, MR. _____ married on 9th inst. to Mrs. Martha Wood, relict of John Wood deceased of Campbell Co., by The Rev. Philip Mathews. Groom of Prince Edward Co.
The Lynchburg Virginian, May 18, 1826, p. 3, c. 3.

JENNINGS, MISS ELIZABETH B. - See entry for Dr. John O. Armistead.

JENNINGS, JOHN married on Nov. 27, 1832 to Miss S. Varnum by The Rev. Samuel Armistead.
The Lynchburg Virginian, Dec. 13, 1832, p. 3, c. 5.

JENNINGS, MISS MARTHA JANE - See entry for Thomas J. Moorman.

JENNINGS, ROBERT G. married on the 6th inst. to Miss Elizabeth Edmunds, dau. of Capt. Henry Edmunds of Halifax, Va., by The Rev. Mr. Mills.
The Lynchburg Virginian, April 18, 1836, p. 3, c. 4.

JENNINGS, SAMUEL B. married on Tues. the 7th inst. to Miss Martha E. Watson, third dau. of Wm. Watson, Esq. of Charlottesville, by The Rev. Mr. Bowman. Groom of Buchanan, Botetourt Co., formerly of Lynchburg.
The Lynchburg Virginian, Oct. 16, 1834, p. 3, c. 4.

JETER, DR. JAMES M. married on Tues., the 23rd inst. to Miss Emeline Dooley, dau. of Mr. James B. Dooley, by The Rev. Vinal Smith. All of the county of Bedford.
The Lynchburg Virginian, Jan. 8, 1835, p. 3, c. 5.

JETER, JESSE married on Jan. 16, 1822 to Miss Susan Robinson, dau. of Benjamin Robinson of Bedford Co. Groom also of Bedford Co.
The Lynchburg Press, Jan. 18, 1822, p. 3.

JOHNS, DR. ANTHONY B. of Pittsylvania Co. married on Dec. 29, 1829 to Miss Eliza M. Rives, dau. of Nathaniel Rives, of Henry Co., Va., by The Rev. Nathan Anderson.
The Lynchburg Virginian, Jan. 7, 1830, p. 3, c. 6.

JOHNS, HOBSON married last evening to Miss Mary Matilda Davis, dau. of
Henry Davis, Esq. of Lynchburg, by The Rev. Wm. S. Reid.
The Lynchburg Virginian, Feb. 25, 1825, p. 3, c. 4.

JOHNSON, ACHILLES D. married on Dec. 8, 1832 at Cedar Creek Meeting
House in Hanover Co., Va. to Miss Lucy Terrell, dau. of late
Joseph Terrell of Caroline. Groom of Lynchburg.
The Lynchburg Virginian, Dec. 20, 1832, p. 3, c. 5.

JOHNSON, ADELINE I. - See entry for Thomas W. Scott.

JOHNSON, ALLEN, ESQ. married on the 3rd inst. to Celina W. Hunter, dau.
of Capt. Hunter of Campbell Co., by The Rev. Wm. S. Reid.
The Lynchburg Virginian, Nov. 6, 1826, p. 3, c. 4.

JOHNSON, MISS CAIRA ANN C.M. - See entry for Jacob M. Tilman.

JOHNSON, CAJAH T. married Jan. 5, 1830 to Edna Todd, dau. of Robert Todd,
married at Wayne Oak Meeting House, in Charles City Co., Va. All
members of Society of Friends.
The Lynchburg Virginian, Jan. 14, 1830, p. 3, c. 6.

JOHNSON, CHRISTOPHER, ESQ. married on the 12th inst. in Bedford Co. to
Pelina Johnson by The Rev. H. Kabler. Bride of Bedford Co.
The Lynchburg Virginian, Nov. 14, 1823, p. 3, c. 3.

JOHNSON, FRANCIS married on Jan. 14, 1824 to Miss Susan Holland, dau. of
Drury Holland of Bedford, by The Rev. Wm. Harris. Groom of Bedford.
The Lynchburg Virginian, Jan. 23, 1824, p. 3.

JOHNSON, JAMES married on May 4th to Miss Susan Price, dau. of the late
Wm. Price, Esq., by The Rev. Mr. McLeroy. All of Pittsylvania.
The Lynchburg Virginian, May 23, 1836, p. 3, c. 3.

JOHNSON, MR. LAFAYETTE married on Wed. last to Miss Harriet Elvira, dau.
of Mr. John H. Moorman of Bedford, by The Rev. N. H. Cobbs. Groom
of Bedford.
The Lynchburg Virginian, Oct. 31, 1836, p. 3, c. 1.

JOHNSON, LILBOURN married to Miss Frances Jordan, dau. of Hezekiah
Jordon. All of Lynchburg.
The Lynchburg Virginian, June 19, 1827, p. 3, c. 4.

JOHNSON, MISS MARIA - See entry for John B. Tilden.

JOHNSON, MISS MARTHA - See entry for Thomas Hight.

JOHNSON, MISS MARTHA ANN - See entry for Marshall B. Jones.

JOHNSON, MISS MARY - See entry for Nelson Thomas.

JOHNSON, MISS MARY VIRGINIA - See entry for Robert M. Omahundre.

JOHNSON, MRS. MILDRED - See entry for Micajah Mosely.

JOHNSON, MISS PHOEBE - See entry for Ira R. Allcock.

JOHNSON, MISS VIRGINIA - See entry for James W. Pegram.

JOHNSON, WILLIAM S. married on Thursday the 8th inst. to Miss Elizabeth Hare, dau. of Wm. Hare, deceased, by The Rev. H. B. Cowles. All of this place.
The Lynchburg Virginian, Oct. 12, 1835, p. 3, c. 4.

JOHNSON, EDWARD P., ESQ. married on 6th inst. to Miss Ann Chilton, dau. of Maj. Thomas Chilton of Fauquier Co. Groom of Botetourt Co.
The Lynchburg Virginian, Jan. 12, 1832, p. 3, c. 5.

JOHNSON, MISS MARY - See entry for William Fosdick.

JOHNSON, MRS. MARY - See entry for Dr. Lewis Shanks.

JOHNSTON, MISS MARY JANE WOOD - See entry for Mr. Harvey Mitchell.

JOHNSON, MISS PELINA - See entry for Christopher Johnson.

JOHNSON, MR. ROBERT G. married on 14th inst. to Miss Sarah Ann Dixon, dau. of John Dixon, Esq., by The Rev. Edward L. Warror. All of Nelson Co.
The Lynchburg Virginian, Mar. 21, 1833, p. 3, c. 3.

JOINER, MR. JAMES H. married on 29th ult. to Miss Sophia B. Tiller of Amherst Co. Groom of Botetourt Co.
The Lynchburg Virginian, Feb. 9, 1835, p. 3, c. 4.

JONES, MISS ANN E. - See entry for Robert M. Briggs.

JONES, DR. DAVID C. married on 10th inst. to Eliza A. Walton, dau. of Wm. Walton of Buckingham, by The Rev. Thos. Burge.
The Lynchburg Virginian, Jan. 18, 1827, p. 3, c. 4.

JONES, MISS ELIZA - See entry for Alfred Elder.

JONES, MISS ELIZA ANN - See entry for Ira Maupin.

JONES, MISS ELIZA B. - See entry for Dr. G. Gilliam.

JONES, MISS ELIZABETH - See entry for Mr. James S. Hendrick.

JONES, MISS ELIZABETH - See entry for William R. Chaplin.

JONES, HEZEKIAH married on Wed. last at residence of Capt. John H. Goodwin in Amherst Co. to Miss Virginia Goodwin, dau. of late John Goodwin, by The Rev. Mr. Davis. Groom of Nelson Co.
The Lynchburg Virginian, Dec. 4, 1834, p. 3, c. 3.

JONES, JAMES S. married on Sept. 14, 1830 to Elizabeth Bernard of Lynchburg by The Rev. Robert Ryland. Groom of Campbell Co.
The Lynchburg Virginian, Sept, 16, 1830, p. 3, c. 5.

JONES, JOHN married to Abigail P. Hale, dau. of Joseph Hale. Both bride and groom of Franklin Co.
The Lynchburg Virginian, Feb. 9, 1826, p. 3.

JONES, MR. JOSEPH married on 7th inst. to Miss Nancy McIver by The Rev. William Hammesley. All of Campbell Co.
The Lynchburg Virginian, Oct. 19, 1835, p. 3, c. 4.

JONES, MISS JULIA ANN - See entry for Mr. Jacob H. Robinson.

JONES, MISS LUCY - See entry for Norborne M. Taliaferro.

JONES, MR. MARSHALL B. married on 4th inst. to Miss Martha Ann Johnson, dau. of Chas. Y. Johnson, deceased, by The Rev. Mr. Fisher. Both formerly of Lynchburg.
The Lynchburg Virginian, Aug. 9, 1832, p. 3, c. 4.

JONES, MISS MARTHA - See entry for _____ Davenport.

JONES, MISS MARY - See entry for John Nelson.

JONES, MISS MARY A. - See entry for James Dixon.

JONES, MISS MARY ANN - See entry for Thomas R. Marshall.

JONES, MISS MARY FRANCES ANN MARIA - See entry for Benjamin Perkins.

JONES, MISS OLIVIA - See entry for Calvin Ford.

JONES, MISS POLLY - See entry for Ambrose McDaniel.

JONES, RICHARD MANDOX married to Elizabeth Lancaster, dau. of Joseph Lancaster of Philadelphia.
The Lynchburg Virginian, July 13, 1824, p. 3.

JONES, MISS SARAH S. - See entry for Coleman D. Bennett, Esq.

JONES, MISS SUSAN - See entry for Joseph B. Nowlin.

JONES, TARLTON married on Oct. 28th last to Mrs. Bagby by The Rev. Samuel Armistead.
The Lynchburg Virginian, Nov. 20, 1828, p. 3, c. 5.

JONES, MR. THOMAS married Thurs. evening the 10th inst. to Miss Frances Watts, dau. of Capt. James Watts, deceased, by The Rev. Samuel Phillips. All of Bedford County.
The Lynchburg Virginian, Sept. 24, 1824, p. 3, c. 3.

JONES, CAPT. THOMAS P. married on 24th ult. to Miss Agnes Watkins, dau. of Benjamin Watkins, Esq. of Pittsylvania Co., by The Rev. Mr. Rankin.
The Lynchburg Virginian, June 7, 1832, p. 3, c. 3.

JONES, THOMAS S. married on Dec. 20, 1827 to Ann B. Calland, dau. of Mrs. Elizabeth C. Calland, by The Rev. John W. Kelly. All of Pittsylvania. The Lynchburg Virginian, Jan. 14, 1828, p. 3, c. 4.

JONES, MR. WIATT married on Jan. 13, 1824 to Miss Mary A. Phelps, dau. of Richard Phelps, deceased, by The Rev. William Duncan. Groom of Nelson Co. The Lynchburg Virginian, Jan. 16, 1824, p. 3.

JORDAN, AMANDA - See entry for Mr. Joel Wright.

JORDAN, MISS ANN - See entry for M. D. Gray, Esq.

JORDAN, MR. EDWIN H. married Dec. 28th to Miss Virginia Jackson, dau. of Capt. Miles Cary of Campbell, by The Rev. Nicholas H. Cobbs. Groom of Scottsville, Va. The Lynchburg Virginian, Jan. 2, 1837, p. 3, c. 2.

JORDAN, MISS ELIZABETH - See entry for William M. Shoemaker.

JORDAN, MISS FRANCES - See entry for Lilbourn Johnson.

JORDAN, MISS JANE - See entry for Robert H. Gray.

JORDAN, MISS REBECCA B. - See entry for Christopher S. Roane.

JORDAN, SAMUEL married on Dec. 20, 1827 to Sarah Walker, dau. of Edmund W. Walker, by The Rev. Samuel Armistead. The Lynchburg Virginian, Jan. 3, 1828, p. 3, c. 2.

JORDAN, MISS W. SARAH - See entry for James M. Loving.

K

KASEY, MISS MARY ANN - See entry for Henry Saunders.

KEARNEY, MAJOR S. N. married Sept. 5, 1830 to Mary Radford at S. Louis, Missouri by The Rev. Mr. Horrel. Groom of the U.S. Army. The Lynchburg Virginian, Sept. 27, 1830, p. 3, c. 5.

KEITH, JAMES W. married on July 10, 1833 to Miss Cary Jane Mays, dau. of George Mays of Nelson, by The Rev. Charles H. Page. Groom of Amherst. The Lynchburg Virginian, July 15, 1833, p. 3, c. 6.

KENERLY, SUSAN - See entry for Doct. C. I. Terrell.

KENNERLY, MISS MARTHA - See entry for Mr. Jackson Penn.

KENNERLY, MISS MARY - See entry for Thomas Penn, Esq.

KENT, GEORGE W. married on 22nd inst. to Miss Mary Fear of Lynchburg by The Rev. Robert Ryland. Groom of Oxford, Granville Co., N.C. The Lynchburg Virginian, Jan. 2, 1832, p. 3, c. 5.

KERR, MATTHEW MORRIS married on Wed. evening last to Miss Nancy E. Ward, dau. of Seth Ward, Esq. of this place, by The Rev. F. G. Smith. Groom formerly of Baltimore.
The Lynchburg Virginian, Feb. 20, 1832, p. 3, c. 4.

KEY, MISS ELIZABETH - See entry for Dr. James G. Turner.

KIDD, MISS SARAH A. - See entry for Robert Watkins.

KINCAID, FRANCES E. - See entry for George Williams.

KING, MISS CLARISSA - See entry for H. M. Andrews.

KING, MISS MARY - See entry for Achilles M. Goodman.

KING, THOMAS married on Sept. 30, 1830 to Nancy Witcher of Franklin Co. by The Rev. Joseph Pedigo. Groom of Henry Co., Va.
The Lynchburg Virginian, Oct. 14, 1830, p. 3, c. 3.

KINGSTON, REUBEN married to Sally Burchett, dau. of Young Burchett of Henry Co.
The Lynchburg Virginian, Aug. 3, 1826, p. 3.

KINNEY, NICHOLAS C., ESQ. married on 10th inst. to Miss Mary Ann Ambler Fisher, dau. of George Fisher, Esq. of Richmond, by Bishop Moore. Groom resident of Staunton.
The Lynchburg Virginian, March 26, 1835, p. 3, c. 5.

KNIGHT, MISS FRANCES ANN - See entry for Wm. B. Murrell.

KNIGHT, MISS MARY - See entry for Mr. Richard J. Waugh.

KRAUTH, WILLIAM T. married on 12th inst. in Paperville, Tenn. to Miss Judith T. Price, dau. of Mr. Edward Price, all of Lynchburg, by The Rev. F. L. B. Shaver.
The Lynchburg Virginian, Feb. 23, 1835, p. 3, c. 5.

KYLE, DAVID married to Harriet Wetherill, dau. of John Wetherill of Chalkly Hall, Philadelphia.
The Lynchburg Virginian, Dec. 14, 1826, p. 3.

KYLE, MISS DIANA R. - See entry for Abner O. Nash.

KYLE, JOHN D. married on 6th ult. to Mrs. Sarah Ann Miles by The Rev. Charles H. Page. All of New Glasgow, Amherst Co.
The Lynchburg Virginian, Aug. 10, 1835, p. 3, c. 4.

KYLE, MISS SOPHIA - See entry for John T. Gregory.

KYLE, MISS SUSAN - See entry for Edwin Hudson.

L

LABBY, MISS MARY J. See entry for Lafayette Neville.

LABBY, PLEASANT married on Feb. 9, 1815, to Miss Elizabeth Rucker by The
Rev. Robert Barnes. Bride of Amherst; groom of Lynchburg.
The Lynchburg Press, Feb. 16, 1815, p. 3.

LACY, MOSES married on Thurs. evening, 8th inst. to Miss Ann Tyree, dau.
of Richard Tyree, Esq. of this place, by The Rev. Wm. S. Reid.
Groom merchant of Tuscaloosa, Ala.
The Lynchburg Virginian, Oct. 12, 1835, p. 3, c. 4.

LACY, JOSEPH formerly of Lynchburg married to Miss Emily A. Moody of
Tuscaloosa, Ala. by The Rev. R. L. Kennon. Married in Tuscaloosa.
The Lynchburg Virginian, Feb. 1, 1830, p. 3, c. 4.

LAIN, JOHN S. married on 4th inst. to Miss Elizabeth Dawson, dau. of
Jacob Dawson, by The Rev. Charles Callaway. All of this place.
The Lynchburg Virginian, April 6, 1827, p. 3, c. 2.

LAIN, LORENZO D. married on 4th inst. to Miss Delilah Dawson, dau. of
David Dawson, deceased, by The Rev. Charles Callaway.
The Lynchburg Virginian, April 6, 1827, p. 3, c. 2.

LAMBERT, MISS HENRIETTA M. P. - See entry for Zachariah Moorman.

LAMBETH, MISS ANN - See entry for Ralph Smith.

LAMBETH, MISS ELIZABETH - See entry for Joseph Echols.

LAMBETH, MISS MARY JANE - See entry for Charles L. Dibrell.

LAMBETH, MISS SARAH LUCINDA - See entry for Abram R. North.

LAMBETH, MISS SUSAN - See entry for John Cary.

LAMBETH, DR. WILLIAM L. married on Nov. 10, 1824, to Miss Susan Davenport,
dau. of late Glover Davenport of Campbell Co., by The Rev. Edmond
Jones. Groom of Lynchburg.
The Lynchburg Virginian, Nov. 16, 1824, p. 3.

LAMKIN, JAMES L. married on July 22, 1823 to Miss Ann G. Dawson, dau. of
Nelson Dawson, Esq. of Amherst, by The Rev. Lewis Dawson. Groom of
Amherst Co.
The Lynchburg Virginian, July 25, 1823, p. 3.

LANCASTER, MISS ELIZABETH - See entry for Richard Mandox Jones.

LANCASTER, SAMUEL married on Dec. 3, 1823 to Miss Ann Lynch, dau. of
John Lynch of Lynchburg, by The Rev. Wm. S. Reid.
The Lynchburg Virginian, Dec. 12, 1823, p. 3.

LANE, MRS. ANN - See entry for Winston S. Blair.

LANE, MISS CLARI - See entry for Thomas Smoot.

LANE, MISS MARY T. - See entry for Thomas J. Sale.

LANGHORNE, MISS ELIZABETH - See entry for Anderson H. Armistead.

LANGHORNE, MISS MARY ELIZABETH - See entry for George P. Taylor.

LANIER, MISS PAULINA V. - See entry for Milton L. Lovell.

LANKFORD, EDWARD C. married on 12th inst. to Miss Ann G. Fowler by The
Rev. Dr. Wm. I. Waller. All of this place.
The Lynchburg Virginian, Nov. 16, 1829, p. 3, c. 6.

LATHAM, HENRY married last evening to Miss Rebecca Jane Owens by The
Rev. F. G. Smith.
The Lynchburg Virginian, Jan. 29, 1829, p. 3, c. 4.

LATHAM, MISS JANE L. - See entry for Dr. William Owens.

LATHAM, WOODVILLE married March 21, 1833 to Miss Sarah M. Bowen by The
Rev. John Woodville. Both of Culpeper.
The Lynchburg Virginian, May 2, 1833, p. 3, c. 5.

LAVENDER, JAMES married on April 6, 1823 to Miss Elizabeth C. Tyree,
dau. of John Tyree, Esq. of Amherst Co., by The Rev. John Allcock.
Groom also of Amherst Co.
The Lynchburg Virginian, April 25, 1823, p. 3.

LAVENDER, WILLIAM married on Dec. 24, 1823 to Miss Sarah Pamplin, dau.
of James Pamplin of Amherst Co., by The Rev. Poindexter P. Smith.
Groom also of Amherst Co.
The Lynchburg Virginian, Jan. 2, 1824, p. 3.

LAWHORNE, MR. JOHN married on Thurs. 26th inst. to Miss Elizabeth Briant
by The Rev. John Alcock. Both of Amherst Co.
The Lynchburg Virginian, March 30, 1835, p. 3, c. 6.

LAWRENCE, THE HON. GOV. HAWLEY SAMUEL married to Maria Hester Monroe,
dau. of President James Monroe. Groom is Governor of New York.
The Lynchburg Press, March 21, 1820, p. 3, c. 6.

LAWSON, GEORGE W. married on 21st inst. to Miss Angeline Marshall, dau.
of Mr. Thomas I. Marshall of Halifax, by The Rev. Elijah Roach.
Groom of Charlotte Co.
The Lynchburg Virginian, Jan. 2, 1837, p. 3, c. 2.

LAZENBY, RESIN married to Elizabeth Hopkins, dau. of Capt. Wm. Hopkins,
deceased. All of Bedford.
The Lynchburg Virginian, April 13, 1827, p. 3, c. 4.

LAYNE, GARRETT C. married at Capt. West's in Caswell Co., N.C. to Miss
Elizabeth W. Pryor, dau. of Col. John Pryor, by The Rev. Geo.
Sterns. All of Amherst.
The Lynchburg Virginian, Dec. 22, 1834, p. 3, c. 3.

LECKIE, ROBERT married Sept. 1, 1830 to Ann Williams, dau. of The Rev. Daniel Williams of Lynchburg, Va., by The Rev. Robert Ryland.
The Lynchburg Virginian, Sept. 6, 1830, p. 3, c. 3.

LEDBEITER, HERBERT M. married on Wed. the 23rd inst. to Harriet W. Patterson, dau. of David Patterson of Campbell, by The Rev. Samuel Davisson. Groom of Lynchburg.
The Lynchburg Virginian, Feb. 28, 1831, p. 3, c. 4.

LEE, MISS ANN C. - See entry for Jessee L. Salmons.

LEE, MR. CHARLES C. married on Thurs. the 15th inst. to Miss Louisa W. Finny, eldest dau. of Mr. Peter Finny, by The Rev. William Davis. All of Franklin County, Va.
The Lynchburg Virginian, Oct. 29, 1835, p. 3, c. 6.

LEE, MISS ELIZABETH - See entry for Patrick Henry Cabell.

LEE, MISS ELIZABETH C. - See entry for Capt. Richard W. Chick.

LEE, GUY married on 9th inst. to Miss Delilah Martin, dau. of Stephen Martin, Esq., by The Rev. Sam'l Davidson. All of Campbell.
The Lynchburg Virginian, Oct. 13, 1828, p. 3, c. 5.

LEE, JOHN married Sept. 16, 1824 to Miss Mary C. E. Manson, dau. of Nathaniel J. Manson, Esq. of Bedford, by The Rev. Nicholas Cobbs. Groom of Lynchburg.
The Lynchburg Virginian, Sept. 21, 1824, p. 3.

LEE, JOHN R., ESQ. married on 7th inst. to Miss Elizabeth Mann P. Nelson by The Rev. Charles Dresser. All of Halifax.
The Lynchburg Virginian, Jan. 21, 1836, p. 3, c. 4.

LEE, THE REV. LEROY M. married on 28th ult. to Miss Virginia Addington by The Rev. Mr. Doggett. bride of Norfolk, Va. Groom of Richmond, Virginia.
The Lynchburg Virginian, Dec. 8, 1836, p. 3, c. 5.

LEE, MISS MARY JANE - See entry for Alexander H. Wilson.

LEE, MISS NANCY E. - See entry for Buford Wills.

LEE, RICHARD A. married on Thurs. evening to Miss Mary Jane Shoemaker, dau. of Mr. Lindsey Shoemaker of this place, by The Rev. E. Wadsworth.
The Lynchburg Virginian, Oct. 31, 1836, p. 3, c. 1.

LEE, MISS SUSAN ANN - See entry for Louis Phillip Burwell.

LEFTWICH, MISS ANN - See entry for Calohil Mennis.

LEFTWICH, MISS ANN MARIA - See entry for John Goode.

LEFTWICH, CAPT. AUGUSTINE married on Tues. evening last to Miss Ann
Elizabeth W. Clark, dau. of James Clark, Esq. of this town, by
The Rev. Samuel Capers. Groom of Lynchburg, Va.
The Lynchburg Virginian, July 19, 1830, p. 3, c. 4.

LEFTWICH, CAPT. AUGUSTINE married on June 17, 1823 to Miss Mildred
Ward, dau. of John Ward, Esq. of Pittsylvania, by The Rev. Mr.
Kelly. Groom of Lynchburg.
The Lynchburg Virginian, June 27, 1823, p. 3.

LEFTWICH, MISS BETSY - See entry for Owil Loving.

LEFTWICH, BIRD S. married on Oct. 22, 1823 to Miss Judith Fuqua, dau.
of Caleb Fuqua of Bedford, by The Rev. William Leftwich. Groom
son of Capt. John Leftwich.
The Lynchburg Virginian, Nov. 7, 1823, p. 3.

LEFTWICH, MISS ELIZABETH - See entry for Mr. William L. Bell.

LEFTWICH, JACKY married to Caroline Snodgrass, dau. of Josephus
Snodgrass. Groom of Alabama.
The Lynchburg Virginian, Jan. 4, 1827, p. 3.

LEFTWICH, THE REV. JAMES married on Jan. 15, 1833 to Miss Ann Bilbro
of Botetourt Co. by The Rev. Absolom Dempsey. Groom of Bedford Co.
The Lynchburg Virginian, Jan. 28, 1833, p. 3, c. 4.

LEFTWICH, JOHN O. married on Oct. 31, 1821 to Sarah P. North, dau. of
Mr. John North of Bedford, by The Rev. Wm. S. Reid. Groom of
Lynchburg.
The Lynchburg Press, Nov. 9, 1821, p. 3.

LEFTWICH, LILBOURN W. married on June 6, 1821 to Maria B. Scott, dau.
of Mrs. Robert Scott of Campbell Co., by The Rev. Wm. S. Reid.
The Lynchburg Press, June 15, 1821, p. 1.

LEFTWICH, MISS LUCY - See entry for Mr. Stephen Terry.

LEFTWICH, MISS SARAH - See entry for John W. Smith.

LEFTWICH, THOMAS married to Maria M. Warwick, dau. of Maj. Wm. Warwick.
Bride of Amherst; groom of Bedford.
The Lynchburg Virginian, Nov. 13, 1826, p. 3.

LEFTWICH, DR. WILLIAM married on Oct. 13, 1814 to Mrs. Eliza Calland
by The Rev. James Mitchell. Bride is widow of late Ralph
Calland, Esq. and dau. of Samuel Smith, Esq. of Bedford. Groom
is physician of Bedford Co.
The Lynchburg Press, Oct. 27, 1814, p. 3.

LEFTWICH, WM. C. married to E. Matilda Woodroof, dau. of Mrs. Elizabeth
Woodroof of Bedford.
The Lynchburg Virginian, Jan. 28, 1828, p. 3.

LEIGH, MISS MARY SUSAN - See entry for Conway Robinson.

LENAS, LEONARD married on Nov. 10, 1826 to Kate Muman at Woodstock.
The Lynchburg Virginian, Dec. 7, 1826, p. 2.

LEROY, MISS CAROLINE - See entry for The Hon. Daniel Webster.

LEUBA, HENRY married to Miss Catherine Goddard, dau. of Mr. Michael
Goddard, by The Rev. F. R. Palmer. All of Georgetown, Ky. Groom
formerly of Lynchburg.
The Lynchburg Virginian, Jan. 17, 1831, p. 3, c. 4.

LEWELLIN, ELIZABETH B. - See entry for Edward B. Wells.

LEWELLIN, MR. JOHN married on 20th of Dec. 1832 to Miss Sarah S. Martin,
dau. of Mr. Charles Martin, by The Rev. Thomas Jones of Lynchburg.
All of Campbell.
The Lynchburg Virginian, Jan. 7, 1833, p. 3, c. 3.

LEWELLIN, MISS MARY ANN - See entry for Mr. Wm. H. Waddell.

LEWELLIN, MISS SARAH - See entry for Samuel S. Robertson.

LEWIS, MR. DAVID P. married on 20th inst. to Miss Martha A. Lilly by
The Rev. Chas. Callaway. All of Pittsylvania.
The Lynchburg Virginian, Dec. 31, 1832, p. 3, c. 2.

LEWIS, MR. HENRY HARRISON married on Wed. evening last to Mrs. Lucy
M. Davis, dau. of Mr. Benjamin Schoolfield of this place, by The
Rev. E. Wadsworth.
The Lynchburg Virginian, Oct. 31, 1836, p. 3, c. 1.

LEYBURN, THE REV. GEORGE W. married on 27th ult. in Bedford Co. to Miss
Elizabeth W. Mosely, dau. of the late Dr. Bennett Mosely, by The
Rev. A. W. Campbell.
The Lynchburg Virginian, Nov. 10, 1836, p. 3, c. 4.

LIGGAN, SARAH - See entry for Wm. W. Dickerson.

LIGGAT, ALEXANDER married on May 13, 1819 to Miss Mary Lynch, dau. of
John Lynch, Sr. of Lynchburg, by The Rev. William S. Reid. Groom
also of Lynchburg.
The Lynchburg Press & Public Advertiser, May 17, 1819, p. 3, c. 5.

LIGON, RICHARD married to Mary Ann Bridgeland. Both bride and groom
of Lynchburg.
The Lynchburg Virginian, March 31, 1828, p. 3.

LILLINGTON, MISS SARAH JANE - See entry for Octavius N. Corbin.

LILLY, MISS MARTHA A. - See entry for David P. Lewis.

LINCOLN, MISS ARIETTA - See entry for Timothy Dwight.

LIPSCOMB, LEONARD married on Aug. 24, 1830 to Miss Jane Hunter of Campbell by The Rev. Samuel Armistead.
The Lynchburg Virginian, Sept. 21, 1830, p. 3, c. 2.

LIVINGSTON, MISS CORA - See entry for Thomas Pennant Barton.

LIVINGSTON, JAMES married to Jane Williams, dau. of The Rev. Daniel
Williams. Bride of Campbell Co.
The Lynchburg Virginian, June 1, 1826, p. 3.

LOFTUS, MISS WILMOUTH - See entry for Martin Mason.

LOGAN, MR. JOHN married on Thurs. evening last to Miss Eliza A. Strange
by The Rev. Nicholas Cobb. Bride of Bedford; groom of Greensboro
North Carolina.
The Lynchburg Virginian, July 13, 1829, p. 3, c. 4.

LOGAN, JOSEPH A. married on Thurs. the 10th inst. at Fotheringay,
Montgomery Co. to Miss Alice, dau. of Henry Edmondson, Esq., by
The Rev. M. Wallace.
The Lynchburg Virginian, Dec. 31, 1835, p. 3, c. 4.

LOGWOOD, THOMAS married on Nov. 10, 1797 to Miss Polly Patterson at
home of Capt. Henry Flood in Buckingham. Groom of Powhatan Co.
The Lynchburg & Farmer's Gazette, Nov. 13, 1797, p. 3, c. 1.

LONDON, MATILDA ANN W. - See entry for Mr. Henry W. Haggard.

LONDON, WIATT married on Thurs. evening the 21st inst. to Miss Rachel
Mahala Scott by The Rev. Daniel Day. All of Amherst.
The Lynchburg Virginian, May 25, 1835, p. 3, c. 5.

LONG, ALBERT C. married on Nov. 6, 1823 to Miss Maria Cralle at
Horgemond, in Campbell Co. by The Rev. Edmund Johns.
The Lynchburg Virginian, Nov. 14, 1823, p. 3.

LOVE, MISS ELEANOR B. - See entry for Edward B. Price.

LOVELL, MILTON L. married on 22nd Jan. to Miss Paulina V. Lanier,
eldest dau. of Mr. John Lanier, by The Rev. John H. Watson.
All of Pittsylvania Co., Va.
The Lynchburg Virginian, Feb. 19, 1829, p. 3, c. 5.

LOVING, MISS ELIZABETH ANN - See entry for George R. Watts.

LOVING, JAMES M. married to Sarah W. Jordan, dau. of Wm. Jordan.
Groom son of Samuel Loving.
The Lynchburg Virginian, Dec. 3, 1827, p. 3.

LOVING, MISS MARY ANN - See entry for David R. McAlexander.

LOVING, OWIL married on Nov. 12, 1823 to Miss Betsy Leftwich, dau. of
Maj. Jesse Leftwich of Bedford Co., by The Rev. William Leftwich.
Groom son of Capt. Lunsford Loving of Nelson Co.
The Lynchburg Virginian, Nov. 21, 1823, p. 3, c. 4.

LOVING, SEATON HENRY married on Oct. 22nd to Miss Louisa Miller Montgomery,
dau. of Capt. Joseph Montgomery., by The Rev. James Boyd. All of
Nelson Co.
The Lynchburg, Virginian, Nov. 6, 1828, p. 3, c. 5.

LOVING, WILLIAM T. married on Dec. 25th, 1834 to Miss Sarah W. Tucker by
The Rev. J. J. Hicks. Bride and groom of Nelson Co., Va.
The Lynchburg Virginian, Jan. 8, 1835, p. 3, c. 5.

LOWE, MISS POLLY - See entry for Thomas O. Staton.

LUCAS, WILLIAM HENRY, ESQ. married on Tues. evening, 12th inst. to Miss
Maria Champe Bradfute, dau. of Davidson Bradfute, Esq. of this
place, by The Rev. F. G. Smith. Groom from Alabama.
The Lynchburg Virginian, July 14, 1836, p. 3, c. 4.

LUCK, MR. JAMES A. married on 19th inst. to Miss Susan H., dau. of Col.
Daniel Coleman, by The Rev. John W. Kelly. All of Pittsylvania.
The Lynchburg Virginian, Dec. 31, 1832, p. 3, c. 2.

LUCK, MISS LUCY ANN - See entry for John Richardson.

LUCKE, MISS ROSINA - See entry for Mr. Giles W. B. Hale.

LUMPKINS, MOORE married on Thurs., Dec. 17, 1829 to Miss Catherine
Richardson, age 18, dau. of John Richardson of Pittsylvania Co.,
by The Rev. Abner Anthony. Groom age 90.
The Lynchburg Virginian, Jan. 4, 1830, p. 3, c. 6.

LUSTER, MISS SUSAN F. - See entry for John E. Curd.

LYLE, MISS JANE - See entry for Henry Morris.

LYMAN, MR. DAVID R. married April 4th to Miss Elizabeth H. Roberts, dau.
of Enock Roberts, Esq., by The Rev. David S. Doggett. All of this
place.
The Lynchburg Virginian, April 5, 1832, p. 3, c. 3.

LYMAN, MEDAD married Wed. night last to Miss Elizabeth Essex, dau. of
The Rev. Benjamin Essex, by The Rev. Wm. S. Reid. All of this place.
The Lynchburg Virginian, Dec. 1, 1828, p. 3, c. 5.

LYNCH, MISS ANN - See entry for Samuel Lancaster.

LYNCH, MISS ELIZA - See entry for Malcolm McNeill.

LYNCH, MISS MARY - See entry for Alexander Liggat.

LYNCH, CAPT. MICAJAH married on June 27, 1821 to Ann Moorman, dau. of
James C. Moorman, Esq., by The Rev. Wm. S. Reid. Married in the
vicinity of Lynchburg.
The Lynchburg Press, June 29, 1821, p. 3.

LYNCH, MISS SARAH CLARK - See entry for John Haywood Hicks.

LYNCH, MISS ZELINDA - See entry for Nathaniel Winston.

Mc

MCALEXANDER, DAVID R. married Oct. 22nd to Miss Mary Ann Loving, dau. of James Loving, Esq., by The Rev. Wm. Hamersley. All of Nelson Co.
The Lynchburg Virginian, Nov. 6, 1828, p. 3, c. 5.

MCCABE, MISS SARAH - See entry for The Rev. Wm. H. Starr.

MCCLAN, MISS SARAH - See entry for James Meador.

MCCLANAHAN, MISS SARAH JANE - See entry for Dr. John H. Griffin.

MCCLURE, MR. REDMUND married on 3rd ult. to Miss Mary Cunningham by The Rev. Charles Bullard. All of Montgomery Co.
The Lynchburg Virginian, Feb. 9, 1835, p. 3, c. 4.

MCCORKLE, CAPT. SAMUEL married last evening to Miss Sarah B. Perry, dau. of Collin M. Perry, by The Rev. Wm. S. Reid. All of this place.
The Lynchburg Virginian, Feb. 4, 1830, p. 3, c. 3.

M'COY, JAMES married on 6th ult. to Miss Mahala Thomas in Hartford, N.C. at the residence of Mr. Wm. M'Coy, by Henry W. Barbour, Esq.
The Lynchburg Virginian, March 5, 1835, p. 3, c. 4.

MCCRAW, MISS CATHERINE - See entry for James R. Mason.

MCCRAW HILL married on 11th inst. in the County of Charlotte to Miss Ann E. Elliott, eldest dau. of the late Jno. Elliott of Prince Edward Co., by The Rev. Mr. Davidson.
The Lynchburg Virginian, Feb. 26, 1829, p. 3, c. 5.

MCCRAW, MISS MATILDA M. - See entry for James W. Wauhop.

MCCRAW, RICHARD married on Dec. 27, 1832 to Miss _____ Carwile by The Rev. Samuel Armistead. Bride and groom both of Campbell Co.
The Lynchburg Virginian, Jan. 21, 1833, p. 3, c. 4.

MCDANIEL, AMBROSE M. married to Polly Jones, dau. of Capt. Chas. Jones of Nelson Co. and of Amherst Co.
The Lynchburg Virginian, April 17, 1828, p. 3.

MCDANIEL, MISS ELIZABETH - See entry for Zach Ogden.

MCDANIEL, JOHN R. married Thurs. 6 o'clock a.m. to Elizabeth F. Chaplin, dau. of Wm. R. Chaplin, Esq., by The Rev. F. G. Smith. All of this place.
The Lynchburg Virginian, Aug. 21, 1837, p. 3, c. 4.

MCDANIEL, MISS LUCY - See entry for John Crenshaw.

MCDANIEL, MISS MARY JANE - See entry for James M. Moorman.

MCDANIEL, MISS SOPHIA - See entry for Thomas Strange.

MCDEARMAN, MISS JUDITH - See entry for Richard Overstreet.

MCDEARMAN, MR. SAMUEL D. married on 10th inst. to Miss Mary Frances
Philadelphia Walton, dau. of William Walton, Esq. of Buckingham Co.
Groom of Prince Edward Co.
The Lynchburg Virginian, June 25, 1835, p. 3, c. 4.

MCDONALD, W. K., ESQ. married on the 19th inst. to Hannah Carnahan,
youngest dau. of The Rev. James Carnahan, D.D. President of the
College of N. Jersey. Married at Princeton. Groom is of Alexandria, D.C., attorney-at-law.
The Lynchburg Virginian, Oct. 28, 1830, p. 3, c. 4.

MCDOUGOLD, MISS SARAH - See entry for Geo. P. Richardson.

MCDOWELL, MRS. ANN D. - See entry for James E. Brown, Esq.

MCDUFFIE, GEO. M. (HON.) married on 27th ult. at Columbia, S.C. to
Miss Mary Rebecca Singleton, dau. of Richard Singleton, Esq. of
Sumpter Dist., S.C., by The Rev. Mr. Converse.
The Lynchburg Virginian, June 25, 1829, p. 3, c. 4.

MCGHEE, WM. T. married to Miss Mary Mosley Green, dau. of Capt. Wm.
Green. Bride and groom of Bedford.
The Lynchburg Virginian, April 20, 1827, p. 3.

MCIVER, CHRISTOPHER married on 12th inst. to Miss Eliza Halsey by The
Rev. Robert Ryland. All of this place.
The Lynchburg Virginian, Nov. 24, 1828, p. 3, c. 5.

MCIVOR, MISS NANCY - See entry for Mr. Joseph Jones.

MCKINNEY, MR. GEORGE married to Miss E. Martin of Campbell by The Rev.
Samuel Armistead.
The Lynchburg Virginian, Dec. 22, 1931, p. 3, c. 5.

MCKINNEY, MISS MARTHA LOUSA - See entry for Capt. David Bridges.

MCKINNEY, CAPT. THOMAS married to Jane G. Dupuy, dau. of Peter Dupuy
of Richmond. Bride of Richmond.
The Lynchburg Virginian, July 10, 1826, p. 3.

MCNEILL, MALCOLM married Nov. 20, 1829 to Miss Eliza Lynch, dau. of
Capt. John Lynch formerly a citizen of Lynchburg, by The Rev.
Edmund Jones, formerly of Petersburg, Va. Married in Jackson,
Tenn. Groom of Christian Co., Ky.
The Lynchburg Virginian, Jan. 14, 1830, p. 3, c. 6.

MCPHAIL, JOHN BLAIR married to Nancy Carrington, 2nd dau. of Col.
Clement Carrington of Charlotte, by The Rev. John H. Rice.
Groom is an attorney-at-law.
The Lynchburg Virginian, Sept. 30, 1830, p. 3, c. 3.

MCREYNOLDS, ROBERT S. married Thurs. the 23rd ult. to Miss Frances M.
White, of Charlotte. Groom of Campbell.
The Lynchburg Virginian, Jan. 3, 1831, p. 1, c. 3.

M

MABRY, MISS GEORGIA A. - See entry for The Rev. Martin P. Parks.

MACKARVIS, MISS CROE - See entry for Col. Darius Hobson.

MACKINDER, JOHN A., ESQ. married on Sunday morning, 7th inst. at Christ Church in Williamsburg to Miss Mary Jane White, eldest dau. of late William M. White of Botetourt Co., by The Rev. Adam Emole. Groom merchant of Williamsburg.
The Lynchburg Virginian, Dec. 15, 1834, p. 3, c. 4.

MADDOX, MISS NANCY - See entry for Thomas M. Massie.

MAGRUDER, ALLAN B., ESQ. married on 17th inst. at Waterview, Fluvanna Co. to Miss Sarah E. Timberlake, dau. of John Timberlake, Esq. of the former place by The Rev. Samuel B. Wilson.
The Lynchburg Virginian, Oct. 1, 1835, p. 3, c. 4.

MAJOR, MISS ANGELINA H. - See entry for Cyrus Robinson.

MAJOR, MR. HARWOOD married on 7th to Miss Cleopatria Tinsley, eldest dau. of Mr. Wm. Tinsley, by The Rev. Nicholas H. Cobbs. All of Bedford.
The Lynchburg Virginian, Dec. 15, 1831, p. 3, c. 3.

MAJORS, MISS LUCY - See entry for Roderick Dawson.

MANNING, CLAIBORNE married to Miss Sarah Huff, dau. of James Huff, by The Rev. Michael Howery. All of Floyd Co.
The Lynchburg Virginian, Oct. 24, 1836, p. 3, c. 3.

MANSFIELD, JOHN married to Martha Wakefield of Medfield. Groom of Brownfield. Married in Newfield.
The Lynchburg Virginian, April 14, 1828, p. 3, c. 5.

MANSON, MISS MARY C. E. - See entry for John Lee.

MAPES, JOSEPH married in Columbus Ohio to Mrs. Eleanor S. Wodou by W. D. Martin, Esq.
The Lynchburg Virginian, Sept. 18, 1834, p. 3, c. 5.

MARKHAM, MISS ANN MARIA - See entry for John Myrick.

MARR, DR. AMBROSE R. married on 5th inst. to Miss Sarah L. Williams, dau. of David Williams of Pittsylvania, by The Rev. Wm. B. Leftwich. Groom of Bedford.
The Lynchburg Virginian, May 18, 1835, p. 3, c. 3.

MARR, JAMES married on Thurs. last to Elizabeth Shields by The Rev. James Boyd. Bride of Nelson; groom of Bedford.
The Lynchburg Virginian, Oct. 26, 1826, p. 3, c. 4.

MARSHALL, MISS ANGELINA - See entry for George W. Lawson.

MARSHALL, MISS MARY JANE - See entry for Hix Bates.

MARSHALL, MISS MARY M. - See entry for Yancey Bailey.

MARSHALL, THOMAS R. married Aug. 18, 1830 in Campbell Co. to Miss Mary Ann Jones, dau. of James S. Jones, Esq. of Campbell Co., Va.
The Lynchburg Virginian, Aug. 26, 1830, p. 3, c. 4.

MARTIN, MISS ANN G. - See entry for John Fowler.

MARTIN, MR. DABNEY married on 18th ult. to Miss Elizabeth Perkins, dau. of Mr. Wm. Perkins of Bedford, by The Rev. Wm. I. Holcomb.
The Lynchburg Virginian, Oct. 8, 1832, p. 3, c. 2.

MARTIN, MISS DELILAH - See entry for Guy Lee.

MARTIN, MISS DOLLY - See entry for John Anderson.

MARTIN, MR. DUDLEY married on Thurs., 8th inst. to Miss Susan Poindexter, dau. of Wm. Poindexter, Esq. of Campbell.
The Lynchburg Virginian, Dec. 22, 1831, p. 3, c. 5.

MARTIN, MISS E. - See entry for Mr. George McKinney.

MARTIN, CAPT. GEORGE W. married on 22nd to Miss Elizabeth Ann Starling by The Rev. John C. Traylor. All of Henry.
The Lynchburg Virginian, Jan. 6, 1831, p. 3, c. 4.

MARTIN, MR. JAMES married on the 15th ult. to Miss Polly Powell, dau. of Mr. David Powell, by The Rev. Samuel Armistead. All of Campbell.
The Lynchburg Virginian, Oct. 6, 1836, p. 3, c. 3.

MARTIN, JAMES E. married on 11th inst. to Miss Elmira J. Cardwell, eldest dau. of Mr. James J. Cardwell, by The Rev. Thomas Jones. All of Campbell County.
The Lynchburg Virginian, Dec. 18, 1834, p. 3, c. 4.

MARTIN, MR. JAMES F. married on March 22nd to Miss Ann A. Feazle, dau. of Mr. Jacob Feazle, by The Rev. Mr. Mitchell. All of Lynchburg.
The Lynchburg Virginian, April 5, 1832, p. 3, c. 3.

MARTIN, JONATHAN married to Sarah Day, dau. of Evan Day of Botetourt Co. Groom of Campbell Co.
The Lynchburg Virginian, Nov. 23, 1826, p. 3.

MARTIN, MR. JOSIAH married on 10th inst. to Miss Martha Ann Pankey of Buckingham by The Rev. Samuel Davidson.
The Lynchburg Virginian, Dec. 18, 1834, p. 3, c. 4.

MARTIN, MISS MALINDA - See entry for Mr. John Scott.

MARTIN, MISS MARY W. - See entry for John C. Staples.

MARTIN, MR. ROBERT C. married on 8th inst. to Miss Nancy Dickey by The Rev. Robert Carson. All of Campbell Co.
The Lynchburg Virginian, Oct. 19, 1835, p. 3, c. 4.

MARTIN, ROGER married on Wed. evening last to Miss Martha Elizabeth
   Corneal by The Rev. Edward Cannon. Bride and groom are of this
   place.
   The Lynchburg Virginian, Oct. 24, 1831, p. 3, c. 5.

MARTIN, MISS SARAH S. - See entry for John Lewellin.

MARTIN, MISS SUSAN - See entry for Major Robert Cook.

MARTIN, WILLIAM married to Eliz. Boon, dau. of Abraham Boon of Franklin
   County.
   The Lynchburg Virginian, June 12, 1828, p. 3.

MASON, MISS ELIZA - See entry for Micajah Clark.

MASON, GILBERT, THE REV. married on Tues. the 6th inst. in Nottoway Co.
   to Miss Mary Dabney Morris, dau. of Capt. Dabney Morris, by The
   Rev. Joseph Baker. Groom of Petersburg.
   The Lynchburg Virginian, Mar. 19, 1832, p. 3, c. 3.

MASON, JAMES R. married on 28th ult. to Miss Catharine McCraw by The
   Rev. Samuel Armistead.
   The Lynchburg Virginian, Feb. 11, 1833, p. 3, c. 3.

MASON, CAPT. JOHN T. married on Feb. 16, 1820 to Miss Nancy T. School-
   field, dau. of Benjamin Schoolfield, by The Rev. Henry Brown.
   Bride and groom of Lynchburg.
   The Lynchburg Press & Public Advertiser, Feb. 18, 1820,

MASON, MARTIN, ESQ. married on Sat. night the 13th Feb. 1830 to Miss
   Wilmouth Lofftus, dau. of Mr. Reuben Lofftus, by The Rev. Abner
   Early. All of Campbell Co.
   The Lynchburg Virginian, Mar. 15, 1830, p. 3, c. 3.

MASON, WATKINS married on Dec. 20, 1832 to Miss Frances Bailey, dau. of
   the late Mr. Thomas Bailey, by The Rev. Nathaniel Lovelace.
   The Lynchburg Virginian, Dec. 24, 1832, p. 3, c. 2.

MASSIE, MISS MARY C. - See entry for Samuel W. Venable.

MASSIE, MISS MARY L. P. - See entry for John H. Pleasants, Esq.

MASSIE, NATHANIEL married on Sept. 4, 1821 to Susan A. Woods, dau. of
   Michael Woods of Nelson Co. by The Rev. Wm. H. Foote. Groom of
   Nelson Co.
   The Lynchburg Press, Sept. 14, 1821, p. 3.

MASSIE, MISS SARAH - See entry for Wm. O. Goode.

MASSIE, M. THOMAS married on Dec. 5, 1823 to Miss Nancy Maddox, dau. of
   John Maddox, Esq. of Amherst Co., by The Rev. Wm. Duncan.
   The Lynchburg Virginian, Dec. 19, 1823, p. 3.

MASSIE, DR. THOMAS married to Sarah J. Cabell, dau. of Col. Wm. Cabell.
Bride and groom of Nelson Co.
The Lynchburg Virginian, April 10, 1826, p. 3.

MASSIE, WILLIAM, ESQ. married on Thurs. 7th inst. to Miss Martha V.
Wiatt of Lynchburg by The Rev. F. G. Smith. Groom resident of
Nelson Co.
The Lynchburg Virginian, May 11, 1829, p. 3, c. 4.

MASSIE, WILLIAM, ESQ. married on 21st inst. to Miss Sarah U. Clark, dau.
of the late Bolling Clark, Esq. of Campbell Co., by The Rev. Wm. S.
Reid. Groom of Nelson Co.
The Lynchburg Virginian, May 28, 1833, p. 3, c. 3.

MASSIE, WILLIAM married on Oct. 20, 1814 to Miss Sarah Steptoe, dau. of
J. Steptoe of near New London, by The Rev. Wm. S. Reid. Groom of
New London.
The Lynchburg Press, Nov. 10, 1814, p. 3.

MASSIE, W. M., ESQ. married recently at Harrisonburg, Rockingham Co. to
Miss Maria C. Effinger, dau. of Mr. Michael Effinger of the former
place, by A. W. Kirkpatrick. Groom from Nelson Co.
The Lynchburg Virginian, Jan. 5, 1835, p. 3, c. 3.

MASSY, MISS MARY L. - See entry for W. M. Harvey.

MATHEWS, MISS ELIZABETH - See entry for Alfred Edgar.

MATHEWS, MISS MARTHA E. - See entry for Mr. Edward Taylor.

MATTHEW, PASCAL married on Nov. 1, 1822 to Miss Barbara Smith by The Rev.
Samuel Armistead. Bride and groom of Charlotte Co.
The Lynchburg Virginian, Nov. 15, 1822, p. 3.

MATTHEWS, EDWIN M. married on Dec. 23, 1828 to Miss Emily Mildred Goggin,
eldest day. of Pleasant M. Goggin of Bedford, by The Rev. Wm. S.
Reid. Groom of Lynchburg.
The Lynchburg Virginian, Jan. 1, 1829, p. 3, c. 4.

MATTHEWS, GEORGE W. married on Wed., Feb. 8th to Miss Dolly A. Hubbard,
dau. of Mr. Joel Hubbard of Halifax, by The Rev. John Hubbard.
Groom from Campbell.
The Lynchburg Virginian, Feb. 20, 1832, p. 3, c. 4.

MATTHEWS, MR. THOMAS married on Wed. last to Miss Mary Randolph Brown,
eldest dau. of Matthew Brown, Esq. of this place, by The Rev. Mr.
Parks. Groom of Greenbriar Co.
The Lynchburg Virginian, Jan. 17, 1831, p. 3, c. 4.

MATTHEWS, WILLIAM W. married on Thurs. last at Mr. William Collins in
Halifax Co., to Miss Mary Stone, dau. of the late John Stone, by
The Rev. Mr. Anderson. Groom of Campbell Co.
The Lynchburg Virginian, Jan. 10, 1828, p. 3, c. 2.

MATOON, MISS ELIZABETH - See entry for Daniel Butts.

MAUNCER, MISS MARY T. - See entry for William H. Morgan.

MAUPIN, MR. IRA married on 17th inst. to Miss Eliza Ann Jones, dau. of
Capt. Wm. R. Jones of Bedford, by The Rev. Henry S. Peyton.
The Lynchburg Virginian, Nov. 22, 1832, p. 3, c. 4.

MAYS, MISS CARY JANE - See entry for James W. Keith.

MAYS, JOSEPH married on Sept. 4, 1817 to Miss Mary Ann Roberts, dau. of
Enoch Roberts of Campbell, by The Rev. J. C. Burruss. Groom of
Lynchburg.
The Lynchburg Press, Sept. 12, 1817, p. 3.

MEAD, WM. married on 22 inst. to Mary W. Crenshaw, youngest dau. of
David Crenshaw, by The Rev. Dr. Philips. Bride and groom of Bedford.
The Lynchburg Virginian, Feb. 25, 1825, p. 3, c. 4.

MEADOR, JAMES married Dec. 23, 1829 to Miss Sarah McClan, dau. of Mr.
James McClan of Bedford, Va., by The Rev. James Leftwich.
The Lynchburg Virginian, Jan. 4, 1830, p. 3, c. 6.

MEADOW, MRS. NANCY - See entry for Abner Skrudbin.

MENNIS, CALOHIL married May 7, 1823 to Miss Ann Leftwich by The Rev.
William Leftwich. Bride and groom of Bedford Co.
The Lynchburg Virginian, May 16, 1823, p. 3, c. 4.

MERRIWETHER, MISS ELIZABETH - See entry for Walker G. Merriwether.

MERRIWETHER, WALKER G. married Nov. 27, 1817 to Miss Elizabeth Merriwether by The Rev. Mr. Anderson. Bride of Bedford; groom of Richmond.
The Lynchburg Press, Dec. 5, 1817, p. 3.

METCALFE, JAMES married Tues. evening, Sept. 1st to Miss Margaret
Harrison, youngest dau. of Samuel J. Harrison, Esq. of this town,
by The Rev. F. G. Smith.
The Lynchburg Virginian, Sept. 3, 1835, p. 3, c. 4.

MICHAUX, MISS VIRGINIA A. - See entry for Peter Hamlin.

MIDDLETON, WALTER H. married to Sarah Williams, dau. of Capt. Francis
Williams. Bride of Nottoway Co., Groom of Lynchburg.
The Lynchburg Virginian, Nov. 26, 1827, p. 3.

MIEURE, THOMAS married on the 15th inst. in Richmond to Miss Catherine
M. Dibrell formerly of Lynchburg, by The Rev. Anthony Dibrell.
Groom is of Richmond.
The Lynchburg Virginian, Dec. 24, 1835, p. 3, c. 5.

MIGANN, MOSES H. married on the 24th inst. at the house of Mr. Joseph
Migann to Miss Jane W. Hill by The Rev. James M. Boyd. All of
Amherst Co.
The Lynchburg Virginian, March 30, 1829, p. 3, c. 4.

MIGGINSON, JOSEPH, ESQ. married on Tues. the 14th inst. to Almira
Montgomery by The Rev. James Boyd. Bride and groom of Nelson Co.
The Lynchburg Virginian, Nov. 23, 1826, p. 3.

MILES, BENJAMIN married on Dec. 23, 1819 to Miss Sally Wilson by The
Rev. Wm. Duncan. Bride and groom both of Amherst Co. Groom 70
years; bride 15 yrs.
The Lynchburg Press & Public Advertiser, Jan. 7, 1825, p. 3, c. 3.

MILES, MISS SARAH ANN - See entry for John D. Kyle.

MILLER, FRANCIS married Nov. 27, 1823 to Miss Maria Perry, dau. of
Collin M. Perry of Lynchburg, by The Rev. Wm. S. Reid. Groom
also of Lynchburg.
The Lynchburg Virginian, Nov. 28, 1823, p. 3.

MILLER, MISS JANE C. - See entry for Wm. C. Roberts.

MILLER, JOHN C. married on the 3rd inst. to Miss Martha A. M. Munford
of Davidson Co., Tenn., by the Rev. F. E. Pitts. Groom is of
Nashville, formerly of Lynchburg.
The Lynchburg Virginian, March 19, 1835, p. 3, c. 5.

MILLER, ROBERT H. married in St. Clairsville, Ohio to Miss Mary Barton.
The Lynchburg Virginian, June 15, 1829, p. 3, c. 6.

MILLNER, MR. JOHN married on 18th inst. to Miss Eliza A. Trotter. All
of Pittsylvania.
The Lynchburg Virginian, Dec. 31, 1832, p. 3, c. 2.

MITCHELL, MISS C. C. - See entry for Yelverton U. Oliver.

MITCHELL, MISS HANNAH ANN - See entry for Fordice F. Bowen.

MITCHELL, MR. HARVEY married in Washington Co., Va. to Miss Mary Jane
Wood Johnston, only dau. of the late Judge Peter Johnston, by The
Rev. D. R. Preston. Groom formerly of Lynchburg.
The Lynchburg Virginian, Oct. 4, 1832, p. 3, c. 4.

MITCHELL, HARVEY married July 22, 1828 to Miss Elizabeth Griffin by The
Rev. Wm. S. Reid. All of Lynchburg.
The Lynchburg Virginian, July 24, 1828, p. 3, c. 5.

MITCHELL, JAMES R. married on May 7th to Miss Elizabeth Franklin, dau.
of Col. Robert Franklin of Campbell, by The Rev. Samuel D. Rice.
Groom son of James Mitchell of Bedford.
The Lynchburg Virginian, May 21, 1835, p. 3, c. 2.

MITCHELL, MISS MARY CHARLOTTE - See entry for John Harvey.

MITCHELL, GEN. PHILO L. Married on 6th ult. to Miss Varina P. Stanton,
dau. of Wm. Stanton, Esq, by The Rev. P. Connelly. Groom formerly
of Lynchburg. Residence of bride and groom, Natchez, Mississippi.
The Lynchburg Virginian, Dec. 1, 1834, p. 3, c. 4.

MITCHELL, MISS SARAH C. - See entry for Hiram Nelms.

MITCHELL, MISS SARAH E. - See entry for Isaac W. Oliver.

MITCHELL, MR. SOCRATES married Thurs. evening, 21st ult. to Miss Martha
Byars of this place, by The Rev. Edward Cannon.
The Lynchburg Virginian, May 2, 1831, p. 3, c. 3.

MITCHELL, DR. THOMAS L. married on May 3, 1825 to Miss Ann D. Saunders,
dau. of Col. David Saunders of Bedford, by The Rev. Wm. S. Reid.
Groom also of Bedford.
The Lynchburg Virginian, May 12, 1825, p. 3.

MITCHELL, WILLIAM, SENIOR married on Feb. 25th to Miss Ann Hagood, dau.
of Gregory Hagood, Esq. of Patrick Co., by The Rev. Joshua Adams
of Patrick. Groom, age 53, of Patrick Co.; bride, age 16.
The Lynchburg Virginian, Mar. 15, 1830, p. 3, c. 3. & Mar. 25, 1830.

MONROE, MISS MARIA HESTER - See entry for Gov. Hawley Samuel Lawrence.

MONROE, CAPT. WILLIAM married on Wed., 20th inst. to Mary Ann Hersey,
eldest dau. of Benj. Hersey of Amherst, by The Rev. Edward Cannon.
Groom of Albemarle.
The Lynchburg Virginian, Feb. 25, 1828, p. 3, c. 5.

MONTAGUE, MISS SARAH L. - See entry for Mr. James A. Dillard.

MONTGOMERY, MISS ALMIRA - See entry for Joseph Megginson.

MONTGOMERY, MISS LOUISA MILLER - See entry for Seaton Henry Loving.

MONTGOMERY, MISS MARY W. - See entry for Champe Carter.

MOODY, MISS EMILY A. - See entry for Joseph Lacy.

MOODY, MISS SUSAN - See entry for Peyton Venable.

MOON, ARTHUR H. married to Miss Rebecca S. Duffel of Lynchburg, dau. of
Mr. James Duffel, by the Rev. E. Cannon. Groom of Buckingham Co.
The Lynchburg Virginian, Mar. 25, 1830, p. 3, c. 3.

MOON, HENRY married on Jan. 10, 1833 to Miss Jemima Bailey by The Rev.
Samuel Armistead. Both bride and groom of Campbell Co.
The Lynchburg Virginian, Jan. 21, 1833, p. 3, c. 4.

MOON, MISS JANE M. - See entry for Shelton Roberts.

MOON, MISS LUCY ANN - See entry for Daniel Brown.

MOON, MISS NANCY S. - See entry for Fenton North.

MOON, RICHARD D. married Aug. 5, 1832 to Miss Syrena L. Mountcastle, dau.
of John Mountcastle, deceased, of Amherst Co., by the Rev. Robert
Carson. Groom of Scottsville.
The Lynchburg Virginian, Sept. 10, 1832, p. 3, c. 4.

MOON, MISS SOPHIA - See entry for Joseph Davis.

MOORE, DR. ALFRED married on 22nd ult. in Richmond at residence of Mr.
Geo. L. Sampson to Miss Mary Jane Watson, dau. of Mr. Matthew
Watson, deceased, formerly of Lynchburg, by Bishop Moore. Groom
of Huntsville, Ala.
The Lynchburg Virginian, Oct. 6, 1836, p. 3, c. 3.

MOORE, DAVID married on Tues. last to Miss Polly Brafford at the Maple
Swamp by The Rev. William Harris. Bride and groom are of Bedford.
The Lynchburg Virginian, Oct. 10, 1831, p. 3, c. 4.

MOORE, DR. DAVID married July 22, 1833 at Preston's Ridge to Miss Marthal
Harrison, dau. of Col. Benjamin Harrison of Brunswick Co., by The
Rev. John Early. Groom of Huntsville, Ala.
The Lynchburg Virginian, Aug. 5, 1833, p. 3, c. 4.

MOORE, EDWIN D. married on 29th ult. to Miss Sarah Woodson by The Rev.
Nicholas H. Cobbs. Bride of Botetourt; groom of Bedford.
The Lynchburg Virginian, May 11, 1829, p. 3, c. 4.

MOORE, MISS ELIZA - See entry for Peter Walker.

MOORE, JESSE married on 5th inst. to Miss Mary Watkins, dau. of Mr.
_____ Watkins of this county, by The Rev. Samuel Armistead.
The Lynchburg Virginian, Nov. 20, 1828, p. 3, c. 5.

MOORE, MARTHA - See entry for Matthew Thompson.

MOORE, MISS MARY ANN - See entry for John Petticrew.

MOORE, MISS MARY ARCHER - See entry for Mr. Albert M. Wilkerson.

MOORE, MISS NANCY - See entry for Benjamin Doe, Esq.

MOORMAN, ACHILLES H. married to Elizabeth S. Calland, dau. of Capt.
Sam'l Calland. Bride and groom from Pittsylvania Co.
The Lynchburg Virginian, Jan. 5, 1826, p. 3.

MOORMAN, MISS ANN - See entry for Capt. Micajah Lynch.

MOORMAN, CHARLES H. married on Thurs. evening last to Miss Ann S. Chilton
of this county, dau. of Mr. Richard Chilton. Groom of Kentucky.
The Lynchburg Virginian, Nov. 2, 1829, p. 3, c. 5.

MOORMAN, MISS ELIZABETH - See entry for James H. Norfolk.

MOORMAN, MISS HARRIET ELVIRA - See entry for Lafayette Johnson.

MOORMAN, MR. JAMES M. married on Tues. the 4th to Miss Mary J. McDaniel, dau. of Mr. Alexander McDaniel, by The Rev. N. H. Cobbs. All of Bedford.
The Lynchburg Virginian, Oct. 31, 1836, p. 3, c. 1.

MOORMAN, MISS JUDITH - See entry for Henry Clark.

MOORMAN, MR. LODOWICK married on Wed. evening, 14th inst. to Miss Elizabeth Davies, dau. of the late Boyle Davies, Esq., by The Rev. N. H. Cobbs. Both of Bedford, Va.
The Lynchburg Virginian, Oct. 19, 1835, p. 3, c. 4.

MOORMAN, MISS LUCINDA - See entry for Mr. John S. Brown.

MOORMAN, MISS LUCY - See entry for Tarlton Brown.

MOORMAN, MISS LUCY JANE - See entry for John D. Gibbs.

MOORMAN, MR. THOMAS J. married on Tues. evening last to Miss Martha Jane Jennings, dau. of Mr. Clement A. Jennings of this place, by The Rev. William J. Holcombe.
The Lynchburg Virginian, May 9, 1831, p. 3, c. 5.

MOORMAN, ZACHARIAH married on 11th ult. to Miss Henrietta M. P. Lambert, dau. of Capt. George Lambert of Bedford, by The Rev. Nicholas H. Cobbs. Groom of Campbell Co.
The Lynchburg Virginian, Dec. 8, 1828, p. 3, c. 6.

MORFORD, MISS CAROLINE FITZRANDOLPH - See entry for James W. Morgan.

MORGAN, DIXON C. married on Sat., 31st inst. to Miss Elizabeth Emmons, youngest dau. of Mr. James Emmons of Fauquier Co., by The Rev. Alexander H. Bennett. Groom of Lynchburg.
The Lynchburg Virginian, Jan. 15, 1835, p. 3, c. 6.

MORGAN, JAMES W. married to Caroline Fitz Randolph, dau. of Maj. Stephen Morford. Bride of New Jersey; groom of Lynchburg.
The Lynchburg Virginian, Oct. 19, 1826, p. 3.

MORGAN, JOHN married to Susan Saunders of Bedford, dau. of Dan'l Saunders.
The Lynchburg Virginian, Feb. 21, 1828, p. 3.

MORGAN, THOMAS married on April 2, 1828 to Susan Hendricks by The Rev. Nicholas H. Cobbs. Groom of Buckingham Co., formerly of Richmond. Bride of Campbell Co.
The Lynchburg Virginian, April 7, 1828, p. 3, c. 5.

MORGAN, WILLIAM married on April 3, 1825 to Mrs. Ann Gwathmey by The Rev. John Early. All of this place. William Morgan was a merchant.
The Lynchburg Virginian, April 8, 1825, p. 3, c. 3.

MORGAN, MR. WM. H. married Thurs. 13th inst. to Miss Mary T. Mounger of
Greensborough, Georgia by The Rev. Louice Pierce. Groom formerly
of Lynchburg, Va.
The Lynchburg Virginian, May 27, 1830, p. 3, c. 6.

MORRIS, GEORGE W. married on 17th to Miss Susan G. Davis by The Rev.
John Davis.
The Lynchburg Virginian, March 3, 1831, p. 3, c. 5.

MORRIS, HENRY married to Jane Lyle, youngest dau. of Joseph Lyle of
Henry Co., by The Rev. Josiah Pedigo.
The Lynchburg Virginian, Jan. 11, 1827, p. 3, c. 2.

MORRIS, MRS. MARY - See entry for Richard Steagall.

MORRIS, MISS MARY DABNEY - See entry for The Rev. Gilbert Mason.

MORRIS, MISS MARY H. - See entry for James Davis, Esq.

MORRIS, MR. MICAJAH married on 20th inst. to Miss Lively Scott of
Pittsylvania by The Rev. Charles Callaway. Groom of Campbell Co.
The Lynchburg Virginian, Dec. 31, 1832, p. 3, c. 2.

MORRIS, RICHARD G. married on Sept. 7, 1825 to Mrs. Elizabeth R. Williams,
dau. of Charles Yancey of Buckingham, by The Rev. Wm. S. Reid.
Groom of Gloucester.
The Lynchburg Virginian, Sept. 15, 1825, p. 3.

MORRIS, MISS SARAH A. - See entry for Dr. William Carter.

MORRISS, MISS MISSOURI - See entry for David R. Edley, Esq.

MORTON, MISS ELIZA J. - See entry for Wm. A. Bennett.

MOSBY, MISS SARAH ANN - See entry for Hardin Perkins.

MOSBY, WILLIAM W., ESQ. married on 11th inst. in Powhatan to Miss
Elizabeth H. Goode, dau. of the late Francis Goode, Esq. of
Powhatan, by The Rev. J. E. Curtis.
The Lynchburg Virginian, Oct. 24, 1836, p. 3, c. 3.

MOSELEY, MISS ELIZABETH W. - See entry for The Rev. Geo. W. Leyburn.

MOSELEY, MISS MARY - See entry for The Rev. Alexander W. Campbell.

MOSELEY, MICAJAH married on 19th inst. at Liberty Chapel to Mrs. Mildred
Johnson, age 28, by The Rev. Samuel Davidson. Both of Bent Creek,
Buckingham Co.
The Lynchburg Virginian, July 27, 1835, p. 3, c. 4.

MOSELY, GEORGE C. married on 17th inst. at Fancy Farm in Bedford to Miss
Mary Whitlocke, dau. of Izard Bacon Whitlocke, Esq., deceased, for-
merly of Richmond, by The Rev. Jacob D. Mitchell. Groom of Lynchburg.
The Lynchburg Virginian, Dec. 21, 1835, p. 3, c. 3.

MOSES, MISS ELIZA - See entry for David Coleman.

MOSLY, MISS ELIZABETH A. - See entry for Charles A. Holcombe.

MOTLEY, MISS MARTHA - See entry for Calohill Yates.

MOUNTCASTLE, MISS SYRENA K. - See entry for Richard D. Moon.

MUMAN, KATE - See entry for Leonard Lenas.

MUNDAY, MISS ANN - See entry for Joseph Pettyjohn.

MUNDY, MISS MARY - See entry for James M. Dillard.

MUNFORD, JOHN D. married on 21st April at St. Catharines to Miss Eliza M. Northrop, dau. of Commodore Northrop.
The Lynchburg Virginian, May 20, 1833, p. 3, c. 5.

MUNFORD, MISS MARTHA A. M. - See entry for John C. Miller.

MURAT, ACHILLES married to Mrs. Catherine Dangerfield Gray, dau. of Major Byrd C. Willis. Bride of Fredericksburg; groom of Florida.
The Lynchburg Virginian, Aug. 24, 1826, p. 3.

MURAT, PRINCE LUCIEN married on Thurs. 18th inst. in St. Michael's Church Trenton, N.J. to Carolina Georgiana, youngest dau. of late Major Thones Frazer of S.C., by The Rev. Dr. Beasley. Groom was second son of Joachim Murat, late ex-king of Naples.
The Lynchburg Virginian Extra, Sept. 1, 1831, p. 3, c. 4.

MURPHEY, J. REMIAR married on Jan. 7, 1829 to Miss Nancy Hawkins, dau. of Joseph H. Hawkins of Bedford, by The Rev. Mr. Whesley. Groom of Lynchburg.
The Lynchburg Virginian, Jan. 15, 1829, p. 3, c. 5.

MURRAY, CAPTAIN WILLIAM married on April 22, 1823 to Miss Rebecca Shelton by The Rev. John Baptist. Bride and groom both from Powhatan Co.
The Lynchburg Virginian, May 9, 1823, p. 3, c. 5.

MURRELL, CHARLES married on Sat., the 6th inst. to Miss Eliza Ann Whittington, dau. of Mr. Stark Whittington, by The Rev. Wm. Leftwich. All of Bedford.
The Lynchburg Virginian, Dec. 14, 1829, p. 3, c. 5.

MURRELL, DAVID G. married on Feb. 2, 1820 to Miss Alice Tate, dau. of Col. Edmund Tate of Campbell Co., by The Rev. Wm. S. Reid. Groom of Lynchburg.
The Lynchburg Press & Public Advertiser, Feb. 4, 1820, p. 3, c. 4.

MURRELL, ANSLON G. married to Elizabeth Emmerson, dau. of the Hon. Thomas Emmerson. Bride of Washington Co., Tenn. Groom of Athens, Tenn.
The Lynchburg Virginian, Sept. 15, 1825, p. 3.

MURRELL, MISS REBECCA C. - See entry for George W. Turner.

MURRELL, MISS ROSANNA E. - See entry for Samuel Claytor.

MURRELL, MR. WILLIAM B. married Thurs. evening, 28th ult. to Miss Frances Ann Knight, dau. of Mr. William H. Knight of Amherst, by The Rev. John B. Tilden. Groom of this place.
The Lynchburg Virginian, June 1, 1835, p. 3, c. 4.

MUSGROVE, MISS RACHEL - See entry for Owen Wilkerson.

MYRICK, JOHN married on Wed. 25th inst. to Miss Ann Maria Markham, dau. of Capt. George Markham of Amherst Co., by The Rev. James Boyd.
The Lynchburg Virginian, Aug. 30, 1830, p. 3, c. 3.

N

NALLY, MR. WILLIAM married on Sept. 21, 1825 to Miss Elizabeth Roberts, dau. of Mr. Alexander Roberts of Nelson, by The Rev. James Boyd. All of Nelson Co.
The Lynchburg Virginian, Sept. 29, 1825, p. 3.

NANCE, MISS CELIA ANN - See entry for Mr. Williamson Burnett.

NASH, ABNER married on August 2nd to Miss Rebecca Scott by The Rev. Samuel Armistead. All of Campbell.
The Lynchburg Virginian, Aug. 12, 1830, p. 3, c. 4.

NASH, ABNER O. married on Thurs. last to Miss Diana R. Kyle by The Rev. Wm. S. Reid. All of this place.
The Lynchburg Virginian, Feb. 9, 1829, p. 3, c. 4.

NASH, ABNER O. married on Tues. the 26th ult. at Hannibal, Missouri to Miss Andasia E. Fontain, late of Maryland. Groom formerly of Lynchburg.
The Lynchburg Virginian, Oct. 29, 1835, p. 3, c. 6.

NASH, FRANCES married on Tues. last to Miss Lucy Adeline Winfree, dau. of Christopher Winfree, Esq. of this vicinity, by The Rev. Wm. I. Holcombe. Groom of Missouri.
The Lynchburg Virginian, May 16, 1836, p. 3, c. 3.

NEAL, STEPHEN R. married Thurs. evening, 16th inst. at Halifax Court House to Miss Sarah A. Royster by The Rev. Mr. Baker. Groom was merchant of Danville.
The Lyncburg Virginian, April 23, 1835, p. 3, c. 5.

NEILSON, HALL married on 17th inst. at the residence of Col. R. Jones in Washington City to Miss Edmonia Lee Page, dau. of the late Wm. Byrd Page of Fairfield, Frederick Co., Va. Married by The Rev. Mr. Jones.
The Lynchburg Virginian, Jan. 26, 1832, p. 3, c. 5.

NELMS, CHARLES, JR. married Wed. the 4th inst. to Mildred J. Preston, only dau. of Isaac Preston, by The Rev. N. H. Cobbs. All of Bedford.
The Lynchburg Virginian, Nov. 16, 1835, p. 3, c. 4.

NELMS, HIRAM married on 21st inst. to Miss Sarah C. Mitchell, dau. of Maj. Samuel Mitchell, by The Rev. James Mitchell. All of Bedford Co.
The Lynchburg Virginian, Jan. 2, 1832, p. 3, c. 5.

NELSON, MISS ELIZABETH MANN P. - See entry for John R. Lee, Esq.

NELSON, JOHN married on 9th inst. to Miss Mary Jones by The Rev. William Harris. All of Liberty.
The Lynchburg Virginian, Feb. 16, 1832, p. 3, c. 4.

NELSON, PETER C. married on Dec. 4, 1823 to Miss Sarah S. Cary, dau. of Miles Cary of Campbell Co., by The Rev. Wm. S. Reid. Groom of Lynchburg.
The Lynchburg Virginian, Dec. 12, 1823, p. 3.

NEVILLE, LAFAYETTE married on Wed. evening, the 7th inst. to Miss Mary J. Labby, dau. of Pleasant Labby, Esq. of this place, by The Rev. Wm. S. Reid. Groom of Lovingston, Nelson Co.
The Lynchburg Virginian, Oct. 12, 1835, p. 3, c. 4.

NEWELL, MISS ISABELLA - See entry for Richard Watts.

NICHOLS, BARTHOLOMEW married on Thurs., July 23rd to Miss Mary Richardson by The Rev. Abner Anthony. All of Pittsylvania.
The Lynchburg Virginian, July 30, 1829, p. 3, c. 4.

NICHOLS, JOSEPH married on Dec. 9, 1824 to Mrs. Mary Ramsey, widow, by The Rev. Mr. Webb. Bride and groom both of Lynchburg.
The Lynchburg Virginian, Dec. 11, 1824, p. 3.

NICKOLLS, MISS ANNA B. - See entry for Sidney S. Baxter.

NICKS, COL. JOHN married on Aug. 13, 1824 in Crawford Co., Ark. to Miss Sarah Price Perkins, dau. of Elisha Perkins, Esq. of Bedford Co., by William F. Vaill.
The Lynchburg Virginian, Sept. 28, 1824, p. 3.

NIMMO, MISS MARION F. - See entry for Caswell Poe.

NIXON, MISS MARGARET JANE - See entry for Samuel Hobart.

NOAH, M. M. married to Rebecca Jackson, dau. of Dan'l Jackson of New York.
The Lynchburg Virginian, Dec. 6, 1827, p. 3.

NOELL, MISS CAROLINE - See entry for Thomas F. Hatcher.

NOELL, THOMAS E. married Jan. 16, 1833 to Miss Susan Ann Saunders, dau. of William Saunders, by The Rev. William Leftwich. Bride and groom of Bedford.
The Lynchburg Virginian, Jan. 31, 1833, p. 3, c. 4.

NORFOLK, MR. JAMES H. married on 6th inst. near St. Louis, Mo. to Miss
Elizabeth Moorman, dau. of Mr. James C. Moorman of Lynchburg, by
The Rev. A. Monroe.
The Lynchburg Virginian, Dec. 31, 1832, p. 3, c. 2.

NORMAN, MISS LUCINDA - See entry for Francis M. Cousins.

NORTH, ABRAM R. married on Nov. 21, 1822 to Miss Sarah Lucinda Lambeth,
dau. of Meredith Lambeth of Campbell Co., by The Rev. George W.
Charlton. Groom of Lynchburg.
The Lynchburg Virginian, Nov. 29, 1822, p. 3.

NORTH, MISS DOLLY P. - See entry for _____ Wooleryming.

NORTH, FENTON married on Thurs., 21st inst. near Red House to Miss Nancy
S. Moon, dau. of Wm. C. Moon of Charlotte Co., by The Rev. Samuel
Armistead of Campbell.
The Lynchburg Virginian, May 28, 1829, p. 3, c. 3.

NORTH, THE REV. HENRY B. married on Jan. 4th at Clarksville, Tenn. to
Mrs. Martha J. Bailey by The Rev. Newton J. Berryman.
The Lynchburg Virginian, Feb. 13, 1832, p. 3, c. 4.

NORTH, MR. RICHARD P. married on 21st of Oct. to Miss Nancy G. Phelps
by The Rev. Samuel Davidson. All of Buckingham.
The Lynchburg Virginian, Nov. 7, 1836, p. 3, c. 4.

NORTH, MISS SARAH P. - See entry for John C. Leftwich.

NORTHROP, MISS ELIZA M. - See entry for John D. Munford.

NORTON, JAMES married on Thurs., July 17th to Miss Theresa Ann Truslow,
eldest dau. of Townsend Truslow, by The Rev. James Taylor. All
of Terra Salis, Kanawha Co.
The Lynchburg Virginian, Aug. 9, 1832, p. 3, c. 4.

NORVELL, MISS ANN E. - See entry for Daniel I. Warwick, Esq.

NORVELL, MISS ANNE ELIZA - See entry for Edwin M. Brown.

NORVELL, CAPT. BENJAMIN married on 8th inst. to Mrs. Flora B. Foster
by The Rev. Isaac Paul. Bride of Amherst; groom of Nelson.
The Lynchburg Virginian, Dec. 15, 1831, p. 3, c. 3.

NORVELL, MISS ELIZA - See entry for George W. Gains.

NORVELL, FAYETTE HENRY, ESQ. married last evening to Miss Mary C. Roane,
dau. of Wm. R. Roane, Esq. of Amherst, by The Rev. W. S. Reid.
Groom of Lynchburg.
The Lynchburg Virginian, Dec. 1830, p. 3, c. 4.

NORVELL, JAMES married on Thurs., the 1st inst. to Miss Francis G.
Powell, dau. of Geo. Powell, deceased, of Amherst Co., by The
Rev. Charles H. Page. Groom is from Kentucky.
The Lynchburg Virginian, July 15, 1830, p. 3, c. 6.

NORVELL, MAJ. JOHN E. married on 3rd inst. to Miss Elizabeth E. Whitteker,
dau. of Mr. Aaron Whitteker, by The Rev. D. H. Hoge. All of Charleston, Va. (now West Va.) Groom formerly of Lynchburg.
The Lynchburg Virginian, Aug. 11, 1836, p. 3, c. 2.

NORVELL, MISS JOSEPHINE - See entry for The Rev. Robert Ryland.

NORVELL, LORENZO, ESQ. married on Wed., Dec. 8th to Miss Lucy, dau. of
Samuel J. Harrison, Esq., by The Rev. F. G. Smith. All of this
place. Groom is a merchant.
The Lynchburg Virginian, Dec. 13, 1830, p. 3, c. 4.

NORVELL, MISS LUCY MINOR - See entry for Capt. John M. Otey.

NORVELL, MISS MARIA - See entry for Dr. William I. Waller.

NORVELL, MISS MARTHA JANE - See entry for John Caskie.

NORVELL, CAPT. WILLIAM WIATT married on Dec. 10, 1818 to Miss Ann
Harrison, dau. of Samuel J. Harrison, by The Rev. Wm. S. Reid.
All of Lynchburg.
The Lynchburg Press & Public Advertiser, Dec. 17, 1818, p. 3.

NOWLIN, CAPT. BRYON W. married to Miss Fanny M. Scott, eldest dau. of
the late Thomas Scott, Esq. of Campbell Co. Married at Col. James
McClanahan's near Big Lick, Botetourt Co. Groom of Brookneal.
The Lynchburg Virginian, June 30, 1828, p. 3, c. 6.

NOWLIN, BRYANT W., ESQ. married on Wed., Nov. 19th, to Miss Ann B. D.
Spencer, eldest dau of Dr. Mace C. Spencer, by The Rev. Wm.
Wittendrick. All of Buckingham. Groom merchant of Oakville.
The Lynchburg Virginian, Dec. 11, 1834, p. 3, c. 3.

NOWLIN, DAVID W. married on 17th inst. to Miss Elizabeth Berger, dau. of
Mr. Jacob Berger, Jr. deceased, by The Rev. Griffith Dickenson.
All of Pittsylvania.
The Lynchburg Virginian, Nov. 30, 1835, p. 3, c. 4.

NOWLIN, MISS HANNAH - See entry for James Harbour.

NOWLIN, JOSEPH B. married on Tues. evening, the 15th inst. to Miss
Susan Jones, dau. of the late Rowland Jones, Esq., all of Lynchburg, by The Rev. Wm. S. Reid.
The Lynchburg Virginian, Dec. 17, 1835, p. 3, c. 3.

NOWLIN, THOMAS W. married on Tues. evening the 15th inst. to Miss Ann T.
Cannefax, dau. of Mr. Chesley Cannefax of Campbell, by The Rev.
Samuel Davisson. Groom from Buckingham.
The Lynchburg Virginian, March 22, 1832, p. 3, c. 4.

NUNNELLY, DANIEL married May 12th to Miss Mary Ann Armistead, dau. of
Francis Armistead of Campbell Co., by The Rev. Samuel Armistead.
Groom of Western District of Tenn.
The Lynchburg Virginian, June 16, 1836, p. 3, c. 4.

O

OGDEN, ELIAS, ESQ. married last evening to Miss Maria Louisa Gordon, dau.
of John M. Gordon, Esq. of this place, by The Rev. Wm. S. Reid.
Groom a merchant of Abingdon.
The Lynchburg Virginian, Feb. 12, 1829, p. 3, c. 4.

OGDEN, ZACK married Nov. 17, 1825 to Miss Elizabeth McDaniel, dau. of
Wm. McDaniel, Esq. of Amherst, by The Rev. Lewis Dawson. All of
Amherst.
The Lynchburg Virginian, Nov. 24, 1825, p. 3, c. 4.

OGLESBY, MISS FRANCES - See entry for John Wingfield.

OGLESBY, CAPT. JOHN S. married on Tues. the 14th inst. in Milton, N.C.
to Miss Sarah P. Allen by The Rev. D. A. Penick. Groom formerly
of Lynchburg.
The Lynchburg Virginian, Oct. 27, 1834, p. 3, c. 4.

OGLESBY, MISS MARY JANE - See entry for Wm. H. Floyd.

OKY, MR. WILLIAM married on 19th inst. to Miss Ann G. Snead, dau. of Mr.
Wm. Snead, by The Rev. Wm. I. Holcombe. All of this place.
The Lynchburg Virginian, Nov. 24, 1834, p. 3, c. 4.

OLIVER, ISAAC W. married on Wed. evening last to Miss Sarah E. Mitchell
of this place by The Rev. F. G. Smith. Groom of Botetourt.
The Lynchburg Virginian, Oct. 10, 1831, p. 3, c. 4.

OLIVER, YELVERTON U. married Sept. 15, 1830 to Miss C. C. Mitchell of
Lynchburg by The Rev. Nicholas H. Cobbs. Groom of Botetourt Co.
The Lynchburg Virginian, Sept. 16, 1830

OMEHUNDRE, ROBERT M. married on 21st inst. at Brook Neal [sic] to Miss
Mary Virginia Johnson, youngest dau. of the late Mr. Charles Y.
Johnson of Lynchburg, by The Rev. Elijah Roach.
The Lynchburg Virginian, Jan. 2, 1837, p. 3, c. 2.

ORANGE, MISS CATHERINE J. - See entry for Abel Frazier.

ORMSBY, MISS MARY JANE - See entry for Dr. Henry B. Caldwell.

ORR, ROBERT married on April 28, 1824 to Miss Elizabeth Bailey by The
Rev. John Early. Bride and groom both of Lynchburg.
The Lynchburg Virginian, April 30, 1824, p. 3.

OTEY, JOHN B. married March 27, 1817 to Miss Anoflina M. Brown, dau. of
Mr. Reid Brown of Amherst, by The Rev. W. S. Reid. Groom of Bedford.
The Lynchburg Press, April 4, 1817, p. 3, c. 2.

OTEY, CAPT. JOHN M. married Dec. 10, 1817 to Miss Lucy Minor Norvell, dau.
of Capt. Wm. Norvell, by The Rev. Wm. S. Reid. All of Lynchburg.
The Lynchburg Press, Dec. 12, 1817, p. 3.

OVERALL, MISS SUSAN - See entry for Edmund M. Rucker.

OVERSTREET, MISS ELIZABETH - See entry for Bailor Rice.

OVERSTREET, RICHARD married on 1st inst. to Miss Judith McDearman, dau.
of Mr. Thomas McDearman of Charlotte, by The Rev. Samuel Armistead.
The Lynchburg Virginian, June 20, 1831, p. 3, c. 4.

OWENS, DR. B. F. married on Nov. 7th at Milledgewille, Ga. to Mrs.
Elmira A. Hargrove, eldest dau. of the Rev. Mr. Williamson. Groom
of Lynchburg.
The Lynchburg Virginian, Dec. 4, 1828, p. 3, c. 5.

OWENS, MISS REBECCA JANE - See entry for Henry Latham.

OWENS, DR. WILLIAM married on Aug. 26, 1819 to Miss Jane L. Latham by
The Rev. Mr. Woodville. Bride of Culpeper; groom of Lynchburg.
The Lynchburg Press & Public Advertiser, Aug. 31, 1819, p. 3, c. 5.

P

PADGETT, TINSLEY married Jan. 14, 1833 to Miss Elizabeth C. Powell of
Amherst Co. Groom of Lynchburg.
The Lynchburg Virginian, Jan. 17, 1833, p. 3, c. 4.

PAGE, THE REV. CHAS. H. married to Gabriella Sophia Crawford of Amherst.
The Lynchburg Virginian, July 12, 1827, p. 3.

PAGE, MISS EDMONIA LEE - See entry for Hall Neilson.

PAGE, MISS MATILDA - See entry for Charles B. Christain.

PALMER, DR. JEFFREY D. married on 4th inst. to Miss Martha Philadelphia
Christian, dau. of Henry Christian of Buckingham Co., by The Rev.
Mr. Berg. Groom of Halifax Co.
The Lynchburg Virginian, Dec. 10, 1832, p. 3, c. 4.

PAMPLIN, MISS SARAH - See entry for Wm. Lavender.

PANKEY, MISS MARTHA ANN - See entry for Mr. Josiah Martin.

PANNILL, MISS CATHARINE A. - See entry for Capt. Robert Wilson.

PANNILL, MISS ELIZABETH S. - See entry for Archibald Stuart.

PANNILL, JEREMIAH married June 3, 1819 to Miss Anne Payne, 3rd dau. of Philip Payne, Esq. of Campbell, by The Rev. John S. Lee. Groom of Culpeper.
The Lynchburg Press & Public Advertiser, June 10, 1819, p. 3, c. 5.

PANNILL, MISS JUDITH A. - See entry for Abram W. Wimbush.

PARKER, MISS ELIZABETH - See entry for J. Pitman.

PARKER, MISS MARTHA - See entry for Joseph Harker.

PARKS, THE REV. MARTIN P. married on Aug. 21, 1832 to Miss Georgia A. Mabry, dau. of Lewis Mabry, Esq. of Petersburg, by The Rev. Wm. J. Waller.
The Lynchburg Virginian, Sept. 10, 1832, p. 3, c. 4.

PARKS, MISS SARAH ANN S. - See entry for Whiting Davies.

PARRISH, BARNETT L. married on 4th ult. to Miss Elizabeth Jane Davies by The Rev. J. D. Mitchell. All of Lynchburg.
The Lynchburg Virginian, Jan. 1, 1835, p. 3.

PARROW, MISS POLINA - See entry for William Stewart.

PARVIN, MISS ELIZABETH E. - See entry for Robert Robson.

PATE, EDMUND married Jan. 1, 1823 to Miss Sarah Bailey by The Rev. Wm. S. Reid. Bride of Lynchburg; groom of Botetourt.
The Lynchburg Virginian, Jan. 7, 1823, p. 3.

PATRICK, DAVID, ESQ. married on 30th ult. to Miss Clementina Walker, dau. of the late John Walker of Buckingham, by The Rev. Wm. Hendrick. Groom of Charlotte.
The Lynchburg Virginian, Oct. 16, 1834, p. 3, c. 4.

PATTEN, JONATHAN T. married on Jan. 15, 1829 to Miss Ann F. Swift, dau. of late Jonathan Swift, Esq. of Alexandria, by The Rev. Wm. S. Reid. Groom of Lynchburg.
The Lynchburg Virginian, Jan. 15, 1829, p. 3, c. 5.

PATTEN, MISS MARY - See entry for Daniel Roff.

PATTERSON, MR. DAVID B. married to Miss Elizabeth Camm, youngest dau. of Mrs. Camm of Amherst, by the Rev. Wm. S. Reid. Groom of Bedford, formerly of Buckingham Co.
The Lynchburg Virginian, Jan. 7, 1833, p. 3, c. 3.

PATTERSON, HARRIET W. - See entry for Herbert M. Ledbeiter.

PATTERSON, MISS JULIA - See entry for Mr. Henry Wade.

PATTERSON, MISS POLLY - See entry for Thomas Logwood.

PATTESON, DR. JOHN H. married to Frances Irvine. Both of Lynchburg.
The Lynchburg Virginian, Jan. 2, 1826, p. 3.

PATTESON, MISS MALINDA - See entry for Edmund Rosser.

PATTESON, COL. SAM'L. A. married to Eliz H. Revely, dau. of Geo.
Revely of Campbell. Groom of Buckingham.
The Lynchburg Virginian, April 10, 1828, p. 3.

PATTESON, WILLIAM married on June 23, 1824 to Miss Amanda M. F. Burd,
dau. of William Burd of Lynchburg, by The Rev. Mr. Howard. Groom
of Lynchburg.
The Lynchburg Virginian, June 25, 1824, p. 3.

PAULET, _____ married on 28th ult. to Miss Martha, dau. of
William C. Moon of Charlotte, by The Rev. Samuel Armistead.
The Lynchburg Virginian, June 11, 1829, p. 3, c. 5.

PAYNE, MISS ANN - See entry for Wm. B. Giles.

PAYNE, MISS ANNE - See entry for Jeremiah Pannill.

PAYNE, MISS CAMILLA - See entry for Samuel M. Scott.

PAYNE, CORNELIUS married Sept. 1, 1817 to Miss Eliza Walton, dau. of
William Walton of Pittsylvania Co. Groom of Lynchburg.
The Lynchburg Press, Sept. 12, 1817, p. 3.

PAYNE, MISS EVELINA - See entry for Edward Wethers.

PAYNE, JOHN W. married Wed. the 9th inst. to Miss Sally Ann Poindexter
by The Rev. John Hubbard. Bride and groom of Campbell.
The Lynchburg Virginian, Sept. 17, 1835, p. 3, c. 5.

PAYNE, MISS MARY JANE - See entry for James A. Turner, Esq.

PEACOCK, MISS SARAH - See entry for John Simmerton.

PEAK, MRS. E. A. PEAK - See entry for H. Henneger.

PEARMAN, MISS ELIZABETH - See entry for Archibald Sneed.

PEASLEE, THE HON. DANIEL married to Lucy Pepper of Washington, Vt.
Groom age 49; bride age 17.
The Lynchburg Virginian, Jan. 24, 1823, p. 1, c. 6.

PEATROSS, MISS LOUISA M. - See entry for John Anthony.

PEGNAM, JAMES W., ESQ. married Tues. 16th inst. at Oakland to Miss
Virginia Johnson, dau. of Wm. R. Johnson, Esq. of Chesterfield,
by The Rev. Mr. Symmes. Groom of this place.
The Lynchburg Virginian, June 25, 1829, p. 3, c. 4.

PENCE, ISAAC married on 22nd inst., 1828 in Shenandoah to Miss Catharine
Showman by The Rev. Mr. Graves. All of this county.
The Lynchburg Virginian, June 9, 1828, p. 3, c. 5.

PENDLETON, HENRY T. married to Miss Sarah Ann Reese at Mrs. Sarah
Chappel's by The Rev. Thomas Jeter. Bride is of Charlotte.
Groom is of Amherst.
The Lynchburg Virginian, June 21, 1830, p. 3, c. 3.

PENDLETON, MISS LETITIA B. - See entry for Mr. Hudson M. Garland, Jr.

PENDLETON, MACE married to Susan Ballinger, dau. of Henry Ballinger of
Lynchburg.
The Lynchburg Virginian, April 14, 1825, p. 3.

PENN, THE REV. DR. ABRAM married on 22nd ult. to Miss Mary E. Thomas of
Louisburg, N.C. by The Rev. M. Brock. Groom of the Virginia
Conference.
The Lynchburg Virginian, July 18, 1836, p. 3, c. 3.

PENN, MISS BARBARA A. L. - See entry for Maj. Clark Penn.

PENN, CLARK married to Mary M. Harriss of Bedford County. Groom of
Patrick County.
The Lynchburg Virginian, May 4, 1826, p. 3.

PENN, MAJ. CLARK married on Thursday, 21st ult. to Miss Barbara A. L.
Penn, daughter of Mr. James Penn, by The Rev. John C. Traylor. All
of Patrick County.
The Lynchburg Virginian, July 11, 1831, p. 3, c. 4.

PENN, MR. EDMUND married on Thursday, 19th inst. to Miss Mary Ann Reid
of Patrick, Va., by The Rev. Mr. Traylor. Groom of Edgefield, S.C.
The Lynchburg Virginian, June 6, 1831, p. 3, c. 4.

PENN, MISS ELIZABETH - See entry for Henry T. Day.

PENN, MISS FRANCES ANN - See entry for Lewis L. Bolling.

PENN, MR. JACKSON married on 2nd inst. to Miss Martha Kennerly by The
Rev. Abram Penn. Both of Patrick County.
The Lynchburg Virginian, Oct. 11, 1832, p. 3, c. 4.

PENN, JAMES married on Nov. 4, 1818 to Miss Martha A. N. Harrison, dau.
of Nicholas Harrison of Lynchburg, by The Rev. Wm. S. Reid. Groom
of Lynchburg.
The Lynchburg Press & Public Advertiser, Nov. 5, 1818, p. 3.

PENN, MISS LUVENIA S. - See entry for Archiless Critz.

PENN, MISS MARY - See entry for Joseph Farris.

PENN, ROBERT C., ESQ. married on June 15, 1814 to Miss Lucindo Steptoe
by The Rev. A. Early.
The Lynchburg Press, June 30, 1814, p. 3, c. 2.

PENN, THOMAS, ESQ. married on Dec. 27, 1818 to Miss Mary Kennerly, dau. of
Joseph Kennerly of Patrick Co. Groom also of Patrick Co.
Lynchburg Press & Public Advertiser, Jan. 7, 1819, p. 3.

PEPPER, LUCY - See entry for Hon. Daniel Peaslee.

PERKINS, BENJ. married on Nov. 27, 1817 to Miss Mary Frances Ann Maria
Jones, dau. of Lewellin Jones, near Huntsville Madison Co., Alabama
Territory, by The Rev. Wm. S. Reid. Bride of Bedford Co. Groom of
Lynchburg.
The Lynchburg Press, Dec. 5, 1817, p. 3.

PERKINS, MISS ELIZABETH - See entry for Mr. Dabney Martin.

PERKINS, HARDIN married on Nov. 10, 1825 to Miss Sarah Ann Mosby, dau. of
John H. Mosby of Nelson, by James Boyd, minister. Groom of Lovingston.
The Lynchburg Virginian, Nov. 17, 1825, p. 3.

PERKINS, HARDIN married on Wed. the 15th inst. at "Mountain Grove"
Albemarle Co., the residence of her mother, to Miss Jane Ann Harris,
dau. of the late Capt. Benjamin Harris. Groom was a merchant at
Lovingston, Nelson Co.
The Lynchburg Virginian, Apr. 23, 1835, p. 3, c. 5.

PERKINS, MISS SARAH PRICE - See entry for Col. John Nicks.

PERRY, JESSE married Elizabeth Curl of Lynchburg, dau. of Richardson Curl.
The Lynchburg Virginian, Nov. 29, 1821, p. 3.

PERRY, DR. LILBURN P. married on 3rd. ult. to Miss Mary Ann Tilfin Clayton,
dau. of Dr. Clayton, both of St. Louis, Missouri. Married by The Rev.
Mr. Lutz.
The Lynchburg Virginian, May 18, 1835, p. 3, c. 2.

PERRY, MISS MARIA - See entry for Francis Miller.

PERRY, MISS SARAH B. - See entry for Capt. Samuel McCorkle.

PETERS, MISS CYRENA BYRON - See entry for David C. Thomas.

PETERS, MISS ELIZABETH - See entry for Mr. Willis H. Wills.

PETERS, DR. FREDERICK G. married to Ann J. Read, dau. of Dr. John T. W.
Read. All of Bedford.
The Lynchburg Virginian, Sept. 13, 1828, p. 3.

PETERS, JACOB married on Monday evening to Miss Rebecca Maria Engiliken
by The Rev. E. Wadsworth.
The Lynchburg Virginian, Dec. 15, 1836, p. 3, c. 4.

PETERS, MISS JULIA D. B. - See entry for Seth Halsey.

PETICOLUS, ADOLPHUS married to Miss Mildred Warner Brown, dau. of Benj. Brown of Amherst.
The Lynchburg Virginian, April 21, 1828, p. 3.

PETTICREW, JOHN married Thurs., Jan. 28, 1830, to Mary Ann Moore, dau. of Predham Moore, all of Campbell County, by The Rev. Isaac Cochran.
The Lynchburg Virginian, Feb. 1, 1830, p. 3, c. 4.

PETTIT, MISS FRANCIS BAKER - See entry for Gustaus Campbell.

PETTIT, MISS SARAH A. - See entry for John H. Watts.

PETTYJOHN, GEORGE W. married on Tuesday 1825 to Miss Ann Reynolds, dau. of Archelans Reynolds of Amherst, by The Rev. William Duncan.
The Lynchburg Virginian, May 12, 1825, p. 3, c. 5.

PETTYJOHN, JOSEPH married on Nov. 14, 1822 to Ann Munday, dau. of Charles Munday of Amherst, by The Rev. William Duncan. Groom of Amherst.
The Lynchburg Virginian, Nov. 22, 1822, p. 3.

PEYTON, HENRY S. married last Thurs. evening to Miss Caroline Winston, dau. of Edmund Winston, Esq. of Amherst, by The Rev. John Early and The Rev. Henry S. Peyton.
The Lynchburg Virginian, Jan. 12, 1832, p. 3, c. 5.

PHAUP, WILLIAM married on Feb. 16, 1819 to Miss Elizabeth H. Chandler, dau. of Samuel Chandler of Lexington, by The Rev. Wm. S. Reid. Groom of Lynchburg.
The Lynchburg Press & Public Advertiser, Feb. 18, 1819, p. 3.

PHELPS, MISS MARY A. - See entry for Mr. Wiatt Jones.

PHELPS, MISS NANCY G. - See entry for Richard P. North.

PHELPS, CAPT. RICHARD R. married at "Bell Air" on Wed. the 12th to Miss Asbury Ann Tilden, youngest dau. of Doct. John B. Tilden of New Town, Frederick Co., Va., by The Rev. Geo. Reed of Methodist Prot. Church.
The Lynchburg Virginian, Jan. 24, 1831, p. 3, c. 5.

PHELPS, DR. ROBERT P. married on Thurs., Nov. 3rd. to Miss Elizabeth Dawson by The Rev. Samuel Davidson. All of Amherst.
The Lynchburg Virginian, Nov. 7, 1836, p. 3, c. 4.

PHELPS, THOMAS married on Dec. 4, 1814 to Miss Nancy Carter by The Rev. John Ayres. Bride and groom both of Bedford.
The Lynchburg Press, Jan. 5, 1815, p. 3.

PHILLIMAN, MISS ELIZABETH - See entry for Fleming Hillhouse.

PHILLIPS, MISS ANN S. - See entry for John S. Blair.

PHILLIPS, MISS FRANCES W. - See entry for Jefferson L. Hill.

PHILLIPS, MR. JAMES W. married on 19th inst. in North Carolina to Miss
Mary M. Pryor, dau. of Col. John Pryor, by The Rev. Thos. Thompson.
All of Amherst.
The Lynchburg Virginian, Sept. 22, 1836, p. 3, c. 4.

PHILPOTT, MISS JANE - See entry for Milton R. Dodson.

PICKETT, BRIGHT married at Market house to Eliza Cole of North Carolina.
Taken from the Augusta Chronicle
The Lynchburg Virginian, March 20, 1828, p. 3, c. 4.

PIERCE, CORNELIUS W. married on July 27, 1814 to Miss Polly Davis, dau.
of Wm. Davis, Sen., by The Rev. Wm. S. Reid. Groom of Lynchburg.
The Lynchburg Press, Aug. 4, 1814, p. 3.

PINKARD, MISS CATHARINE - See entry for Joseph Coleman.

PITMAN, J.   married on 3rd. inst. to Miss Elizabeth Parker by David
D. Reamer, Esq. All of New Hanover, Burlington County.
The Lynchburg Virginian, Nov. 29, 1832, p. 3, c. 4.

PITTIE, POLLY - See entry for M. Michael Waltman.

PLEASANTS, JOHN H., ESQ. married on 15th inst. at Falling Spring, Alleghany
to Miss Mary L. P. Massie, dau. of Henry Massie, Esq. of Falling
Spring, Alleghany Co.
The Lynchburg Virginian, Dec. 28, 1829.

PLUCKETT, MISS WINIFRED ANN ELIZA - See entry for David P. Boaz.

PLUNKETT, MISS FRANCES - See entry for John Shields.

PLUNKETT, JOHN married to Cynthia Ann Staples, dau. of David Staples of
Amherst. Groom of Buckingham.
The Lynchburg Virginian, Feb. 9, 1826, p. 3.

POE, MISS ANN TATE - See entry for Dr. John P. Harrison.

POE, CASWELL married on Sept. 9, 1823 to Miss Marion F. Nimmo by The Rev.
Mr. Hart. Bride of Richmond; groom of Lynchburg.
The Lynchburg Virginian, Sept. 26, 1823, p. 3.

POE, WILLIAM, ESQ. married on 11th inst. to Miss Margaret Tippett by The
Rev. Wm. S. Reid. All of this place. Groom: merchant of house of
John, Wm. & Caswell Poe.
The Lynchburg Virginian, Aug. 13, 1829, p. 3, c. 4.

POINDEXTER, GARLAND married on the 19th inst. to Miss Julia Bingham of
this place by The Rev. Wm. I. Waller. Groom of Bedford County.
The Lynchburg Virginian, Nov. 26, 1829, p. 3, c. 6.

POINDEXTER, JAS. married on Nov. 26, 1823 to Miss Susan D. Shelton, dau.
of William Shelton of Amherst, by The Rev. Mr. Freeman. Groom of
Bedford.
The Lynchburg Virginian, Nov. 28, 1823, p. 3, c. 3.

POINDEXTER, MISS SALLY ANN - See entry for John W. Payne.

POINDEXTER, MISS SUSAN - See entry for Mr. Dudley Martin.

POINDEXTER, WILLIS married on 13th inst. to Miss Emily Slaughter, dau. of Jos. Slaughter, Esq. by The Rev. Nicholas H. Cobbs. All of Bedford.
The Lynchburg Virginian, Oct. 20, 1836, p. 3, c. 3.

POINTER, MISS ELIZA - See entry for William R. Dawson, Esq.

POLK, LUCIUS J., ESQ. married on 10th inst. in Washington, at the mansion of the President, to Miss Mary A. Eastin of Tennessee, a member of the President's family (Andrew Jackson). Married by The Rev. Mr. Hawley.
The Lynchburg Virginian, April 26, 1832, p. 3, c. 5.

POLLARD, MISS MARGARET C. - See entry for James P. Henderson, Esq.

POORE, WILLIAM A., ESQ. married on 19th inst. in Buckingham Co. to Miss Eliza Bolling Flood, only dau. of Dr. Joel W. Flood of said Co., by The Rev. Poindexter P. Smith. Groom of Richmond.
The Lynchburg Virginian, Nov. 30, 1835, p. 3, c. 4.

PORTER, CLAIBORN married to Sarah Early of Lynchburg, dau. of Rev. Abner Early.
The Lynchburg Virginian, Dec. 14, 1826, p. 3.

PORTER, MISS FRANCES ANN - See entry for Kenneth Urquhart.

PORTER, MISS FRANCES H. - See entry for Rufus A. Putnam.

PORTER, JAMES, SR. married to Mrs. Catharine Borge at Canterbury, England. His 6th wife.
The Lynchburg Virginian, Jan. 24, 1823, p. 1, c. 6.

PORTER, MR. MADISON C. married on 15th inst. at Scottsville, Albemarle Co., to Miss Emily Staples, dau. of Mr. Beverly Staples of the former place. Married by The Rev. Edward Wadsworth.
The Lynchburg Virginian, Oct. 29, 1835, p. 3, c. 6.

PORTER, MISS SARAH F. - See entry for Wm. A. Staples.

POWELL, MISS ELIZA - See entry for Mr. John Smith.

POWELL, MISS ELIZABETH - See entry for Samuel Roberts.

POWELL, MISS ELIZABETH C. - See entry for Tinsley Padgett.

POWELL, MISS FRANCIS G. - See entry for James Norvell.

POWELL, MISS MILDRED - See entry for Samuel G. Garland.

POWELL, MISS NANCY - See entry for Beverly Wade.

POWELL, DR. NATHANIEL R. married on 25th ult. to Miss Sophonisba Anne
Carrington, dau. of Capt. Benjamin Carrington of Cumberland, by
The Rev. C. H. Page of Amherst. Groom is of Nelson.
The Lynchburg Virginian, March 19, 1835, p. 3, c. 5.

POWELL, MISS POLLY - See entry for Mr. James Martin.

POWELL, RICHARD married on 28th inst. to Miss Belinda Griffith of
Franklin by The Rev. Moses Greer, Jr. Groom is of Amherst.
The Lynchburg Virginian, Sept. 3, 1835, p. 3, c. 4.

POWERS, JOHN married on July 28th in Nelson Co. to Miss Sophia Harvey
of same county by The Rev. James Boyd.
The Lynchburg Virginian, Aug. 6, 1829, p. 3, c. 5.

PRATHER, MISS MARIA JULIA - See entry for Henry Clay, Jr.

PRESTON, MISS MILDRED J. - See entry for Charles J. Nelms.

PRESTON, MOSES H. married to Elizabeth D. Tyree, eldest dau. of Richard
Tyree of Lynchburg.
The Lynchburg Virginian, Sept. 20, 1827, p. 3, c. 2.

PRESTON, WM. B. married on 22nd inst. to Miss Matilda, dau. of Charles
Nelms, Esq., by The Rev. James Leftwich. All of Bedford Co.
The Lynchburg Virginian, Jan. 2, 1832, p. 3, c. 5.

PRICE, EDWARD B. married on 26th ult. at Abingdon to Miss Eleanor B. Love,
dau. of Mr. John J. Love of the former place, by The Rev. F. L. V.
Shaver. Groom formerly of Lynchburg.
The Lynchburg Virginian, July 6, 1835, p. 3, c. 3.

PRICE, MISS ELIZABETH - See entry for Martin Wheelan.

PRICE, MISS JUDITH T. - See entry for William T. Krauth.

PRICE, MISS MARTHA CORNELIA - See entry for George Edward Dabney.

PRICE, MISS MARY A. - See entry for Isaac H. Dennis.

PRICE, PHILIP M. married to Matilda Greentree of Washington. Groom of
Philadelphia.
The Lynchburg Virginian, May 15, 1826, p. 3.

PRICE, RANSOM married to Mary A. Spencer, dau. of Col. Guidian Spencer of
Charlotte. Groom of Prince Edward Co.
The Lynchburg Virginian, Nov. 30, 1826, p. 3.

PRICE, WILSON married to Susan Rose of Buckingham Co. Groom of Amherst Co.
The Lynchburg Virginian, April 13, 1827, p. 3.

PRYOR, MISS ELIZABETH W. - See entry for Garrett C. Layne.

PRYOR, MISS JANE - See entry for William H. Bibb.

PRYOR, MISS MARY W. - See entry for Mr. James W. Phillips.

PUCKETT, RICHARDSON married on Dec. 20, 1827 to Polly Epperson of Campbell Co. by The Rev. Samuel Armistead.
The Lynchburg Virginian, Jan. 3, 1828, p. 3, c. 2.

PUGH, MISS ELIZABETH - See entry for William Beckham.

PULLING, MISS JULIA ANN - See entry for Thos. A. Fourqurean.

PURCELL, MISS SARAH J. - See entry for James H. Hopkins.

PURVIS, MISS LUCINDA - See entry for Joel M. Wheeler.

PURYEAR, MISS MAHALA - See entry for Samuel Burch.

PUTNAM, THE REV. RUFUS A. married in Worcester, Mass. to Miss Frances H. Porter of Worcester. Groom of Fitchburg. Taken from National Aegis.
The Lynchburg Virginian, June 9, 1825, p. 3, c. 3.

Q

QUARLES, FRANCIS E. married on March 29, 1828 to Miss Belinda Ann Thornton, dau. of P. P. Thornton, by The Rev. Charles H. Page. Bride and groom both of Amherst Co.
The Lynchburg Virginian, April 14, 1828, p. 3, c. 5.

QUARLES, WILLIAM J. A. married on Thursday 31, Jan. to Miss Eliza A. Hopkins by The Rev. Samuel Phillips. All of Bedford.
The Lynchburg Virginian, Feb. 7, 1828, p. 3, c. 5.

R

RAGLAND, MISS F. - See entry for William Wauhop.

RADFORD, MISS MARY - See entry for Major S. N. Kearney.

RAILY, MISS ELIZABETH - See entry for Mr. David Hodge.

RAMSEY, MISS EMILY - See entry for Joab Cumpton.

RAMSEY, MRS. MARY - See entry for Joseph Nichols.

RAMSEY, THOMAS married on 3rd inst. to Miss Susan Hazlwood of Charlotte Co. by The Rev. Samuel Armistead.
The Lynchburg Virginian, Feb. 7, 1831, p. 3, c. 4.

RANDOLPH, B. H. married on 7th inst. at residence of Dr. Clifford Cabell in Buckingham to Miss Sarah Eliza Anthony, dau. of the late Christopher Anthony, by The Rev. Mr. Wilmer. Groom of Richmond.
The Lynchburg Virginian, Dec. 15, 1836, p. 3, c. 4.

RANDOLPH, MISS CATHERINE C. - See entry for Josiah B. Abbott, Esq.

RANDOLPH, MARY GABRIELLA - See entry for John Biddle Chapman.

RANDOLPH, MISS VIRGINIA JEFFERSON - See entry for Nicholas Philip Trist.

RAY, C. BARNETT married on Thursday, Dec. 31, 1829 to Eveline D. Bibb
of Amherst County.
The Lynchburg Virginian, Jan. 7, 1830, p. 3, c. 6.

READ, MISS ELIZA - See entry for Nathan Reid.

READ, MRS. ISABELLA - See entry for Capt. Lindsey Coleman.

READ, LANDON CABELL married on 12th inst. in Richmond to Miss Adelaide
Matilda Cox, dau. of Edward Cox, Esq., by The Rev. Mr. Plummer.
Groom was formerly of Lynchburg. Bride is of that city.
The Lynchburg Virginian, Feb. 23, 1835, p. 3, c. 5.

READ, SAMUEL married on May 19, 1814 to Miss Elizabeth Callaway, dau. of
Col. William Callaway of Bedford.
The Lynchburg Press, June 2, 1814, p. 3.

READ, SAMUEL, ESQ. married on 29th ult. to Mrs. Elizabeth Woodroof of
Bedford. Groom is a merchant of Bedford.
The Lynchburg Virginian, May 6, 1830, p. 3, c. 5.

READ, WILLIAM A. married on Thursday evening last to Miss Mary Jane Hare,
dau. of Mr. Jesse Hare of this place, by The Rev. Wm. S. Reid. Groom
from Campbell Co.
The Lynchburg Virginian, Sept. 15, 1834, p. 3, c. 5.

REAMEY, COL. DANIEL married on August 11th to Miss Susan L. Starling,
eldest dau. of Thomas Starling of Henry Co., by The Rev. John C.
Traylor. All of Henry Co. Virginia.
The Lynchburg Virginian, Sept. 8, 1825, p. 3, c. 3.

REDD, JAMES M. married Nov. 17, 1825 to Miss Ruth Staples, dau. of the
late Col. Samuel Staples. Married at Patrick Co. by The Rev. Mr.
Lowe. Groom of Henry County C. H.
The Lynchburg Virginian, Nov. 24, 1825, p. 3, c. 4.

REDD, MISS LUCINDA - See entry for John Wooton.

REED, ISAAC SHELBY, ESQ. married June 26th in Washington City to Miss
Ann Laura Green, dau. of Gen. Duff Green, by The Rev. O. B. Brown.
Groom is of Mississippi.
The Lynchburg Virginian, July 5, 1832, p. 3, c. 4.

REESE, MISS ELIZABETH M. - See entry for Mr. Spotswood Hawkins.

REESE, MISS SARAH ANN - See entry for Henry T. Pendleton.

REESE, MISS SOPHIA S. - See entry for Robert J. Thurmon.

REESE, WASHINGTON married May 8, 1828 to Mary Robertson, dau. of Nicholas
Robertson, Esq. of Bedford, by The Rev. John Ayres.
The Lynchburg Virginian, May 22, 1828, p. 3, c. 5.

REEVES, MR. RICHARD married on 3rd inst. to Miss Elizabeth Harker by
David D. Reamer, Esq. All of New Hanover - Burlington County.
The Lynchburg Virginian, Nov. 29, 1832, p. 3, c. 4.

REID, JOHN C. married April 2, 1818 to Miss Esther Austin of Bedford by
The Rev. Wm. S. Reid. Groom of Lynchburg.
The Lynchburg Press, April 10, 1818, p. 3.

REID, JOHN O. married May 20, 1819 to Miss Martha Rosser, dau. of Wm.
Rosser, Sen. of Campbell, by The Rev. Mr. Johns. Groom of Campbell.
The Lynchburg Press & Public Advertiser, May 27, 1819, p. 3.

REID, DR. JOHN T. W. married in this place on Wednesday, 4th inst. to
Miss Elizabeth Douthat, dau. of the late Major Robert Douthat of
Rockbridge, by The Rev. Wm. S. Reid. Groom of Bedford.
The Lynchburg Virginian, Feb. 9, 1835, p. 3, c. 4.

REID, MISS MARTHA F. - See entry for Josiah Shepperson.

REID, MISS MARY ANNE - See entry for Mr. Edmund Penn.

REID, NATHAN, ESQ. married on 3rd inst. to Miss Eliza Read, dau. of Dr.
J. T. W. Read, by The Rev. Nicholas H. Cobbs. All of Bedford Co.
The Lynchburg Virginian, March 8, 1830, p. 3, c. 3.

REID, MISS SARAH - See entry for Mr. James Wood.

REVELY, MISS ELIZ. H. - See entry for Col. Sam'l. A. Patteson.

REYNOLDS, MISS ANN - See entry for George W. Pettyjohn.

REYNOLDS, CHAS. married March 26, 1825 to Miss Harriet Cocke, dau. of
the late Capt. Drury Cocke, by The Rev. Frederick Kabler. Groom
of Bedford.
The Lynchburg Virginian, April 1, 1825, p. 3.

REYNOLDS, ISAAC R. married July 30, 1833 to Mrs. Sarah Rucker by The
Rev. Thomas Jones. All of Amherst Co.
The Lynchburg Virginian, Aug. 5, 1833, p. 3, c. 4.

REYNOLDS, MR. ISAAC R. married on 6th inst. to Miss Ann Cox, dau. of
the late Milner Cox, by The Rev. Wm. S. Reid. All of Amherst Co.
The Lynchburg Virginian, Aug. 17, 1829, p. 3, c. 4.

REYNOLDS, O. F. married Dec. 8, 1825 to Miss Lucy R. S. Bell, dau. of
Capt. Drury Bell of Amherst, by The Rev. Lewis Dawson. All of
Amherst Co.
The Lynchburg Virginian, Dec. 15, 1825, p. 3, c. 3.

REYNOLDS, WILLIS married Oct. 17, 1822 by The Rev. Geo. W. Charlton to
Miss Jane Dawson, dau. of The Rev. Lewis Dawson of Amherst Co.
The Lynchburg Virginian, Nov. 1, 1822, p. 3.

RHODES, MR. DAVID married Thurs. evening, 21st inst. to Miss Martha Yancey, dau of Mr. Joel Yancey of Bedford County, by The Rev. Joseph Carson. Groom of Lynchburg.
The Lynchburg Virginian, Nov. 29, 1822, p. 3, c. 5.

RICE, BAILOR married on 18th inst. to Elizabeth Overstreet, dau. of John Overstreet, by The Rev. Nicholas H. Cobbs. All of Bedford.
The Lynchburg Virginian, Dec. 24, 1827, p. 3, c. 4.

RICE, CAPT. JOHN married on Thursday last to Mrs. Phebe Callahan by The Rev. J. Cole.
The Lynchburg Virginian, Nov. 23, 1829, p. 3, c. 5.

RICHARDS, MR. GUSTARVUS married to Miss Electra B. Wilder, dau. of S. V. S. Wilder of Bolton, Mass. Groom of New York, Bride of Bolton, Mass.
The Lynchburg Virginian, Aug. 19, 1833, p. 3, c. 4.

RICHARDS, HENRY B. married on 10th inst. to Miss Angelina L. Barnes, dau. of Doct. Asa Barnes of Lunenburg Co., Va., by The Rev. Henderson Lee.
The Lynchburg Virginian, May 19, 1836, p. 3, c. 3.

RICHARDSON, MISS CATHERINE - See entry for Moore Lumpkins.

RICHARDSON, MISS ELIZABETH - See entry for James Banagh.

RICHARDSON, GEO. P. married in Richmond to Miss Sarah McDougald by The Rev. Wm. H. Hart. Bride of Richmond; groom formerly of Lynchburg.
The Lynchburg Virginian, Nov. 20, 1824, p. 3.

RICHARDSON, GEORGE P. married Oct. 8, 1818 to Miss Ann Gavan, dau. of James Gavan of Powhite, Hanover Co., by The Rev. John D. Blair. Groom of Lynchburg.
The Lynchburg Press & Public Advertiser, Oct. 12, 1818, p. 3, c. 2.

RICHARDSON, JOHN married Jan. 16, 1833 to Miss Lucy Ann Luck at home of Mr. L. F. Luck by The Rev. N. W. Cobbs. Bride of Botetourt, groom attorney-at-law of Bedford.
The Lynchburg Virginian, Jan. 24, 1833, p. 3, c. 6.

RICHARDSON, HILLARY G. married on Wednesday, Oct. 21st to Miss Lucinda M. Clark, dau. of Littleberry Clark, Esq. of Prince Edward, by The Rev. Daniel Witt. Groom of Charlotte.
The Lynchburg Virginian, Nov. 2, 1835, p. 3, c. 4.

RICHARDSON, MISS MARY - See entry for Bartholomew Nichols.

RICHESON, JOHN married Feb. 5, 1828 to Miss Susan Rucker, dau. of Reuben Rucker.
The Lynchburg Virginian, Feb. 7, 1828, p. 3, c. 5.

RISQUE, MISS HARRIET - See entry for Capt. G. C. Hutter.

RITCHIE, MISS MARY ROANE - See entry for Thomas Green, Esq.

RIVES, MISS ANN M. - See entry for Dr. James Saunders.

RIVES, MISS ELIZA M. - See entry for Dr. Anthony B. Johns.

RIVES, MISS LUCY S. - See entry for Alexander Brown.

RIVES, MISS MARY W. - See entry for Orville C. Rives.

RIVES, ORVILLE C., ESQ. married on 10th inst. to Miss Mary W., dau. of the late Nath'l Rives, Esq. of Lynchburg, by The Rev. J. W. Childs. Groom of Fayette County, Tennessee.
The Lynchburg Virginian, Dec. 17, 1835, p. 3, c. 3.

RIVES, WILLIAM C., ESQ. married March 24, 1819 to Miss Judith P. Walker, dau. of the late Col. Francis Walker, by The Rev. Mr. Wyrdown at Castle Hill in Albemarle. Groom of Nelson.
The Lynchburg Press & Public Advertiser, April 5, 1819, p. 3, c. 4.

ROANE, CHRISTOPHER S. married on 13th inst. to Miss Rebecca B. Jordan of Prince George Co. by The Rev. H. B. Coles. Groom of Amherst.
The Lynchburg Virginian, Sept. 22, 1836, p. 3, c. 4.

ROANE, MISS MARY C. - See entry for Fayette Henry Norvell.

ROBERTS, MISS ELIZABETH - See entry for Wm. Nally.

ROBERTS, MISS ELIZABETH H. - See entry for Mr. David R. Lyman.

ROBERTS, JOSEPH F. married on 10th inst. to Miss Mary P. White by The Rev. Mr. Smith. All of Charlotte.
The Lynchburg Virginian, Dec. 21, 1829, p. 3, c. 5.

ROBERTS, MR. MARK married at Stratham, N.H. to Miss Sarah Wiggin. "On this occassion the grandmother was present being in her 100th year. Nobody could recollect in the town of Stratham her 2nd marriage which took place over 75 years ago."
The Lynchburg Virginian, Jan. 10, 1833, p. 3, c. 4.

ROBERTS, MISS MARY ANN - See entry for Joseph Mays.

ROBERTS, MISS MATILDA - See entry for Abram F. Biggers.

ROBERTS, SAMUEL married Nov. 10, 1814 to Miss Elizabeth Powell by The Rev. W. P. Martin. Bride and groom both of Lynchburg.
The Lynchburg Press, Nov. 17, 1814, p. 3.

ROBERTS, MISS SARAH - See entry for W. M. Turner.

ROBERTS, SHELTON married Wed. 22nd inst, 1830 to Miss Jane M. Moon of Buckingham Co. by The Rev. John Ayres. Groom of Nelson Co.
The Lynchburg Virginian, Jan. 3, 1831, p. 1, c. 3.

ROBERTS, WILLIAM C. married 18th inst. in Rockingham to Miss Jane C. Miller, dau. of John Miller of Rockingham, by The Rev. William Coffin.
The Lynchburg Virginian, Nov. 10, 1836, p. 3, c. 4.

ROBERTSON, A. married May 6, 1819 to Miss Sarah F. Brown, dau. of Doctor Brown of New Glasgow, by The Rev. Mr. Herndon. Groom of Lynchburg.
The Lynchburg Press & Public Advertiser, May 10, 1819, p. 3.

ROBERTSON, MARY - See entry for Washington Reese.

ROBERTSON, MR. THEODERICK married on 20th ult. to Miss Susan Rush, dau. of James J. Rush, Esq. of Philadelphia, by The Rev. Mr. Chambers. Groom of Richmond (late of Lynchburg).
The Lynchburg Virginian, Oct. 8, 1832, p. 3.

ROBERTSON, WYNDHAM, ESQ. married on 16th inst. near Abingdon to Miss Mary F. T. Smith, only dau. of Francis Smith, Esq. of Washington County, by The Rev. Stephen Bovell. Groom member of Executive Council of Va.
The Lynchburg Virginian, Aug. 25, 1831, p. 3, c. 4.

ROBINSON, CONWAY married on 14th inst. to Miss Mary Susan Leigh, dau. of Benj. Watkins Leigh, Esq., by The Rev. Bishop Moore. All of Richmond.
The Lynchburg Virginian, July 25, 1836, p. 3, c. 3.

ROBINSON, CYRUS married on 17th ult. to Miss Angelina H. Major, dau. of John Major, by The Rev. Nicholas Cobbs. Bride and groom both of Bedford.
The Lynchburg Virginian, Oct. 26, 1826, p. 3, c. 4.

ROBINSON, EDWIN married on Oct. 6th to Miss Frances Brown, dau. of Mr. Henry Brown, Sr. of Bedford, by The Rev. Wm. S. Reid.
The Lynchburg Virginian, Oct. 10, 1836, p. 3, c. 4.

ROBINSON, HENRY married on Nov. 10th at Wamseyville, Ohio to Miss Mary Timberlake, eldest dau. of Christopher I. Timberlake of Bedford Co.
The Lynchburg Virginian, Dec. 19, 1831, p. 3, c. 4.

ROBINSON, MR. JACOB H. married on 14th inst. to Miss Julia Ann, Dau. of The Rev. Thomas Jones, by The Rev. H. B. Cowles. All of this place.
The Lynchburg Virginian, Oct. 19, 1835, p. 3, c. 4.

ROBINSON, JOSEPH married on Dec. 2, 1832 to Miss Catharine Callahan by The Rev. Samuel Armistead.
The Lynchburg Virginian, Dec. 13, 1832, p. 3, c. 5.

ROBINSON, MISS MARTHA L. - See entry for Taliaferro Wallace.

ROBINSON, ROBERT married Jan. 20, 1825 to Miss Martha J. Harrison, dau. of Samuel J. Harrison, by The Rev. Wm. S. Reid. Mr. Robinson of McKee-Robinson & Co.
The Lynchburg Virginian, Jan. 25, 1825, p. 3.

ROBINSON, MR. SAMUEL S. married on 10th inst. to Miss Sarah Lewellin, dau. of Mr. James Lewellin, by The Rev. Mr. Parks.
The Lynchburg Virginian, June 14, 1830, p. 3, c. 4.

ROBINSON, MISS SUSAN - See entry for Jesse Jeter.

ROBSON, ROBERT married to Elizabeth E. Parvin of Princeton, Ind. Groom Groom of Washington.
The Lynchburg Virginian, May 15, 1826, p. 3.

ROCK, WILLIAM married on 30th inst. at Richmond to Miss Sarah Ann Brown, dau. of Mr. Edward Brown of Lynchburg, by The Rev. Dr. Penn. Groom of Richmond.
The Lynchburg Virginian, Feb. 6, 1832, p. 3, c. 5.

RODIER, MISS MARY ANN - See entry for A. C. Settle.

ROFF, DANIEL married in Danube, N.Y. to Mary Patten.
The Lynchburg Virginian, June 25, 1824, p. 3, c. 3.

ROHR, MISS LUCINDA S. - See entry for Henry R. Goulder.

ROOSEVELT, JAMES I., JR., ESQ. married on May 30th at Hotel of American Minister in Paris, to Miss Cornelia Van Ness, dau. of The Honorable P. Van Ness, Minister of United States to Court of Madrid. The groom is of New York.
The Lynchburg Virginian, Aug. 11, 1831, p. 3, c. 4.

RORAR, MISS NANCY - See entry for Jacob Crider.

ROSE, DR. GEORGE N. married Dec. 23, 1829 to Mary Jane Eubank, dau. of Capt. Thomas N. Eubank of Amherst County, Va. Groom of Nelson Co.
The Lynchburg Virginian, Jan. 7, 1830, p. 3, c. 6.

ROSE, MISS LURITTA - See entry for The Hon. Thomas D. Arnold.

ROSE, MISS MARY E. - See entry for D. C. Mitchell.

ROSE, MISS SUSAN - See entry for Wilson Price.

ROSS, MISS CATHERINE L. - See entry for Robert J. Yancey.

ROSS, MISS JANE B. - See entry for Thomas D. Evans.

ROSSER, EDMUND married Feb. 7, 1828 to Malinda Patteson of Campbell Co., dau. of David Patteson, by The Rev. Samuel Davidson.
The Lynchburg Virginian, Feb. 19, 1828, p. 3, c. 4.

ROSSER, MR. EDMUND W. married March 26th to Miss Ann Elizabeth Gilbert, dau. of Capt. George Gilbert of Pittsylvania, by The Rev. John Hubbard. Groom of Campbell Co.
The Lynchburg Virginian, April 13, 1835, p. 3, c. 3.

ROSSER, MISS ELIZABETH ANN - See entry for Thomas O. Cheatham.

ROSSER, CAPT. JOHN married Jan. 24, 1833 to Miss Mary Cocke by The Rev. David Fisher. Bride and groom of Campbell Co.
The Lynchburg Virginian, Jan. 28, 1833, p. 3, c. 4.

ROSSER, MISS MARTHA - See entry for John O. Reid.

ROSSER, THOMAS married to Miss Ariana W. West, step.-dau. of Peter Francisco of Buckingham Co., Va. Groom of Campbell Co.
The Lynchburg Virginian, Feb. 18, 1828, p. 3, c. 4.

ROYALL, MR. BENJAMIN FRANKLIN married on 22nd inst. to Miss Louisa Shelton,
dau. of the late Wm. Shelton of Nelson, by The Rev. Henry Peyton.
Groom of Lynchburg.
The Lynchburg Virginian, May 28, 1833, p. 3, c. 3.

ROYAL, MISS ELIZA - See entry for Fortunatus Sydnor.

ROYALL, JOHN   married to Miss Anna K. Taylor, dau. of the late George
Keith Taylor, Esq., by The Rev. Mr. Hamner.
The Lynchburg Virginian, Mar. 29, 1830, p. 3, c. 3.

ROYALL, JOSEPH EDWIN, ESQ. married on the 21st to Miss Elizabeth Gwatkyns,
dau. of James Gwatkyns, Esq. of Bedford Co., Va., by The Rev. Wm.
Reid. Groom from Lynchburg.
The Lynchburg Press, Jan. 4, 1822, p. 1, c. 3.

ROYALTY, MISS ELIZABETH - See entry for John Crumpecker.

ROYSTER, MISS SARAH A. - See entry for Stephen R. Neal.

RUCKER, ALFRED married on Tuesday evening last to Miss Elizabeth M., dau.
of Mr. Wm. Burd, by The Rev. D. Doggett. All of this place.
The Lynchburg Virginian, Aug. 9, 1832, p. 3, c. 5.

RUCKER, CLIFTON H. married to Miss Mary Jane Staples, dau. of Mr. James
Staples of Campbell, on Thursday last by The Rev. John Early. Groom
of this place.
The Lynchburg Virginian, Jan. 17, 1831, p. 3, c. 4.

RUCKER, EDMUND M. married on 9th inst. in Rutherford Co., Tenn. to Miss
Susan Overall by The Rev. Mr. Clark. Bridegroom member of the
Baltimore Humbug.
The Lynchburg Virginian, Oct. 1, 1835, p. 3, c. 4.

RUCKER, MISS ELIZABETH - See entry for Gilbert Hayth.

RUCKER, MISS ELIZABETH - See entry for Pleasant Labby.

RUCKER, JOHN married on Tues. evening last to Mrs. Elizabeth Duval by
The Rev. Wm. S. Reid. All of this place.
The Lynchburg Virginian, Aug. 6, 1835, p. 3, c. 5.

RUCKER, JONATHAN married on the 6th inst. to Miss Ann Y. Cawthon by The
Rev. John Davis. All of Amherst.
The Lynchburg Virginian, March 12, 1832, p. 3, c. 4.

RUCKER, MISS MARY ANN - See entry for Capt. Isaac Rucker.

RUCKER, NATHANIEL married on the 24th inst. to Miss Mary Woodroof, dau. of
Mr. David Woodroof, by The Rev. Jas. Reid. All of Amherst Co.
The Lynchburg Virginian, Sept. 29, 1828, p. 3, c. 6.

RUCKER, MRS. SARAH - See entry for Isaac R. Reynolds.

RUCKER, MISS SUSAN - See entry for John Richeson.

RUDD, LIEUT. JOHN married Wed. evening, the 6th inst. to Miss Elizabeth Y.
Speed of Powhatan by The Rev. James Doughen. Groom is of U.S. Navy.
The Lynchburg Virginian, Oct. 21, 1830, p. 3, c. 1.

RUDD, MISS MARTHA M. - See entry for William L. Thornton.

RUDD, MISS PAULINA CATHERINE - See entry for Nathan H. Hancock.

RUSH, MISS SUSAN - See entry for Mr. Theoderick Robertson.

RUSSELL, MISS FRANCES - See entry for John Flood.

RUSSEL, JOHN married on 13th inst. to Miss Jane Duncan, dau. of the late
Flemming H. Duncan, by The Rev. John Davies. All of Amherst.
The Lynchburg Virginian, June 21, 1830, p. 3, c. 3.

RUTHERFOORD, SAMUEL, ESQ. married on Thurs. last to Miss Frances Watson,
dau. of Mrs. Watson of this place, by The Rev. F. G. Smith. Groom
of Richmond.
The Lynchburg Virginian, Nov. 24, 1834, p. 3, c. 4.

RYLAND, REV. ROBERT married on 27th inst. to Miss Josephine Norvell, dau.
of Thomas Norvell, Esq. of Richmond, Va. Married in Richmond by The
Rev. Mr. Keeling.
The Lynchburg Virginian, June 7, 1830, p. 3, c. 5.

S

ST. JOHN, _____ Married on Dec. 17, 1828 to Miss Eliza Sublett of
Campbell Co.
The Lynchburg Virginian, Jan. 5, 1829, p. 3, c. 5.

SALE, MISS CLARA LEWIS - See entry for Wm. H. Blair.

SALE, JOHN married Feb. 3, 1824 to Miss Mahala S. Barker, dau. of John
Barker, dec'd., by The Rev. John Sledd. All of Bedford.
The Lynchburg Virginian, Feb. 13, 1824, p. 3.

SALE, NELSON, ESQ. married on Dec. 5, 1822 to Ann A. Wharton, dau. of
Capt. John Wharton of Bedford, by The Rev. Dr. Samuel Philips.
The Lynchburg Virginian, Dec. 20, 1822, p. 3.

SALE, MISS PAMELIA F. - See entry for Samuel Floyd.

SALE, THOMAS J. married on Feb. 3rd, 1824 to Miss Mary T. Lane, dau. of
Henry Lane, Jr., by The Rev. John Sledd.
The Lynchburg Virginian, Feb. 13, 1824, p. 3.

SALMONS, JESSE L. married on 30th ult. to Miss Ann C. Lee, dau. of James
Lee of Amherst, by The Rev. Dr. Waller. Groom of Bedford.
The Lynchburg Virginian, May 4, 1829, p. 3, c. 5.

SALMONS, CAPT. WILLIAM married May 30, 1827 to Miss Evalina P. Cobbs,
dau. of John Cobbs, by The Rev. James Leftwich. All of Bedford.
The Lynchburg Virginian, June 1, 1827, p. 3, c. 3.

SAMPLE, MISS ABIGAIL - See entry for George Woods.

SAMPSON, MR. GEORGE L. married Friday, 16th inst. to Mrs. Martha Graham
by The Rev. F. G. Smith. Bride of Lynchburg. Groom of Richmond.
The Lynchburg Virginian, Dec. 19, 1831, p. 3, c. 4.

SANDIDGE, MISS ELIZABETH - See entry for Seaton Hamlet.

SANDIDGE, MISS MAHALA - See entry for John T. Hunt.

SAUNDERS, MISS ANN D. - See entry for Dr. Thomas L. Mitchell.

SAUNDERS, DAVID, JR. married June 26, 1823 to Miss Anzoletta M. Warwick,
dau. of Maj. Wm. Warwick, of Amherst, by The Rev. Wm. S. Reid.
Groom of Lynchburg.
The Lynchburg Virginian, June 27, 1823, p. 3.

SAUNDERS, MISS ELIZA N. - See entry for Giles Fuqua.

SAUNDERS, MISS ELVIRA - See entry for Charles P. Craghead.

SAUNDERS, THE REV. FLEMING EARLY A. married May 19, 1814 to Miss Alice
Watts. Bride of Campbell Co. Groom of Franklin.
The Lynchburg Press, June 2, 1814, p. 3.

SAUNDERS, MISS FRANCES - See entry for Thomas Helms.

SAUNDERS, HENRY married on the 2nd inst. to Miss Mary Ann Kasey, eldest
dau. of Col. John Kasey, by The Rev. John Ayres. All of Bedford.
The Lynchburg Virginian, Feb. 13, 1832, p. 3, c. 4.

SAUNDERS, DR. JAMES. married on Nov. 19, 1823 to Miss Ann M. Rives, dau.
of Nathaniel Rives of Rockingham Co., N.C., by the Rev. Ira Ellis.
Groom of Lynchburg.
The Lynchburg Virginian, Nov. 25, 1823, p. 3, c. 5.

SAUNDERS, MR. JAMES married on 24th inst. to Miss Mary Ann Stanley, only
dau. of Mr. William Stanley, by The Rev. Thos. Jones. Bride of
Campbell Co. Groom of Rockbridge Co.
The Lynchburg Virginian, Aug. 15, 1833, p. 3, c. 3.

SAUNDERS, MISS MARY - See entry for Mr. John W. Timberlake.

SAUNDERS, MISS MELINDA L. - See entry for James E. Bouldin, Esq.

SAUNDERS, MISS SUSAN - See entry for John Morcan.

SAUNDERS, MISS SUSAN ANN - See entry for Thomas E. Noell.

SAUNDERS, WILLIAM married April 4, 1822 to Miss Mary Camm by The Rev. Wm.
S. Reid. Both of Lynchburg.
The Lynchburg Press, April 5, 1822, p. 3.

SAVAGE, MISS MARY - See entry for Thomas M. Gabbert.

SCHOOLFIELD, MISS ELIZA M. - See entry for Cephas Webb.

SCHOOLFIELD, MISS LUCY - See entry for Mr. Addison Davis.

SCHOOLFIELD, MISS NANCY T. - See entry for Capt. John T. Mason.

SCHOOLFIELD, MISS SARAH B. - See entry for Thomas Davis.

SCOTT, MISS ANN - See entry for Charles Cobbs.

SCOTT, MISS ANN - See entry for James P. Taylor.

SCOTT, MISS FANNY M. - See entry for Capt. Bryan W. Nowlin.

SCOTT, MISS FRANCES H. - See entry for Robert E. Wilbourn.

SCOTT, HENRIETTA D. - See entry for William Bailey.

SCOTT, MR. HUGH R. married on 20th inst. to Miss Elizabeth Jane Burks, dau. of Samuel Burks dec'd. of Amherst, by The Rev. James Boyd.
The Lynchburg Virginian, Jan. 24, 1831, p. 3, c. 5.

SCOTT, MISS JEANETTE - See entry for Thomas Aldridge.

SCOTT, MR. JOHN married on 8th inst. at Yancyville to Miss Malinda Martin by Thomas D. Johnson, Esq. All of Bedford Co., Va.
The Lynchburg Virginian, July 18, 1836, p. 3, c. 3.

SCOTT, JOHN C. married Dec. 23, 1829 to Miss Margaret Fields, youngest dau. of Mr. Wm. Fields of Bedford, Va., by The Rev. John Ayers.
The Lynchburg Virginian, Jan. 4, 1830, p. 3, c. 6.

SCOTT, MISS LIVELY - See entry for Micajah Morris.

SCOTT, MISS MARIA B. - See entry for Lilbourn W. Leftwich.

SCOTT, MISS MARISSE FRANCES - See entry for John W. West.

SCOTT, MISS RACHEL MAHALA - See entry for Wiatt London.

SCOTT, MISS REBECCA - See entry for Abner Nash.

SCOTT, MISS ROBIN A. - See entry for Dr. Thomas J. Gardin.

SCOTT, MISS SALLY - See entry for Hotchkiss Carver.

SCOTT, SAMUEL M. married June 3, 1819 to Miss Camilla Payne, 5th dau. of Philip Payne, Esq., by The Rev. John S. Lee. All of Campbell Co.
The Lynchburg Press & Public Advertiser, June 10, 1819, p. 3, c. 5.

SCOTT, THOMAS H. married on the 3rd inst. to Margaret P. Burks, dau. of Sam. Burks, dec'd. of Amherst Co., by The Rev. Nicholas H. Cobb. Groom of Campbell Co.
The Lynchburg Virginian, Aug. 10, 1826, p. 3, c. 3.

SCOTT, THOMAS W. married in Scott Co. to Miss Adeline I. Johnson, dau. of
The Hon. Richard M. Johnson, Rep. from Ky. to the Congress of the U.S.
The Lynchburg Virginian, July 16, 1835, p. 3, c. 4.

SCRUGGS, BENJAMIN E. married on Thursday last to Miss Emeline S., dau. of
late Samuel J. Cabell, Esq., by The Rev. Wm. S. Reid. All of this
place.
The Lynchburg Virginian, Dec. 21, 1829, p. 3, c. 5.

SCRUGGS, MRS. CHARLOTTE - See entry for Capt. Tubal Early.

SEAY, JOHN married Sept. 9, 1830 to Mrs. Mary G. Wills, widow of Elias
Wills of Amherst, by The Rev. Wm. I. Holcombe.
The Lynchburg Virginian, Sept. 13, 1830, p. 3, c. 3.

SEBRAY, MISS - See entry for Mr. Thomas Nance.

SELDEN, SAMUEL M. married on 3rd inst. at Person Co., N.C. to Miss Caroline
Elizabeth Hare, dau. of Mr. Jesse Hare of Lynchburg, by The Rev. Mr.
Bailey. Groom formerly of Fredericksburg, Va.
The Lynchburg Virginian, Dec. 12, 1836, p. 3, c. 6.

SETTLE, A. C. married April 17th in Washington, D.C. to Miss Mary Ann
Rodier by The Rev. Mr. Levering. Bride of Georgetown; groom of Va.
The Lynchburg Virginian, June 2, 1836, p. 3, c. 3.

SHACKLEFORD, MR. JOHN C. married on Thursday last to Miss Nancy C.
Davenport, dau. of Capt. Stephen Davenport of Halifax, by The Rev.
David B. McGehee.
The Lynchburg Virginian, Dec. 3, 1832, p. 3, c. 3.

SHANDS, WILLIAM married Oct. 25, 1832 to Miss Martha M. Bingham by The
Rev. John Early. Bride of Lynchburg; groom of Bedford.
The Lynchburg Virginian, Nov. 5, 1832, p. 3, c. 5.

SHANKS, DR. LEWIS married on 21st inst. to Mrs. Mary Johnston by The Rev.
Jeptha Harrison. Bride of Stafford Co. Groom of Fincastle.
The Lynchburg Virginian, Nov. 5, 1835, p. 3, c. 3.

SHARP, MISS FRANCES - See entry for William Bigbie.

SHARPE, WM. married at Mrs. Sarah Chappels to Miss Lucy Reese by The
Rev. Thomas Jeter.
The Lynchburg Virginian, June 21, 1830, p. 3, c. 3.

SHELTON, MISS ELIZA - See entry for Richard H. Burks.

SHELTON, GEO. W. married Dec. 3, 1822 to Miss Elizabeth Harris, dau. of
Mr. Anderson Harris, by The Rev. James Mitchell. All of Bedford Co.
The Lynchburg Virginian, Dec. 6, 1822, p. 3.

SHELOR, MISS JANE - See entry for Col. Joseph Howard.

SHELTON, JOHN G. married to Ann Burd, dau. of Wm. Burd of Lynchburg, by
The Rev. Caleb Leach.
The Lynchburg Virginian, Jan. 7, 1828, p. 3.

SHELTON, JOHN G. married on 11th ult. to Miss Mary W. Burd, dau. of Mr. William Burd. Married by The Rev. Mr. Drummond in St. Louis Mo. All of that place. Bride formerly of Lynchburg.
The Lynchburg Virginian, March 12, 1835, p. 3, c. 4.

SHELTON, JOHN P. married May 17, 1825 to Miss Sarah Bell, eldest dau. of Capt. Drury Bell of Amherst, by The Rev. Lewis Dawson. Groom of Amherst.
The Lynchburg Virginian, May 19, 1825, p. 3, c. 5.

SHELTON, MISS LOUISA - See entry for Mr. Benjamin Franklin Royall.

SHELTON, MISS REBECCA W. - See entry for Capt. Wm. Murray.

SHELTON, SAMUEL married on Wednesday last to Miss Mary M. Didlake, dau. of Mr. Henry Didlake of this place, by The Rev. Dr. Holcombe. Groom of Nelson.
The Lynchburg Virginian, Sept. 12, 1836, p. 3, c. 3.

SHELTON, MISS SUSAN D. - See entry for Joseph Poindexter.

SHELTON, DR. T. C. married Nov. 10, 1824 to Miss Letitia Calland, dau. of late Capt. Samuel Calland of Pittsylvania Co., by The Rev. James Beck.
The Lynchburg Virginian, Dec. 24, 1824, p. 3.

SHEPPERSON, MR. JOSIAH married Thurs., Dec. 9th, to Miss Martha F. Reid of Amherst by The Rev. Robert Ryland. Groom of Prince Edward.
The Lynchburg Virginian, Dec. 13, 1830, p. 3, c. 4.

SHERMAN, ALBERT A. married Nov. 27, 1822 to Miss Anneliza Cheetwood by The Rev. Dr. Phillips. Bride and groom of Bedford.
The Lynchburg Virginian, Dec. 13, 1822, p. 3, c. 4.

SHIELDS, MISS ELIZABETH - See entry for James Marr.

SHIELDS, JOHN married on 10th inst. to Frances Plunkett, dau. of Ambrose Plunkett of Campbell Co. Groom of Nelson Co.
The Lynchburg Virginian, Oct. 26, 1826, p. 3, c. 4.

SHIELDS, MISS MARY - See entry for Patrick P. Burton.

SHIELDS, MISS MARY ANN - See entry for James M. Wilcox.

SHILLING, MR. DAVID married in Columbus, Ohio to Miss Mary Wait.
The Lynchburg Virginian, June 30, 1836, p. 3, c. 3.

SHOEMAKER, MISS ANN - See entry for James M. Yancey.

SHOEMAKER, LINDSEY married June 2, 1814 to Miss Elizabeth Doyle. Bride and groom both of Lynchburg.
The Lynchburg Press, June 9, 1814, p. 3.

SHOEMAKER, MISS MARY JANE - See entry for Richard A. Lee.

SHOEMAKER, WILLIAM M. married last Wednesday to Miss Elizabeth Jordon, dau. of Hezekiah Jordon, by The Rev. W. S. Reid. All of this place. The Lynchburg Virginian, June 20, 1831, p. 3, c. 4.

SHOWMAN, MISS CATHARINE - See entry for Isaac Pence.

SHUSTER, PHILIP, ESQ. married May 23, 1823 to Miss Polly Cairns by The Rev. Dr. Phillips. Bride and groom of Bedford. The Lynchburg Virginian, June 6, 1823, p. 3.

SIMMERTON, JOHN married June 22, 1820 to Miss Sarah Peacock by The Rev. William Duncan. Bride and groom of Amherst. The Lynchburg Press & Public Advertiser, June 27, 1820, p. 3.

SIMPSON, JAMES H. married Feb. 20, 1828 to Eleanor Hudgins, dau. of Capt. Wescomb Hudgins of Fredericksburg, by The Rev. George W. Charlton at home of John Thurman. Groom of Lynchburg. The Lynchburg Virginian, Feb. 28, 1828, p. 3, c. 6.

SINGLETON, MISS MARY REBECCA - See entry for Geo. M. McDuffie.

SKENK, JOHN W. married on 4th inst. to Miss Caroline L. Cofer, dau. of Mr. Geo. Cofer of Bedford Co., by The Rev. Nicholas H. Cobbs. Groom formerly of Albemarle. The Lynchburg Virginian, Mar. 15, 1830, p. 3, c. 3.

SKRUDBIN, ABNER married on 1st inst. to Mrs. Nancy Meadow by The Rev. Stephen Wood. All of Bedford. The Lynchburg Virginian, Nov. 21, 1836, p. 3, c. 4.

SLAUGHTER, MISS EMILY - See entry for Willis Poindexter.

SLAUGHTER, SARAH - See entry for James Spencer.

SMITH, MR. CHAMNESS married on 2nd inst. to Miss Mary Jane Tinsley, dau. of Mr. Rodney Tinsley, by The Rev. Thomas Jones. All of Bedford. The Lynchburg Virginian, Nov. 7, 1836, p. 3, c. 4.

SMITH, MISS BARBARA - See entry for Pascal Matthew.

SMITH, MISS ELIZABETH - See entry for Micajah Wheeler.

SMITH, JAMES M. married on Thurs., 13th inst. to Mrs. Martha W. Clarke, dau. of Maj. John Redd, by The Rev. John C. Traylor. All of Henry Co. The Lynchburg Virginian, April 3, 1828, p. 3.

SMITH, JAMES M., ESQ. married on 26th ult. to Miss Mary Miller Northana Bell, youngest dau. of Capt. James M. Bell of Culpepper Co., by The Rev. Mr. Law. The Lynchburg Virginian, Jan. 8, 1835, p. 3, c. 5.

SMITH, MR. JOHN married on 8th ult. to Miss Eliza Powell, dau. of Mr. David Powell, by The Rev. Samuel Armistead. All of Campbell. The Lynchburg Virginian, Oct. 6, 1836, p. 3, c. 3.

SMITH, JOHN, JR. married Wed., 2nd inst. at residence of Mrs. E. Callands, Pittsylvania Co., to Miss Matilda Ann Callaway, Dau. of Dr. Henry Callaway. Groom merchant of this place.
The Lynchburg Virginian, Mar. 8, 1825, p. 3, c. 5.

SMITH, JOHN W. married last Wed. to Miss Sarah Leftwich, dau. of The Rev. Wm. Leftwich of Bedford, by The Rev. Thompson. Groom of Pittsylvania Co.
The Lynchburg Virginian, Mar. 16, 1827, p. 3, c. 2.

SMITH, MAJOR JOHN W. married on 18th inst. to Miss Martha Ann Bullock, dau. of John Bullock, by The Rev. Wm. S. Reid. All of this place.
The Lynchburg Virginian, March 19, 1829, p. 3, c. 4.

SMITH, MISS JULIA - See entry for John Craghead.

SMITH, MISS MARIA L. - See entry for Micajah R. Foot.

SMITH, MISS MARY - See entry for Ezra Walker.

SMITH, MISS MARY - See entry for William Booth.

SMITH, MISS MARY F. T. - See entry for Wyndham Robertson.

SMITH, MISS MARY JANE - See entry for Park Street.

SMITH, MISS PAULINE - See entry for James L. Claytor.

SMITH, RALPH married Feb. 20, 1822 to Miss Ann Lambeth, dau. of Meredith Lambeth of Campbell Co., by The Rev. G. W. Charlton. Groom of Pittsylvania Co.
The Lynchburg Press, Feb. 22, 1822, p. 3, c. 5.

SMITH, MISS SARAH - See entry for Wright Smith.

SMITH, WILLIAM married Dec. 13, 1832 to Miss Catharine C. Clark, dau. of Paulet Clark, Esq. of Campbell Co., by The Rev. Sam Armistead.
The Lynchburg Virginian, Dec. 24, 1832, p. 3, c. 2.

SMITH, WILLIAM W. married on 8th inst. to Miss Sarah Ann Davis, dau. of Henry Davis, Esq., by The Rev. Nicholas M. Cobbs. All of this place.
The Lynchburg Virginian, July 12, 1830, p. 3, c. 5.

SMITH, WRIGHT married on Tues. 21st inst. to Miss Sarah Smith, dau. of Mr. Wm. Smith, by The Rev. Abner Anthony. All of Franklin Co.
The Lynchburg Virginian, Jan. 6, 1831, p. 3, c. 4.

SMOOT, THOMAS, ESQ. married 22nd inst. to Miss Clari Lane. All of Amherst Co., Va.
The Lynchburg Virginian, Aug. 30, 1830, p. 3, c. 3.

SNEAD, MISS ANN G. - See entry for Mr. William Oky.

SNEAD, MISS ELIZABETH - See entry for Warner Gannaway.

SNEED, ARCHIBALD married on 4th inst. to Miss Elizabeth Pearman by The
Rev. Dr. Holcombe. All of this place.
The Lynchburg Virginian, Nov. 12, 1835, p. 3, c. 3.

SNODGRASS, MISS CAROLINE - See entry for Jacky Leftwich.

SNOW, MR. ABNER married on 30th ult. to Miss Mary Ann Brown, dau. of Mr.
Henry Brown dec'd., by The Rev. Mosby Arnold. All of this place.
The Lynchburg Virginian, Dec. 8th, 1836, p. 3, c. 5.

SPARHAWK, EDWARD V. married to Miss Eloise Worrell in Richmond, Va. Groom
is editor of Petersburg Intelligencer.
The Lynchburg Virginian, Aug. 21, 1837, p. 3, c. 4.

SPARROW, MISS MARY JANE - See entry for Samuel B. Hardy.

SPEECE, NATHAN married Sept. 22, 1830 to Miss Eliza Allen of Campbell Co.,
Va. by The Rev. Frederick Kabler.
The Lynchburg Virginian, Sept. 27, 1830, p. 3, c. 5.

SPEED, MISS ELIZABETH Y. - See entry for Lieut. John Rudd.

SPENCER, MISS ANN B. D. - See entry for Bryant W. Nowlin, Esq.

SPENCER, MISS CATHERINE - See entry for Jefferson Clark.

SPENCER, JAMES married April 24, 1821 to Miss Sarah Slaughter by The Rev.
Mr. Boyd. All of Amherst Co.
The Lynchburg Press, May 4, 1821, p. 3.

SPENCER, MISS MARY A. - See entry for Ransom Price.

SPENCER, MISS SOPHIA W. - See entry for Col. James Campbell.

SPENCER, MISS SUSAN - See entry for William T. Harvey.

SPOONER, ALDEN B., ESQ. married Aug. 14, 1814 to Miss Elizabeth H.
Crawford, dau. of Wm. S. Crawford of Amherst Co. Married at
Tusculum, Amherst Co. by The Rev. Charles Crawford. Groom,
attorney-at-law of Petersburg, Va.
The Lynchburg Press, Aug. 25, 1814, p. 3, c. 3.

SPURLOCK, THOMAS W. married Dec. 12, 1832 to Miss Martha Ann Davis by The
Rev. M. Reuben L. Coleman. Bride and groom of Lynchburg.
The Lynchburg Virginian, Dec. 24, 1832, p. 3, c. 2.

STABLER, ROBINSON married on 16th inst. to Miss Mary A. Davis, dau. of Wm.
Davis, Jr. of this County. Married at Friend's Meeting House. Groom
of Alexandria.
The Lynchburg Virginian, Oct. 23, 1828, p. 3, c. 5.

STAGG, MR. JOHN married Thurs. Feb. 6, 1823 to Miss Elizabeth K. Fox at
residence of B. F. Coke, Esq. in Henrico Co. Groom of Charles City Co.
The Lynchburg Virginian, Mar. 18, 1823, p. 1, c. 6.

STAPLES, MISS CYNTHIA ANN - See entry for John Plunkett.

STAPLES, MISS EMILY - See entry for Mr. Madison C. Porter.

STAPLES, GEORGE W. married March 26, 1833 at home of Dr. Gilbert in Amherst Co. to Miss Leanna Lee Dibrell by The Rev. William Hendrick. Bride and groom of Amherst.
The Lynchburg Virginian, April 8, 1833, p. 3, c. 5.

STAPLES, JAMES married on 2nd inst. to Miss Lavinia M. A. Elliott, dau. of Robert Elliott of Campbell Co., by The Rev. John S. Lee. Groom formerly of this place.
The Lynchburg Virginian, Aug. 3, 1837, p. 3, c. 4.

STAPLES, JOHN C. married to Miss Mary W. Martin, dau. of Col. Joseph Martin of Henry Co. Groom of Patrick Co.
The Lynchburg Virginian, July 13, 1826, p. 3, c. 4.

STAPLES, MISS MARY JANE - See entry for Clifton H. Rucker.

STAPLES, MISS RUTH - See entry for James M. Redd.

STAPLES, MRS. SARAH - See entry for Lawson Turner.

STAPLES, WM. A. married Thurs. 25th inst. to Miss Sarah F. Porter of Campbell Co. by The Rev. Thomas Burge.
The Lynchburg Virginian, Nov. 29, 1830, p. 3, c. 4.

STAPLES, WILLIAM A. married on 21st inst. to Miss Martha Ann L. Cox, youngest dau. of the late Milner Cox of Amherst, by The Rev. Wm. I. Holcombe. Groom of Bedford.
The Lynchburg Virginian, Mar. 28, 1833, p. 3, c. 4.

STARLING, MISS ELIZABETH ANN - See entry for Capt. George W. Martin.

STARLING, MISS SUSAN G. - See entry for Col. Daniel Reamey.

STARR, THE REV. WM. H. married April 14, 1825 to Miss Sarah McCabe by The Rev. Wm. Leftwich. Bride and groom of Bedford.
The Lynchburg Virginian, May 5, 1825, p. 3.

STANLEY, MISS MARY ANN - See entry for James Saunders.

STANTON, MISS VIRGINIA P. - See entry for Gen. Philo L. Mitchell.

STATON, THOMAS O. married July 28th to Miss Polly Lowe by The Rev. James Boyd. All of Nelson Co.
The Lynchburg Virginian, Aug. 6, 1829, p. 3, c. 5.

STEAENS, DOCTOR JAS. T. married on Nov. 17, 1817 to Miss Towns, dau. of Capt. Towns of Amelia. Groom of Lynchburg.
The Lynchburg Press, Dec. 12, 1817, p. 3.

STEAGALL, RICHARD married on 9th inst. to Mrs. Mary Morris, widow of the late Henry Morris, Esq., by The Rev. Joseph Pedigo.
The Lynchburg Virginian, June 20, 1831, p. 3, c. 4.

STEDMAN, NATHAN, ESQ. married on 13th inst. to Miss Euphenia White, dau.
of Mr. Thos. W. White of Richmond, by The Rev. Wm. S. Plummer. Groom
was Comptroller of State of N.C.
The Lynchburg Virginian, Jan. 21, 1836, p. 3, c. 4.

STEEL, MISS MARTHA - See entry for John Holmes.

STEEN, MISS JULIAN ANN T. - See entry for Julian R. Henley.

STEEN, MISS PAULINA P. - See entry for Thomas O. Acree.

STEPHEN, MISS CAROLINE - See entry for John M. B. Stevens.

STEPTOE, MISS LUCINDA - See entry for Robert C. Penn.

STEPTOE, MISS SARAH T. - See entry for Wm. Massie.

STEPTOE, THOMAS married on 28th ult. to Miss Catharine Yancey, eldest dau.
of Maj. Joel Yancey of Bedford, by The Rev. Nicholas H. Cobbs.
The Lynchburg Virginian, Aug. 5, 1830, p. 3, c. 5.

STEVENS, MISS ELIZABETH - See entry for Thomas J. DuVal.

STEVENS, JOHN M. B. married on 9th inst. to Miss Caroline Stephen, dau. of
Capt. Stephen, by The Rev. Mr. Carson. All of Campbell Co.
The Lynchburg Virginian, Dec. 17, 1835, p. 3, c. 3.

STEVENS, MISS SUSAN - See entry for The Rev. Norval D. Howe.

STEVENS, THOMAS B. married Sept. 22, 1814 to Miss Martha B. Heath by The
Rev. Joab Watson. Bride and groom of Lynchburg.
The Lynchburg Press, Sept. 29, 1814, p. 5.

STEWARD, WM. married last Sunday to Polina Parrow, dau. of Stephen Parrow[sic]
of Campbell Co., by The Rev. Mr. Webb.
The Lynchburg Virginian, March 23, 1826, p. 3, c. 4.

STEWART, LORENZO, ESQ. married to Miss Sarah Ann Anderson, dau. of Mrs.
Elizabeth W. Anderson of Bedford, by The Rev. Nicholas Hamner Cobbs.
Groom was an attorney-at-law of Oglethorpe Co., Georgia.
The Lynchburg Virginian, Jan. 10, 1831, p. 3, c. 3.

STINNER, SARAH - See entry for Reuben Wilmore.

STOCKER, MRS. ELIZABETH H. - See entry for Robert Walsh.

STONE, MISS MARY - See entry for Daniel Aunspaugh.

STONER, MISS MATILDA M. - See entry for Albert G. Williams.

STOREY, JOSEPH E. married last Thurs. evening to Miss Elizabeth L. Gregory
by The Rev. Thomas Burge. All of Amherst.
The Lynchburg Virginian, Nov. 19, 1829, p. 3, c. 4.

STRANGE, MISS ELIZA A. - See entry for John Logan.

STRANGE, CAPT. NATHANIEL S. married July 9, 1833 to Miss Caroline D.
Alexander, dau. of Reuben Alexander, Esq. of Marrow Bone, Ky.
Groom lately of Bedford, Va.
The Lynchburg Virginian, July 25, 1833, p. 3, c. 4.

STRANGE, THOMAS married on Nov. 11, 1823 to Miss Sophia McDaniel, dau. of
Capt. John McDaniel of Amherst, by The Rev. Daniel Day. Groom of
Bedford.
The Lynchburg Virginian, Nov. 14, 1823, p. 3.

STRATTON, CAPT. ASA married Jan. 29, 1833 to Miss Elizabeth Whitehead by
The Rev. Isaac Paul. Both of Nelson Co.
The Lynchburg Virginian, Feb. 14, 1833, p. 3, c. 4.

STRATTON, FRAZER O. married on the 18th inst. to Miss Charlotte Turner,
dau. of Benj. Turner, Esq., by The Rev. John Ayres. All of Bedford Co.
The Lynchburg Virginian, Dec. 4, 1828, p. 3, c. 5.

STRATTON, SAMUEL married on 2nd inst. at residence of Capt. Thomas Jones
to Miss Catharine Trible, dau. of G. W. Trible of Nelson, by The Rev.
Wm. Duncan. Groom merchant of Jonesborough.
The Lynchburg Virginian, Aug. 16, 1827, p. 3, c. 3.

STRATTON, THOMAS J. married Thurs. 11th inst. to Ann W. Dillon, dau. of
Wm. Dillon of Buckingham, by The Rev. Thomas Burge. Groom of Powhatan.
The Lynchburg Virginian, Sept. 24, 1827, p. 3, c. 5.

STREET, PARK married July 28th at residence of Mr. John W Cook to Miss
Mary Jane Smith by The Rev. James Reed. Bride of Franklin Co. Groom
of vicinity of Nashville, Tenn.
The Lynchburg Virginian, Aug. 6, 1829, p. 3, c. 5.

STRICKLAN, DR. JOHN married on 10th inst. to Miss E. Edmonds, eldest dau.
of William Edmonds dec'd. of Nelson Co., by The Rev. James Boyd.
All of Nelson Co.
The Lynchburg Virginian, Aug. 17, 1826, p. 3, c. 3.

STUART, ALEXANDER H. H., ESQ. married to Miss Frances Peyton Baldwin,
eldest dau. of Gen. Briscoe G. Baldwin, by The Rev. Mr. Watts.
All of Staunton, Va.
The Lynchburg Virginian, Aug. 15, 1833, p. 3, c. 4.

STUART, ARCHIBALD married June 27, 1817 to Miss Elizabeth S. Pannill, dau.
of David Pannill dec'd. of Pittsylvania Co., by The Rev. Griffith
Dickerson. Groom was attorney-at-law of Campbell Co.
The Lynchburg Press, July 4, 1817, p. 3.

STUART, MISS NANCY - See entry for Addison Armistead.

SUBLETT, ELIZA - See entry for _____ St. John.

SUMPTER, MISS MARY JANE - See entry for Kalita B. Townly.

SYDNOR, FORTUNATUS married Nov. 13, 1817 to Miss Eliza Royal by The Rev.
Wm. S. Reid. Bride and groom of Lynchburg.
The Lynchburg Press, Nov. 14, 1817, p. 3, c. 3.

TAIT, MISS ANN - See entry for Robert T. Woods.

TAIT, MISS LOUISA O. - See entry for W. H. Fox.

TALBOT, MISS ELIZA W. - See entry for Samuel W. Dickens.

TALIAFERRO, MR. CHARLES B. married on 13th inst. to Miss Elizabeth C.
Carter of Halifax, dau. of Capt. Samuel Carter. Groom of Danville.
The Lynchburg Virginian, Nov. 20, 1834, p. 3, c. 4.

TALIAFERRO, LANDON married on 25th inst. to Miss Ann Divers formerly of
Richmond by The Rev. Matthew Jackson. Groom is of Rocky Mount.
The Lynchburg Virginian, Sept. 3, 1835, p. 3, c. 4.

TALIAFERRO, MISS MARY JANE - See entry for Henry Dillard.

TALIAFERRO, NORBORNE M., ESQ. married on Oct. 29, 1823 to Miss Lucy
Jones, dau. of the late Roland Jones of Lynchburg, by The Rev.
John Early. Groom attorney-at-law of Lynchburg.
The Lynchburg Virginian, Oct. 31, 1823, p. 3.

TALIAFERRO, MISS SARAH ANNE - See entry for John Crews.

TALIAFERRO, TAZEWELL married Sept. 1, 1836 to Miss Amanda Callaway, dau.
of Henry T. Callaway, by The Rev. Moses Green. All of Franklin Co.
The Lynchburg Virginian, Oct. 24, 1836, p. 3, c. 3.

TALLIAFERRO, MISS CAROLINE - See entry for Leonard H. Childress.

TANNER, MISS NANCY - See entry for Nathan Tanner.

TANNER, NATHAN married on 9th inst. to Miss Nancy Tanner, dau. of Mr.
Branch Tanner, by The Rev. Samuel Armistead. All of Campbell Co.
The Lynchburg Virginian, Feb. 23, 1829, p. 3, c. 5.

TARDY, MISS LUCY ANN - See entry for George E. Thurman.

TARDY, SAMUEL married Nov. 13, 1814 to Miss Jane Haden, dau. of Benj.
Haden, Esq., by The Rev. A. Early. All of Campbell Co.
The Lynchburg Press, Nov. 17, 1814, p. 3.

TATE, MISS ALICE - See entry for David G. Murrell.

TATE, MISS CATHARINE - See entry for Major Moses G. Carper.

TATE, MISS SELINE - See entry for Linneus Dupuy.

TATUM, EDWARD married on Wed., 17th inst. to Miss Ruth S. Foster, dau. of
Capt. Charles Foster, by The Rev. John Washburn. All of Patrick Co.
The Lynchburg Virginian, Feb. 29, 1836, p. 3, c. 4.

TAYLOE, GEORGE P. married on 14th inst. to Miss Mary Elisabeth Langhorne,
dau. of Wm. Langhorne, Esq., by The Rev. Mr. Cobbs. All of Botetourt
Co. Groom of "Cloverdale", Botetourt Co.
The Lynchburg Virginian, Oct. 28, 1830, p. 3, c. 4.

TAYLOR, MISS ANNA K. - See entry for John Royall.

TAYLOR, MR. EDWARD married on 10th inst. to Miss Martha E. Mathews by The Rev. Samuel Davidson. All of Campbell Co.
The Lynchburg Virginian, Dec. 18, 1834, p. 3, c. 4.

TAYLOR, JAMES P. married on 4th inst. to Miss Ann Scott of New Glasgow (Amherst Co.), by The Rev. Washington Carter.
The Lynchburg Virginian, Feb. 9, 1835, p. 3, c. 4.

TAYLOR, JEFFERSON married on Thurs., Dec. 1st, to Miss Mary Adams, dau. of Isaac Adams, by The Rev. Stephen Hubbard. All of Patrick Co.
The Lynchburg Virginian, Dec. 22, 1825, p. 3, c. 3.

TAYLOR, JORDAN married on 13th inst. to Miss Frances Williamson by The Rev. Samuel Armistead. All of Charlotte.
The Lynchburg Virginian, Dec. 27, 1822, p. 3, c. 5.

TAYLOR, MR. SILAS married on 18th inst. to Miss Mary A. S. Walker by The Rev. Henry S. Peyton. All of Bedford Co.
The Lynchburg Virginian, April 23, 1832, p. 3, c. 5.

TAYLOR, MISS SUSAN - See entry for Mr. George W. Beuford.

TERREL, DOCTOR C. I. married on 20th ult, 1822 to Miss Susan Kenerly. Bride of Patrick, Va. Groom formerly of Lynchburg.
The Lynchburg Virginian, Sept. 6, 1822, p. 3, c. 5.

TERRELL, MISS LUCY - See entry for Achilles D. Johnson.

TERRILL, MISS SARAH - See entry for John L. Douglas.

TERRY, MISS ANN HENRY - See entry for William T. Campbell.

TERRY, MISS LETITIA W. - See entry for Dr. Achilles Whitlocke.

TERRY, MISS MARY A. M. - See entry for Laurence H. Hall.

TERRY, MR. STEPHEN married on 9th of last month to Miss Lucy Leftwich, dau. of Capt. Peyton Leftwich, by The Rev. Griffith Dickerson of Pittsylvania. All of Campbell Co.
The Lynchburg Virginian, Dec. 1, 1828, p. 3, c. 5.

THOMAS, MISS DELIGHT - See entry for Mr. John F. Davis.

THOMAS, DAVID C. married June 8, 1825 to Miss Cyrena Byron Peters, dau. of Mr. Elisha Peters of Nelson Co., by The Rev. James Boyd. Groom of Buckingham Co.
The Lynchburg Virginian, June 9, 1825, p. 3.

THOMAS, MISS LUCY - See entry for George Turner.

THOMAS, MISS MAHALA - See entry for James M'Coy.

THOMAS, MISS MARY E. - See entry for The Rev. Dr. Abram Penn.

THOMAS, NELSON married Dec. 17, 1818 to Miss Mary Johnson by The Rev.
Pleasant Thurman. Bride of Amherst Co. Groom of Lynchburg.
The Lynchburg Press & Public Advertiser, Dec. 21, 1818, p. 3.

THOMPSON, MISS ANNE C. - See entry for Charles Whitley.

THOMPSON, MISS ELENOR - See entry for Robert S. Andrews.

THOMPSON, MISS LOUISA - See entry for Robert M. Warwick.

THOMPSON, MRS. LOUISA A. - See entry for George Tucker, Esq.

THOMPSON, MATTHEW married Feb. 3, 1828 to Miss Martha Moore, dau. of Mrs.
Mary Moore, by The Rev. Henry Brown. All of Campbell Co.
The Lynchburg Virginian, Feb. 14, 1828, p. 3, c. 5.

THOMPSON, CAPT. STITH married Feb. 17, 1818 to Miss Sarah Warwick, dau. of
Maj. Wm. Warwick of Amherst, by The Rev. Wm. Jones. Groom of Dinwiddie.
The Lynchburg Press, Feb. 20, 1818, p. 3.

THOMPSON, WILLIAM DANIEL married Jan. 17, 1828 to Getty K. Green of Tenn.,
formerly of Lynchburg. Married in Fayetteville, Tenn.
The Lynchburg Virginian, Feb. 14, 1828, p. 3, c. 5.

THOMPSON, WILLIAM, JR. married June 19, 1823 to Miss Sarah Cheatham, dau.
of Mr. Peter Cheatham, by The Rev. John McLane. All of Campbell Co.
The Lynchburg Virginian, July 5, 1823, p. 3.

THORNHILL, WILLIAM married June 8, 1820 to Miss Lucy Walton. Bride and
groom both of Buckingham Co.
The Lynchburg Press & Public Advertiser, June 13, 1820, p. 3.

THORNTON, MISS S. - See entry for Wm. Arnold.

THORNTON, WILLIAM L. married on 24th ult. to Miss Martha M. Rudd, dau. of
Maj. Thomas Rudd, by The Rev. E. Collins.
The Lynchburg Virginian, Dec. 1, 1831, p. 3, c. 4.

THURMAN, MISS ANN SOPHIA - See entry for Littleton V. Creasey.

THURMAN, GEORGE E. married May 29, 1833 to Miss Lucy Ann Tardy by The Rev.
David S. Doggett. All of Lynchburg.
The Lynchburg Virginian, June 3, 1833, p. 3, c. 5.

THURMON, ROBERT J. married on 26th inst. to Miss Sophia S. Reese, dau. of
the late William Reese, by The Rev. William Leftwich. Bride and
groom of Bedford.
The Lynchburg Virginian, Sept. 3, 1835, p. 3, c. 4.

THURMAN, MR. ROBERT W. married on 10th inst. to Miss Louisa Anderson, dau.
of Mr. John Anderson of Campbell Co., by The Rev. Henry B. Cowles.
Groom of Lynchburg.
The Lynchburg Virginian, Dec. 15, 1834, p. 3, c. 4.

TILDEN, MISS ASBURY ANN - See entry for Capt. Richard R. Phelps.

TILDEN, MISS [CORNELIA MEYER] - See entry for Christopher Winfree.

TILDEN, MR. JOHN B. married on Tuesday last in Lynchburg to Miss Maria Johnson of this place, by The Rev. William S. Reid.
The Lynchburg Virginian, Oct. 25, 1835, p. 3, c. 6.

TILDEN, RICHARD S. married Jan. 1, 1818 to Miss Evaline Burd, dau. of Wm. Burd. All of Lynchburg.
The Lynchburg Press, Jan. 2, 1818, p. 3.

TILLER, MISS SOPHIA B. - See entry for James H. Joiner.

TILMAN, JACOB H. married on 16th inst. to Miss Caira Ann C. M. Johnson, dau. of Capt. James Johnson, by The Rev. James Boyd. All of Nelson Co.
The Lynchburg Virginian, Aug. 23, 1827, p. 3, c. 2.

TIMBERLAKE, JOHN W. married in Highland Co., Ohio to Miss Mary Saunders, dau. of Jonathan Saunders, Esq. Groom formerly of Campbell Co., Va.
The Lynchburg Virginian, May 28, 1833, p. 3, c. 3.

TIMBERLAKE, MISS MARY - See entry for Henry Robinson.

TIMBERLAKE, MISS SARAH E. - See entry for Allan B. Magruder.

TINSLEY, ALFRED married Dec. 27, 1829 to Ann D. Farnsworth of Amherst Co.
The Lynchburg Virginian, Jan. 7, 1830, p. 3, c. 6.

TINSLEY, MISS ANN M. - See entry for Rowland P. Burks.

TINSLEY, MISS CHARLOTTE ANN - See entry for Charles B. Gwatkins.

TINSLEY, MISS CLEOPATRIA - See entry for Mr. Harwood Major.

TINSLEY, JOHN T. married on 22nd inst. to Miss Matilda W. Burford, dau. of Ambrose Burford, by The Rev. Lewis Dawson. All of Amherst Co., Va.
The Lynchburg Virginian, Aug. 28, 1826, p. 3, c. 4.

TINSLEY, MARTIN D. married on 14th inst. to Miss Emily Davis by The Rev. C. H. Page. All of Amherst Co., Va.
The Lynchburg Virginian, Nov. 19, 1832, p. 3, c. 4.

TINSLEY, MISS MARY JANE - See entry for Chamness Smith.

TINSLEY, ROBERT, ESQ. married last Thurs. evening to Miss Eliza L. Davenport, dau. of the late Glover L. Davenport of Campbell Co., Va. Groom of Amherst Co., Va.
The Lynchburg Virginian, Oct. 19, 1829, p. 3, c. 4.

TIPPETT, MISS MARGARET - See entry for William Poe.

TODD, MISS MARGARET - See entry for Charles Calhoun.

TOLER, RICHARD H. married Dec. 20, 1832 to Miss Mary Ann Frances Duval, dau. of Jamor Wm. Duval of Buckingham Co., Va., by The Rev. Thomas Burge. Groom one of editors of The Virginian.
The Lynchburg Virginian, Dec. 24, 1832, p. 3, c. 2.

TOMINSON, ARTHUR married on 21st inst. to Mrs. Caroline Matilda Coleman, relic of John Coleman, by The Rev. Wm. Harris. All of Bedford.
The Lynchburg Virginian, Jan. 2, 1832, p. 3, c. 5.

TOMPKINS, QUARLES, ESQ. married on 9th inst. to Miss Evelyn Byrd by The Rev. F. G. Smith. All of Lynchburg.
The Lynchburg Virginian, Feb. 11, 1825, p. 3, c. 4.

TOWLES, MISS ELIZABETH L. - See entry for John Blair Dabney.

TOWNLEY, MISS ELIZA H. - See entry for Willis Bradley.

TOWNLEY, MISS MARTHA - See entry for Samuel Bailey.

TOWNLY, ALVA R. married last Tuesday to Miss Emily Worsham, dau. of Mr. Littlebury Worsham of Caswell Co., North Carolina. Groom of Danville, Va.
The Lynchburg Virginian, June 14, 1830, p. 3, c. 5.

TOWNLY, KALITA B. married Wednesday last to Miss Mary Jane Sumpter by The Rev. Richard Lattimore. All of Lynchburg.
The Lynchburg Virginian, Dec. 3, 1829, p. 3, c. 5.

TOWNS, MISS - See entry for Dr. James T. Steaens.

TRACE, MRS. DOLLY - See entry for Jesse Glancy.

TREADWAY, THE REV. AMOS married Dec. 28, 1824 to Miss Minerva B. Grant, dau. of J. Grant, Esq. Groom late of Lynchburg. Married at Verona, New York by The Rev. Mr. Hollister.
The Lynchburg Virginian, Jan. 28, 1825, p. 3.

TREADWELL, ALEXANDER PHILIP SOCRATES AMELIUS CAESAR HANNIBAL MARCELLUS GEORGE WASHINGTON married at New Orleans to Miss Caroline Sophia Maria Julianne Wortley Montague Joan of Arc Williams. All of New Orleans.
The Lynchburg Virginian, Nov. 13, 1828, p. 3, c. 5.

TRENT, JAMES married on 8th inst. to Miss Mary Carwiles, dau. of Mr. Jacob Carwiles, by The Rev. Samuel Armistead. All of Campbell Co.
The Lynchburg Virginian, Aug. 16, 1832, p. 3, c. 5.

TRENT, MISS NANCY ELIZABETH - See entry for James R. Bridges.

TRIBLE, MISS CATHARINE - See entry for Samuel Stratton.

TRIST, NICHOLAS PHILIP married Sept. 10, 1824 to Miss Virginia Jefferson Randolph, dau. of Col. Tho. M. Randolph of Albemarle; [granddaughter of Thomas Jefferson.] Married at Monticello by The Rev. F. W. Hatch.
The Lynchburg Virginian, Sept. 28, 1824, p. 3, c. 5.

TROTTER, MISS ELIZA A. - See entry for John Millner.

TRUSLOW, MISS THERESA ANN - See entry for James Norton.

TUCKER, GEORGE, ESQ. married on 9th inst. to Mrs. Louisa A. Thompson of
Baltimore by The Rev. Dr. Wyatt. Groom formerly of this place and
is a professor at the University of Virginia.
The Lynchburg Virginian, Dec. 18, 1828, p. 3, c. 4.

TUCKER, MISS SARAH W. - See entry for William T. Loving.

TURNER, MISS ANN B. - See entry for Reuben Carver.

TURNER, MISS ADELINE - See entry for William G. Harlin.

TURNER, MISS CHARLOTTE - See entry for Fraser O. Stratton.

TURNER, DAVID married to Almira Brown of Liberty,[now Bedford City, Va.]
Copied from a Middletown newspaper.
The Lynchburg Virginian, June 12, 1828, p. 3, c. 4.

TURNER, GEORGE married Feb. 13, 1827 to Miss Lucy Thomas of Nelson Co.,
Va. Groom of Amherst Co., Va. Married in Nelson Co.
The Lynchburg Virginian, March 2, 1827, p. 3, c. 3.

TURNER, GEORGE W. married May 20th to Miss Rebecca C. Murrell by The
Rev. F. G. Smith. Bride and groom of Lynchburg.
The Lynchburg Virginian, May 21, 1829, p. 3, c. 3.

TURNER, JAMES A., ESQ. married on 15th inst. to Miss Mary Jane Payne, dau.
of John R. D. Payne, Esq. of Lynchburg, by The Rev. Wm. I. Holcombe.
Groom of Lexington, Va.
The Lynchburg Virginian, April 20, 1835, p. 3, c. 5.

TURNER, DR. JAMES G. married June 14, 1825 to Miss Elizabeth Key, dau. of
the late Capt. Thomas Key of Bedford, by The Rev. Jackson. Groom of
Franklin Co., Va.
The Lynchburg Virginian, June 23, 1825, p. 3.

TURNER, LAWSON married on 17th inst. to Mrs. Sarah Staples of Buckingham
Co., Va. by The Rev. Thomas Burge. Groom of Amherst Co., Va.
The Lynchburg Virginian, Nov. 22, 1830, p. 3, c. 4.

TURNER, W. M. married Jan. 11, 1825 to Miss Sarah Roberts, dau. of Capt.
Zachariah Roberts of Nelson Co., by The Rev. James Boyd. Groom of
Amherst.
The Lynchburg Virginian, Jan. 14, 1825, p. 3.

TURNER, ZACHARIAH married Sept. 28th at Oakville to Miss E. Call of
Buckingham Co., Va. by The Rev. Mr. Fisher of the Buckingham Circuit.
The Lynchburg Virginian, Oct. 10, 1836, p. 3, c. 4.

TYREE, MISS ANN - See entry for Moses Lacy.

TYREE, MISS ELIZABETH C. - See entry for James Lavender.

TYREE, MISS ELIZABETH D. - See entry for Moses H. Preston.

TYREE, JOHN H. married last Tues. to Miss Ann P. Bransford, dau. of Samuel
Bransford, Esq. by The Rev. John Early. All of this place.
The Lynchburg Virginian, Oct. 16, 1828, p. 3, c. 6.

U

URQUHART, MR. KENNETH married on 6th inst. to Miss Frances Ann Porter, eldest dau. of Capt. Benjamin W. Porter, by The Rev. John W. Watson. All of Campbell Co., Va.
The Lynchburg Virginian, Nov. 17, 1834, p. 3, c. 4.

V

VALENTINE, GEORGE married on 9th inst. to Miss Ann Ballentine by The Rev. M. P. Parks. All of this place.
The Lynchburg Virginian, Feb. 14, 1831, p. 3, c. 5.

VANNESS, CORNELIA - See entry for James Roosevelt, Jr., Esq.

VARNUM, MISS S. - See entry for John Jennings.

VAUGHAN, MISS MARY M. - See entry for Richard C. Fortune.

VAWTER, MRS. MILDRED - See entry for Obadiah Echols.

VAWTER, SILAS married on 28th inst. 1830 to Miss Sarah Fear by The Rev. Robert Ryland. All of this place.
The Lynchburg Virginian, Jan. 3, 1831, p. 1, c. 3.

VENABLE, JOSEPH E. married Dec. 6, 1832 at Capt. R. Venable's residence in Prince Edward Co., Va. to Miss Mary Ann Dunnington, dau. of late Walter Dunnington of Lynchburg, by The Rev. M. Dance. Groom merchant at Farmville.
The Lynchburg Virginian, Dec. 13, 1832, p. 3, c. 5.

VENABLE, NATHANIEL I., ESQ. married Aug. 6, 1833 to Miss Elizabeth J. Dennis, dau. of Mrs. Elizabeth Dennis of Campbell, by The Rev. Mr. Dance. Groom of Prince Edward.
The Lynchburg Virginian, Aug. 8, 1833, p. 3, c. 4.

VENABLE, PEYTON married Wed. the 24th ult. to Miss Susan Moody by The Rev. Robert B. Thompson. All of Lynchburg.
The Lynchburg Virginian, Jan. 1, 1835, p. 3, c. 3.

VENABLE, MR. SAMUEL W. married on 4th inst. to Miss Mary C. Massie by The Rev. John S. Lee. All of this place.
The Lynchburg Virginian, April 5, 1832, p. 3.

VEST, MISS MARGARET CATHERINE - See entry for Thomas W. Watts.

W

WADDELL, MR. WM. H. married on 26th inst. to Miss Mary Ann Lewellin of Lynchburg by The Rev. Edward Cannon. Groom formerly of Charles City Co., Va.
The Lynchburg Virginian, April 30, 1832, p. 3, c. 3.

WADDILL, MR. PLEASANT married on 20th inst. to Miss Martha Wilson by The
Rev. William Blair. All of Pittsylvania Co.
The Lynchburg Virginian, Dec. 31, 1832, p. 3, c. 2.

WADE, BEVERLY married on 6th inst. to Miss Nancy Powell by The Rev. Wm.
Duncan. All of Amherst Co.
The Lynchburg Virginian, Nov. 9, 1829, p. 3, c. 5.

WADE, MR. HENRY married to Miss Julia Patterson. All of Franklin County.
The Lynchburg Virginian, Dec. 15, 1834, p. 3, c. 4.

WAIT, MISS MARY - See entry for Mr. David Shilling.

WAKEFIELD, MISS MARTHA - See entry for John Mansfield.

WALFORD, MISS SARAH W. - See entry for John V. Hardwick.

WALKER, MISS CLEMENTINA - See entry for David Patrick, Esq.

WALKER, EZRA, ESQ. married on 1st. inst. to Miss Mary Smith, dau. of
Abram Smith, Esq. of Rockingham, by The Rev. Henry Ruffner. Groom
an editor of the Charleston Banner.
The Lynchburg Virginian, Nov. 22, 1832, p. 3, c. 4.

WALKER, HENRY F. married March 13, 1823 to Miss Cynthia Ferguson by The
Rev. Moses Greer. All of Franklin Co., Va.
The Lynchburg Virginian, March 28, 1823, p. 3.

WALKER, MR. JOSEPH M. married on 19th inst. to Miss Eleanor Amyx by The
Rev. Henry S. Peyton. All of Bedford Co.
The Lynchburg Virginian, April 23, 1832, p. 3, c. 5.

WALKER, MISS JUDITH P. - See entry for William C. Rives, Esq.

WALKER, MISS LUCY - See entry for Charles Cobbs.

WALKER, MISS MARY A. S. - See entry for Mr. Silas Taylor.

WALKER, PETER married March 10, 1819 to Miss Eliza Moore, dau. of Col.
Thomas Moore of Bedford, by The Rev. Wm. S. Reid. Groom of Lynchburg.
The Lynchburg Press & Public Advertiser, March 15, 1819, p. 3.

WALKER, MR. SAMUEL J. married on Tues. 8th inst. to Miss Martha Ann Walton,
dau. of Col. William Walton of Buckingham Co., Va.
The Lynchburg Virginian, June 17, 1830, p. 3, c. 4.

WALKER, MISS SARAH - See entry for Samuel Jordan.

WALLACE, MISS SUSANNA - See entry for Josiah Cole.

WALLACE, TALIAFERRO married on 3rd inst. to Miss Martha L. Robinson, dau.
of The Rev. Wm. Robinson, dec'd., by The Rev. Lewis Dawson. All of
Amherst Co.
The Lynchburg Virginian, May 11, 1827, p. 3, c. 3.

WALLER, MISS LUCY ANN - See entry for Archibald Goven.

WALLER, DR. WILLIAM I. married last evening to Miss Maria Norvell, dau. of
William Norvell, Esq., by The Rev. John Early. Bride of Lynchburg;
groom of Petersburg, Va.
The Lynchburg Virginian, Nov. 10, 1831, p. 3, c. 4.

WALLER, WM. M., ESQ. married Sept. 17, 1824 to Miss Sarah A. Garland, dau.
of David S. Garland, Esq., by The Rev. James Boyd. All of Amherst.
The Lynchburg Virginian, Sept. 24, 1824, p. 3.

WALTHALL, R. H. married on 6th inst. to Julian Dinwiddie, dau. of Maj.
Joseph Dinwiddie of Campbell Co., by The Rev. Thomas Burge. Groom
of Buckingham Co., Va.
The Lynchburg Virginian, Dec. 13, 1827, p. 3, c. 4.

WALSH, ROBERT married Thursday evening to Mrs. Elizabeth H. Stocker by The
Rev. Dr. Delancy. Groom editor of the National Gazette.
The Lynchburg Virginian, Nov. 20, 1834, p. 3, c. 4.

WALTMAN, M. MICHAEL married May 15, 1828 to Polly Pittie in Harbaugh's
Valley "after courtship of 50 years". Married by The Rev. Mr. Hemick.
The Lynchburg Virginian, June 12, 1828, p. 3, c. 4.

WALTON, MISS ELIZA - See entry for Cornelius Payne.

WALTON, MISS ELIZA A. - See entry for Dr. David C. Jones.

WALTON, MISS ELIZABETH - See entry for William Bailey.

WALTON, LUCY - See entry for William Thornhill.

WALTON, MISS MARTHA ANN - See entry for Samuel J. Walker.

WALTON, MISS MARY FRANCES PHILADELPHIA - See entry for Samuel D. McDearman.

WARD, BENJAMIN, ESQ. married on 6th inst., 1827 to Miss Elizabeth White,
dau. of Samuel White of Fort Lewis. Married at Fort Lewis, Botetourt
Co., Va. by The Rev. F. G. Smith.
The Lynchburg Virginian, March 9, 1827, p. 3, c. 2.

WARD, MR. CHARLES married on 6th inst. to Miss Martha Ann, dau. of Dr.
Lynch Dillard, by The Rev. G. Dickerson. Both of Pittsylvania Co.
The Lynchburg Virginian, Oct. 25, 1835, p. 3, c. 6.

WARD, HENRY, ESQ. married on 17th inst. to Miss Sarah Cabell, dau. of Dr.
John J. Cabell, by The Rev. Wm. S. Reid. Groom of Pittsylvania,
bride of this place.
The Lynchburg Virginian, March 21, 1831, p. 3, c. 5.

WARD, MISS MILDRED - See entry for Capt. Augustine Leftwich.

WARD, MISS NANCY E. - See entry for Mathew Morris Kerr.

WARD, SETH, JR. married Dec. 30, 1818 to Miss Anne Hendrick by The Rev.
Wm. S. Reid. Both bride and groom of New London.
The Lynchburg Press & Public Advertiser, Jan. 7, 1819, p. 3.

WARD, WILLIAM married on 9th inst. to Miss Eliza M. Adams, dau. of Maj.
John L. Adams, by The Rev. Mr. Burns. All of Pittsylvania.
The Lynchburg Virginian, Nov. 21, 1836, p. 3, c. 4.

WARD, THE REV. WILLIAM NORVELL married on Tues., the 9th ult., to Miss
Mary Blincoe at the home of bride's mother in Leesburg by The Rev.
George Adie. Groom of Bowling Green, Caroline Co., Va.
The Lynchburg Virginian, Aug. 22, 1836, p. 3, c. 5.

WARE, CAPT. JAMES married on 6th inst. to Miss Lucy Eubank, dau. of the
late Geo. Eubank, by The Rev. Chas. H. Page. All of Amherst.
The Lynchburg Virginian, Aug. 13, 1829, p. 3, c. 4.

WARWICK, MISS ANZOLETTA M. - See entry for David Saunders, Jr.

WARWICK, DANIEL I. ESQ. married last Wed. night to Miss Ann E. Norvell,
youngest dau. of the late Wm. Norvell, Esq. of Lynchburg, by The Rev.
Wm. S. Reid. Groom of Amherst Co.
The Lynchburg Virginian, Jan. 12, 1835, p. 3, c. 5.

WARWICK, MISS MARIA M. - See entry for Thomas Leftwich.

WARWICK, ROBERT M. married on 9th ult. to Miss Louisa Thompson, dau. of D.
Thompson of Nottoway Co., Va., by The Rev. Wm. A. Smith. Groom of
Amherst Co.
The Lynchburg Virginian, March 11, 1830, p. 3, c. 3.

WARWICK, MISS SARAH - See entry for Capt. Stith Thompson.

WATERS, MR. JUNIUS married at Towanda, Pa., age 16 to Mrs. Rosina Whiskey,
age 84. "The very best receipt for grog is fresh water and old
whiskey." From the Petersburg Constelation.
The Lynchburg Virginian, July 18, 1836, p. 3, c. 3.

WATKINS, MISS AGNESS - See entry for Capt. Thomas P. Jones.

WATKINS, MISS JUSTINIA - See entry for George Adams.

WATKINS, MISS MARY - See entry for Jesse Moore.

WATKINS, ROBERT married Jan. 31, 1828 to Sarah A. Kidd, dau. of James
Kidd of Nelson Co., by The Rev. James Boyd.
The Lynchburg Virginian, Feb. 21, 1828, p. 3, c. 5.

WATSON, MR. married on 6th inst. to Miss Sarah Wyatt of Charlotte Co. by
The Rev. Sam uel Armistead. Groom of Prince Edward Co.
The Lynchburg Virginian, Nov. 27, 1834, p. 3, c. 5.

WATSON, MRS. - See entry for John Willis.

WATSON, MISS ANNE ELIZA - See entry for James E. Horner.

WATSON, MISS FRANCES - See entry for Samuel Rutherfoard, Esq.

WATSON, MISS MARTHA E. - See entry for Samuel B. Jennings.

WATSON, MISS MARY JANE - See entry for Dr. Alfred Moore.

WATSON, MISS PAMELIA H. - See entry for Mr. Jones W. Burton.

WATSON, WILLIAM B. married on May 28, 1833 to Miss Amanda Melvina Bagby, dau. of Mr. Wm. S. Bagby of Lynchburg, by The Rev. Mr. Thompson of the Methodist Protestant Church. Groom of Danville.
The Lynchburg Virginian, June 6, 1833, p. 3, c. 5.

WATT, MISS JANE M. - See entry for Ludwell L. Dawson.

WATT, MISS LOUISA M. - See entry for Archbald M. Webster.

WATTS, MISS ALICE - See entry for The Rev. Fleming Early A. Saunders.

WATTS, ARTHUR married on 15th ult. near Chillicothe, Ohio to Miss Ellen S. Worthington, dau. of the late Gov. Worthington of Ohio. Groom formerly of Bedford, Va.
The Lynchburg Virginian, July 11, 1831, p. 3, c. 4.

WATTS, MISS FRANCES - See entry for Thomas Jones.

WATTS, GEORGE R. married Sept. 22, 1825 to Miss Elizabeth Ann Loving, dau. of Joseph Loving of Nelson Co., by The Rev. James Boyd. Groom of Nelson Co.
The Lynchburg Virginian, Sept. 29, 1825, p. 3.

WATTS, MR. JOHN H. married on 20th inst. to Miss Sarah A. Pettit, dau. of Mr. James Pettit of Campbell Co., by The Rev. Mr. Abner Early.
The Lynchburg Virginian, Dec. 31, 1832, p. 3, c. 3.

WATTS, RICHARD married on 18th ult. to Isabella Newell, dau. of Capt. Thomas Newell of Botetourt Co., by The Rev. Mr. Houston. Groom of Bedford Co.
The Lynchburg Virginian, June 1, 1826, p. 3, c. 3.

WATTS, ROBERT married Thurs., the 24th inst. to Miss Mary Ann, dau. of Capt. Isaac Rucker, by The Rev. Benjamin R. Dawson. All of Amherst.
The Lynchburg Virginian, Dec. 31, 1835, p. 3, c. 4.

WATTS, THOMAS W. married on 18th inst. to Miss Margaret Catharine Vest by The Rev. Robert Ryland. All of Campbell Co.
The Lynchburg Virginian, Nov. 30, 1829, p. 3, c. 5.

WAUGH, MR. RICHARD J. married to Miss Mary Knight at the home of Wm. H. Knight of New Glasgow (Amherst Co., Va.), by The Rev. Chas. H. Page. All of Amherst Co.
The Lynchburg Virginian, April 30, 1832, p. 3, c. 3.

WAUHOP, JAMES W. married to Miss Matilda M. McCraw, dau. of Wm. McCraw of
   Surry, N. C. Groom of Patrick Co., Va.
   The Lynchburg Virginian, March 30, 1827, p. 3.

WAUHOP, WILLIAM married last Thurs. evening at the residence of Mr. Richard
   Borum to Miss F. Ragland by The Rev. Mr. Dresser. All of Halifax, Va.
   The Lynchburg Virginian, May 21, 1835, p. 3, c. 2.

WEAVER, CAPT. WM. married on 5th inst. to Mrs. Mary Cawthon, widow of
   Robert Cawthon of Amherst Co., by The Rev. Wm. Duncan. Groom of
   Fluvannia Co., Va.
   The Lynchburg Virginian, April 20, 1826, p. 3, c. 4.

WEBB, CEPHAS married on Thurs., 22nd inst., to Miss Eliza M. Schoolfield,
   dau. of Benjamin Schoolfield of this place, by The Rev. Henry B.
   Cowles. Groom of St. Louis, Missouri.
   The Lynchburg Virginian, Nov. 2, 1835, p. 3, c. 4.

WEBB, JAMES, ESQ. married Nov. 14, 1822 to Miss Eliza Irvin by The Rev.
   Dr. Phillips. Bride and groom of Bedford.
   The Lynchburg Virginian, Jan. 7, 1823, p. 3.

WEBB, MISS JANE - See entry for Mr. George Abbitt.

WEBB, Murry married Aug. 3rd to Miss Delana Davidson, dau. of Mr. Stephen
   Davidson, by The Rev. Gabriel Walker. All of Buckingham Co., Va.
   The Lynchburg Virginian, Aug. 19, 1830, p. 3, c. 4.

WEBBER, PETER married March 12th, 1828 to Miss Mildred Frazier, dau. of
   Wm. Frazier, Esq., by The Rev. Abner Early. All of Campbell Co., Va.
   The Lynchburg Virginian, March 19, 1829, p. 3, c. 4.

WEBSTER, MR. ARCHIBALD M. married on 8th inst. to Miss Louisa M. Watt, dau.
   of Col. James Watt of Buckingham Co. by The Rev. John Early.
   The Lynchburg Virginian, Nov. 19, 1832, p. 3, c. 4.

WEBSTER, THE HON. DANIEL married last Sat. in the city of New York to Miss
   Caroline, dau. of Hermon Leroy, Esq. of New York City, by The Rev.
   Dr. Wainwright.
   The Lynchburg Virginian, Dec. 24, 1829, p. 3, c. 6.

WEIDEMYER, HENRY M. married last evening to Miss Sarah Jane Williams,
   eldest dau. of Jehu Williams of the firm of Williams & Victor of
   this town, by The Rev. Dr. Wm. Holcombe. Groom of New York.
   The Lynchburg Virginian, June 23, 1836, p. 3, c. 5.

WELCH, MISS NANCY - See entry for Pleasant Ingram.

WELLS, EDWARD B. married last evening to Miss Elizabeth B. Lewellin by
   The Rev. Edward Cannon. All of Campbell Co., Va.
   The Lynchburg Virginian, Nov. 30, 1826, p. 3.

WEST, MISS ARIANA W. - See entry for Thomas Rosser.

WEST, JOHN W. married Nov. 1, 1832 to Miss Mariar Francis Scott, dau. of
Col. Thomas Scott of Prince Edward Co., by The Rev. Mr. Dance. Groom
of Buckingham Co., Va.
The Lynchburg Virginian, Nov. 12, 1832, p. 3, c. 5.

WEST, MRS. MARY R. - See entry for Henry L. Duffel.

WETHERILL, MISS HARRIET - See entry for David Kyle.

WETHERS, EDWARD married June 3, 1819 to Miss Evelina Payne, dau. of Philip
Payne, Esq. of Campbell Co., by The Rev. John S. Lee. Groom of
Fauquier Co.
The Lynchburg Press & Public Advertiser, June 10, 1819, p. 3, c. 5.

WHARTON, MISS ANN A. - See entry for Nelson Sale, Esq.

WHARTON, JOHN A. married on 23rd ult. to Miss Isabella Brown, dau. of
Lyman Brown, Esq. of New Boston, Mass., by The Rev. Levi White.
Married at New Boston, Mass.
The Lynchburg Virginian, April 5, 1830, p. 3, c. 3.

WHARTON, MISS SOPHIA - See entry for Capt. Richard Davis.

WHEATLY, DR. JAMES married Nov. 9, 1824 to Miss Mildred L. Williams in
Lynchburg by The Rev. Wm. S. Reid. Groom of Fauquier Co., Va.
The Lynchburg Virginian, Nov. 12, 1824, p. 3.

WHEELAN, MARTIN married Dec. 25, 1828 married to Miss Elizabeth Price from
Unity, Montgomery Co., Md. Groom from Falls of St. Anthony, Miss.
The Lynchburg Virginian, Jan. 12, 1829, p. 3, c. 5.

WHEELER, GEORGE married March 31, 1825 to Miss Rhoda Cannifax, dau. of Mrs.
Isabella Cannifax, by The Rev. Samuel Davidson. Bride of Campbell Co.
The Lynchburg Virginian, April 14, 1825, p. 3, c. 4.

WHEELER, JOEL M. married on 21st inst. to Miss Lucinda, dau. of Mr. Charles
Purvis. Bride and groom of Nelson Co., Va.
The Lynchburg Virginian, Jan. 2, 1832, p. 3, c. 5.

WHEELER, MICAJAH married Tues., July 29, 1828, to Miss Elizabeth Smith by
The Rev. James Boyd. A.. of Nelson Co., Va.
The Lynchburg Virginian, Aug. 7, 1828, p. 3, c. 5.

WHEELER, MR. SAMUEL O. married Nov. 15th to Miss Mary Ann Furbush, dau. of
Mr. Wm. Furbush, by The Rev. David Fisher. Both of Campbell Co., Va.
The Lynchburg Virginian, Dec. 31, 1832, p. 3, c. 3.

WHISKEY, MRS. ROSINA - See entry for Mr. Junius Waters.

WHITE, CASANDRA CAROLINE - See entry for Dr. John L. Cole

WHITE, MISS EDITHA - See entry for Dr. Gabriel S. Fisher.

WHITE, MISS ELIZABETH - See entry for Benj. Ward, Esq.

WHITE, MISS EUPHENIA - See entry for Nathan Stedman.

WHITE, MISS FRANCES M. - See entry for Robert S. McReynolds.

WHITE, MR. HUGH, JR. married Tues. the 13th inst. to Miss Ann B. J. Gordon, dau. of John M. Gordon, Esq. of this place, by The Rev. Jacob D. Mitchell. Groom is merchant of Abingdon, Va.
The Lynchburg Virginian, Oct. 25, 1835, p. 3, c. 6.

WHITE, MISS JANE G. R. WHITE - See entry for Samuel Carroll.

WHITE, MISS JULIA ANN - See entry for William Harvey.

WHITE, MISS MARTHA - See entry for Robert Andrews.

WHITE, MISS MARY JANE - See entry for John A. Mackinder.

WHITE, MISS MARY P. - See entry for Joseph F. Roberts.

WHITE, SAMUEL married on 13th inst. to Miss Martha Jackson, dau. of Josiah Jackson of Campbell Co., by The Rev. Samuel Armistead. Groom of Charlotte Co., Va.
The Lynchburg Virginian, Oct. 27, 1831, p. 3, c. 4.

WHITEHEAD, MISS ELIZABETH - See entry for Capt. Asa Stratton.

WHITLEY, CHARLES married Oct. 17, 1822 to Miss Anne C. Thompson, dau. of Capt. Anderson Thompson of Bedford Co., by The Rev. Samuel Phillips. Groom of Bedford.
The Lynchburg Virginian, Nov. 1, 1822, p. 3.

WHITLOCKE, DR. ACHILLES married April 22, 1833 at Caswell Co., N.C. to Miss Letitia W. Terry, eldest dau. of Wm. Terry, Esq. of Liberty, Bedford Co., Va., by Elder John P. Harrison of the Methodist Church.
The Lynchburg Virginian, April 29, 1833, p. 3, c. 5.

WHITLOCKE, MISS MARY - See entry for George C. Mosely.

WHITLOW, MISS ELIZABETH ANN - See entry for Robert Callaway.

WHITLOW, JOSIAH H. married on 26th ult. at Milton, N.C. to Miss Lucy Ann Bradley, dau. of Mr. Collin Bradley of Campbell Co., Va., by The Rev. Samuel Bryant.
The Lynchburg Virginian, May 9, 1836, p. 3, c. 3.

WHITTEKER, MISS ELIZABETH E. - See entry for Maj. John E. Norvell.

WHITTINGTON, MISS ELIZA ANN - See entry for Charles Murrell.

WIATT, MISS MARTHA V. - See entry for Wm. Massie.

WIATT, MISS MARY - See entry for David Hoffman.

WIGGIN, MISS SARAH - See entry for Mark Roberts.

WILBOURN, ROBERT E. married on 11th inst. to Miss Frances H. Scott of Nelson Co., Va. Married at residence of Dr. Frederick G. Peters.
The Lynchburg Virginian, Oct. 17, 1836, p. 3, c. 3.

WILCOX, JAMES M., ESQ. married on 15th inst. to Miss Mary Ann Shields Lamb, only dau. of John F. Lamb, M.D. of Frankfort, Pa., by The Rt. Rev. Bishop White.
The Lynchburg Virginian, Nov. 29, 1832, p. 3, c. 4.

WILCOX, MISS MARY E. - See entry for John Thompson Brown, Esq.

WILCOX, MRS. - See entry for Gen. Wm. R. Ashley.

WILDER, MISS ELECTRA B. - See entry for Gustarvus Richards.

WILEY, FERDINAND M. married on 21st inst. at Fincastle, (Botetourt Co., Va.) to Miss Jane M. Cawthorn by The Rev. Jacob Carper.
The Lynchburg Virginian, July 30, 1835, p. 3, c. 5.

WILKERSON, OWEN married on 4th inst. to Miss Rachel Musgrove, age 19, dau. of Benjamin Musgrove. Groom aged 56. Married in Bedford Co., Va.
The Lynchburg Virginian, March 11, 1830, p. 3, c. 3.

WILKINS, ROBERT S. married Nov. 15, 1821 to Miss Elizabeth Hardwick by The Rev. Joseph Carson. Bride and groom of Lynchburg.
The Lynchburg Press, Nov. 16, 1821, p. 3.

WILKINSON, MR. ALBERT M. married on 14th inst. to Miss Mary Archer, dau. of Mr. William Moore of Prince Edward Co., by The Rev. Thomas Jones. Groom of Campbell Co.
The Lynchburg Virginian, Oct. 19, 1835, p. 3, c. 4.

WILKS, BENJAMIN married Dec. 20, 1827 to Miss Matilda Duffel by The Rev. Mr. Ryland. All of Lynchburg.
The Lynchburg Virginian, Jan. 3, 1828, p. 3, c. 2.

WILLIAMS, ALBERT G. married on 2nd inst. to Miss Matilda M. Stoner, dau. of Mr. Dan'l Stoner of Botetourt Co., by The Rev. Sam'l Philips. Groom of Bedford Co.
The Lynchburg Virginian, June 23, 1836, p. 3, c. 5.

WILLIAMS, MISS ANN - See entry for Robert Leckie.

WILLIAMS, MISS CAROLINE SOPHIA MARIA JULIANNE WORTLEY MONTAGUE JOAN OF ARC - See entry for Alexander Philip Socrates Amelius Caesar Hannibal Marcellus George Washington Treadwell.

WILLIAMS, DOC. married in Knoxville, Tenn. to Miss Nancy, dau. of Mr. James Isreal, by E. Nelson, Esq. Groom age 100. All of Knox Co., East Tennessee.
The Lynchburg Virginian, Sept. 4, 1934, p. 3, c. 4.

WILLIAMS, MRS. ELIZABETH - See entry for Richard G. Morris.

WILLIAMS, MISS ELMIRA - See entry for Samuel Christopher Clark.

WILLIAMS, MISS EMILY LOUISA - See entry for Bethel Washburn Henson.

WILLIAMS, FIELDING L. married on 14th inst. to Miss Frances Boyd, dau. of
Wm. Boyd, by The Rev. Metcalf. Married in Mecklinburg Co. Groom of
Lynchburg.
The Lynchburg Virginian, Feb. 20, 1827, p. 3, c. 6.

WILLIAMS, GEORGE married on 14th inst. to Frances E. Kincaid by The Rev.
Isaac Paul. All of Nelson Co., Va.
The Lynchburg Virginian, Nov. 23, 1826, p. 3.

WILLIAMS, MISS JANE - See entry for James Livingston.

WILLIAMS, MISS MILDRED L. - See entry for Dr. James Wheatly.

WILLIAMS, COL. R. W. married Tues. evening last in Washington to Miss
Rebecca Branch, dau. of the Hon. John Branch of North Carolina.
Groom from Tallahasse.
The Lynchburg Virginian, April 28, 1831, p. 3, c. 4.

WILLIAMS, MISS SARAH - See entry for Walter H. Middlton.

WILLIAMS, MISS SARAH JANE - See entry for Henry M. Weidmeyer.

WILLIAMS, MISS SARAH L. - See entry for Dr. Ambrose R. Marr.

WILLIAMSON, BENJAMIN married March 26, 1822 to Miss Margaret Hubbard, dau.
of Stephen Hubbard, by The Rev. Dr. Samuel Phillips. Both of Bedford
County.
The Lynchburg Press, April 5, 1822, p. 3, c. 4.

WILLIAMSON, CAPT. DANIEL W. married on 15th inst. to Miss Martha Ann
Armistead, dau. of The Rev. Samuel Armistead of Campbell Co., Va.,
by The Rev. John Davidson. Groom of Charlotte Co., Va.
The Lynchburg Virginian, Feb. 28, 1831, p. 3, c. 4.

WILLIAMSON, MISS FRANCES - See entry for Jordan Taylor.

WILLIAMSON, WILLIAM married Dec. 19, 1822 to Miss Parmelia F. Jackson by
The Rev. Samuel Armistead. Bride and groom of Charlotte Co.
The Lynchburg Virginian, Dec. 27, 1822, p. 3.

WILLIS, JOHN married June 18, 1817 to Mrs. Watson. Broth bride and groom
of Amherst Co., Va.
The Lynchburg Press, June 20, 1817, p. 3.

WILLIS, MR. WESTERN married on 20th inst. to Miss Louisa Chaney. All of
Pittsylvania.
The Lynchburg Virginian, Dec. 31, 1832, p. 3, c. 2.

WILLS, BURFORD married Dec. 31, 1829 to Miss Nancy E. Lee, second dau. of
Francis L. Lee of Montgomery Co., Va., by The Rev. N. H. Cobbs.
Groom lived in Bedford Co. Married in New London.
The Lynchburg Virginian, Jan. 4, 1830, p. 3, c. 6.

WILLS, MISS ELIZABETH - See entry for Richard Adams.

WILLS, MISS FRANCES - See entry for George Griggs.

WILLS, MRS. MARY G. - See entry for John Seay.

WILLS, MISS MILDRED - See entry for Willis P. Wills.

WILLS, MISS REBECCA ANN - See entry for James Alexander.

WILLS, MR. WILLIS H. married Sept. 22, 1825 to Miss Elizabeth Peters, dau. of Mr. Elisha Peters, by The Rev. James Boyd. All of Nelson Co.
The Lynchburg Virginian, Sept. 29, 1825, p. 3, c. 5.

WILLS, WILLIS P. married July 28th to Miss Mildred Wills by The Rev. James Boyd. All of Nelson Co., Va.
The Lynchburg Virginian, Aug. 6, 1829, p. 3, c. 5.

WILMORE, REUBEN married on Feb. 28, 1828 to Miss Sarah Stinner by The Rev. Charles H. Page. All of Amherst Co., Va.
The Lynchburg Virginian, March 13, 1828, p. 3, c. 5.

WILSON, ALEXANDER H. married on 10th inst. to Miss Mary Jane, eldest dau. of Mr. Wm. K. Lee, by The Rev. Wm. Hammersly. All of Campbell Co.
The Lynchburg Virginian, Dec. 17, 1835, p. 3, c. 3.

WILSON, JOSEPH, ESQ. married on 13th inst. to Mary J. Campbell, dau. of Robert Campbell, Esq. of Bedford Co., by The Rev. Nicholas Hamner Cobbs. Groom clerk of Bedford Superior Court.
The Lynchburg Virginian, March 19, 1829, p. 3, c. 4.

WILSON, MISS MARTHA - See entry for Pleasant Waddill.

WILSON, CAPT. ROBERT married Nov. 6, 1817 to Miss Catharine A. Pannill, dau. of Samuel Pannill of Campbell Co., by The Rev. Griffith Dickerson. Groom of Pittsylvania Co.
The Lynchburg Press, Nov. 14, 1817, p. 3, c. 3.

WILSON, MISS SALLY - See entry for Benjamin Miles.

WIMBISH, MR. ABRAM W. married March 1, 1827 to Miss Judith A. Pannill, dau. of Sam'l Pannill of Campbell Co., by The Rev. Robert Hurt. Groom of Halifax Co.
The Lynchburg Virginian, March 9, 1827, p. 3, c. 2.

WIMBISH, MISS MARY A. - See entry for John W. Young.

WINFREE, CHRISTOPHER married on 20th ult., 1817 to Miss Cornelia Meyer Tilden, of Fredericksburg, Va. Groom of Lynchburg.
The Lynchburg Press, Dec. 5, 1817, p. 3, c. 4.

WINFREE, MISS LUCY ADELINE - See entry for Francis Nash.

WINFREY, MISS MARY A. - See entry for Watson Cauldwell.

WINGFIELD, MISS JERUSHA - See entry for William M. Bowling.

WINGFIELD, JOHN married on 10th inst. to Miss Frances, eldest dau. of Mr. Wm. Oglesby, by The Rev. Thomas Jones. All of Bedford.
The Lynchburg Virginian, Dec. 17, 1835, p. 3, c. 3.

WINN, MISS ELIZA - See entry for The Hon. Powhatan Ellis.

WINSTON, MISS CAROLINE - See entry for Henry S. Peyton.

WINSTON, DR. FAYETTE married on 6th inst. to Miss Martha A. Dix, dau. of T. Dix, Esq., by The Rev. W. Taylor. All of Henry Co., Va. The Lynchburg Virginian, June 21, 1832, p. 3, c. 4.

WINSTON, MISS NANCY - See entry for Dr. John Dillard.

WINSTON, NATHANIEL married May 6, 1819 to Miss Zelinda Lynch, dau. of Edward Lynch of Lynchburg. Groom of Richmond. The Lynchburg Press & Public Advertiser, May 10, 1819, p. 3.

WITCHER, MISS NANCY - See entry for Thomas King.

WITHERS, CHAS. A. married last Tues. to Miss Matilda Lynch, dau. of Edward Lynch, by The Rev. F. G. Smith. All of this place. The Lynchburg Virginian, Dec. 25, 1828, p. 3, c. 3.

WOLTZ, WILLIAM F. married on 12th inst. to Miss Mary M. Feazel, dau. of Mr. Jacob Feazel of this county, by The Rev. Samuel Phillips. Groom formerly of Botetourt Co., Va. The Lynchburg Virginian, May 26, 1836, p. 3, c. 3.

WOOD, MISS AGNES W. - See entry for Robert G. Branch.

WOOD, MISS ELEANOR - See entry for William A. Harris.

WOOD, MISS ELIZABETH ANN - See entry for Thomas B. Wright.

WOOD, MR. JAMES married on 21st inst. to Miss Sarah Reid, dau. of Obidiah Reid, Esq., by The Rev. Henry Brown. All of Amherst Co. The Lynchburg Virginian, March 25, 1833, p. 3, c. 5.

WOOD, MISS JANE L. - See entry for Joseph Hardy.

WOOD, MRS. MARTHA - See entry for _____ Jennings.

WOODING, NATHANIEL W. married on 26th ult. to Miss Mary Barger by The Rev. Mr. Dickenson. Bride and groom residents of Pittsylvania Co., Va. The Lynchburg Virginian, April 2, 1835, p. 3, c. 4.

WOODROOF, MRS. ELIZABETH - See entry for Samuel Read, Esq.

WOODROOF, MISS E. MATILDA - See entry for Wm. C. Leftwich.

WOODROOF, MISS MARY - See entry for Nathaniel Rucker.

WOODROOF, MISS SARAH ANN - See entry for Walter B. Boswell.

WOODS, GEORGE married Feb. 19, 1824, to Miss Abigail Sample, dau. of John Sample, by The Rev. Jos. Jackson. All of Franklin Co. The Lynchburg Virginian, March 5, 1824, p. 3.

WOODS, MISS MARY - See entry for Hugh Barclay.

WOODS, ROBERT T., ESQ. married on 28th ult. at Franklin Court-house to Miss
   Ann Tait, dau. of Caleb Tait, Esq. All of Franklin Co.
   The Lynchburg Virginian, June 11, 1829, p. 3, c. 5.

WOODS, MISS SUSAN A. - See entry for Nathaniel Massie.

WOODSON, MISS ANN M. - See entry for Jonathan H. Hatcher.

WOODSON, MR. BENJAMIN married last Tues. to Miss Sarah Hood, dau. of Mr.
   Hobson Hood of Campbell Co., by The Rev. John Walker.
   The Lynchburg Virginian, Feb. 16, 1827, p. 3, c. 5.

WOODSON, EDWIN H. married on Sept. 24, 1830 to Mary Goldin of Lynchburg
   by The Rev. John S. Lee.
   The Lynchburg Virginian, Sept. 27, 1830, p. 3, c. 5.

WOODSON, MISS SARAH - See entry for Edwin D. Moore.

WOODY, MISS SARAH - See entry for Lorenza D. Aistrop.

WOOLERYMING, _____ married on Thurs. last, 20th inst. to Miss Dolly P.
   North by The Rev. Mr. Johns. Bride & groom of Campbell Co., Va.
   The Lynchburg Press and Public Advertiser, May 27, 1819, p. 3, c. 5.

WOOTON, JOHN married Dec. 8, 1830 to Miss Lucinda Redd by The Rev. John C.
   Traylor. All of Henry County, Va.
   The Lynchburg Virginian, Dec. 16, 1830, p. 3, c. 2.

WORRELL, MISS ELOISE - See entry for Edward V. Sparhawk.

WORSHAM, MISS EMILY - See entry for Alva R. Townly.

WORSHAM, MR. SAMUEL married on 14th inst. to Miss Frances East by The Rev.
   Benjamin Kidd. All of Pittsylvania Co.
   The Lynchburg Virginian, May 21, 1832, p. 3, c. 3.

WORTHAM, ELLIOTT married Jan. 1, 1824 to Miss Nancy B. Davis, dau. of
   Capt. James Davis, by The Rev. John Davis. Both of Amherst Co.
   The Lynchburg Virginian, Jan. 9, 1824, p. 3, c. 4.

WORTHINGTON, MISS ELLEN S. - See entry for Mr. Arthur Watts.

WRIGHT, JOEL married to Miss Amanda Jordan, dau. of Leroy Jordan, by The
   Rev. James Leftwich. All of Bedford.
   The Lynchburg Virginian, Jan. 17, 1828, p. 3, c. 4.

WRIGHT, MISS MARTHA R. - See entry for The Rev. Geo. W. Charlton.

WRIGHT, THOMAS B. married Aug. 22, 1832 to Miss Elizabeth Ann Wood, dau.
   of Mr. Joseph Wood, by The Rev. Thomas Jones. All of Campbell Co.
   The Lynchburg Virginian, Aug. 27, 1832, p. 3, c. 5.

WYATT, MISS SARAH - See entry for _____ Watson.

WYLLIE, ALLEN J. married June 15, 1820 to Miss Martha Holcombe, dau. of
John Holcombe of Lynchburg.
The Lynchburg Press & Public Advertiser, June 27, 1820, p. 3.

WYLLIE, GEO. A. married in Summer Co., Tenn. to Miss Elizabeth Elliott,
dau. of Col. George Elliott of Summer Co., Tenn. Groom of Halifax,Va.
The Lynchburg Virginian, Jan. 17, 1831, p. 3, c. 4.

X - Y

YANCEY, MISS MARTHA - See entry for David Rhodes.

YANCEY, JAMES M. married June 6, 1833 in Caswell, N.C. to Miss Ann Shoemaker,
dau. of Mr. Lindsey Shoemaker, by Benjamin C. West. All of Lynchburg.
The Lynchburg Virginian, June 13, 1833, p. 3, c. 4.

YANCEY, ROBERT J. married on 21st ult. in Wythe Co. to Miss Catherine L.
Ross of Wythe Co., by The Rev. L. S. Marshall.
The Lynchburg Virginian, Nov. 2, 1829, p. 3, c. 5.

YATES, CALOHILL married Jan. 22, 1828 to Miss Martha Motley, dau. of John
Motley of Pittsylvania Co., Va. Groom of Bedford.
The Lynchburg Virginian, Feb. 14, 1828, p. 3, c. 5.

YEATMAN, MRS. JANE - See entry for The Hon. John Bell.

YOUNG, MR. GEORGE married on 22nd ult. to Miss Nancy Jane Agnew, dau. of
Samuel Agnew, by The Rev. Michael Howery. All of Floyd County, Va.
The Lynchburg Virginian, Feb. 9, 1835, p. 3, c. 4.

YOUNG, JOHN W. married on 23rd inst. to Miss Mary A., dau. of Mrs. Nancy
Wimbish of Halifax, by The Rev. A. M. Poindexter.
The Lynchburg Virginian, Dec. 31, 1835, p. 3, c. 4.

YOUNG, SAMUEL married Dec. 22, 1823 to Miss Frances Beckham by The Rev.
Wm. S. Reid. Bride and groom of Lynchburg.
The Lynchburg Virginian, Jan. 2, 1824, p. 3.

YOUNG, MISS SARAH - See entry for Hezekiah Farris.

Z

Deaths from Lynchburg, Virginia Newspapers

ADAMS, JAMES killed in Alleghany Co., Virginia.
The Lynchburg Press, Dec. 7, 1819, p. 2.

ADAMS, JOHN, President of the United States, died July 4, 1826, in his 90's.
The Lynchburg Virginian, July 17, 1826, p. 3, c. 3.

ADAMS, DR. JOHN died June 26, 1825. He was Mayor of Richmond.
The Lynchburg Virginian, June 27, 1825, p. 3.

ADAMS, PARHAM died Aug. 30, 1831 at Lynchburg. His soda-fountain blew up. He was "in the prime of life."
The Lynchburg Press, Aug. 31, 1831, p. 1.

ADAMS, PETER BOYLSTON, ESQ. died a few weeks ago, age 85, in Quincy, Mass. Brother of President John Adams, late President of the U.S.A.
The Lynchburg Virginian, Aug. 1, 1823, p. 3, c. 4.

ADAMS, WILLIAM A. died Dec. 15, 1822. Age 26. Survived by parents. Son of John Adams, Sr. of Pittsylvania Co.
The Lynchburg Virginian, Jan. 3, 1823, p. 3.

ADCOCK, E. died on the 20th Oct. in the 25th year of his age at Colonel W. Coleman's, Amherst Court House.
The Lynchburg Virginian, Oct. 31, 1831, p. 3, c. 4.

ADIE, MRS. ELEANOR died on 30th ult. in Richmond, Va. Late consort of Mr. Samuel P. Adie of that place. Deceased was Miss Bennett who resided a few months in Lynchburg.
The Lynchburg Virginian, Jan. 8, 1835, p. 3, c. 5.

AKERS, JOHN died on Jan. 9, 1822 in Nelson Co. Survived by parents. He was the son of William Akers.
The Lynchburg Press, Jan. 25, 1822, p. 3, c. 4.

ALDRIDGE, MRS. CATHERINE died on 10th Dec. 1825 in Tuscumbia, Alabama. She was consort of Thomas Aldridge. She was recently of Amherst Co., Va.
The Lynchburg Virginian, Dec. 29, 1825, p. 3, c. 4.

ALDRIDGE, COL. THOMAS died on Dec. 24, 1832, age 54 years, at Tuscaloosa, Alabama. Formerly of Amherst Co. Resident of Ala. for last 8 yrs. From the *Tuscaloosa Alabamian*, Jan. 6th.
The Lynchburg Virginian, Jan. 21, 1833, p. 3, c. 4.

ALEXANDER, WILLIAM died on Friday, the 8th ult. at his residence in Patrick Co., age 79. Became Professor of Religion. Member of Presbyterian Church. He had 3 wives and 21 children.
The Lynchburg Press, April 5, 1822, p. 3, c. 4.

ALLEN, CAPT. ANSON died on Dec. 10, 1832 at Blue Sulphur Springs, Greenbrier Co. formerly of Lynchburg. He died after painful illness of many weeks.
The Lynchburg Virginian, Dec. 20, 1832, p. 3, c. 5.

ALLEN, JAMES died on Feb. 22, 1814 at St. Catharines, Mississippi
   Territory. Was formerly of Virginia.
   The Lynchburg Press, April 28, 1814, p. 3, c. 3.

ALLEN, PAUL died on Saturday. Was of Baltimore. "A writer of considerable
   talents."
   The Lynchburg Virginian, Aug. 31, 1826, p. 3, c. 3.

ANDERSON, CAROLINE K. died on Feb. 25th. Age 18. Was of Lynchburg.
   The Lynchburg Virginian, March 13, 1827, p. 3, c. 5.

ANDERSON, MRS. ELIZABETH died on March 26, 1833, age 19. Deceased was
   of Campbell Co., the wife of Jeremiah E. Anderson. He was member
   of M. E. Church.
   The Lynchburg Virginian, April 11, 1833, p. 3, c. 5.

ANDERSON, FRANCIS died March 13, 1818, age 77. She was consort of
   Col. Nelson Anderson of Bedford Co.
   The Lynchburg Press, March 20, 1818, p. 3, c. 2.

ANDERSON, MR. JACOB died on Nov. 20, 1832 near St. Louis, Mo. Reported
   also in St. Louis Republican. Formerly of the firm of Brown and
   Anderson of Lynchburg and more recently a resident of Campbell Co.
   The Lynchburg Virginian, Jan. 7, 1833, p. 3, c. 3.

ANDERSON, JAMES died Dec. 31, 1821, age 58 years, at his residence in
   Franklin Co. Survived by "affectionate widow and children."
   The Lynchburg Press, Jan. 18, 1822, p. 3, c. 4.

ANDERSON, JAMES C. died July 4th in 23rd year of his age at residence
   of his father in Callaway Co., Missouri. Formerly of Campbell Co.,Va.
   The Lynchburg Virginian, Aug. 10, 1837, p. 3, c. 3.

ANDERSON, JOHN died Jan. 28, 1828 in New Castle, England "in advanced
   age." He and his wife are buried in the same grave.
   The Lynchburg Virginian, April 14, 1828, p. 3, c. 5.

ANDERSON, MRS. JOHN died Jan. 28, 1828 in New Castle, England "in
   advanced age." She and husband buried in same grave.
   The Lynchburg Virginian, April 14, 1828, p. 3, c. 5.

ANDERSON, THE REV. PEYTON died at Culpeper Court House. He was a
   Methodist Preacher, and was the Presiding Elder of the James
   River District.
   The Lynchburg Virginian, Sept. 12, 1823, p. 3.

ANDERSON, SARAH died on Sept. 10th; age 20, in Missouri. She was the
   dau. of James and Elizabeth Cox and granddaughter of Capt. John
   Gills of Bedford County. Member of Methodist Protestant Church.
   The Lynchburg Virginian, March 23, 1835, p. 3, c. 5.

ANDERSON, WILLIAM, ESQ. died on 10th inst. "Struck by lightning at his
plantation on Staunton River in Campbell Co." He was High-Sheriff
of Campbell Co. Was 49 years old. Left widow and 10 children.
The Lynchburg Star, June 19, 1806, p. 3, c. 4.

ANDERSON, WILLIAM W. died April 28, 1828 in his 17th year in Halifax
Co. at residence of Mr. Allen S. Fleshman.
The Lynchburg Virginian, June 5, 1828, p. 3, c. 4.

ANDREWS, PEGGY died on 21st inst. in Amherst Co. She left husband and
an infant. She was consort of William Andrews.
The Lynchburg Virginian, April 13, 1826, p. 3, c. 3.

ANDREWS, WILLIAM died Dec. 18, 1818 in Lynchburg. He was a native of
Scotland. He had lived in Va. for 20 years and also lived at
Charlotte Court House.
The Lynchburg Press & Public Advertiser, Dec. 21, 1818, p. 3, c. 4.

ANTHONY, CHRISTOPHER, ESQ. died yesterday morning in this place.
The Lynchburg Virginian, Oct. 1, 1835, p. 3, c. 4.

ANTHONY, MARY ANN died on 25th ult., the youngest dau. of James Anthony.
The Lynchburg Virginian, Dec. 8, 1825, p. 3, c. 5.

ANTHONY, SALLY died Jan. 14, 1822. She was the dau. of Col. Mark Anthony
of Bedford.
The Lynchburg Press, Feb. 1, 1822, p. 3, c. 3.

ANTHONY, THOMAS died Jan. 17, 1822 at father's residence. Was son of Col.
Mark Anthony of Bedford Co.
The Lynchburg Press, Feb. 1, 1822, p. 3, c. 3.

APPLING, THOMAS died Sept. 6, 1835, age 80, in Amherst Co., Va. He was
"A soldier of the Revolution when he served three short tours, at
that time living in Albemarle."
The Lynchburg Virginian, Sept. 17, 1835, p. 3, c. 5.

ARMISTEAD, MRS. FRANCES died on Friday, Nov. 11, inst. Age 21. Was of
Campbell Co. and consort of Mr. Samuel M. Armistead.
The Lynchburg Virginian, Nov. 27, 1834, p. 3, c. 5.

ARMISTEAD, JOHN S. of Lexington, Kentucky, cadet at West Point, drowned.
He was a nephew of Col. W. K. Armistead.
The Lynchburg Virginian, Feb. 22, 1825, p. 3, c. 1.

ARMSTRONG, MISS SARAH B. died on 25th ult., age 21, at Dr. Kincaid's in
Nelson Co.
The Lynchburg Virginian, March 21, 1836, p. 3, c. 2.

ASGILL, GEN. SIR CHARLES, BART. died in England, age about 70. Was
Captain and Prisoner to the American Arms in Revolutionary War.
Gen. Washington countermanded the orders given for his execution.
The Lynchburg Virginian, Oct. 3, 1823, p. 3, c. 4.

AUSTIN, MISS ANN died on April 18, 1833, age 23 years. Was eldest dau. of Dr. Wm. W. Austin of Bedford.
The Lynchburg Virginian, May 6, 1833, p. 3, c. 4.

AUSTIN, MRS. LOCKY died on 29th of April, age 44 years. Was mother of Miss Ann Austin who had died on April 18th. Survived by husband and 11 children, the youngest 11 days old. She was the wife of Dr. Wm. W. Austin.
The Lynchburg Virginian, May 6, 1833, p. 3, c. 4.

B

BABBIT, LT. F. H. killed on board the U.S. Frigate President.
The Lynchburg Press, March 9, 1815, p. 3, c. 5.

BABER, GEORGE died Jan. 5, age 48. He was of Liberty. He left a widow and children.
The Lynchburg Press & Public Advertiser, Jan. 28, 1819, p. 3, c. 4.

BAGWELL, COL. CHARLES died on the 24th ult. Deceased of Accomac Co., Eastern Shore. Murdered while driving home from Drummond Town.
The Lynchburg Press & Public Advertiser, June 14, 1819, p. 3, c. 5.

BAILEY, JOHN died Aug. 29, 1823 at Warm Springs. Was 27 years old and from Lynchburg.
The Lynchburg Virginian, Sept. 5, 1823, p. 3.

BAILEY, MRS. MARY died June 11, 1819; of Pulaski, Giles Co., Tenn. Consort of Mr. Parks Bailey of Pulaski. Formerly of Lunenburg Co., Va.
The Lynchburg Press & Public Advertiser, July 27, 1819, p. 3, c. 5.

BAILEY, VINCENT S. died on Thursday last, age 33. Resident of this place. He left a wife and infant.
The Lynchburg Virginian, Jan. 2, 1826, p. 3.

BAKER, MRS. MARY ANN R. died at Wilmington, N.C. She was formerly Miss Gilliam of Lynchburg.
The Lynchburg Virginian, June 25, 1829, p. 3, c. 4.

BALDWIN, DR. CORNELIUS died on Sunday last. Deceased was of Middletown. Copied from Winchester Republican of Sept. 16, 1828.
The Lynchburg Virginian, Oct. 2, 1828, p. 3, c. 5.

BALDWIN, DR. ZEBULON died on July 14, 1795 in Lynchburg. He was a resident of Lynchburg and is survived by his wife.
The Lynchburg & Farmer's Gazette, July 18, 1795, p. 3, c. 4.

BALL, THE HON. WILLIAM LEE died in Washington City, age 45 years. He was a member of the House of Representatives from State of Virginia.
The Lynchburg Virginian, March 12, 1824, pp. 2 and 3.

BANE, CAPT. JAMES died at father's residence in Montgomery Co., age 30 yrs.
Survived by his father. "An honest man is the noblest work of God
and such was Capt. Bane."
The Lynchburg Virginian, Jan. 21, 1836, p. 3, c. 4.

BANGHAM,   Died July 12, 1795, age 14 years. Drowned at
Ferrall's Mill, a few miles from Lynchburg. He was the son of
Humphrey Bangham.
The Lynchburg & Farmer's Gazette, July 18, 1795, p. 3, c. 4.

BARKSDALE, MRS. HARRIET T. died May 3, 1828, age 24 years, at"Locust Hill"
in Halifax Co. She was the wife of Dr. Claiborne Barksdale. She was
survived by her husband and 3 children.
The Lynchburg Virginian, June 9, 1828, p. 3, c. 5.

BARKSDALE, ROBERT died on 7th inst., age 18.
The Lynchburg Virginian, Feb. 13, 1826, p. 3, c. 4.

BARNEY, COMMANDER a veteran Officer.
The Lynchburg Press, Dec. 21, 1818, p. 3.

BARTEE, WILLIAM D. died on Sunday the 17th ult. in Fincastle, Botetourt
Co., Va. He was formerly of Lynchburg.
The Lynchburg Press, Feb. 1, 1819, p. 3, c. 5.

BASSHAM, JOHN died on the 12th inst. at his residence in Franklin Co., Va.
He left a numerous family.
The Lynchburg Virginian, July 27, 1826, p. 3, c. 2.

BEAUMONT, MRS. CHARLES W., JR. died on Sunday, 7th of August. Deceased
was an instructress.
The Lynchburg Virginian, August 22, 1831, p. 3, c. 4.

BECKHAM, MRS. MARY died on May 4, 1833. She was long a resident of this
place and a member of the M. E. Church.
The Lynchburg Virginian, May 6, 1833, p. 3, c. 5.

BECKHAM, MRS. SARAH died Feb. 4th in Amherst, age 59 years. She is
survived by husband and 4 children.
The Lynchburg Press, March 8, 1822, p. 3.

BECKWITH, SIR JENNINGS died on Nov. 13th, age 72, at Mt. Airy, Richmond
Co., Va. Deceased was son of Jonathan Beckwith and grandson of Sir
Marmaduke Beckwith, Bart.
The Lynchburg Virginian, Nov. 30, 1835, p. 3, c. 4.

BEDELL, THE REV. DR. died on Saturday morning at Baltimore, Md.
The Lynchburg Virginian, Sept. 11, 1834, p. 3, c. 5.

BEIRNE, GEORGE, ESQ. died on Dec. 1, 1832 at Union, Monroe Courthouse,
Va. (now W. Va.) He was for many years a highly respected citizen
of Union. He leaves a wife and 9 children.
The Lynchburg Virginian, Dec. 20, 1832, p. 3, c. 5.

BELL, MRS. EVELINE B. died Dec. 11, 1834, age 25 years. She was the consort of Alfred A. Bell.
The Lynchburg Virginian, Jan. 19, 1835, p. 3, c. 4.

BELTON, WILLIAM H. died on Florida side of St. Mary's River, Traders Hill. Member of 4th regiment U.S. Infantry and died of a bullet wound.
The Lynchburg Press, May 13, 1819, p. 3, c. 2.

BERGER, MRS. CATHERINE died on 24th inst. 1830, in the 51st year of her age. She was the consort of Mr. J. Berger of the County of Pittsylvania. "An affectionate mother." She was a member of the Baptist Church for 34 years.
The Lynchburg Virginian, Feb. 7, 1831, p. 3, c. 4.

BERGER, MR. JACOB, JR. died 13th inst., age 57 years, 2 months, 15 days. Died at his residence in Pittsylvania Co.
The Lynchburg Virginian, March 21, 1833, p. 3, c. 3.

BERKELY, PRINCESS died Jan. 12th in Naples. Formerly known as Lady Craven. "Celebrated in America because of the ardent part she took in the American Cause."
The Lynchburg Virginian, April 14, 1828, p. 3, c. 5.

BERNARD, JANE died on 1st inst., June 1828 in her 18th year.
The Lynchburg Virginian, June 5, 1828, p. 3, c. 4.

BERNARD, SPENCER D. died on Feb. 17, 1833 at Scottsville, Va. She was formerly of Lynchburg.
The Lynchburg Virginian, March 7, 1833, p. 3, c. 3.

BETZ, CONRAD F.M. died on the 11th inst. in 77th year of his age at his residence in Franklin Co. at Taylor's Store. He left a wife and numerous offspring.
The Lynchburg Virginian, June 21, 1830, p. 3, c. 3.

BIBB, WILLIAM W. died lately at his residence in Alabama. He was Governor of Alabama.
The Lynchburg Press & Public Advertiser, Aug. 11, 1820, p.3, c. 3.

BIGBIE, RHODAM died on 21st inst. near Rogerville, East Tenn. Formerly of Buckingham Co., but more recently of Lynchburg.
The Lynchburg Virginian, Oct. 26, 1829, p. 3, c. 5.

BIRKS, JOHN died Dec. 25, 1827, age 88 years. He was of Buckingham Co., Va. and was a Lieutenant in Revolution.
The Lynchburg Virginian, Jan. 3, 1828, p. 3.

BISHOP, JONATHAN died a few weeks ago at Camp Branch, Mo. Deceased was formerly of this vicinity.
The Lynchburg Virginian, Sept. 29, 1834, p. 3, c. 5.

BLACK, REV. J. L. died at the residence of Capt. Wm. M. Waller in Amherst Co., Va. Was minister of Episcopal Church and native of Ireland, and graduate of Trinity College, Dublin.
The Lynchburg Virginian, Mar. 12, 1835, p. 3, c. 4.

BLACK, MISS MILLICENT died Nov. 10, 1814 at the home of Mr. James Jones
in Lynchburg. She was dau. of Wm. Black, Sr. of Campbell Co.
The Lynchburg Press, Nov. 17, 1814, p. 3, c. 3.

BLAIR, ALLEN died on Thurs., April 23, 1835 in his 81st year at his
residence in Amherst Co.
The Lynchburg Virginian, May 4, 1835, p. 3, c. 4.

BLAIR, JANE died on 5th inst. in her 26th year. She was consort of
Winston S. Blair of Lynchburg.
The Lynchburg Virginian, July 12, 1827, p. 3, c. 3.

BLAIR, GRIZEL C. H. died on 27th ult. age 24, at the residence of Mrs.
Lucy R. Spencer in Amherst Co. She was consort of Wm. H. Blair
of Amherst Co. and left besides her husband, an infant.
The Lynchburg Virginian, Aug. 10, 1826, p. 3, c. 3.

BLAIR, MRS. POLLY died on 24th March 1831, age 55, at her residence in
Pittsylvania Co. Was wife of Capt. James Blair.
The Lynchburg Virginian, April 4, 1831, p. 3, c. 4.

BLAIR, DR. THOMAS D. died on 4th inst, age 24 at Buffalo Ridge Springs
in Nelson Co. Deceased left father and mother.
The Lynchburg Virginian, Sept. 14, 1826, p. 3, c. 4.

BLAIR, WILLIAM H. died on Tuesday the 12th inst., age 30, at his residence
in Union; son of Mr. Allen Blair of Amherst Co., Va. Left infant
son and widow.
The Lynchburg Virginian, Sept. 8, 1834, p. 3, c. 4.

BLAIR, MR. WINSTON S. died on Sunday morning last at his residence in
Amherst Co. Was formerly of this place.
The Lynchburg Virginian, Dec. 15, 1831, p. 3, c. 3.

BLANCHARD, J. was of Salisbury, Eng.
The Lynchburg Virginian, June 9, 1825, p. 3, c. 3.

BLOOMFIELD, ROBERT died Aug. 19, 1823, age 57, at Sheffield.
The Lynchburg Virginian, Oct. 21, 1823, p. 3.

BLOUNT, CAPTAIN CHARLES died on Monday, 14th inst. Age 67. Was of
Campbell Co. and member of Baptist Church.
The Lynchburg Virginian, March 31, 1831, p. 3, c. 4.

BOAL, ALEXANDER died on March 17, 1827 in his 23rd year. He was of the
firm of James and Alexander Boal of Lynchburg.
The Lynchburg Virginian, March 20, 1827, p. 3, c. 4.

BOAL, SAMUEL died on the 19th inst. in the 26th year of his age. Was a
native of County Antrim, Ireland.
The Lynchburg Virginian, Dec. 31, 1835, p. 3, c. 4.

BOARD, MRS. ANNA died on 6th inst. in 37th year of her age, at residence, Walnut Grove, in Bedford Co. Mother of 9 children and was consort of Francis Board.
The Lynchburg Virginian, Aug. 12, 1830, p. 3, c. 4.

BOARDMAN, DANIEL H., M.D. died on 13th ult. at New Orleans. He was of New Milford, Litchfield Co., Conn.
The Lynchburg Virginian, Nov. 13, 1834, p. 1, c. 4.

BOLEY, JOHN W. died Nov. 24th at his father's residence in Campbell Co.
The Lynchburg Virginian, Jan. 10, 1831, p. 3, c. 3.

BOLLING, ARCHIBALD, JR. died April 13, 1825 at his home in Campbell Co. Age 46; is survived by wife and 8 children.
The Lynchburg Virginian, May 12 and 26, 1825, p. 3.

BOLLING, ARCHIBALD, SR. died on Saturday, 14th ult. Was of Campbell Co.
The Lynchburg Virginian, July 23, 1827, p. 3, c. 4.

BOLLING, MRS. ELIZABETH R. died May 13, 1835. Consort of John R. Bolling of Campbell County.
The Lynchburg Virginian, May 19, 1825, p. 3, c. 5.

BOLLING, LINNEUS, ESQ. died on 7th inst., age 63, at residence in Buckingham Co. "Active and faithful magistrate; member of General Assembly 1799-1800 and thereafter." He was a Republican of Jeffersonian school and husband and father.
The Lynchburg Virginian, Feb. 1, 1836, p. 3, c. 4.

BONAPARTE, NAPOLEON died May 6, 1821 at St. Helena. Notice carried also in the Lynchburg Press of Aug. 31, p. 1, and p. 3.
The Lynchburg Press, Aug. 17, 1821, p. 3.

BOOKER, HENRY died April 7th, age 52. For many years a resident of Powhatan Co.
The Lynchburg Virginian, April 12, 1832, p. 3, c. 3.

BOOTH, ABRAM died on 10th inst. at the residence of Mr. W. W. Reese, in Bedford. Deceased was of the firm of Booth and Hatcher of Franklin Co.
The Lynchburg Virginian, Sept. 19, 1831, p. 3, c. 5.

BOOTH, MRS. FRANCES COX died Jan. 9, 1832. She was wife of Thomas Booth.
The Lynchburg Virginian, Jan. 9, 1832, p. 3, c. 1.

BOOTH, MISS MARIA died on 23 inst. at her father's residence in Franklin Co. She was daughter of Benjamin Booth, Esq.
The Lynchburg Virginian, Feb. 3, 1831, p. 3, c. 4.

BORLAND, JAMES B. died on 13th inst. about 30 years of age at house of Mr. Seiver, 7 miles west of Kingeton, Tenn. Deceased was formerly merchant here. A native of Ireland - came to Lynchburg in February 1834 - was on trip to purchase goods when he died.
The Lynchburg Virginian, Aug. 10, 1835, p. 3, c. 4.

BORRIE, ETIENNA died near New Orleans. He was the first man to cultivate cane sugar in the Mississippi.
The Lynchburg Press, March 17, 1820, p. 3.

BOSWELL, MRS. SARAH ANN died on 16th inst. in her 25th year at Bethel, Amherst Co. Left a husband, Walter B. Boswell, and 2. children.
The Lynchburg Virginian, July 28, 1828, p. 3.

BOURNE, ROSE B. died on 4th inst. in her 33rd year. Was wife of Wm. Bourne of Amherst Co. She leaves 5 small children.
The Lynchburg Virginian, May 11, 1827, p. 3, c. 3.

BOWLING, JAMES, SR. died on 12th inst., age 87. Deceased was of Amherst and a soldier of the Revolution.
The Lynchburg Virginian, Nov. 24, 1836, p. 3, c. 4.

BOWYER, COL. HENRY died on 13th inst. at an advanced age at his residence near Fincastle. Deceased was a soldier of the Revolution and for many years Clerk of the Court of Botetourt County.
The Lynchburg Virginian, June 21, 1832, p. 3, c. 4.

BOYD, MRS. CATHARINE died on 16th inst. in 31st year. Was consort of John Boyd of Lynchburg.
The Lynchburg Virginian, June 19, 1827, p. 3, c. 4.

BOYD, GEORGE, ESQ. died on 1st of last month, age 62 years, in Montgomery County, Tenn. while on visit. Deceased was of Amherst County.
The Lynchburg Virginian, Sept. 11, 1834, p. 3, c. 4.

BOYD, THE REV. JAMES died on 1st of July at his residence near Randolph Macon College. Deceased was for many years member of Virginia Conference of the Methodist Episcopal Church.
The Lynchburg Virginian, August 4, 1836, p. 3, c. 4.

BOYD, THOMAS of Halifax County, killed.
The Lynchburg Virginian, Oct. 27, 1825, p. 3.

BRADFUTE, DAVIDSON, ESQ. died on Wed. last at Sweet Springs where he had gone for his health. Deceased was Cashier of Farmers' Bank of Lynchburg.
The Lynchburg Virginian, Sept. 5, 1831, p. 3, c. 5.

BRADFUTE, MISS MARGARET died on April 3, 1833 in Lynchburg at home of Mrs. Bradfute. She was third dau. of Robert Bradfute, Esq. late of Bedford County.
The Lynchburg Virginian, April 8, 1833, p. 3, c. 5.

BRANCH, MRS. WINIFRED I. died on 29th inst., age 40, in Buckingham Co. Deceased was consort of Samuel Branch, Esq. She left husband and 10 children.
The Lynchburg Virginian, Nov. 6, 1828, p. 3, c. 5.

BRANSON, WESLEY H. died on March 30, 1833, age 14 years. Deceased was of Pittsylvania Co. and the second son of James Branson.
The Lynchburg Virginian, April 18, 1833, p. 3, c. 4.

BRECKENRIDGE, GENERAL JAMES died on 13th inst. at his residence near Fincastle (Botetourt Co.). He was a soldier of the Revolution and a member of the Virginia Legislature and of the Congress of the U.S. He was interred with military honors.
The Lynchburg Virginian, May 20, 1833, p. 3, c. 5.

BRENT, RICHARD died Dec. 30, 1815 in Washington. He was a United States Senator from the State of Virginia.
The Lynchburg Press, Jan. 5, 1815, p. 3.

BRENT, ROBERT, ESQ. died Sept. 7, 1819. He was Paymaster General of the Army and Judge of Orphan's Court. Of Washington County.
The Lynchburg Press & Public Advertiser, Sept. 14, 1819, p. 3, c. 5.

BRIDGES, MRS. NANCY E. T. died on Feb. 22, 1833 in 22nd year. Consort of Mr. James R. Bridges of Richmond and only child of Col. William Callaway of Franklin Co.
The Lynchburg Virginian, March 4, 1833, p. 3, c. 5.

BRIGGS, DAVID, ESQ. died on 5th inst. at Richmond, Va. Formerly of Fredericksburg, Va. He was attorney-at-law; filled a seat in the State Legislature
The Lynchburg Virginian, Jan. 28, 1825, p. 3, c. 5.

BRIGGS, ISAAC died on 6th inst. at his residence in Maryland. Formerly Assistant Engineer of the State of Virginia.
The Lynchburg Virginian, Jan. 28, 1825, p. 3, c. 5.

BRIM, RICHARD died on 8th ult., age 33 years, at residence of Ann S. Slappy in Twiggs, County, Ga. He was a native of Pittsylvania Co., Va.
The Lynchburg Virginian, Oct. 27, 1825, p. 3, c. 4.

BROADNAX, GEN. WM. H. died recently at his residence in Dinwiddie Co. "A conspicuous and meritorious citizen of Virginia."
The Lynchburg Virginian, Nov. 8, 1834, p. 3, c. 5.

BROCKENBROUGH, ARTHUR S., ESQ. died on Friday last at the University of Virginia. Formerly resident of Richmond and recently Proctor to the University. Left wife and 9 children.
The Lynchburg Virginian, May 10, 1832, p. 3, c. 3.

BROOKS, JOHN died August 16th at Lovingston, Va.
The Lynchburg Press, Aug. 29, 1817, p. 3, c. 4.

BROSA, SIGNOR died Aug. 22, 1822 in Lynchburg, age 26 years, and a native of Spain. He was with a theatrical group.
The Lynchburg Virginian, Aug. 27, 1822, p. 3, c. 6.

BROWN, MRS. ANN died on Tuesday at her residence in New Orleans. Deceased
was the wife of James Brown, Esq., late Minister Plenipotentiary of
the United States in France.
The Lynchburg Virginian, Nov. 1, 1830, p. 3, c. 5.

BROWN, DANIEL funeral service at Lynchburg on Sunday next.
The Lynchburg Virginian, Aug. 10, 1826, p. 3, c. 2.

BROWN, ELIZABETH died on 16th inst. She was consort of Edward Brown
of this place, formerly of Richmond.
The Lynchburg Virginian, Feb. 23, 1826, p. 3; Mar. 2, 1826, p. 3.

BROWN, FRANCES died on Aug. 14, 1822. She was the wife of Henry Brown,
Esq. of Bedford.
The Lynchburg Virginian, Aug. 30, 1822, p. 2, c. 2.

BROWN, HENRY, JR., ESQ. died on 19th ult. in New York. He was middle
age. Deceased was of Lynchburg and the eldest son of Henry Brown
of "Otter Hills", Bedford. He left a wife and 2 children.
The Lynchburg Virginian, June 2, 1836, p. 3, c. 3.

BROWN, DR. JAMES M. died April 23, 1824 in Amherst. A native of Scotland,
but for many years a resident of Campbell Co., however at the time
of his death he was a resident of Amherst Co.
The Lynchburg Virginian, April 30, 1824, p. 3.

BROWN, JOHN died on April 20th age 87, 5 mos. and 7 days, at his residence
in Campbell Co. Left wife, 4 children, 49 grandchildren and 14
great grandchildren.
The Lynchburg Virginian, May 5, 1836, p. 3, c. 3.

BROWN, GEN. JOHN died on the 6th inst. at Staunton. He was Judge of
Staunton, Greenbriar Co. and Wythe Co. Chancery Courts.
The Lynchburg Virginian, Oct. 19, 1826, p. 3, c. 3.

BROWN, MISS JUDITH died on 12th ult. at the late residence of Mr. Thos.
Whittington of Bedford Co. She was a member of the Baptist Church.
The Lynchburg Virginian, March 28, 1833, p. 3, c. 4.

BROWN, MARY ELIZABETH died on 30th ult., age 10 mos., at the residence
of father in Campbell Co. She was an only child of Henry J. and
Lucy C. Brown.
The Lynchburg Virginian, April 16, 1835, p. 3, c. 5.

BROWN, NANCY HARRISON died on 15th ult. in the 19th year of her age. She
was the dau. of Read and Elizabeth Brown and a member of the Methodist Episcopal Church
The Lynchburg Virginian, Aug. 19, 1833, p. 3, c. 4.

BROWN, PHILIP DANIEL died on Sunday last, age 18 mos. at the home of his
father, Mr. Henry J. Brown of this County. He was an only child.
The Lynchburg Virginian, May 28, 1832, p. 3, c. 5.

BROWN, MR. RODERICK died 21st Oct. last at residence of his mother in
this place. He was a member of Methodist Church.
The Lynchburg Virginian, Nov. 8, 1834, p. 3, c. 5.

BROWN, CAPT. SAMUEL died on Sunday morning last at his grandfathers in
Bedford Co.
The Lynchburg Virginian, May 14, 1835, p. 3, c. 3.

BROWN, THOMAS R., ESQ. died on 20th inst., 31 years of age. He was of
Booth's Tavern in the county of Alleghany, four miles from the
Sweet Springs. Deceased was of Caroline Co. but also formerly of
Lynchburg. Son of the late Dr. James M. Brown of Amherst.
The Lynchburg Virginian, August 27, 1835, p. 3, c. 5.

BRUCE, THE REV. PHILIP died in Tenn. He was the next oldest travelling
preacher of the M. E. Church in the United States.
The Lynchburg Virginian, June 15, 1826, p. 3, c. 2.

BUCKNER, MAJOR COLIN died on 28th ult. He was from Lynchburg and an
Officer of Regular Army. During last war served on Canada Frontier.
He was Postmaster, also Ruling Elder of First Presbyterian Church.
The Lynchburg Virginian, March 10, 1836, p. 3, c. 5.

BULLARD, JOSEPH P. died on July 10, 1825. He was of Cavendish, Vermont
but had been a resident of Lynchburg for several months.
The Lynchburg Virginian, July 14, 1825, p. 3, c. 4.

BULLOCK, MRS. ISABELLA died on Feb. 26, 1820. She was consort of James
Bullock of Lynchburg.
The Lynchburg Press & Public Advertiser, Feb. 29, 1820, p. 3, c. 5.

BULLOCK, JAMES P. died on Sunday. He was of Lynchburg.
The Lynchburg Virginian, May 25, 1826, p. 3, c. 3.

BURCH, CAPT. DANIEL E. died on 8th inst., age 37 years, in Louisville,
Kentucky. Native of New Jersey. Leaves wife and 1 child.
The Lynchburg Virginian, May 30, 1833, p. 3, c. 4.

BURFORD, AMBROSE died on Oct. 31st, age 67, at his residence in the
County of Amherst.
The Lynchburg Virginian, Nov. 9, 1835, p. 3, c. 4.

BURGE, THE REV. THOMAS died on May 29, 1833, 46 years old, at his residence in Buckingham Co., Va. Leaves wife and 6 children. He was
a member of the Methodist Episcopal Church.
The Lynchburg Virginian, June 3, 1833, p. 3, c. 5.

BURKS, DAVID, SR. died on Feb. 28, 1828, age 99. Of Amherst Co.
The Lynchburg Virginian, April 7, 1828, p. 3, c. 5.

BURKS, MRS. JUDITH died on June 17, 1825, age 37 years. Consort of
George Burks of Amherst.
The Lynchburg Virginian, June 23, 1825, p. 3, c. 4.

BURNETT, HARRISON died on the 19th, age 25, at Chester, N. J. He was the son of Mr. John Burnett of Chester, N. J.
The Lynchburg Virginian, Dec. 1, 1836, p. 3, c. 5.

BURNETT, HOWELL died on the 13th, age 28, at Chester, N. J. He was son of Mr. John Burnett of Chester, N. J.
The Lynchburg Virginian, Dec. 1, 1836, p. 3, c. 5.

BURNETT, JAMES died on 24th at Chester, N.J. He was the son of Mr. John Burnett of Chester, N.J.
The Lynchburg Virginian, Dec. 1, 1836, p. 3, c. 5.

BURNETT, KETURAH died on the 9th ult. at Chester, N.J. She was the consort of Mr. John Burnett.
The Lynchburg Virginian, Dec. 1, 1836, p. 3, c. 5.

BURNETT, MARTIN died at residence of Thomas Walker of Smith Co., Tenn., late of Campbell Co., Va. Was 23 years old.
The Lynchburg Virginian, Aug. 19, 1830, p. 3, c. 4.

BURNETT, MISS PATSEY died Nov. 6, 1814. Dau. of Edmund Burnett of Bedford.
The Lynchburg Press, Nov. 17, 1814, p. 3, c. 3.

BURNETT, RICHARD died on the 17th, age 18, at Chester, N.J. He was the son of Mr. John Burnett of Chester, N.J.
The Lynchburg Virginian, Dec. 1, 1836, p. 3, c. 5.

BURNEY, WILLIAM killed in Powder Mill explosion. News account from Newark dated April 26. Left wife and 1 child.
The Lynchburg Press, May 12, 1814, p. 2.

BUROT, MISS VIRGINIA died on Oct. 19, 1814, age 17 years. She was of Richmond, Va. and died at Mrs. Garraur's in Lynchburg.
The Lynchburg Press, Oct. 27, 1814, p. 3, c. 2.

BURR, JOSEPH no date of death given. Age 54 years. He was of Manchester, Vermont.
The Lynchburg Virginian, May 12, 1828, p. 3, c. 6.

BURROWS, JOHN died April 26, 1824, age 32, at Goose Creek, his father's home in Bedford Co. Also see The Virginian, July 16, 1824, p. 3, c.5, under name Burress, John.
The Lynchburg Virginian, June 25, 1824, p. 3, c. 5.

BURRUSS, EDMUND died on Sept. 17th, 1830, age 80 years. Deceased was of Bedford Co. and was a Revolutionary soldier. He fought at Battle of Guilford Court House.
The Lynchburg Virginian, Oct. 21, 1830, p. 3, c. 1.

BURRUSS, MRS. HANNAH died on the 13th inst., age 79, at her residence in Bedford Co. She was consort of Edmund Burruss, dec'd. She left 5 children.
The Lynchburg Virginian, Dec. 23, 1836, p. 3, c. 2.

BURTON, THE REV. ALBERT G. died recently in Mississippi on a visit. He
was a minister of the M. E. Church in Virginia.
The Lynchburg Virginian, Nov. 17, 1836, p. 3, c. 4.

BURTON, MISS BETSY died Dec. 12th at 9 p.m. at Dr. Paul Cabell's home.
The Lynchburg Virginian, Dec. 22, 1834, p. 3, c. 3.

BURTON, MRS. ELIZABETH died on the 7th inst. age 25. She was wife of
Woodson A. Burton of Campbell. Left a husband and infant child.
The Lynchburg Virginian, Feb. 19, 1829, p. 3, c. 5.

BURTON, MRS. EMILY died on 5th inst., in 37th year.
The Lynchburg Virginian, April 13, 1827, p. 3, c. 4.

BURTON, CAPT. JESSE died on the 7th inst. at an advanced age at his
Seat in Campbell Co., Va. He left wife and large family. "A kind
husband, a fond parent.
The Lynchburg & Farmer's Gazette, May 2, 1795, p. 3, c. 2.

BURTON, JOHN H., ESQ. died on 9th inst., age 46, at his residence in
Campbell Co. He left wife and 9 children.
The Lynchburg Virginian, Dec. 11 & Dec. 15, 1828, p. 3, c. 5.

BURTON, CAPT. ROBERT died on 9th of present month, age 67. He was
Secretary to Patrick Henry, Esq. when he was Governor of Va.
Left one daughter and grandchildren. He was of Bedford.
The Lynchburg Press & Public Advertiser, Feb. 18, 1819, p. 3, c. 5.

BURTON, DR. WILLIAM L. died Oct. 10th at house of Mr. R. Mitchell in
Liberty. He was late of Big Lick, Va. (Present day Roanoke, Va.)
The Lynchburg Virginian, Oct. 25, 1822, p. 3, c. 4.

BURWELL, BLAIR R. died Nov. 23rd, age 25, at Natchez. The deceased was
of Franklin, Va.
The Lynchburg Virginian, Jan. 2, 1837, p. 3, c. 2.

BURWELL, HARRIET F. died on 11th inst. at residence of Mrs. Goode in
Mecklenburg, Va. She was the dau. of John S. Burwell, Esq. of
Franklin Co.
The Lynchburg Virginian, Nov. 1, 1827, p. 3, c. 4.

BURWELL, MRS. LUCY CARTER died Dec. 10, 1824, age 36. She was the wife
of Nathaniel Burwell, Esq. of Botetourt Co.
The Lynchburg Virginian, Dec. 24, 1824, p. 3, c. 4.

BUTLER, MRS. DEBORAH died at her mother's in Campbell Co. Sept. 3, 1822.
She was the wife of William Butler and the dau. of Achilles Douglass.
The Lynchburg Virginian, Sept. 6, 1822, p. 3, c. 5.

BUTLER, MRS. NANCY died Wednesday the 29th day of December 1830. Was
consort of Mr. Edward Butler. She leaves husband and 7 children,
youngest child 2 hours old. Joined Methodist Church 18 months
earlier.
The Lynchburg Virginian, Jan. 10, 1831, p. 3, c. 3.

C

CABANISS, EDWIN G., ESQ. died on 17th ult. at Danville, Va. Editor of the <u>Danville Reporter</u>.
The <u>Lynchburg Virginian</u>, June 6, 1836, p. 3, c. 3.

CABELL, MRS. ELIZABETH B. died Tuesday, the 26th inst., age 21 years. Deceased was the relict of William Lewis Cabell, dec'd. late of Lynchburg. Died at Union-Hill the residence of Mayo Cabell, Esq. in Nelson Co.
The <u>Lynchburg Virginian</u>, Nov. 1, 1830, p. 3, c. 5.

CABELL, FREDERICK of Nelson Co. "Funeral sermon will be preached by The Rev. Wm. S. Reid at Mr. Frederick Cabells in Nelson Co. on Sunday the 30th of this month."
The <u>Lynchburg Press & Public Advertiser</u>, July 21, 1820, p. 3, c. 2.

CABELL, DR. GEORGE died Nov. 30, 1823, age 27. Survived by wife and children. Disease originated in fall from his horse.
The <u>Lynchburg Virginian</u>, Dec. 2, 1823, p. 3, c. 5.

CABELL, NICHOLAS C., ESQ. died Oct. 14, 1821 in Buckingham Co., age 26. Was son of William H. Cabell.
The <u>Lynchburg Press</u>, Oct. 19, 1821, p. 3, c. 5.

CABELL, COL. WILLIAM died Nov. 2nd at his Seat in Nelson County.
The <u>Lynchburg Virginian</u>, Nov. 8, 1822, p. 3, c. 6.

CABELL, WILLIAM LEWIS, ESQ. died Monday, the 21st inst. at Red Sulphur Springs (Monroe Co., Va. now West Va.)
The <u>Lynchburg Virginian</u>, June 28, 1830, p. 3, c. 4.

CALDWELL, JUDGE died on 11th inst. "Killed in duel with Col. Sam'l Gwinn"; both of State of Mississippi.
The <u>Lynchburg Virginian</u>, Feb. 4, 1836, p. 2, c. 4.

CALLAHAN, STEPHEN died at Marseilles, France. U.S. Consul at Marseilles.
The <u>Lynchburg Press</u>, July 27, 1819, p. 3.

CALLAND, ELIZABETH died on Feb. 4, 1828 in 70th year in Pittsylvania Co. Relict of Samuel Calland.
The <u>Lynchburg Virginian</u>, Feb. 18, 1828, p. 3, c. 4.

CALLAND, CAPT. SAMUEL died on 22nd ult. in 31st year. Leaves wife and 5 small children. He was of Pittsylvania Co.
The <u>Lynchburg Press</u>, April 13, 1818, p. 3, c. 3.

CALLAWAY, AMARICAI consort of Capt. John Callaway of Franklin Co. and dau. of Col. George Hairston of Henry Co.
The <u>Lynchburg Virginian</u>, April 13, 1826, p. 3.

CALLAWAY, ANN ELIZA died on 15th of June, age 14. Died at residence of Dr. Thos. Massie in Nelson Co. Dau. of Dr. George Callaway.
The <u>Lynchburg Virginian</u>, June 23, 1831, p. 3, c. 3.

CALLAWAY, MRS. ANNAH B. died Nov. 2, 1834 at her residence in Bedford Co. Relict of Col. Wm. Callaway dec'd; died age 83. Member Presbyterian Church for nearly half a century.
The Lynchburg Virginian, Nov. 13, 1834, p. 3, c. 4.

CALLAWAY, CAPT. (RICHARD) killed by Indians on 1st inst. Was formerly of Bedford. From St. Louis, Mo. paper of March 1. "Capt. Calloway was known to all and his loss will be regretted by all who estimate his worth and sterling courage."
The Lynchburg Press, April 20, 1815, p. 3, c. 1.

CALLAWAY, CHAS, SEN. died June 30, 1827 in 78th year, at residence in Pittsylvania Co. Youngest brother of Col. James, Col. John and Col. William Callaway all of whom were officers in Revolutionary War. Left 9 children.
The Lynchburg Virginian, July 12, 1827, p. 3, c. 3.

CALLAWAY, MRS. ELIZA died on 26th ult., age 34 yrs., 3 mos., 26 days. She was consort of Francis Calloway of Lynchburg. She leaves 2 children, a son and daughter.
The Lynchburg Virginian, Dec. 11, 1834, p. 1, c. 4.

CALLAWAY, MRS. ELIZABETH (ELIZA) died on 23rd ult., age 41, at residence in the "Forest", Bedford Co. Relict of Wm. Callaway, Jr., and the daughter of Mr. Samuel Calland, Sr. dec'd. and Mrs. Elizabeth Calland of Pittsylvania Co.
The Lynchburg Virginian, March 23, 1827, p. 3, c. 2.

CALLAWAY, JOHN died Aug. 22nd, age 46. Son of Capt. Charles Callaway of Pittsylvania Co. Left wife and 3 children.
The Lynchburg Virginian, Sept. 8, 1831, p. 3, c. 4.

CALLAWAY, LANGDON CHEEVES died on 27th inst., age 20. Was son of Col. James Callaway of Franklin City, Va.
The Lynchburg Virginian, Dec. 3, 1835, p. 3, c. 2.

CALLAWAY, MRS. MARY died on 30th ult., age 58, at Brookneal. Deceased was wife of Mr. Frank Callaway.
The Lynchburg Virginian, Sept. 15, 1836, p. 3, c. 3.

CALLAWAY, MRS. MARY died Dec. 11, 1821, age 76. Widow of Col. James Callaway.
The Lynchburg Press, Dec. 21, 1821, p. 3, c. 4.

CALLAWAY, COL. WILLIAM of Bedford Co., age 73. Died at house of Samuel Reid, Sept. 22, 1821. Survived by aged widow and one child.
The Lynchburg Press, Oct. 5, 1821, p.3, c. 4.

CALQUHOUN, THOMAS, ESQ. died last Tues. in this place. Formerly of Petersburg
The Lynchburg Virginian, Feb. 16, 1832, p. 3, c. 4.

CAMDEN, MRS. died on 30th ult. in 26th year of age. Consort of Benjamin Camden of Amherst.
The Lynchburg Virginian, Jan. 10, 1835, p. 3, c. 3.

CAMDEN, LEROY died March 31, 1824, age 38. Deceased was of Amherst Co.
Died at his residence.
The Lynchburg Virginian, April 16, 1824, p. 3.

CAMPBELL, MRS. JENNET consort of Col. James Campbell, Cashier of State
Bank, North Carolina.
The Lynchburg Press & Public Advertiser, Jan. 14, 1820, p. 3, c. 5.

CAMPBELL, JOHN, SR. died on 17th inst. age 84 years and 8 months, at his
residence. Deceased was of Washington, Virginia.
The Lynchburg Virginian, Jan. 9, 1826, p. 3.

CAMPBELL, COL. JOHN B. died Sept. 1, 1814 at Williamsville, near Buffalo.
Was in the 11th U.S. Infantry.
The Lynchburg Press, Nov. 10, 1814, p. 3, c. 1.

CAMPBELL, JOHN B. died Dec. 20, 1821 age 24 at house of Mr. James
McReynolds of Campbell Co. Deceased was of Campbell Co.
The Lynchburg Press, Jan. 18, 1822, p. 1.

CAMPBELL, JOHN QUINCY died on Feb. 22nd, age 11 years and 58 days. Died
in St. Charles Co., Missouri. Son of Capt. James Campbell, recently
of Bedford Co., Va.
The Lynchburg Virginian, April 14, 1836, p. 3, c. 4.

CAMPBELL, LUCINDA S. died on Feb. 24, 1827. Consort of Capt. James
Campbell of Bedford. Survived by husband and 8 children.
The Lynchburg Virginian, March 16, 1827, p. 3, c. 2.

CAMPBELL, MRS. MARGARET died on 14th inst., in 26th year. Consort of
James Campbell of Campbell Co. twelve miles below Lynchburg.
Survived by husband and 2 small children.
The Lynchburg Virginian, April 20, 1827, p. 3, c. 5.

CAMRON, DANIEL died on 2nd inst. in 88th year of age at his residence in
Pittsylvania Co. The Fredericksburg Herald asked to copy.
The Lynchburg Virginian, Aug. 10, 1837, p. 3, c. 3.

CANDLER, WILLIAM SEN. died on 3rd inst. age 85, at his residence in
Campbell Co. Was a Revolutionary soldier.
The Lynchburg Virginian, May 16, 1836, p. 3, c. 3.

CANN, JAMES died of hydrophobia as result of a dog's bite. Survived by
a large family.
The Lynchburg Press, Feb. 25, 1820, p. 3.

CANNON, THE REV. EDWARD died on Sunday night last at residence of The Rev.
Mr. Kabler near Lynchburg. Long-time active member of the Virginia
Conference of the Methodist Episcopal Church. Resident of Lynchburg
for past ten or twelve years. Deceased left a wife and three small
children.
The Lynchburg Virginian, Aug. 15, 1833, p. 3, c. 3.

CARDOZO, MRS. ELIZABETH died April 24, 1821 at Lynchburg. She was of
Lynchburg and left a husband and 6 children.
The Lynchburg Press & Public Advertiser, April 27, 1821, p. 3, c. 4.

CARLTON, MR. HENRY died on 14th inst. at Red Sulphur Springs, Bath Co.
Deceased was a merchant of Lynchburg.
The Lynchburg Virginian, Sept. 22, 1828, p. 3, c. 5.

CARNOT, COUNT died at Magdeburg, Pennsylvania. Connected with the French
Revolution. Minister of War to Napoleon. Age 70 years.
The Lynchburg Virginian, Oct. 21, 1823, p. 3.

CARR, DABNEY OVERTON died Sept. 17, 1830 in 24th year of his age. Son of
Col. Samuel Carr of Albemarle Co., Va. Died at Bogota, Colombia.
Was a student at West Point.
The Lynchburg Virginian, Dec. 20, 1830, p. 3, c. 2 and 3.

CARROLL, CHARLES of Carrolton died on Wed. last at home of his son-in-law,
R. Catou, Esq. He was born 20 Sept. 1737, Annapolis. A most
impressive 2 column obituary from the Baltimore American Nov. 15.
The Lynchburg Virginian, Nov. 22, 1832, p. 1, c. 3 and 4.

CARSON, MRS. MARY ANN died April 13, 1823 at Lynchburg. Was the consort
of The Rev. Joseph Carson.
The Lynchburg Virginian, May 2, 1823, p. 3.

CARTER, MRS. BETTY died on 9th inst., age 65 years, at Audley, in Frederick Co., Va. Was relict of late Charles Carter, Esq. and niece of
late Gen. George Washington.
The Lynchburg Virginian, May 3, 1830, p. 3, c. 4.

CARTER, CAPT. EDWARD died on 10th inst at his residence in Amherst Co.
Died in his 57th year.
The Lynchburg Virginian, Dec. 22, 1825, p. 3.

CARTER, CAPT. JOHN CHAMP died at his residence in Nelson Co. at age 68.
Deceased was an officer in Revolutionary War.
The Lynchburg Virginian, April 20, 1826, p. 3, c. 4.

CARTER, MRS. ELIZABETH died on 7th of May in 82nd year of age. She was
consort of Mr. Levin Carter of Pittsylvania Co., Va.
The Lynchburg Virginian, June 7, 1832, p. 3, c. 3.

CARTER, HILL died Sept. 2, 1830 in Amherst Co.
The Lynchburg Virginian, Sept. 6, 1830, p. 3, c. 3.

CARTER, MRS. NANCY died on 3rd inst. in 36th year of age. Wife of Edward
Carter, Esq., merchant of New London. Member of Methodist Episcopal
Church.
The Lynchburg Virginian, Aug. 10, 1837, p. 3, c. 3.

CARTMILL, COL. JAMES died on Dec. 16, 1836 suddenly at residence of James
S. Wood, Esq. in Botetourt Co., Va. President of Bank of Virginia at
Buchanan and for many years a citizen of Buchanan.
The Lynchburg Virginian, Dec. 26, 1836, p. 3, c. 4.

CASSIN, LIEUT. COMMANDER JOSEPH of U.S. Navy died on board U.S. Sch'r,
Grampus, on her passage from Pensacola to Havanna, on 30th of Nov.
and at 4 o'clock in the afternoon of the same day, his remains
were committed to the deep.
The Lynchburg Virginian, Jan. 15, 1827, p. 3.

CATLETT, R. P., ESQ. died lately at Clinton, Mississippi. Was editor
of the Mississippian.
The Lynchburg Virginian, July 22, 1833, p. 3, c. 6.

CHAMBERS, DR. HENRY died in Dinwiddie Co., Va. Senator of U.S. from
Alabama and a native of Lunenburg County.
The Lynchburg Virginian, Feb. 2, 1826, p. 3, c. 5.

CHANDLER, CLARK, ESQ. died in Cohaine, Mass., Feb. 27, 1824 at age 54.
Survived by son, John D. Chandler.
The Lynchburg Virginian, March 23, 1824, p. 3.

CHAPLIN, PAUL JONES died Friday night the 29th ult. at age 9. Died at
residence of Mrs. Betts in the county of Botetourt, Va. Deceased
was of Danville, Va. son of Wm. R. Chaplin, Esq., Cashier of branch
of the Bank of Virginia at Danville.
The Lynchburg Virginian, Sept. 8, 1834, p. 3, c. 4.

CHEATHAM, PETER of Campbell County died.
The Lynchburg Virginian, May 18, 1826, p. 3, c. 5.

CHEATHAM, MRS. SARAH died June 19, 1833, age 57, at residence in Campbell
Co. Was member of Presbyterian Church and relict of Eli Cheatham.
The Lynchburg Virginian, June 29, 1833, p. 3, c. 5.

CHICKLAY, W. died on Sunday last on his way to Kingston Church to be
married. Age 44. Groom had been married twice before.
The Lynchburg Press & Public Advertiser, June 14, 1819, p. 3, c. 2.

CHILDERS, CAPT. DRURY died on 25th ult., age 52, in this place.
The Lynchburg Virginian, Dec. 5, 1836, p. 3, c. 3.

CHILDS, FRANCIS died in Burlington, Vermont; age 67 years. Born at
Philadelphia Oct. 23, 1763. "Lost his father at an early age.
John Jay took him under his protection, educated him. Dec'd came
to Va., was in Charlottesville when Tarleton raided for Jefferson.
At war's end he settled in New York. Publisher of first daily New
York City paper."
The Lynchburg Virginian, Nov. 1, 1830, p. 3, c. 5.

CHILTON, RICHARD, SR. died August 4, 1821.
The Lynchburg Press, Aug. 10, 1821, p. 1, c. 6.

CHRISTIAN, MISS ANN died Oct. 5, 1818 in this place on Monday last at the
residence of Dr. Rose. She was of Lynchburg.
The Lynchburg Press & Public Advertiser, Oct. 8, 1818, p. 3, c. 1.

CHRISTIAN, DRURY died May 28, 1821, age 19. Was son of Capt. John
Christian of Amherst Co. He was of New Glasgow.
The Lynchburg Press & Public Advertiser, June 15, 1821, p. 3, c. 5.

CHRISTIAN, ELISHA died on the 5th inst., age 41, at his residence in
Amherst Co., Va.
The Lynchburg Virginian, Dec. 14, 1829, p. 3, c. 5.

CHRISTIAN, MRS. JANE died May 9, 1821, age 44. Wife of Charles H.
Christian of Amherst.
The Lynchburg Press & Public Advertiser, June 1, 1821, p. 3, c. 3.

CHRISTIAN, JOHN died on Sept. 26, 1823 in Amherst Co., age 30. Resident
of Amherst Co., Va.
The Lynchburg Virginian, Oct. 10, 1823, p. 3.

CHRISTIAN, MRS. JUDITH died on the 18th inst., 80th year of her age.
Deceased was of Amherst.
The Lynchburg Virginian, July 19, 1830, p. 3, c. 4.

CHRISTIAN, MISS MARTHA A. died on 18th inst., age 23, at Mountain View,
Buckingham Co., Va. at residence of father. Dau. of Col. Samuel
P. Christian.
The Lynchburg Virginian, Aug. 25, 1834, p. 3, c. 4.

CHRISTIAN, MRS. MILDRED died on July 7th at advanced age at her residence
in Amherst Co. She was the relict of Drury Christian, deceased.
Belonged to Presbyterian Church.
The Lynchburg Virginian, Aug. 10, 1837, p. 3, c. 3.

CHRISTIAN, ROBERT died on the 26th inst., age 18, at his father's
residence. He was of Buckingham Co., Va. and 4th son of Col.
Samuel P. Christian.
The Lynchburg Virginian, Oct. 2, 1834, p. 3, c. 4.

CHRISTIAN, SIDNEY died on Feb. 2, 1833, infant son of Samuel P. Christian,
Esq. of Buckingham Co., Va.
The Lynchburg Virginian, Feb. 8, 1833, p. 3, c. 5.

CHRISTIAN, DR. WILLIAM H. B. died Tuesday nite last in this place.
Deceased was of Campbell Co., Va.
The Lynchburg Virginian, Aug. 17, 1835, p. 3, c. 4.

CLARK, MRS. ANNE died on the night of 27th ult. at residence of Capt. A.
Leftwich of this place. Deceased was of Camden S. C. and was the
relict of the late James Clark, Esq.
The Lynchburg Virginian, Sept. 1, 1836, p. 3, c. 4.

CLARK, JOHN, SR. died April 2, 1819, age 74, at his home in Campbell Co.
The Lynchburg Press & Public Advertiser, April 8, 1819, p. 3, c. 4.

CLARKE, BOWLING, SR. died Dec. 4th, age 60. He was of Campbell Co.
The Lynchburg Press & Public Advertiser, Dec. 10, 1818, p. 3, c. 2.

CLARKE, CHRISTOPHER (HENDERSON), ESQ. died on 4th inst., age 61, at
residence of Mr. James Hendrick near New London.
The Lynchburg Virginian, Nov. 20, 1828, p. 3, c. 5.

CLARKE, MRS. MARY relict of Christopher Clarke, Esq. of New London
vicinity. Died Dec. 17, 1819. [Maiden name was Norvell.]
The Lynchburg Press & Public Advertiser, Dec. 21, 1819, p. 3, c. 5.

CLARKSON, GEN. MATTHEW died on April 25, 1825 in New York. Revolutionary
Patriot.
The Lynchburg Virginian, May 9, 1825, p. 3, c. 6.

CLARKSON, VIRGINIA died Saturday morning the 6th inst. at the residence
of Mr. David Herndon. Infant daughter of Menoah P. and Zerilda
S. Clarkson, aged 25 days.
The Lynchburg Virginian, Dec. 17, 1835, p. 3, c. 3.

CLAY, CYRUS B. died on Sept. 8, 1820 at residence of Dr. Howell Davies
in Lynchburg. Son of The Rev. Charles Clay of Bedford.
The Lynchburg Press & Public Advertiser, Sept. 12, 1820, p. 3, c. 5.

CLAYTON, CAPT. JOHN (Press recorded Claytor in error) died on 21st inst.
at residence of Jasper Clayton in Bedford. Aged veteran of American
Revolution. Member of Va. Legislature several years after war. [See
Bedford Co. C.O.B. #18. Also Estate Settlement, Bedford Co., Va.
March 24, 1821.]
The Lynchburg Press & Public Advertiser, Aug. 25, 1820, p. 3, c. 5.

CLAYTOR, ELIZABETH CHARLOTTE died last Thursday, aged about 8 years.
Was eldest daughter of the late Samuel Claytor, Esq. who preceded
her to the grave just one week.
The Lynchburg Virginian, Sept. 26, 1831, p. 3, c. 5.

CLAYTOR, MAJOR JOHN died on 25th inst., age about 75 years. Died at his
place, White Oak Grove, in Bedford Co. He was a Revolutionary
soldier. Officer in the militia. [Gwathmey, Virginians in The
Revolution p. 156 gives name as Clayton.]
The Lynchburg Virginian, Dec. 1, 1828, p. 3, c. 5.

CLAYTOR, MRS. MARY of Bedford, wife of Samuel Claytor and daughter of
Henry Brown.
The Lynchburg Press & Public Advertiser, Nov. 16, 1818, p. 3, c. 4.

CLAYTOR, SAMUEL, ESQ. died last Thursday afternoon at age 37 at Leewood,
in the neighborhood of Lynchburg. Deceased was a member of the late
Convention of Virginia.
The Lynchburg Virginian, Sept. 19, 1831, p. 3, c. 5.

CLEMENT, DANIEL died Dec. 24th, age 30, at residence of mother in this
place.
The Lynchburg Virginian, Jan. 3, 1833, p. 3, c. 4.

CLEMENT, MISS ELIZA C. C. died on 10th inst. in 35th year of her age. Dau. of William Clement, deceased.
The Lynchburg Virginian, April 23, 1832, p. 3, c. 5.

CLEMENT, MARTHA died March 3, 1825, from pulmonary disease.
The Lynchburg Virginian, March 15, 1825, p. 3.

CLEMENT, MRS. MARY died Jan. 25, 1827. Wife of William Clement of Campbell Co. Member of Baptist Church. Left husband and three children.
The Lynchburg Virginian, Feb. 1, 1827, p. 3, c. 4.

CLEMENT, MRS. STELLA died on 9th inst. in 40th year. Wife of Dr. George W. Clement of Franklin. Leaves husband and 10 children. Was dau. of Major John Smith of Pittsylvania Co., Va.
The Lynchburg Virginian, Aug. 15, 1833, p. 3, c. 3.

CLOP, LORENZO died Jan. 12, 1828 in 89th year. Was of Pittsylvania Co. "Mr. Clop had said he was hired by King George, III to come to America and fight the Americans under command of Lord Cornwallis; was in battle of Guilford Court House. He escaped and joined Americans."
The Lynchburg Virginian, Jan. 21, 1828, p. 3.

CLOPTON, THE REV. ABNER W. died on March 20, 1833, age 50 years. Was of Charlotte Co., Va. Educated at University of N.C., later instructor there. Later Baptist preacher. (copied from Richmond Enquirer)
The Lynchburg Virginian, April 11, 1833, p. 3, c. 4 & 5.

COATS, JEREMIAH died Jan. 1, 1833. Formerly of Amherst Co., Va.
The Lynchburg Virginian, Feb. 21, 1833, p. 3, c. 4.

COBBS, ANTHONY died Sept. 4, 1814 at Norfolk. Was of Lynchburg and was member of the Lynchburg Rifle Co.
The Lynchburg Press, Sept. 15, 1814, p. 5, c. 5.

COBBS, CHARLES G. died Dec. 26, 1826 "very suddenly".
The Lynchburg Virginian, Jan. 11, 1827, p. 3, c. 3.

COBBS, CHARLES G. died on 8th inst. at the home of his step-father, Mr. Jacob Fetzel. Age about four years and ten months.
The Lynchburg Virginian, Sept. 17, 1832, p. 3, c. 5.

COBBS, LINNAEUS BOLLING died on 23rd inst., age 13 months. Child of Dr. John L. Cobbs of Lynchburg. Lost his mother only few weeks ago. Was of Buckingham Co., Va.
The Lynchburg Virginian, May 28, 1832, p. 3, c. 5.

COBBS, MRS. MARY died Tuesday last, wife of Dr. John L. Cobbs of this town. Dau. of Linneus Bolling, Esq. of Buckingham Co. Age 22 yrs.
The Lynchburg Virginian, April 19, 1832, p. 3, c. 4.

COBBS, DR. MERIWETHER L. died Sunday 14th ult. at residence at Surry
Court House, Va. Formerly of Campbell Co. He had just commenced
practice of his profession.
The Lynchburg Virginian, Nov. 19, 1827, p. 3, c. 5.

COBBS, CAPT. ROBERT died on Friday 21st inst. in 72nd year. Died at
his residence in Campbell Co.
The Lynchburg Virginian, Sept. 3, 1829, p. 3, c. 5.

COCKE, MRS.   died on 25th in Albemarle Co. Wife of Dr. Charles
Cocke of that county. Died on return from the Springs.
The Lynchburg Virginian, Nov. 8, 1834, p. 3, c. 5.

COCKE, MR. JOHN LEWIS died May 28, 1825. Of Powhatan,"shot himself in
his temple while hunting in the woods."
The Lynchburg Virginian, May 30, 1825, p. 3.

COCKE, LUCY ANN died on Nov. 23, age 7, at her uncle's Wm. Herndon in
Campbell Co. Dec'd dau. of Thomas Cocke. Left father and sisters.
The Lynchburg Virginian, Dec. 15, 1836, p. 3, c. 4.

COCKE, THOMAS W. died lately at Louisville, Ky. Youngest son of the late
Col. Thomas W. Cocke of this place.
The Lynchburg Virginian, Jan. 26, 1832, p. 3, c. 5.

COFER, MRS. HOPE died Nov. 5, 1836, age 70, near Goose Creek. Wife of
Joseph Cofer.
The Lynchburg Virginian, Nov. 21, 1836, p. 3, c. 4.

COFER, LUCRETIA died Jan. 10, 1828. Consort of Thomas Cofer of Bedford.
The Lynchburg Virginian, Jan. 17, 1828, p. 3, c. 4.

COFFER, MR. JESSE died on morning of the 7th inst. at residence in
Bedford County.
The Lynchburg Virginian, March 14, 1836, p. 3, c. 4.

COLEMAN, CATHERINE F. died Dec. 13, 1824 at residence of her father, Capt.
Robert S. Coleman of Bedford Co.
The Lynchburg Virginian, Dec. 24, 1824, p. 3.

COLEMAN, MRS. ELIZABETH died and buried in Amherst Co. Funeral sermon
on the 10th Oct. by Rev. Wm. S. Reid.
The Lynchburg Press & Public Advertiser, Sept. 10, 1819, p. 3, c. 5.

COLEMAN, FLEMING died July 22nd at Hinds Co., Miss. Was formerly of
Amherst Co. Left in this Section 2 parents, numerous brothers
and sisters.
The Lynchburg Virginian, Aug. 10, 1835, p. 3, c. 4.

COLEMAN, MAJOR REUBEN died March 29, 1822, age 38. Was of Amherst Co.
The Lynchburg Press, April 5, 1822, p. 3, c. 4.

COLEMAN, CAPT. ROBERT S. died on 2nd inst. near Lynchburg. Was 47. Left
wife and 10 children.
The Lynchburg Virginian, Jan. 18, 1827, p. 3, c. 3.

COLLINS, HESTER AND ANNE EDWARDS "Of Moorestown, New Jersey, died at
Dunks Ferry, when carriage broke through the ice." Headed Feb. 9,
Philadelphia.
The Lynchburg Press & Public Advertiser, Feb. 25, 1820, p. 3, c. 2.

COLVIN, RUSSELL killed in Manchester, Vermont several years since.
The Lynchburg Press, Dec. 7, 1819, p. 3, c. 5.

COOK, THE REV. JOSEPH died March last on Red Sea. A missionary.
The Lynchburg Virginian, Oct. 31, 1825, p. 3, c. 5.

COOK, JOHN L. died on 22nd inst., age 53. One of the editors of the
Richmond Enquirer.
The Lynchburg Virginian, April 28, 1836, p. 3, c. 5.

COOK, SAMUEL, ESQ. died March 7, 1830, age 40, at his residence in
Franklin Co. "Lost in short period, during last seven months,
three (out of four) of his children." Leaves widow and a dau.
The Lynchburg Virginian, Mar. 18, 1830, p. 3, c. 3.

COOK, SARAH died April 6, 1824, age 61. Wife of Maj. Benjamin Cook of
Franklin County.
The Lynchburg Virginian, April 16, 1824, p. 3.

COOK, MRS. SARAH M. died on 1st inst., age 43, at Liberty (Bedford Co.).
Wife of Maj. William Cook.
The Lynchburg Virginian, June 7, 1832, p. 3, c. 3.

COOPER, THE HON. F. ASHLEY died in pugilist contest. Son of Earl of
Shaftsbury. (Sunday last), from a late London paper.
The Lynchburg Virginian, April 25, 1825, p. 3, c. 2.

CORN, SUSANNAH died on 25th ult., age 46, at house of Mr. John Slaughter,
Sr. in Patrick Co. Was widow of late Samuel Corn and 2nd dau. of
Mr. Slaughter. Member of Baptist Church.
The Lynchburg Virginian, Feb. 22, 1836, p. 3, c. 4.

CORNELIUS, GEORGE died on 10th inst. in 49th year of age. Was of
Amherst Co.
The Lynchburg Virginian, Sept. 27, 1827, p. 3, c. 4.

CORNELIUS, JAMES T. died on 28th ult, 1827 in 20th year. Was of
Amherst Co. Died at father's residence.
The Lynchburg Virginian, April 10, 1827, p. 3.

COUSINS, RICHARD H. died on May 21, 1828, age 24. Was of Pittsylvania Co.
The Lynchburg Virginian, June 2, 1828, p. 3, c. 6.

COVENTRY, WILLIAM died in Powder Mill explosion. Single man.
The Lynchburg Press, May 12, 1814, p. 2.

COWARDIN, MRS. MARY RHODES died on Friday the 3rd inst. at residence of
her husband, John L. Cowardin, near Danville, Pittsylvania Co., Va.
From Danville Statesman.
The Lynchburg Virginian, Dec. 20, 1830, p. 3, c. 3.

COX, JOHN died Aug. 21, 1817 in Patrick Co. while on visit. Resident of
Henry Co. Hero of American Revolution.
The Lynchburg Press, Sept. 5, 1817, p. 3, c. 5.

COX, MARTHA died on Dec. 31, 1827, consort of Reuben Cox of Amherst.
Survived by husband and large family of children.
The Lynchburg Virginian, Jan. 17, 1818, p. 3, c. 4.

COX, MILLNER,   died on Thursday, 23rd of this inst., age 55. Was of
Amherst Co. Left a bereaved consort; sorrowing children.
The Lynchburg Virginian, Jan. 1, 1829, p. 3, c. 4.

COZEUS, HORATIO, ESQ. died on 13th inst. by assasination by Mr. French
Strother. Deceased was of St. Louis, Missouri and a distinguished
member of the bar.
The Lynchburg Virginian, Aug. 24, 1826, p. 2, c. 6.

CRALLE, MRS. JUDITH SCOTT died on 19th inst. in 27th year of age in this
town. Dau. of Dr. John J. Cabell. Left one child.
The Lynchburg Virginian, April 27, 1835, p. 3, c. 5.

CRALLE, LINDSEY H. died on 13th July last, age 23, in vicinity of Vicks-
burg, Miss. on transitory trip from Campbell Co., Va. his native
County and State.
The Lynchburg Virginian, Aug. 21, 1834, p. 3, c. 5.

CRAWFORD, CHARLES died in April 1824 in Montgomery, Ala., (brother of
the Secretary of the Treasury).
The Lynchburg Virginian, May 28, 1824, p. 3, c. 5.

CRAWFORD, THE REV. CHARLES died lately in Shelbyville, Ky. A native of
Amherst, moved to Kentucky about 10 years ago. Member of Protestant
Episcopal Church.
The Lynchburg Virginian, June 26, 1828, p. 3, c. 5.

CRAWFORD, D. W. died on Saturday last in a duel at Mobile, Ala. Deceased
was of the firm of Armstrong and Crawford.
The Lynchburg Press, May 3, 1819, p. 3, c. 2.

CRAWFORD, MISS ELIZABETH died in Shellyville, Ky. Dau. of late Rev.
Charles Crawford formerly of Amherst Co.
The Lynchburg Virginian, July 7, 1831, p. 3, c. 4.

CRAWFORD, MRS. HANNAH H. died Nov. 9, 1823 at Nelson Crawford's home in
Amherst Co. Consort of Bennet A. Crawford.
The Lynchburg Virginian, Nov. 14, 1823, p. 3, c. 3.

CRAWFORD, NELSON, JUN, died on Sunday 20th inst. at residence on Rockfish
in Nelson Co.
The Lynchburg Virginian, Dec. 28, 1829, p. 3, c. 5.

CRAWFORD, WILLIAM SIDNEY, ESQ. died at Tusculum, his seat in Amherst Co.,
Va. Was of Amherst Co.
The Lynchburg Press, March 23, 1815, p. 3, c. 1.

CRAWFORD, MR. NATHAN died March 4th at his residence in Nelson Co., in
his 89th year. Was an efficient patriot of the Revolution. Left
only son and two duaghters and many grandchildren. Did not want
to apply for a Pension for his military services. "I fought for
the liberty of my country; I obtained it - I have enjoyed it and
I leave it as a rich inheritance for my children - I ask no more."
The Lynchburg Virginian, May 28, 1833, p. 3, c. 3.

CREMORNE, PHILADELPHIA HANNAH died on Friday 14th inst. Relict of Thomas
Viscount Cremorne. "Dowager Viscountess". From a London paper.
The Lynchburg Virginian, June 5, 1826, p. 3, c. 4.

CRENSHAW, HENRIETTA died on Oct. 29th, age 19. Eldest dau. of Mr.
Samuel Crenshaw of Bedford Co.
The Lynchburg Virginian, Nov. 16, 1835, p. 3, c. 4.

CREWS, JOHN died Nov. 11, 1825, age 16. Was of Amherst Co.
The Lynchburg Virginian, Nov. 17, 1825, p. 3.

CREWS, MISS SALLIE died on June 25, 1835, age 65, at Montpelier, near
Amherst Court House.
The Lynchburg Virginian, July 13, 1835, p. 3, c. 4.

CRIDER, HENRY died on 19th ult., age 31, at his residence in Pittsylvania
Co. Left a wife.
The Lynchburg Virginian, Sept. 15, 1834, p. 3, c. 5.

CRIGAN, MRS. JANET L. died on 10th inst. in Richmond, Va. Consort of Mr.
Robert B. Crigan.
The Lynchburg Virginian, March 23, 1835, p. 3, c. 5.

CROES, JOHN (REV. D.D.) died on 30th ult. at New Brunswick, N.J. at age
70. Bishop of Protestant Episcopal Church in State of New Jersey.
The Lynchburg Virginian, Aug. 6, 1832, p. 3, c. 5.

CROSBY, ENOCH died on 26th ult., age 88, at Putnam Co., N.Y. From West-
chester Herald.
The Lynchburg Virginian, July 16, 1835, p. 3, c. 5.

CRUMP, MARTHA died on 11th inst. in Amherst Co. Was of Amherst.
The Lynchburg Virginian, Nov. 5, 1824, p. 3, c. 5.

CURLE, CAPT. JOHN died on 28th inst., in 69th year. An officer of the
Revolutionary army. Member of Methodist Church.
The Lynchburg Virginian, March 30, 1827, p. 3, c. 3.

CURLE, JUDITH died March 20, 1823, age 60, in Lynchburg. Consort of
John Curle.
The Lynchburg Virginian, April 1, 1823, p. 3, c. 5.

CURRY, DAVID died Feb. 25th, 1820 at Natchez. Was of Second Creek.
The Lynchburg Press & Public Advertiser, Mar. 31, 1820.

CURTIS, BARTHOLOMEW died Dec. 14, 1821. Age between 70 and 80 years.
The Lynchburg Press, Dec. 21, 1821, p. 3, c. 3.

CUTLER, MRS. REBECCA E. died May 16, 1833 in 42nd year. Deceased was wife of Robert C. Cutler of Lovingston, Nelson Co. Member of M. E. Church. Leaves husband and one son.
The Lynchburg Virginian, June 13, 1833, p. 3, c. 4.

D

DABBS, THE REV. RICHARD of Davidson County, Tenn. Pastor of Baptist Church in Nashville, Tenn.
The Lynchburg Virginian, June 23, 1825, p. 3.

DABNEY, MRS. ANN died on 1st inst., age 34. Wife of Chiswell Dabney.
The Lynchburg Virginian, Aug. 18, 1834, p. 3, c. 4.

DABNEY, JOHN died Monday morning, July 2nd, one o'clock a.m., aged 13 years, 5 months, 11 days. Died at residence of his father in Amherst. Deceased was son of Chiswell Dabney, Esq.
The Lynchburg Virginian, July 9, 1832, p. 3, c. 4.

DADE, DR.   died in duel on 22nd ult. near Buffalo. Dr. Dade, Surgeon of 10th Infantry.
The Lynchburg Press, Dec. 29, 1814, p. 3.

DALE, COMMODORE RICHARD died on Friday, age 70, at Philadelphia. Deceased was officer in the American Navy in the Revolution.
The Lynchburg Virginian, March 9, 1826, p. 3, c. 2.

DALTON, JOHN SPIKE died on Friday, March 2, 1827, about 70 years old. Was of Pittsylvania Co.
The Lynchburg Virginian, March 16, 1827, p. 3, c. 2.

DALTON, MRS. MARY died March 17th in Rockingham Co., N.C. Wife of Col. Sam'l Dalton and dau. of James Scales, Esq.
The Lynchburg Virginian, May 30, 1836, p. 3, c. 3.

DANDRIDGE, MRS. SARAH died on 12th inst. Deceased was wife of Dr. Charles F. Dandridge and granddaughter of Patrick Henry.
The Lynchburg Virginian, Sept. 25, 1834, p. 3, c. 5.

DANIEL, MISS LOUISA died on the 27th of May, age 19. Was of this place.
The Lynchburg Virginian, June 2, 1836, p. 3, c. 3.

DANIEL, MRS. MARGARET died on the 11th inst. Wife of The Hon. William Daniel of Lynchburg.
The Lynchburg Virginian, Oct. 15, 1824, p. 3.

DAUNS, CAPT. JOHN killed by lightning while on his ship.
The Lynchburg Press & Public Advertiser, Feb. 18, 1820, p. 3.

DAVENPORT, MRS. MARY died on May 10, 1828, age 77 years. Widow of
Joseph Davenport of Amherst Co. Member of Methodist Church
The Lynchburg Virginian, May 22, 1828, p. 3.

DAVENPORT, PETER died August 29th, 39 years old, at the residence of Mr.
John Adams in the county of Fluvanna. He was a painter.
The Lynchburg Virginian, Sept. 10, 1835, p. 3, c. 4.

DAVIDSON, THE REV. JOHN A. died August 14, 1832 at Chilton's Tavern,
Campbell Co. Son of The Rev. Samuel Davidson of Campbell Co.
Age 28. He was a Baptist.
The Lynchburg Virginian, Aug. 23, 1832, p. 3, c. 3.

DAVIES, MRS. ELIZABETH died on Sunday the 2nd inst. Was relict of
Nicholas Davies of Amherst Co., age 56.
The Lynchburg Press & Public Advertiser, April 7, 1820, p. 3, c. 6.

DAVIES, MRS. ELIZABETH died on 20th day of March, age 61. Consort of the
late Samuel B. Davies of Bedford Co.
The Lynchburg Virginian, March 28, 1833, p. 3, c. 4.

DAVIES, MRS. HARRIET HOWELL died Sept. 14, 1820. Consort of Dr. Howell
Davies of Lynchburg.
The Lynchburg Press & Public Advertiser, Sept. 19, 1820, p. 3, c. 5.

DAVIES, JULIA SOPHIA died on Nov. 27, age 5, at Amherst Courthouse.
Deceased youngest dau. of Dr. Harvey L. Davies.
The Lynchburg Virginian, Dec. 15, 1836, p. 3, c. 4.

DAVIES, NICHOLAS on the 28th inst., departed this life, of Bedford Co.,
(therefore date of death was Sept. 28, 1794). Notice signed by
Henry L. Davis, Sept. 30, 1794.
The Lynchburg & Farmer's Gazette, Nov. 1, 1794, p. 4, c. 3.

DAVIES, WILLIAM S. died yesterday morning, age 19.
The Lynchburg Virginian, Oct. 24, 1823, p. 3, c. 4.

DAVIS, ADDISON died on 15th Sept. last, age 34, in Pike Co., Mo. Was
married to Miss Lucy M. Schoolfield, dau. of Mr. Benj. Schoolfield
of Lynchburg.
The Lynchburg Virginian, Oct. 30, 1834, p. 3, c. 5.

DAVIS, JOHN died in a Powder Mill explosion. News account from Newark, N.J.
dated April 26. Accident occurred on Wednesday last at Belleville;
works owned by Messrs Bullus, Decatur and Rucker.
The Lynchburg Press, May 12, 1814, p. 2, c. 3.

DAVIS, MRS. LUCY W. died Jan. 2, 1819. Widow of Henry L. Davis of Lynchburg.
The Lynchburg Press & Public Advertiser, Jan. 7, 1819, p. 3, c. 5.

DAVIS, MRS. MARTHA died Wed., 11th of this month. Deceased was wife of
Micajah Davis of Lynchburg.
The Lynchburg Virginian, July 19, 1832, p. 3, c. 3.

DAVIS, MRS. MARY died 20th of last March at her residence. Aged 85 or 86 years. Widow of William Davis. Member of the Society of Friends.
The Lynchburg Virginian, April 1, 1839, p. 3, c. 4.

DAVIS, MRS. MARY C. died on Thursday last, age 45, in this place. Consort of Micajah Davis, Jr.
The Lynchburg Virginian, Aug. 25, 1828, p. 3, c. 6.

DAVIS, SAMUEL A. died Sept. 13, 1821, age 21. Was of Lynchburg. Son of Mr. Henry Davis.
The Lynchburg Press & Public Advertiser, Sept. 21, 1821, p. 1.

DAVIS, SAMUEL L. died on Tuesday last at residence of Wm. Davis, Jr. near this place (Lynchburg).
The Lynchburg Virginian, July 31, 1828, p. 3, c. 6.

DAVIS, MRS. SARAH died March 9, 1824, age 42. Survived by husband and children.
The Lynchburg Virginian, March 19, 1824, p. 3.

DAVIS, SUSAN died Feb. 16, 1833 at residence of her mother, Mrs. Mary Davis, the widow of the late Wm. Davis, Sr. She was the eldest dau.
The Lynchburg Virginian, Feb. 25, 1833, p. 3, c. 5.

DAVIS, WILLIAM, SR. died on Tues., 1st inst. in 75th year at his residence in Lynchburg, Va.
The Lynchburg Virginian, Sept. 3, 1829, p. 3, c. 4.

DAVIS, MRS. ZELINDA died Thursday the 9th inst., age 68, at her residence in this town. Wife of William Davis, Jr. and dau. of the late John Lynch, Sr. Member of The Society of Friends.
The Lynchburg Virginian, May 20, 1839, p. 3, c. 4.

DAVOUST, LOUIS NICHOLAS, Duke of Averstadt (France).
The Lynchburg Virginian, August 12, 1823, p. 3.

DAWSON, MAJOR HENRY died Monday night, the 10th of Oct. Was tavern keeper at Lovingston.
The Lynchburg Virginian, Oct. 13, 1831, p. 3, c. 4.

DAWSON, CAPT. PLEASANT died Feb. 10, 1833. Was of Bedford Co., but for many years a citizen of Amherst Co.
The Lynchburg Virginian, Feb. 14, 1833, p. 3, c. 4.

DAWSON, DR. SAMUEL G. died on 7th inst. in Putnam, Ohio. Was late of Virginia and many years ago one of the Editors of the Lynchburg Press.
The Lynchburg Virginian, Dec. 21, 1835, p. 3, c. 3.

DAY, CATHARINE widow of Joseph Day and dau. of Mordecai Yarnell.
The Lynchburg Virginian, May 8, 1828, p. 3.

DAY, JOHN died on June 5th, age 62. Son of Mrs. Mary Ann Day of Amherst Co., Va. Died at Prince Edward Co.
The Lynchburg Virginian, July 22, 1830, p. 3, c. 5.

DAY, MRS. MARY ANN died on 28th of June, aged 86 years, in Amherst Co., Va.
The Lynchburg Virginian, July 22, 1830, p. 3, c. 5.

DEAN, JOHN died on 2nd inst., upwards of 70 yrs. Died at residence in Powhatan Co. Left widow and several children.
The Lynchburg Virginian, June 8, 1829, p. 3, c. 4.

DECATUR, COMMODORE STEPHEN died March 23, 1820. Killed in a duel in Washington. Also in press March 31, 1820, p. 3.
The Lynchburg Press & Public Advertiser, Mar. 28, 1820, p. 3.

DEHON, THE REV. died on Aug. 6, 1817 at Charleston, S.C. Bishop of S.C.
The Lynchburg Press, Aug. 29, 1817, p. 3, c. 1.

DEISON, CHARLES died on 10th inst. in Florence, Ala. but was a resident of Lynchburg.
The Lynchburg Virginian, Feb. 2, 1826, p. 3, c. 5.

DELIESSELINE, THOMAS J. of Dewee's Island, son of Capt. Deliesseline; died at Dewee's Island. **From Charleston Times.**
The Lynchburg Press & Public Advertiser, Feb. 25, 1820, p. 3.

DEMETRIADES, CONSTANTINE of Oxford, England but a native of Greece.
The Lynchburg Virginian, July 17, 1826, p. 2.

DEMPSEY, MRS. MARTHA died on 27th Sept. 1834 at her residence in Amherst Co. The Richmond Whig and Danville Reporter will oblige a subscriber by copying the above in their papers. Wife of William Dempsey.
The Lynchburg Virginian, June 29, 1835, p. 3, c. 5.

DE NEUEFCHATEAU, FRANCIS died in France. A celebrated French Academician.
The Lynchburg Virginian, April 14, 1828, p. 3, c. 5.

DENNETT, MRS. ELIZABETH D. died on Friday, 15th inst., age 27. Consort of Mr. Joseph Dennet of this place.
The Lynchburg Virginian, Jan. 28, 1836, p. 3, c. 5.

DENNIS, ROBERT H. died on Feb. 29, age about 27. Eldest son of Mrs. Dennis of this county.
The Lynchburg Virginian, March 8, 1832, p. 3, c. 3.

DE NOAILLES, DUKE OF FRANCE died on Nov. 6th, age 85, in France. Father of "Gen. La Fayette's heroic wife".
The Lynchburg Virginian, Jan. 28, 1825, p. 3, c. 5.

DE TOLLY, FIELD MARSHALL BARCLAY died recently in Russia. Renowned in war between France and Russia.
The Lynchburg Virginian, April 14, 1828, p. 3, c. 5.

DETTO, PETER died Tues., last. Was of Lynchburg.
The Lynchburg Press, Aug. 10, 1821, p. 1.

DE WITT, JACOB T. C., wife, daughter age 6, and two men (brothers) by the name of Kniffen, drowned in crossing the Coyuga Lake. Sheriff of Coyuga Co.
The Lynchburg Press, May 12, 1814, p. 3, c. 1.

DEWS, MR. WILLIAM, SR. died on 9th inst. in 82nd year of age at his
residence in Pittsylvania Co., Va. Soldier of the Revolution.
The Lynchburg Virginian, Feb. 16, 1835, p. 3, c. 5.

DIBRELL, ELIZABETH ECHOLS died on 25th inst. at New London. "Child of
Charles L. Dibrell, Esq. being the third which he has lost within
a very brief period."
The Lynchburg Virginian, Dec. 31, 1832, p. 3, c. 3.

DIBRELL, MARY WILMOUTH died on Dec. 15, 1832 at New London. Dau. of
Chas. L. and Mary Jane Dibrell.
The Lynchburg Virginian, Dec. 24, 1832, p. 3, c. 2.

DIBRELL, MEREDITH LAMBETH died on Dec. 19, 1832 at New London, son of
Chas. L. and Mary Jane Dibrell.
The Lynchburg Virginian, Dec. 24, 1832, p. 3, c. 2.

DIBRELL, MRS. LETITIA died Feb. 25, 1822, age 23. Consort of James W.
Dibrell of Lynchburg.
The Lynchburg Press, March 1, 1822, p. 3, c. 4.

DICK, JOHN died April 23, 1824 at New Orleans. Judge of District Court
of U.S. for Eastern Louisiana.
The Lynchburg Virginian, May 28, 1824, p. 3.

DICKENSON, THE REV. CRISPIN died on Oct. 28, 1832, age 45 years, at
home in Pittsylvania Co.
The Lynchburg Virginian, Nov. 8, 1832, p. 3, c. 5.

DICKENSON, MARGARET ANN died on Monday evening last. Was only child of
Mr. William W. Dickenson of this place; aged 4 years, 5 mos., 18 days.
The Lynchburg Virginian, June 21, 1832, p. 3, c. 4.

DICKENSON, MRS. MARY ANN died on Nov. 11th. Wife of Capt. Willis
Dickenson of Amherst.
The Lynchburg Virginian, Nov. 23, 1835, p. 3, c. 3.

DICKERSON, WILLIAM drowned in Rappahannock River, of Middlesex Co.
The Lynchburg Press, Nov. 23, 1821, p. 1.

DIGGES, WILLIAM died on Monday last. Was a native of Elizabeth City Co.
formerly resided in Richmond. Deceased removed to this place.
The Lynchburg Virginian, May 12, 1836, p. 3, c. 4.

DILLARD, CAPT. JAMES died Oct. 16, 1823, age about 79, at his residence
in Nelson Co.
The Lynchburg Virginian, Oct. 24, 1823, p. 3, c. 4.

DILLARD, CAPTAIN JAMES died on April 4th in his 77th year at his residence
in Amherst Co. Officer of the Revolution. Formerly Justice of Peace
for Buckingham Co. and Amherst Co.
The Lynchburg Virginian, April 12, 1832, p. 3, c. 2.

DILLARD, COL. JOHN died on Dec. 1, 1822, age 71 years at home of Gen.
John Dillard of Henry Co.
The Lynchburg Virginian, Jan. 31, 1823, p. 3.

DILLARD, LUCY ANN died at age of 2 years and 20 days. Third dau. of
Thomas and Mary H. Dillard.
The Lynchburg Virginian, Sept. 8, 1831, p. 3, c. 4.

DILLARD, MRS. MILDRED died Jan. 3, 1824, age 34, at residence of husband.
Wife of Dr. Lynch Dillard of Pittsylvania Co. Survived by husband
and 7 small children.
The Lynchburg Virginian, Jan. 9, 1824, p. 3.

DILLARD, THOMAS died on Aug. 7, 1820, age about 45 years, at Fancy Farm
in Bedford. Survived by wife and four children.
The Lynchburg Press, Aug. 15, 1820, p. 3, c. 5.

DILLARD, WILLIAM died on Sat. 3rd inst. Drowned in Rappahannock River;
was of Middlesex Co.
The Lynchburg Press, Nov. 23, 1821, p. 1.

DILLON, DR. JOHN G. died June 12, 1835, age 27. Deceased was of Salem,
Botetort Co. Left wife and one child. Died at Salem, Botetort Co.
The Lynchburg Virginian, July 9, 1835, p. 3, c. 6.

DINWIDDIE, WILLIAM died on 5th of Sept. 23 years old. Died at father's
residence in Campbell County, Virginia.
The Lynchburg Virginian, Sept. 17, 1835, p. 3, c. 5.

DIX, JAMES D., ESQ. died on 28th Nov. last, age 25. Died at residence of
father in Henry County.
The Lynchburg Virginian, Dec. 21, 1829, p. 3, c. 5.

DOAK, ROBERT died in powder mill explosion. Article stated Wed. last,
but news item dated Newark, April 26. Left wife and one child.
The Lynchburg Press, May 12, 1814, p. 2, c. 3.

DONOHO, MAJOR killed on 7th inst. Member of 4th Regiment, U.S. Infantry.
The Lynchburg Virginian, Aug. 21, 1826, p. 3, c. 2.

DONOLD, MRS. ANDREW died on May 28, 1809 in Bedford Co. Relict of Mr.
Andrew Donold deceased.
The Lynchburg Press, June 3, 1809, p. 3, c. 3.

DORSEY, JOHN S., Professor of Anatomy at University of Pennsylvania.
Article dated Philadelphia Nov. 13. Died day before.
The Lynchburg Press, Nov. 19, 1818, p. 3, c. 4.

DOSS, AGNES ANN died May 23, 1830, age 13. Dau. of Mr. Overstreet Doss.
Died in Buckingham Co.
The Lynchburg Virginian, June 14, 1830, p. 3, c. 5.

DOUGLAS, MRS. ANN L. died yesterday morning. Consort of Achilles M.
Douglas.
The Lynchburg Virginian, July 29, 1830, p. 3, c. 4.

DOUGLASS, JOHN died on 15th inst., age 28, in this place. Left father
and mother. Formerly of Madison Co., Ohio.
The Lynchburg Virginian, Sept. 18, 1826, p. 3, c. 4.

DOUGLAS, CAPT. JOHN L. died on 8th inst., age 36, near Staunton River.
The Lynchburg Virginian, Jan. 10, 1832, p. 3, c. 3.

DOW, PEGGY died Jan. 6, 1820 near Hebron, Connecticut. Wife of Lorenzo Dow.
The Lynchburg Press, Jan. 28, 1820, p. 3.

DRAKE, ELIZABETH ADELAIDE died on 12th inst., age 18, at Caxamalca, the
residence of her father, Col. Sam'l Drake in the county of Powhatan.
The Lynchburg Virginian, May 30, 1836, p. 3, c. 3.

DRAKE, MRS. PARMELA died on 19th inst., age 42, in Madison Co., Alabama.
Consort of Mr. Andrew Drake. Left husband and 8 children.
The Lynchburg Virginian, Nov. 12, 1829, p. 3, c. 5.

DREAN, MRS. ELIZABETH died on July 31, 1833, age 22. Consort of Mr.
Thomas A. Drean. Member of Methodist Church.
The Lynchburg Virginian, Aug. 5, 1833, p. 3, c. 4.

DUCHOQUET, FRANCIS died on 9th of January last at Cumberland, Maryland.
Deceased, the benevolent Indian Trader, ransomed Mr. Charles Johnston,
of the Botetourt Springs, from captivity by the Indians in the year
1790. Was on way to Washington as interpreter to Shawnee Chiefs.
The Lynchburg Virginian, June 21, 1832, p. 3, c. 4.

DUDLEY, WILLIAM died May 27, 1823, age 16. Son of Mrs. Ann Dudley of
Lynchburg.
The Lynchburg Virginian, May 30, 1823, p. 3.

DUFFEL, JOHN died March 6, 1819. Was merchant of Lynchburg.
The Lynchburg Press & Public Advertiser, March 11, 1819, p. 3, c. 4.

DUFFEL, JAMES died on 21st inst., age 74 years. Resident of this place.
The Lynchburg Virginian, October 22, 1835, p. 3, c. 3.

DUFFEL, SARAH DANDRIDGE died Friday morning last, age 19. Second dau.
of James Duffel.
The Lynchburg Press & Public Advertiser, Mar. 1, 1819, p. 3, c. 4.

DUKE, MARIA LOUISA died on 18th inst., age 6. Daughter of Capt. A. B.
Duke of Campbell.
The Lynchburg Virginian, Oct. 24, 1836, p. 3, c. 3.

DUNCAN, FLEMING H. died Dec. 26, 1826 in 54th year. Deceased was of
Amherst Co., and a Baptist preacher. Left widow and children.
The Lynchburg Virginian, Jan. 11, 1827, p. 3, c. 3.

DUNCAN, JOHN died on 8th inst., age 12, at father's residence in Bedford Co. Was son of John Duncan.
The Lynchburg Virginian, Dec. 23, 1836, p. 3, c. 2.

DUNCAN, CAPT. SILAS E. died on 16th inst. at White Sulphur Springs, Va. Was Captain in U.S. Navy.
The Lynchburg Virginian, Oct. 2, 1834, p. 3, c. 4.

DUNNINGTON, HENRY died on 26th inst., age 15 mos., 10 days. Son of Henry and Mary Eliza Dunnington of this place.
The Lynchburg Virginian, Nov. 30, 1835, p. 3, c. 4.

DUNSCOMBE, DR. DANIEL L. died Wed. morning the 16th inst., age 35, at residence of Henry Christian, Esq. of Buckingham Co. Moved from Halifax Courthouse where he had resided.
The Lynchburg Virginian, March 21, 1836, p. 3, c. 2.

DURKEE, NATHAN M. died Sept. 6, 1821 at Bedford Courthouse. Formerly of New York.
The Lynchburg Press, Sept. 14, 1821, p. 3, c. 5.

DUSMORE, ALEXANDER died in powder mill explosion. News account from Newark dated April 26. Accident occurred on Wednesday last at Belleville Works owned by Messrs. Bulluss, Decatur and Rucker.
The Lynchburg Press, May 12, 1814, p. 2, c. 3.

DUVAL, THOMAS died on Oct. 2, 1832 at Lynchburg. Formerly of Richmond.
The Lynchburg Virginian, Oct. 25, 1832, p. 3, c. 4.

DYBALL, JOHN died Dec. 14, 1819. Merchant of Lynchburg.
The Lynchburg Press & Public Advertiser, Dec. 21, 1819, p. 3, c. 2.

DYERLE, REBECCA JANE died on Sunday, 15th inst., age 4. Dau. of Mrs. Catherine Dyerle, widow, of near this place.
The Lynchburg Virginian, July 23, 1832, p. 3, c. 4.

E

EADES, JOSEPH died at his home in Buckingham. Formerly of Albemarle Co. Died on 31st ult. at age 65.
The Lynchburg Virginian, Sept. 6, 1827, p. 3, c. 3.

EARL, JAMES H. died at age 25. Was of Alexandria but for a few weeks past he was a resident of Lynchburg.
The Lynchburg Virginian, Sept. 23, 1823, p. 3.

EARLY, CAPT. JOSHUA died Nov. 3, 1814 at Bladensburg, Md. Was of Bedford Co. Survived by wife.
The Lynchburg Press, Dec. 1, 1814, p. 3, c. 2.

EARLY, MRS. RUTH died on 5th inst. Consort of Col. Joab Early of Franklin Co.
The Lynchburg Virginian, April 19, 1832, p. 3, c. 3.

EAST, EZEKIEL A.died on 20th inst. in 40th year of age at his late place
of residence. Was merchant of Amherst Co. Left a wife.
The Lynchburg Virginian, Sept. 27, 1827, p. 3, c. 4.

ECHOLS, DABNEY HERNDON died on 8th inst., age 3 years, at New London. Son
of Peregride and Sarah Echols. Died of scarlet fever.
The Lynchburg Virginian, Jan. 17, 1833, p. 3, c. 5.

ECHOLS, MRS. JANE died Jan. 18, 1819. Wife of Jacob Echols of Liberty.
The Lynchburg Press & Public Advertiser, Jan. 28, 1819, p. 3, c. 4.

ECHOLS, JOSEPH died May 30, 1824, age 36. Was of Lynchburg. Died at his
residence. Survived by a family.
The Lynchburg Virginian, June 4, 1824, p. 3.

ECHOLS, MOSES died at Athens, Alabama Territory.
The Lynchburg Press & Public Advertiser, Nov. 16, 1818, p. 3, c. 4.

ECHOLS, OBIDIAH, ESQ. died Friday morning last in Lynchburg.
The Lynchburg Virginian, July 14, 1836, p. 3, c. 4.

ECHOLS, MISS WILMOUTH E. died on Tuesday morning the 10th inst. in
Pittsylvania at the residence of her brother. Was youngest dau. of
Mr. Obadiah Echols of Lynchburg. Was 20 years of age.
The Lynchburg Virginian, Mar. 19, 1835, p. 3, c. 5.

EDENFIELD, DR. WILLIAM R. died Oct. 20, 1824. Was of Lynchburg, one of
the oldest inhabitants.
The Lynchburg Virginian, Oct. 22, 1824, p. 3, c. 5.

EDGAR, CAPT. THOMAS murdered a few days ago. Of Bedford County.
The Lynchburg Virginian, Nov. 24, 1825, p. 3, c. 3.

EDMOND, ANDREW died Oct. 16, 1826, age 80, at Tranent, England. Interred
in Tranent Church yard.
The Lynchburg Virginian, April 13, 1827, p. 2, c. 6.

EDMOND, HELEN MANNERS died Oct. 15, 1826, age 80. Wife of Andrew Edmond
who died on following day. Died at Tranent, England. Interred in
Tranent Church yard.
The Lynchburg Virginian, April 13, 1827, p. 2, c. 6.

EDWARDS, ANNE died at Dunks Ferry "when carriage broke through the ice."
She was of Moorestown, New Jersey. See entry for: Hester Collins.
The Lynchburg Press & Public Advertiser, Feb. 25, 1820.

EDWARDS, BARNET died "lately" age 38 at Monroe Co., Va. Formerly of
Amherst Co.
The Lynchburg Virginian, Jan. 19, 1832, p. 3, c. 4.

EDWARDS, DANIEL C., SEN. died on Nov. 23, 1832, age 82. Died at his residence in Pittsylvania. Was a soldier of the American Revolutionary War.
The Lynchburg Virginian, Dec. 24, 1832, p. 3, c. 2.

EDWARDS, NINIAN, ESQ. died on 20th ult., at his residence in Belville, Ill. Late Governor of Ill. and member of the U.S. Senate.
The Lynchburg Virginian, Aug. 8, 1833, p. 3, c. 5.

ELLIOTT, MRS. ANN died July 24, 1823, age 32. Consort of Peter Elliott of Lynchburg. Survived by one child. Member of Methodist Church.
The Lynchburg Virginian, Aug. 19, 1823, p. 3, c. 6.

ELLIS, CHARLES WILLIAM died on 11th inst., age 18 months. Third son of Richard S. Ellis of Red Hill, Amherst Co.
The Lynchburg Virginian, Sept. 19, 1831, p. 3, c. 5.

ELLIS, MRS. ELIZA R. died on 3rd inst., age 22, at residence of her father, T. Winn, Esq. in Washington City. Deceased was the consort of Judge Powhatan Ellis, of Mississippi.
The Lynchburg Virginian, Mar. 19, 1835, p. 3, c. 5.

ELLIS, CAPT. JOHN died on Jan. 31, 1826, age 58, at Amherst Co.,"Clover Dale". Died at his residence.
The Lynchburg Virginian, Feb. 9, 1826, p. 3.

ELLIS, MAJOR JOSIAH died June 29, 1810. Resident of Amherst County.
The Lynchburg Star, July 20, 1810, p. 3, c. 4.

ELLIS, CAPT. JOSHUA S. died May 25, 1825 in 37th year. Was of Amherst Co.
The Lynchburg Virginian, June 2, 1825, p. 3, c. 5.

ELLIS, JOSIAH, ESQ. died on 20th inst. at the "Wilderness", Capt. Thos. M. Eubank's residence in Campbell Co.
The Lynchburg Virginian, April 25, 1836, p. 3, c. 3.

ELLIS, MRS. MARY died on 18th ultimo. Consort of The Rev. Ira Ellis of Christian Co., Ky., formerly of Pittsylvania, Va.
The Lynchburg Virginian, Jan. 2, 1832, p. 3, c. 5.

ELLIS, POWHATAN died on July 30, age 20 mos., 6 days. Died in Lexington, Ky. Son of Powhatan Ellis, Esq. of Natchez, Miss.
The Lynchburg Virginian, Aug. 28, 1834, p. 3, c. 5.

ELLSON, WILLIAM murdered May 12, 1825 in his home, and his store robbed. Was of Stafford Co.; died in Fredericksburg, Va.
The Lynchburg Virginian, June 6, 1825, p. 3.

ELY, MRS. MARTHA ANN PAYNE died June 29, 1828 in Huntsville, Ala. Consort of Henry B. Ely formerly of Campbell Co.
The Lynchburg Virginian, July 17, 1828, p. 3, c. 4.

EPPERLY, MRS. ELSPA died on 27th ult., age 20, at her residence in Floyd Co. Consort of Joseph Epperly. Left one small child.
The Lynchburg Virginian, Feb. 9, 1835, p. 3.

EPPES, JOHN W., ESQ. Congressman, serving in both branches of Congress.
Copied from Richmond Compiler of the 17th.
The Lynchburg Virginian, Sept. 23, 1823, p. 3, c. 6.

EPPES, MRS. MARY ELIZABETH CLELAND died on 15th inst. at residence in
Leon Co., near Tallahassee, Fla. Wife of Francis Eppes, Esq. formerly of Virginia.
The Lynchburg Virginian, May 7, 1835, p. 3, c. 4.

ERWIN, MRS. ANN B. died on 9th inst., 29 years old, at Woodlands near
Lexington, Ky. Was consort of James Erwin, Esq. and the last
surviving dau. of The Hon. Henry Clay.
The Lynchburg Virginian, Dec. 31, 1835, p. 3, c. 4.

ESSEX, MRS. ANN died on Christmas Eve, 1835. Age 69. Resident of
Lynchburg. Born in Fredericksburg. Strong worker for Methodists.
The Lynchburg Virginian, Jan. 7, 1836, p. 3, c. 3.

EUBANK, GEORGE died on Thursday last, age 80. Was of Amherst County.
The Lynchburg Virginian, June 22, 1826, p. 3, c. 3.

EVANS, MRS. ABIGAIL died on Thursday last at 2 o'clock. Consort of Mr.
Joseph D. Evans.
The Lynchburg Virginian, March 17, 1836, p. 3, c. 5.

EVANS, DANIEL died on 1st inst., age 80, in Campbell Co. Was of Campbell
Co. and elder of Presbyterian Church.
The Lynchburg Virginian, Jan. 12, 1829, p. 3, c. 5.

EVANS, JAMES died in Chester Co., Pennsylvania at age 95. Was Revolutionary
soldier.
The Lynchburg Press & Public Advertiser, Mar. 28, 1820, p. 3, c. 5.

EVANS, OLIVER, ESQ. died at home of Elijah Ward. He was of Philadelphia.
The Lynchburg Press & Public Advertiser, Apr. 29, 1819, p. 3, c. 4.

EVARTS, JEREMIAH, ESQ. died on 10th inst. at Charleston, S. C. Was
author of, Letters of Wm. Penn.
The Lynchburg Virginian, May 30, 1831, p. 3, c. 3.

EWELL, DR. JAMES died at Covington, Louisiana. Author of Medical
Companion. Recently of New Orleans; formerly of Washington City.
The Lynchburg Virginian, Nov. 29, 1832, p. 3, c. 4.

EYRON, THE REV. ROBERT died on Saturday week. Age 84. Of Cannington,
near Bridgewater.
The Lynchburg Virginian, April 28, 1828, p. 3, c. 1.

F

FARIS, THOMAS died on 13th inst., age 28, at Capt. John M. Otey's. He was of Campbell Co.
The Lynchburg Virginian, Aug. 18, 1828, p. 3, c. 5.

FAULCONER, MRS. ELIZABETH died Jan. 12, 1822, age 33. Consort of Spencer Faulconer of Nelson Co. Survived by husband and 6 children. Died in Nelson Co.
The Lynchburg Press, Jan. 25, 1822, p. 3, c. 4.

FEAZLE, SUSANNAH died July 6th. Consort of Jacob Feazle.
The Lynchburg Virginian, July 10, 1826, p. 3, c. 6.

FEAZLE, WILLIAM died Friday the 18th inst., 54th year of his age. Died at his brother's residence in this place.
The Lynchburg Virginian, June 28, 1830, p. 3, c. 4.

FERGUSON, MRS. JEMIMA died on 20th inst. Consort of Capt. David Ferguson, of Franklin Co. Left children and husband.
The Lynchburg Virginian, Aug. 2, 1833, p. 3, c. 3.

FERGUSON, MRS. MARY died on 2nd inst. at Franklin, Va. Relict of Alexander Ferguson.
The Lynchburg Virginian, July 20, 1826, p. 3, c. 5.

FISHER, JOHN died at Charleston; hanged for highway robbery. Article headed Charleston Feb. 19.
The Lynchburg Press & Public Advertiser, Mar. 7, 1820, p. 3, c. 5.

FISHER, LAVINIA died at Charleston; hanged for highway robbery. Article headed Charleston Feb. 19. See entry for John Fisher.
The Lynchburg Press & Public Advertiser, Mar. 7, 1820, p. 3, c. 5.

FITZHUGH, WILLIAM H., ESQ. died on May 21, 1830 at residence of The Hon. Charles Goldsboro, his father-in-law, one mile from Cambridge, Md. Deceased of Ravensworth, Fairfax Co., Va. Obituary is from The National Intelligencer of May 24th.
The Lynchburg Virginian, May 31, 1830, p. 3, c. 5, 6.

FITZPATRICK, ANN M. died April 1, 1827, age 22. Consort of John E. Fitzpatrick of Pittsylvania Co. Left a two day old child.
The Lynchburg Virginian, April 13, 1827, p. 3.

FLEMING, JUDGE WILLIAM died Feb. 24, 1824, age 90. Was presiding Judge of the Court of Appeals. Died at his seat in Chesterfield.
The Lynchburg Virginian, March 2, 1824, p. 3.

FLOYD, MISS CORRELLY died on July 14, 1833 at residence of her father in Montgomery Co. Dau. of Gov. John Floyd.
The Lynchburg Virginian, July 29, 1833, p. 3, c. 3.

FLOYD, MRS. MARY JANE died July 9, 1833, age 28. Wife of Mr. Wm. Floyd and dau. of the late Mr. Jacob Oglesby. Member of M. E. Church since age 14. Cincinnati papers asked to take note because of relatives there.
The Lynchburg Virginian, July 18, 1833.

FONTAINE, JAMES murdered in his field by several of his Negroes. Was from Cumberland County.
The Lynchburg Virginian, July 2, 1827, p. 2, c. 6.

FORBES, MRS. MARY died Nov. 19, 1821, age 106. Of Nelson County, a native of Ireland.
The Lynchburg Press, Dec. 14, 1821, p. 3, c. 3.

FOSTER, CAPT. CHARLES died May 19, 1828, age 46. Was of Patrick Co.
The Lynchburg Virginian, June 9, 1828, p. 3, c. 5.

FOSTER, LEWIS T. died on 8th of Feb. at his residence in Patrick Co. Age 26. Member of Baptist Church.
The Lynchburg Virginian, Mar. 8, 1830, p. 3, c. 3.

FOUSHEE, DR. WILLIAM, SR. died Aug. 21, 1824. Was of Richmond; a Senator and also in Revolutionary War.
The Lynchburg Virginian, August 31, 1824, p. 3, c. 6.

FOX, ED. J. died in duel with Henry Randall. Fought just without the District of Columbia on the 8th inst. Both of the Treasury Dept.
The Lynchburg Press, Aug. 17, 1821, p. 3, c. 3.

FOWLER, THOMAS died on 19th inst.
The Lynchburg Virginian, July 12, 1830, p. 3, c. 5.

FRANKLIN, MRS. ELIZABETH C. died on 5th inst., age 36, at her husband's residence in the lower part of Campbell Co. Left husband and eight small children.
The Lynchburg Virginian, Sept. 15, 1836, p. 3, c. 3.

FRANKLIN, CAPT. JOHN died on Tuesday last at Amherst Court House.
The Lynchburg Virginian, Nov. 12, 1829, p. 3, c. 5.

FRANKLIN, JOHN R. died Oct. 24, 1825 at his mother's home near Amherst Court House. Was of Amherst County.
The Lynchburg Virginian, Oct. 27, 1825, p. 3, c. 4.

FRANKLIN, MR. WILLIAM died on Tues. last in Lynchburg, the 8th inst. Member of Presbyterian Church of Lynchburg.
The Lynchburg Virginian, Mar. 10, 1836, p. 3, c. 5.

FRANKLIN, WILLIAM L. died on 10th inst. Of Campbell Co. Left wife and three children.
The Lynchburg Virginian, Nov. 20, 1826, p. 3, c. 5.

FREEMAN, COL. CONSTANT died Feb. 27, 1824, age 67. Was of Washington. Auditor of the Treasury for Navy Dept. at Washington City.
The Lynchburg Virginian, March 23, 1824, p. 3.

FREEMAN, MRS. JUDITH died on 21st ult. at father's house. Consort of Mr. Garland H. Freeman. Member of Baptist Church. Left husband and infant son.
The Lynchburg Virginian, Feb. 19, 1835.

FRENCH, MRS. FRANCES died on 11th inst. at Petersburg. Consort of The
   Rev. Dr. French of Norfolk borough.
   The Lynchburg Virginian, Aug. 21, 1837, p. 3, c. 4.

FRETWELL, MRS. RHODA consort of Mr. James Fretwell. Leaves husband
   and child.
   The Lynchburg Virginian, Jan. 29, 1835, p. 3, c. 5.

FULTON, JOHN H., ESQ. died on 28th ult. in Abington. Representative in
   the last Congress of the dist. in which he resided.
   The Lynchburg Virginian, Feb. 11, 1836, p. 3, c. 5.

FULTON, ROBERT, ESQ. died on Thursday 23rd inst. at New York. "His name
   will not be forgotten as long as the Hudson and Mississippi continue
   to flow."
   The Lynchburg Press, March 9, 1815, p. 2, c. 5.

FUQUA, JOSEPH died on 4th inst., age 73, in Bedford Co. near Liberty at
   his residence.
   The Lynchburg Virginian, May 14, 1829, p. 3, c. 5.

G

GALLION, CHARLES E. died Sat. night the 14th inst., age 24, in this place.
   The Lynchburg Virginian, Jan. 23, 1832, p. 3, c. 3.

GALT, WILLIAM, ESQ. died March 29, 1825. A native of Scotland, but
   living in Richmond.
   The Lynchburg Virginian, April 1, 1825, p. 3, c. 5.

GAMBLE, COL. JOHN M. died on 12th inst. at Brooklyn, N.Y. In the U.S.
   Marine Corps - the last of 4 brothers who died in naval service.
   The Lynchburg Virginian, Sept. 22, 1836, p. 3, c. 4.

GARDNER, EBENEZER FRANCIS died Sept. 4, 1830 in Rockbridge Co. Merchant
   in Lynchburg. Native of Massachusetts.
   The Lynchburg Virginian, Sept. 6, 1830, p. 3, c. 3.

GARLAND, EDMUND PENDLETON died Wed., the 4th inst., 9 mos., 24 days of age.
   Died at home of his grandfather, Micajah Pendleton in Nelson Co. Was
   son of Hudson M. Garland, Jr.
   The Lynchburg Virginian, March 16, 1835, p. 3, c. 3.

GARLAND, JAMES died on Tuesday the 10th inst., 2 yrs., 7 mos. Was the
   youngest son of James Garland of Nelson Co.
   The Lynchburg Virginian, July 19, 1832, p. 3, c. 3.

GARLAND, MALVINA died April 11, 1815, age 11. Youngest dau. of Hudson M.
   Garland of Amherst Co.
   The Lynchburg Press, April 27, 1815, p. 3, c. 2.

GARLAND, MISS MARTHA H. died on 28th ult., age 18. Dau. of David S. Garland, Esq. of Amherst Co.
The Lynchburg Virginian, Sept. 8, 1836, p. 3, c. 2.

GARLAND, MRS. PAULINA died on 27th ult., age 16, at residence of Sam'l Garland, Esq. near Lynchburg. Wife of Capt. Burr Garland of Liberty.
The Lynchburg Virginian, Oct. 2, 1828, p. 3, c. 5.

GARTH, MRS. MATILDA died on 5th inst., age 28. Consort of John Garth of Lynchburg. Left husband and two small children.
The Lynchburg Virginian, Jan. 9, 1826, p. 3.

GATES, CAPT. LEMUEL died on 6th ult. at Fort Drane, Florida. Was Capt. in U.S. Army, 1st Artillery.
The Lynchburg Virginian, Sept. 5, 1836, p. 3, c. 4.

GIBSON, WILLIAM H. died Aug. 27, 1823, age about 50. Of Amherst County. Died at his residence.
The Lynchburg Virginian, Sept. 12, 1823, p. 3.

GILBERT, MRS. ANN D. died on 8th inst., age 69, at residence of her son, Dr. E. R. Gilbert, in Amherst Co. She was member of M. E. Church.
The Lynchburg Virginian, Nov. 29, 1830, p. 3, c. 4.

GILBERT, DR. EZEKIEL died Aug. 24, 1822, age 71, at Mr. John Garth's. He was of Amherst Co. Survived by wife and children.
The Lynchburg Virginian, Aug. 30, 1822, p. 3.

GILES, WILLIAM B., ESQ. died Dec. 4th at his seat in Amelia Co. He was one of first parliamentary debaters of his time. Has been in public life for nearly 40 years. Member of State Legislature; in both Houses of Congress, in the Executive Chair and in the Convention of Va.
The Lynchburg Virginian, Dec. 13, 1830, p. 3, c. 4.

GILLESPY, died in Powder Mill explosion. News account dated April 26, Newark, explosion of a Powder Mill at Belleville, owned by Messrs. Bullus, Decatar and Rucker.
The Lynchburg Press, May 12, 1814, p. 2, c. 3.

GILLIAM, MR. ARCHELAUS, SR. died on Saturday morning, 22nd inst., age 82, at his residence in Amherst Co. Soldier of the Revolution.
The Lynchburg Virginian, Oct. 31, 1836, p. 3, c. 1.

GILLIAM, CHARLES died at his residence in this Co. (Campbell) at age 45.
The Lynchburg Virginian, April 9, 1830, p. 3, c. 3.

GILLIAM, JARRATT died on Feb. 8, 1833, age 69, at his residence in Amherst Co. Member of Baptist Church.
The Lynchburg Virginian, Feb. 21, 1833, p. 3, c. 4.

GILMER, PEACHY R., ESQ. died on April 8th, age 57, at his residence in Albermarle. Formerly of Bedford Co.
The Lynchburg Virginian, April 18, 1836, p. 3, c. 4.

GIMBREDE, THOMAS died on 24th ult., age 51, at West Point. Instructor of Drawing in the Military Academy at West Point.
The Lynchburg Virginian, Jan. 10, 1833, p. 3, c. 5.

GIRARD, STEPHEN, ESQ. departed this life yesterday afternoon.
The Lynchburg Virginian, Jan. 2, 1832, p. 3, c. 5.

GLASGOW, MISS REBECCA JANE died on 24th of July in 19th year of age. Died at Rockbridge Co. Dau. of Joseph Glasgow.
The Lynchburg Virginian, Aug. 14, 1837, p. 3, c. 4.

GODFREY, MISS CAROLINE LOUISA died July 14, 1820 at residence of Howell Davies.
The Lynchburg Press & Public Advertiser, July 18, 1820, p. 3, c. 5.

GODFREY, JOHN E. died a few days ago from pulmonary complaint in Charlottesville, Va. Of Lynchburg and Charlottesville.
The Lynchburg Virginian, June 27, 1825, p. 3, c. 5.

GODFREY, JOHN W. died in Wilkerson, Miss. Formerly of Philadelphia.
The Lynchburg Press & Public Advertiser, July 7, 1820, p. 3, c. 4.

GODFREY, MRS. MARTHA K. died Aug. 30, 1820 at Buford's Tavern in Bedford Co. Widow of the late John W. Godfrey.
The Lynchburg Press & Public Advertiser, Sept. 1, 1820, p. 3, c. 5.

GODFREY, MISS MARY VIRGINIA died Jan. 11, 1822 in Bedford Co. at home of Capt. Robert L. Coleman.
The Lynchburg Press, Jan. 18, 1822, p. 1.

GOGGIN, MRS. MARY C. died on evening of 6th of March last, aged 21 years. Died at their residence in Liberty, Bedford Co. Deceased was the consort of Wm. L. Goggin, Esq. and eldest dau. of Maj. Wm. Cook.
The Lynchburg Virginian, March 12, 1835, p. 3, c. 5.

GOGGIN, COL. PLEASANT M. died on Thurs. last. He was of Bedford Co. Long a magistrate, several times a delegate in Legislature.
The Lynchburg Virginian, Feb. 7, 1831, p. 3, c. 4.

GOODE, MARY ANN died on Jan. 13, 1833, age 14, in Botetourt Co. of scarlet fever. Dau. of Dr. Thomas Goode of Bedford Co.
The Lynchburg Virginian, Jan. 17, 1833, p. 3, c. 5.

GOODRICH, CAPT. killed in Battle at Bridgewater near Niagara Falls.
The Lynchburg Press, Aug. 18, 1814, p. 2.

GOODRICH, EDMUND, SR. died on 13th inst. at his residence in Amherst Co. Died in the 68th or 69th year of his age. Member of the Baptist Church for upwards of 45 years.
The Lynchburg Press & Public Advertiser, Sept. 24, 1819, p. 3, c. 5.

GOODWIN, JOHN died Sept. 22, 1823, age 33. Son of Thomas Goodwin of Nelson Co.
The Lynchburg Virginian, Oct. 10, 1823, p. 3.

GOODWIN, JOHN H. died on 6th inst., age 80, at residence in Amherst Co.
The Lynchburg Virginian, July 12, 1832, p. 3, c. 5.

GOODWIN, MRS. MARY died Dec. 15th of this inst., age 70. Was consort
of Mr. John H. Goodwin, Sen. of the Co. of Amherst.
The Lynchburg Virginian, Dec. 25, 1828, p. 3, c. 3.

GOODWIN, MRS. MARY died on 10th inst. at Tate's Springs, Campbell Co.
Consort of John R. Goodwin of Amherst Co. Left husband and 6
young children.
The Lynchburg Virginian, Aug. 22, 1836, p. 3, c. 5.

GOODWIN, CAPT. PHILIP died Feb. 9th at residence of his father in Amherst
Co. Was of Amherst Co. Left brothers and father.
The Lynchburg Virginian, Feb. 16, 1826, p. 3, c. 5.

GOODWIN, MRS. TEMPERENCE died Monday, Jan. 19, 1829 in Nelson Co. Born
in Hanover Co. Resident of Nelson Co. Consort of Mr. Thomas
Goodwin. Survived by husband and children.
The Lynchburg Virginian, Jan. 29, 1829, p. 3, c. 4.

GOOLSBY, WILLIAM died March 22, 1818, age 108. Was of Albermarle Co.
The Lynchburg Press, April 24, 1818, p. 3.

GOUGH, MRS. SARAH C. died Aug. 5, 1830. Wife of William Gough of
Campbell Co.
The Lynchburg Virginian, Aug. 26, 1830, p. 3, c. 4.

GOULD, JACOB killed during a robbery in Stoneham.
The Lynchburg Press, Dec. 14, 1820, p. 2.

GRAHAM, DR. JAMES funeral service at Beaver Creek by The Rev. Wm. S. Reid.
The Lynchburg Press & Public Advertiser, April 8, 1819, p. 3, c. 4.

GRAHAM, JAMES died Mon. morning at the residence of the Editor of this
paper. (paper in Jackson, Tenn.) In 29th year of age. He was
formerly of the neighborhood of Lynchburg. (From Jackson, Tenn. paper.)
The Lynchburg Virginian, Sept. 3, 1827, p. 3, c. 2.

GRAHAM, THE HON. JOHN died in Washington City in August 1820. First Clerk
in Dept. of State and late Minister Plenipotentiary of the U.S. at
Court of the Brazils, Rio de Janeiro.
The Lynchburg Press & Public Advertiser, Sept. 19, 1820, p. 3, c. 5.

GRANTLAND, FLEMING died on 28th ult. at Milledgeville, Ga. Was Junior
Editor of the Georgia Journal. Left wife and two babes.
The Lynchburg Press & Public Advertiser, Feb. 15, 1819, p. 3, c. 3.

GRASTY, PHILIP L. died on Nov. 21, 1827 in Orange Co. Of Pittsylvania Co.
The Lynchburg Virginian, Jan. 3, 1828, p. 3, c. 2.

GRAVIER, JOHN died on 1st inst., age 96 near site of old Gravier Plantation
in New Orleans. Native of France.
The Lynchburg Virginian, Nov. 8, 1834, p. 3, c. 5.

GRAY, MISS MARIA S. died on 9th inst. in the evening in this Town. Only
surviving dau. of the late Francis Gray, Esq. Member of 2nd Baptist
Church. Leaves aged mother.
The Lynchburg Virginian, Feb. 14, 1831, p. 3, c. 5.

GRAY, THE HON. WILLIAM died on Friday morning, age 75 at Boston. He was
a merchant.
The Lynchburg Virginian, Nov. 17, 1825, p. 3, c. 3.

GRAY, WILLIAM died on Sunday the 23rd. Age 80. Was of Patrick Co.
The Lynchburg Virginian, May 18, 1826, p. 3, c. 5.

GREEN, JESSE died Oct. 15, 1824, age 73, at his residence in Monroe Co.,
near Sulphur Springs.
The Lynchburg Virginian, Nov. 26, 1824, p. 3.

GREEN, JOHN W. died on 25th ultimo, age 43, in Nelson Co. Resident of
Nelson Co.
The Lynchburg Virginian, Jan. 8, 1829, p. 3, c. 4.

GREGORY, CAROLINE EARL died on Sunday, 17th inst., age 5, at Buckingham
Courthouse. Only child of John T. and Sophia Gregory.
The Lynchburg Virginian, Sept. 1, 1834, p. 3, c. 5.

GREGORY, ISAAC died May 15th, 1824. Was of Lynchburg, an old inhabitant.
The Lynchburg Virginian, May 21, 1824, p. 3, c. 4.

GREGORY, WILLIAM died on Thurs., 3rd inst., age 60, at residence in
Amherst Co. Father of 12.
The Lynchburg Virginian, Dec. 17, 1829, p. 3, c. 6.

GREGORY, VIRGINIA CAROLINE died on 6th inst., aged 15 mos. Died in
Washington, N.C. She was the dau. of The Rev. Geo. N. Gregory.
The Lynchburg Virginian, Nov. 20, 1834, p. 3, c. 4.

GREGORY, MARY ANN died on 16th inst. in 19th year of age. Consort of
George N. Gregory. Left husband and one infant.
The Lynchburg Virginian, Jan. 25, 1827, p. 3, c. 5.

GREGORY, MRS. MARTHA died Aug. 20, 1832, age 51, at Amherst Co. She was
of Amherst Co. and wife of Wm. Gregory. Left 12 children.
The Lynchburg Virginian, Aug. 30, 1832, p. 3, c. 4.

GREGORY, WILLIAM SULDEN died on 8th inst. Age 24 and 10 mos. Died in
Amherst Co. The St. Louis papers will please copy above.
The Lynchburg Virginian, Sept. 26, 1836, p. 3, c. 3.

GRIFFIN, WILLIAM S., ESQ. died at residence of The Hon. Moses Linell in
Wilkinson Co. Was formerly of Lynchburg, Va. A much respected
member of the bar.
The Lynchburg Virginian, Oct. 25, 1835, p. 3, c. 6.

GUERRANT, TABITHA, MRS. died Sept. 18th, age 55. Consort of Peter
Guerrant of Franklin Co.
The Lynchburg Virginian, Sept. 28, 1826, p. 3, c. 4.

GURLEY, THE HON. H. H. died March 16th at Baton Rouge, La. Was Judge
of 4th District Court of State of Louisiana. Native of Conn.
Representative in Congress from La. Lost his wife earlier.
The Lynchburg Virginian, April 16, 1832, p. 3, c. 4.

GUTHRIE, MRS. ELIZABETH died on Friday last, age 53, at her residence in
Amherst Co. Relict of the late Wm. Guthrie.
The Lynchburg Virginian, Oct. 6, 1828, p. 3, c. 5.

GUTHRIE, WIATT died on 18th inst. in the morning. Son of William Guthrie
of Amherst.
The Lynchburg Virginian, Nov. 1, 1822, p. 3, c. 4.

GUTHRIE, WILLIAM died April 25, 1824, age 53. Killed when thrown from
a horse. Was of Amherst Co.
The Lynchburg Virginian, May 7, 1824, p. 3.

GWATKINS, MRS. MARY died on Monday the 30th ult., age 79, in Bedford Co.
Wife of Col. Charles Gwatkins.
The Lynchburg Virginian, April 27, 1829, p. 3, c. 4.

GWATKINS, COL. EDWARD died Feb. 3, 1833, 43 years old. Died at his
residence in Bedford Co.
The Lynchburg Virginian, Feb. 21, 1833, p. 3, c. 4.

H

HACKWORTH, CAPT JESSE died May 29, 1830, age 47, at his residence in
Franklin Co.
The Lynchburg Virginian, June 17, 1830, p. 3, c. 5.

HAGWOOD, WILLIAM G. died last Saturday morning.
The Lynchburg Press, March 23, 1815, p. 3, c. 1.

HAIRSTON, CONSTANTINE died Feb. 12, 1819, age 13. Son of Colonel George
and Mrs. Elizabeth Hairston of Henry Co.
The Lynchburg Press & Public Advertiser, Feb. 25, 1819, p. 3, c. 4.

HAIRSTON, MRS. ELIZABETH died Jan. 26, 1819, age 60. Consort of Col.
George Hairston of Henry Co.
The Lynchburg Press & Public Advertiser, Feb. 25, 1819, p. 3, c. 4.

HAIRSTON, NICHOLAS P. died July 9, 1822 in Mississippi. Formerly of
Henry Co., Va.
The Lynchburg Virginian, Sept. 27, 1822, p. 3, c. 4.

HALES, THOMAS died Aug. 14, 1823. An inhabitant of Nelson Co., Va. but a
native of Ireland.
The Lynchburg Virginian, October 3, 1823, p. 3.

HALKERSTONE, MRS. MILDRED died on 30th ult. at the Refuge Cabin, near
the Poplar Meeting House. Was wife of Robert Halkerstone, who
fought and bled under Washington's wing 7 years in the Revolutionary
War.
The Lynchburg Virginian, Sept. 8, 1834, p. 3, c. 4.

HALL, CAPT. JOSEPH C. died on 17th inst. in New York. He was of the U.S.
Marine Corp.
The Lynchburg Virginian, May 30, 1833, p. 3, c. 4.

HALSEY, WILLIAM A. died on 23rd inst. at the residence of Mr. John Hollins
in this town. Was 60 years of age.
The Lynchburg Virginian, Feb. 27, 1832, p. 3, c. 5.

HAMILTON, A. killed on board U.S. Frigate President.
The Lynchburg Press, March 9, 1815, p. 3.

HAMNER, MISS LOUISA JANE died at age 16 at Charlotte Court House, Va.
Was sister of The Rev. James K. Hamner.
The Lynchburg Virginian, June 25, 1829, p. 3, c. 4.

HAMPTON, GEN. WADE died a short time since in Alabama.
The Lynchburg Virginian, Sept. 7, 1826, p. 3, c. 4.

HANCOCK, CAPT. EDWARD died on 9th inst., age 82, at his residence in
County of Bedford. Was a member of Baptist Church.
The Lynchburg Virginian, March 17, 1836, p. 3, c. 5.

HANCOCK, COL. GEORGE died at Fothoringay, age 66.
The Lynchburg Press & Public Advertiser, July 28, 1820, p. 3, c. 4.

HANCOCK, MR. JOHN, JR. died on 19th inst., age 38, near Red House in
Charlotte County. He leaves a wife and one son.
The Lynchburg Virginian, May 30, 1833.

HANCOCK, MRS. MARGARET died on 23rd of October in her 73rd year in
Louisville, Ky. Was relic of Col. Geo. Hancock of Montgomery Co., Va.
The Lynchburg Virginian, Nov. 20, 1834, p. 3, c. 4.

HANCOCK, THOMAS died at his home. Was of Edgefield District, South Carolina.
The Lynchburg Press & Public Advertiser, Feb. 18, 1820, p. 3.

HANNOR, CAPT. JOHN died on 21st ult. in his 63rd year at his residence in
Halifax.
The Lynchburg Virginian, Dec. 8, 1825, p. 3.

HANSARD, MRS. MARY died on the 16th inst. in Amherst County. Was wife of
Dr. Ambrose Hansard.
The Lynchburg Virginian, Nov. 26, 1829, p. 3, c. 6.

HANSFORD, JOHN died on Friday last. Was an old citizen of Amherst County.
The Lynchburg Virginian, Nov. 30, 1826, p. 3, c. 3.

HARDY, MR. JOSEPH died Sat. the 22nd. ult., age 80, at his residence in Bedford County.
The Lynchburg Virginian, June 3, 1830, p. 3, c. 6.

HARDY, ROBERT, SR. died on Dec. 16, 1827 in 81st year of age on Staunton River in Bedford County. "He assisted in struggle for independence." (American Revolution)
The Lynchburg Virginian, Feb. 28, 1828, p. 3, c. 6.

HARPER, JESSE died on Oct. 28, 1831 in his 23rd year in St. Louis, Mo. Formerly of Franklin Co., Va. where his widowed mother still resides. Was the eldest child of his parents.
The Lynchburg Virginian, Sept. 17, 1832, p. 3, c. 5.

HARPER, GEN. ROBERT GOODLOVE died at his home suddenly yesterday. Age 60. "For two weeks he had been actively engaged in an important case in the Circuit Court of the United States." Copied from the *Baltimore American*.
The Lynchburg Virginian, Jan. 25, 1825, p. 3, c. 5.

HARPER, WM. T. died on Aug. 4, 1832, age 31, in St. Louis, Mo. His widowed mother resides in Franklin Co., Va.
The Lynchburg Virginian, Sept. 17, 1832, p. 3, c. 5.

HARRIS, CLIFTON G. died a few days since at Lexington, Va. Was of Nelson Co. and a student at Washington College. "Students to wear crepe on left arm for 30 days in his memory."
The Lynchburg Virginian, Aug. 5, 1833, p. 3, c. 4.

HARRIS, CAPT. EDWARD died on Friday the 8th of June, age 62, in Madison Co., Alabama, his home for the last 10 years. Deceased was formerly of Nelson County, Va.
The Lynchburg Virginian, June 28, 1832, p. 3, c. 5.

HARRIS, THE REV. FLETCHER died on 18th inst. Was a methodist preacher of Lynchburg.
The Lynchburg Press & Public Advertiser, Oct. 5, 1818, p. 2, c. 6.

HARRIS, MR. FRANCIS P. died on Friday last. Was of this place.
The Lynchburg Virginian, Feb. 13, 1827, p. 3, c. 5.

HARRIS, JOHN, SR. died Nov. 23, 1824, age 82, at his residence in Buckingham Co. He was a soldier of the Revolution. For 30 or 40 years he had been a member of the Baptist Church.
The Lynchburg Virginian, Dec. 24, 1824, p.3, c.4.

HARRIS, MRS. LUCY died 2nd inst. in her 28th year. Was wife of Mr. James B. Harris of Amherst Co. She died of measles and scarlet fever. She leaves a husband, three children, father, mother, brother and sisters. She was member of the Second Baptist Church.
The Lynchburg Virginian, May 14, 1832, p. 3, c. 4.

HARRIS, MR. LEE W. died on Oct. 31st at Locust Grove in Nelson Co. He left wife and 6 children.
The Lynchburg Virginian, Jan. 2, 1837, p. 3, c. 2.

HARRIS, WILLIAM, SR. died at age 76 at his residence. Was of Southern
part of Campbell Co. and a member of the Methodist Church. He was
a soldier of the Revolution.
The Lynchburg Virginian, Oct. 22, 1832, p. 3, c. 3.

HARRIS, WILLIAM B. died on morning of 10th inst. at his residence near
Winchester, Tenn. Was a native of Virginia and for many years a
resident of Madison County, Ala. Copied from Huntsville Democrat
of November 26.
The Lynchburg Virginian, Dec. 11, 1834, p. 1, c. 4.

HARRISON, AINSWORTH died on 3rd inst., age 71. Was formerly of Pittsylvania
Co., Va. He was a soldier of the Revolution.
The Lynchburg Virginian, Dec. 29, 1834, p. 3, c. 3.

HARRISON, MRS. ANN died at age 49 at Wilson Co., Tenn. at the residence of
son-in-law The Rev. M. C. Henderson. Widow of Nicholas Harrison dec'd,
formerly of Lynchburg, Va.
The Lynchburg Virginian, March 15, 1832, p. 3, c. 3.

HARRISON, HENRIETTA WOODROW died in Pensecola, Fla. Late of Lynchburg.
See entry for Tipton B. Harrison.
The Lynchburg Virginian, Nov. 8, 1822, p. 3, c. 6.

HARRISON, THE REV. JOHN died at age 56 at Preston, England.
The Lynchburg Virginian, Oct. 21, 1823, p. 3.

HARRISON, JOHN CLEVES SYMMES, ESQ. died on 30th ult., age 32, at his
father's home at North Bend, Ohio. The deceased was eldest son of
Gen. Wm. H. Harrison; and his widow was only child of Gen. Z.M. Pike.
The Lynchburg Virginian, Nov. 18, 1830, p. 3, c. 5.

HARRISON, NICHOLAS died on 16th ult., age 50, in the town of Bainbridge,
Alabama. Formerly of Lynchburg.
The Lynchburg Virginian, Aug. 10, 1826, p. 3, c. 3.

HARRISON, SOPHIA died on 5th inst. in 39th year in Amherst. Was consort
of Col. Richard Harrison of Amherst County and leaves 6 infant
children and husband. Was a member of Presbyterian Church.
The Lynchburg Virginian, July 17, 1828, p. 3, c. 4.

HARRISON, TIPTON B. AND "HIS LADY," HENRIETTA WOODROW HARRISON died in
Pensacola, Fla. Both were late of this place (Lynchburg).
The Lynchburg Virginian, Nov. 8, 1822, p. 3, c. 6.

HARRISON, WILLIAM, ESQ. died on Thursday night last. Was "one of the
oldest citizens of Lynchburg and universally esteemed."
The Lynchburg Virginian, Aug. 25, 1834, p. 3, c. 5.

HARVEY, CAPT. JACK D. died May 24, 1825, age 42, at his home in Charlotte Co.
The Lynchburg Virginian, June 2, 1825, p. 3.

HATCHER, CHARLES EDWARD died Monday, 20th inst., age 2 years, 6 months
at home of his father, Mr. Archibald Hatcher.
The Lynchburg Virginian, July 23, 1829, p. 3, c. 5.

HATCHER, CATHERINE S. died on 10th inst., age 32, in Bedford County. Was
wife of Mr. Thomas Hatcher.
The Lynchburg Virginian, Aug. 18, 1834, p. 3, c. 5.

HATCHER, MRS. ELIZABETH died on 27th ult. in her 31st year. Was consort
of Henry Hatcher of Bedford.
The Lynchburg Virginian, Jan. 5, 1826, p. 3.

HATCHER, FRANCES OVERTON died on Sat. last, age 16 mos., at this place.
Deceased was the youngest dau. of Mr. Archibald Hatcher.
The Lynchburg Virginian, Aug. 3, 1826, p. 3, c. 3.

HATCHER, LEANNAH VIRGINIA died on 12th inst. age 2 mo., 9 days. Was dau.
of Julius W. Hatcher, Esq. of this town.
The Lynchburg Virginian, Sept. 20, 1832, p. 3, c. 3.

HATCHER, SARAH L. died on Friday a.m., the 12th inst., age 23 at late
residence of her father. Was dau. of Hardaway Hatcher of Bedford.
The Lynchburg Virginian, Oct. 25, 1827, p. 3, c. 3.

HATCHER, WILSON CARY died on 16th inst., age 22, at King's Tavern near
Prince Edward Courthouse, Va. Deceased of Lynchburg for past 9 or
10 years. Left mother, sisters and brothers.
The Lynchburg Virginian, Aug. 22, 1836, p. 3, c. 5.

HAWKINS, ROBERT died on Feb. 21, 1820 at age 57. Was of Bedford Co.
The Lynchburg Press & Public Advertiser, Feb. 29, 1820, p. 3, c. 5.

HAWKINS, THOMAS died Feb. 1, 1822, age 71. He was of Nelson Co.
The Lynchburg Press, March 8, 1822, p. 3, c. 4.

HAY, CHARLES died April 19, 1833, age 60, at Georgetown. Was son of the
late Judge George Hay of Virginia and formerly Chief Clerk of the
Navy Department.
The Lynchburg Virginian, April 29, 1833, p. 3, c. 5.

HAY, GEORGE died a few days ago. Was Judge of U.S. Circuit Court.
Son-in-law of Ex-Pres. Monroe.
The Lynchburg Virginian, Sept. 30, 1830, p. 3, c. 3.

HAYS, SILAS died on 22nd inst. at Rebecca Furnace, the residence of Mr.
Wm. Ross, in the county of Botetourt. Deceased was late of Richmond.
The Lynchburg Virginian, June 21, 1832, p. 3, c. 4.

HAYWOOD, THE HON. JOHN died at age 66. Was Judge of the Supreme Court
of Tennessee. (Whig & Banner, Dec. 13)
The Lynchburg Virginian, Jan. 15, 1827, p. 3, c. 5.

HAYWOOD, WILLIAM G. died March 18, 1815. Was of Lynchburg.
The Lynchburg Press, March 23, 1815, p. 3, c. 1.

HEADEN, JOHN, ESQ. died on 10th inst., age 56. Was of Bedford Co.
The Lynchburg Virginian, Oct. 19, 1826, p. 3, c. 2.

HEADEN, MISS MARIA died June 16, 1828 at residence of her mother in
Bedford. Was dau. of the late John Headen of Bedford.
The Lynchburg Virginian, June 23, 1828, p. 3, c. 5.

HEDGWICH, DR. AUGUSTUS D. W. died August 26, 1821.
The Lynchburg Press, Aug. 31, 1821, p. 1, c. 6.

HEGEMAN, EMILY died May 7, 1833 at Vicksburg, Miss. Dau. of Dr. J.W. Hegeman.
The Lynchburg Virginian, June 6, 1833, p. 3, c. 5.

HEGEMAN, JANE died May 7, 1833 at Vicksburg, Miss. Dau. of Dr. J.W. Hegeman.
The Lynchburg Virginian, June 6, 1833, p. 3, c. 5.

HEGEMAN, JULIET died May 7, 1833 at Vicksburg, Miss. Dau. of Dr. J.W. Hegeman.
The Lynchburg Virginian, June 6, 1833, p. 3, c. 5.

HENING, WILLIAM WALLER died April 1, 1828 in Richmond. Was Clerk of the
Chancery Court of the Richmond District.
The Lynchburg Virginian, April 7, 1828, p. 3, c. 5.

HENLEY, LEONARD died on 25th inst. in his 85th year at his residence in
Amherst Co.
The Lynchburg Virginian, July 6, 1835, p. 3, c. 3.

HENLY, CAPT. ROBERT,U.S. Navy died on 6th inst., age 45, at his residence
on Sullivans Island. Was of this Borough and was Commandant of the
Naval Station at Charleston, S.C. at time of his death. Copied from
The Norfolk Beacon.
The Lynchburg Virginian, Oct. 23, 1828, p. 3, c. 5.

HENRY, ALEXANDER SPOTTSWOOD died Aug. 16th, age 8 yrs., 6 mos. Was 3rd
son of Capt. A. S. Henry.
The Lynchburg Virginian, Sept. 15, 1828, p. 3, c. 5.

HENRY, MR. EDWARD died Wed. morning at New Glasgow in Amherst Co. He was
an attorney-at-law of Henry Co. and son of Patrick Henry, Esq. of
Campbell Co.
The Lynchburg & Farmers Gazette   1790, p. 3, c. 3.

HENRY, MISS LAURA SACK died Tues., the 29th ult. at age 14. Was eldest
dau. of Alexander S. Henry, Esq. of Campbell Co.
The Lynchburg Virginian, April 11, 1831, p. 3, c. 4.

HENSLEY, WHITEEN died at age 23. Was son of Wm. Hensley of Bedford Co.
The Lynchburg Virginian, Aug. 23, 1827, p. 3, c. 2.

HERON, ROBERT died on Sunday the 24th ult., age 24, at Toronto, Canada.
He was a printer.
The Lynchburg Virginian, Sept. 18, 1834, p. 3, c. 5.

HERRING, JOHN S. died in Lexington, Ky. about 3 weeks since. Was a native of Virginia.
The Lynchburg Virginian, Feb. 18, 1825, p. 3, c. 3.

HERSEY, WILLIAM J. died on 23rd of last month, age 24, at McMinnville, Tenn. Was on his way home from Alabama where he had been visiting relatives.
The Lynchburg Virginian, Sept. 8, 1831, p. 3, c. 4.

HESTON, MRS. SARAH died on 27th inst. Was the consort of Silas Heston. Besides her husband she left 7 children.
The Lynchburg Virginian, Feb. 2, 1826, p. 3.

HEWSON, JOHN WILLIAMS died on 18th inst. in Baltimore at the residence of Mr. N. F. Williams. Deceased was infant son of Mr. B. W. Henson of Cincinnati, and formerly of Lynchburg.
The Lynchburg Virginian, June 28, 1832, p. 3, c. 5.

HICKOK, JOSEPH died on 19th inst., age 21 yrs., 9 mos. 4 days. Died in Lovingston, Nelson Co.
The Lynchburg Virginian, Dec. 31, 1832, p. 3, c. 3.

HICKS, JOHN WESLEY CHILDS. died on Thursday morning, Aug. 21st., age 14 mos., at Buffalo Springs. Was son of The Rev. Jno. J. Hicks.
The Lynchburg Virginian, Sept. 22, 1834, p. 3, c. 5.

HIGGINBOTHAM, MRS. FRANCES died May 30, 1825, age 91, near New Glasgow in Amherst Co.
The Lynchburg Virginian, June 13, 1825, p. 3, c. 6.

HIGGINBOTHAM, MR. JAMES D. died on 10th inst., age 23, at home of his uncle, Thos. Higginbotham of Amherst. Was the son of James Higginbotham, dec'd. of Amherst Co.
The Lynchburg Virginian, Oct. 20, 1825, p. 3, c. 3.

HIGGINBOTHAM, MR. JESSE died on 8th ult., age 57, at Soldier's Joy in Nelson Co.
The Lynchburg Virginian, July 7, 1836, p. 3, c. 4.

HIGGINBOTHAM, JOHN died July 23, 1814, age 83. Was of Amherst Co.
The Lynchburg Press, Aug. 4, 1814, p. 3, c. 3.

HIGGINBOTHAM, DR. SHANNON died Jan. 22, 1819, age 23, in Philadelphia. Was son of Wm. Higginbotham of Amherst Co.
The Lynchburg Press & Public Advertiser, Feb. 11, 1819, p. 3, c. 3.

HIGGINBOTHAM, MR. THOMAS died on Wed. the 4th inst. in his 64th years. He was of Amherst Co., and a merchant. See also Lynchburg Virginian Feb. 9, 1835.
The Lynchburg Virginian, Feb. 16, 1835, p. 3, c. 5.

HIGGINBOTHAM, THOMAS, ESQ. died on 5th inst. at his residence in Amherst. Formerly merchant of this place. See also Lybg. Virginian Feb. 16, 1835.
The Lynchburg Virginian, Feb. 9, 1835.

HILL, JAMES, SR. died Wed., Feb. 2nd in his 90th year at his residence in
the County of Amherst. Soldier of the Revolution.
The Lynchburg Virginian, Feb. 14, 1831, p. 3, c. 5.

HILL, JEREMIAH murdered in Portsmouth. Belonged to the U.S. Frigate.
The Lynchburg Virginian, Aug. 12, 1827, p. 2, c. 5.

HILL, NATHANIEL died on Feb. 7, 1836, age 64, at residence of Mrs. Nancy
Drake in Nelson Co. "This notice is given for information of the
relations of deceased who reside in Tenn."
The Lynchburg Virginian, Feb. 22, 1836, p. 3, c. 4.

HILL, WM. D. died on 19th October, age 48, in Amherst Co.
The Lynchburg Virginian, Nov. 5, 1829, p. 3, c. 5.

HILLSMAN, MRS. CONSTANCE C. died on Wed. last, age 22. Wife of Sherlock
Hillsman and youngest dau. of Mr. Wm. Fowler.
The Lynchburg Virginian, Aug. 18, 1834, p. 3, c. 4.

HITE, MRS. MARY died on 9th inst. in Campbell Co. She was of Campbell Co.
Wife of Samuel Hite and dau. of Samuel Woodall.
The Lynchburg Virginian, June 18, 1835, p. 1, c. 5.

HOFFMAN, MR. SAMUEL died at age 24 at residence of Dr. Phillips at Liberty.
Was native of Maryland.
The Lynchburg Virginian, Oct. 10, 1823, p. 3.

HOLCOMBE, MRS. ELIZABETH H. died Sept. 21st, age 23, in Campbell Co. Was
the wife of Mr. Charles A. Holcombe. Left infant son, age 3.
The Lynchburg Virginian, Oct. 3, 1836, p. 3, c. 5.

HOLCOMBE, JOHN ESQ. died. Was late Marshal of Superior Court of Chancery
for Lynchburg District. He is survived by wife and 6 children.
The Lynchburg Press, March 8, 1822, p. 3, c. 4.

HOLCOMBE, COL. PHILEMON died Nov. 3rd at age 72 at residence of son-in-law,
Thomas Watkins, Esq. in Fayette Co., Tenn. Deceased was of Amelia
County, Virginia.
The Lynchburg Virginian, Dec. 11, 1834, p. 1, c. 4.

HOLLAND, DREWRY, SR. died on 31st ult. at age 72. He was of Bedford and
a soldier of the Revolution.
The Lynchburg Virginian, Aug. 10, 1826, p. 3, c. 3.

HOLLAWAY GEO.d. 4th inst. near Huntsville, Ala. Was of Orange Co., Va.
The Lynchburg Virginian, Aug. 31, 1826, p. 3, c. 3.

HOLLAWAY, CAPT. THOMAS S. died June 28, 1824, age 57, at his residence
in Amherst County.
The Lynchburg Virginian, July 9, 1824, p. 3.

HOLMES, DAVID died Aug. 20, 1832 at Duvall's Sulphur Springs, near
Winchester, Va. Was late Gov. of Mississippi and formerly a U.S.
Senator from that State.
The Lynchburg Virginian, Sept. 3, 1832, p. 3, c. 5.

HOLMES, THE REV. HENRY died Thurs. morning last at his residence in
Edenton, N.C. Was Presiding Elder of Norfolk District of the
Methodist Episcopal Church.
The Lynchburg Virginian, Aug. 10, 1829, p. 3, c. 4.

HOLMES, MR. HARVEY H. died Oct. 17, 1824, age 17, at Lynchburg. Was the
son of Mr. Ira Holmes of Colchester, Conn.
The Lynchburg Virginian, Oct. 22, 1824, p. 3.

HOLMES, THE HON. HUGH died Jan. 27th. He was of Winchester and Judge of
General Courts of Virginia.
The Lynchburg Virginian, Feb. 11, 1825, p. 3,

HOLMES, MRS. SARAH B. died Dec. 28, 1828 in Botetourt Co., Va. Age 28.
The Lynchburg Virginian, Jan. 8, 1829, p. 3, c. 4.

HOLT, MRS. ELSY died on 27th Jan., age 63. Was late of Cumberland Co.
and left husband and 5 children.
The Lynchburg Virginian, Feb. 3, 1831, p. 3, c. 4.

HOLT, WILLIAM C., ESQ. died on 21st inst. in Norfolk. Was Speaker of
the Senate of Va. Was from Norfolk at the time of his death and
President of the Norfolk branch of the Farmers Bank.
The Lynchburg Virginian, Nov. 29, 1832, p. 3, c. 4.

HOOK, ROBERT died Sept. 17, 1821, age 24, in New London.
The Lynchburg Press, Sept. 28, 1821, p. 3, c. 5.

HOPE, WILLIS B. died on 1st of June last at Rockymount, Franklin Court
House, Virginia. Was formerly of this place.
The Lynchburg Virginian, July 9, 1832, p. 3, c. 4.

HOPKINS, "Three children of Mr. Jesse T. Hopkins died in
Bedford of scarlet fever in the space of 6 days; a son 5 years old,
a daughter 3 years old and a daughter 15 mos. old.
The Lynchburg Virginian, April 30, 1832, p. 3, c. 3.

HOUSTON, CAPT. JAMES died. Was of Iredell County, formerly of Ireland.
The Lynchburg Press & Public Advertiser, Sept. 7, 1819, p. 3, c. 6.

HOWARD, MRS. MARY died on 13th inst., age 23, in the Co. of Floyd. Was
consort of Col. Joseph Howard.
The Lynchburg Virginian, March 5, 1835, p. 3, c. 4.

HOWARD, THE REV. THOMAS died Feb. 26, 1827 at the home of Mr. Nathaniel
Smith. Was Presiding Elder in Methodist Church and of Goochland Co.
The Lynchburg Virginian, March 13, 1827, p. 3, c. 5.

HOWARD, THOMAS C. died on 29th ult., age 49, at Red Sulphur Springs. He was Clerk of the Hustings Court of Richmond; Clerk of the Circuit Court of Henrico; Clerk of the Committee for Courts of Justice; and Clerk of the General Court of Virginia.
The Lynchburg Virginian, Sept. 11, 1834, p. 3, c. 5.

HOWELL, DANIEL died March 5th at age 77. He was of Floyd Co. and left a wife and several children.
The Lynchburg Virginian, April 4, 1836, p. 3, c. 4.

HOWELL, E. F. killed on U.S. Frigate President.
The Lynchburg Press, March 9, 1815, p. 3, c. 5.

HOWELL, MRS. MARTHA died Jan. 28, 1819, age 79. Was of Patrick Co.
The Lynchburg Press & Public Advertiser, March 18, 1819, p. 3, c. 4.

HOWELL, PAUL died April 30, 1828 in 96th year. Born in Culpeper Co. At death he had 11 children living; over 80 grandchildren; 165 great grandchildren and 2 great great grandchildren.
The Lynchburg Virginian, May 19, 1828, p. 3, c. 5.

HOYLE, CHARLES died Sept. 13, 1825, age 72. Citizen of Lynchburg.
The Lynchburg Virginian, Sept. 15, 1825, p. 3, c. 4.

HOYLE, MRS. CHRISTIAN died June 12, 1823. Was about 65 years old. She was consort of Charles Hoyle of Lynchburg. (Also in paper of June 20, 1823, p. 3.)
The Lynchburg Virginian, June 13, 1823, p. 3, c. 4.

HUBARD, MISS LOUISIANA died Oct. 18, 1832 at age 21, in Sweet Springs. She was of Buckingham Co. and only dau. of Doct. James T. Hubard of Buckingham Co.
The Lynchburg Virginian, Oct. 25, 1832, p. 3, c. 4.

HUBBARD, WILLIAM died on 13th inst. at age 20. Died at residence of Major and Mrs. Tucker in Halifax Co. Left mother, brothers and sisters.
The Lynchburg Virginian, Oct. 23, 1828, p. 3, c. 5.

HUDSON, CALEB B. died on June 7th last, age 40, near Bellafont, Jackson Co., Alabama at his residence. About 6 years ago he moved to Alabama from Pittsylvania Co., Va.
The Lynchburg Virginian, Aug. 21, 1834, p. 3.

HUDSON, JACOB died on 1st inst., upwards of 60 years, at his residence, Patrick Co. He left children.
The Lynchburg Virginian, April 20, 1826, p. 3, c. 4.

HUGER, THE HON. BENJAMIN died at residence in Georgetown, S.C. Formerly member of House of Representatives of the U.S.
The Lynchburg Virginian, Aug. 1, 1823, p. 3, c. 4.

HUGHES, LAURA SOPHIA died on 7th of August last in Stockholm, Sweden. She was wife of Christopher Hughes, Esq. Charge des Affairs of U.S. of America. Dau. of Gen. Samuel Smith of Baltimore, Md.
The Lynchburg Virginian, Oct. 18, 1832, p. 3, c. 5.

HUGHES, MRS. MARY "and infant babe", died Aug. 3, 1821. Survived by
husband, Nelson B. Hughes, and two children. Was of Lynchburg.
The Lynchburg Press, Aug. 10, 1821, p. 1.

HUGHES, MRS. SUSANNAH died on 6th inst., age 102, in Amherst Co.
The Lynchburg Virginian, June 17, 1830, p. 3, c. 5.

HUMPHREYS, MARY died at age 65. Was consort of Dr. Thomas Humphreys
of Lynchburg.
The Lynchburg Press, Jan. 4, 1822, p. 1.

HUMPHREYS, DR. THOMAS died on 28th inst. at advanced age. He moved to
this place shortly after the Revolution. But one member of his
family survives him.
The Lynchburg Virginian, Jan. 2, 1826, p. 3, c. 4.

HUNT, COL. DAVID died on 19th ult., age 82, at his residence in Pittsylvania
Co. He left 2 children. Was a Revolutionary soldier.
The Lynchburg Virginian, March 23, 1826, p. 3, c. 4.

HUNT, MRS. MAHALA died on Thurs. morning last. Was the consort of Mr.
John T. Hunt of this place.
The Lynchburg Virginian, March 1, 1830, p. 3, c. 3.

HUNT, ROBERT, ESQ. died Dec. 25, 1827 at residence in Campbell Co. He
leaves wife and 3 children. He was late High Sheriff of Campbell
Co. and for many years a Justice of the Peace.
The Lynchburg Virginian, Jan. 10, 1828, p. 3, c. 2.

HUNTER, CHARLES ELLIS of Clover Green, Campbell Co. Son of Capt.
Robert Hunter.
The Lynchburg Virginian, March 27, 1828, p. 3.

HUNTER, MISS ELIZABETH M. died on 14th ult. at her father's residence in
Campbell Co., Va.
The Lynchburg Virginian, March 30, 1826, p. 3, c. 4.

HUNTER, JAMES, ESQ. died on 19th inst. at his residence in Essex Co., Va.
Was a member of the Board of Public Works of Va.
The Lynchburg Virginian, March 9, 1826, p. 3, c. 2.

HUNTER, JEREMIAH died on 4th inst., age 28, in Bedford Co. at the home
of his father, Mr. Peter Hunter.
The Lynchburg Virginian, Sept. 18, 1828, p. 3, c. 6.

HUNTER, MARY died March 29, 1824, age 19 or 20 years, at the home of her
father, Robert Hunter, Esq. of Campbell Co.
The Lynchburg Virginian, April 9, 1824, p. 3.

HUNTER, NANCY E. died May 24, 1823, age 25 or 26 years, at the home of
her father, Robert Hunter, Esq. of Campbell Co.
The Lynchburg Virginian, June 6, 1823, p. 3.

HUNTER, PETER died on 21st inst., age 61, at residence in Bedford Co.
The Lynchburg Virginian, Sept. 28, 1835, p. 3, c. 4.

HUNTINGTON, GENERAL JEDEDIAH died Oct. 9th, age 79, at New London. He
was a Revolutionary officer.
The Lynchburg Press & Public Advertiser, Oct. 12, 1818, p. 3, c. 2.

HUTCHESON, MRS. ELIZABETH B. died Dec. 27, 1832, age 33, in Amherst Co.
Was the consort of Mr. Thomas Hutcheson of Amherst. She is survived
by 7 children.
The Lynchburg Virginian, Feb. 14, 1833, p. 3, c. 4.

HUTCHERSON, JOHN died June 4th at age 60. Was of Amherst Co.
The Lynchburg Virginian, June 29, 1826, p. 3.

HUTCHINGS, CAPT. MOSES died on the 2nd inst., age 83, at his residence in
Pittsylvania Co. Was an officer in the Revolutionary War.
The Lynchburg Virginian, April 18, 1836, p. 3, c. 4.

I

IRVINE, FRANCES died on Sunday, age 10 mos., at residence of father. Dau.
of Dr. John and Frances M. Patterson Irvine.
The Lynchburg Virginian, Sept. 11, 1834, p. 3, c. 4.

IRVINE, MRS. MARTHA died April 26, 1833, age 65, at her residence in
Bedford.
The Lynchburg Virginian, May 6, 1833, p. 3, c. 5.

IRVINE, CAPT. WILLIAM died at his residence in Bedford Co.
The Lynchburg Virginian, May 28, 1829, p. 3, c. 3.

J

JACKSON, FRANCIS JAMES, Minister plenipotentiary to the U.S. Died on
Friday, age 44. From London Courier of Aug. 13. Died at Brighton.
(England)
The Lynchburg Press, Oct. 27, 1814, p. 3, c. 2.

JACKSON, RACHEL died on Dec. 22, 1828 at "Hermitage" near Nashville, Tenn.
Wife of Gen. Andrew Jackson, Pres.-Elect of the United States. Copied from
Nashville Banner of Dec. 23.
The Lynchburg Virginian, Jan. 8, 1829, p. 3, c. 4.

JACOBS, HENRY died Oct. 31, 1814 in the service of his Country. Age
about 21, of Lynchburg.
The Lynchburg Press, Nov. 10, 1814, p. 3, c. 2.

JAMES, FREDERICK, ESQ. died on 11th inst. at Millsburg, Africa. He was
one of the fathers of the Colony. Left U.S. in 1820. From the
Liberia Herald.
The Lynchburg Virginian, May 11, 1835, p. 3, c. 3.

JAMIESON, ANDREW died on August last. Was living in Lynchburg, but
died near Greenock, Scotland, his original home.
The Lynchburg Press, Nov. 23, 1821, p. 1.
The Lync
JEMISON, DR. JACOB, Surgeon's Mate, died on 30th July last at age 29,
on board U.S. Frigate Java. Belonged to the Seneca tribe of Indians.
From the New York Standard.
The Lynchburg Virginian, Jan. 3, 1831, p. 1, c. 3.

JENNINGS, PHILIP died on Friday last, age 47.
The Lynchburg Virginian, June 6, 1836, p. 3, c. 3.

JETER, HENRY, CAPT. died August 6, age 77, at his residence in Bedford Co.
The Lynchburg Press, Aug. 10, 1821, p. 3, c. 5.

JOHNSON, MR. ANDERSON died on 30th ult., age 40, at Williamsburg. Was
formerly of Lynchburg.
The Lynchburg Virginian, Aug. 25, 1836, p. 3, c. 5.

JOHNSON, EDWARD died. An old and highly esteemed resident of Lynchburg.
The Lynchburg Virginian, Jan. 7, 1830, p. 3, c. 6.

JOHNSON, THE HON. JOHN died a few days since at Hancock in Washington Co.
He was Chancellor of Maryland, acting as a Commissioner in the
establishment of the boundary on the Virginia frontier. From the
Baltimore American.
The Lynchburg Virginian, Aug. 17, 1824, p. 3, c. 5.

JOHNSON, SARAH died on 21st inst., age 45. Wife of Newby Johnson of
Campbell Co.
The Lynchburg Virginian, Sept. 28, 1826, p. 3, c. 4.

JOHNSON, MR. THOMAS H. died July 20th, age 87, at residence in Bedford
Co. Left wife and 4 children.
The Lynchburg Virginian, Sept. 19, 1836, p. 3, c. 4.

JOHNSTON, CHARLES, ESQ. died a few days since in Botetourt Co. Proprietor
of the Botetourt Springs.
The Lynchburg Virginian, Jan. 31, 1833, p. 3, c. 4.

JOHNSTON, MRS. ELIZABETH P. died at home of her father, Mr. John
Steptoe of New London. Wife of Charles Johnston, Esq. of Botetourt
Co. Survived by husband and children.
The Lynchburg Press & Public Advertiser, April 7, 1820, p. 3, c. 5.

JOHNSTON, MISS MARTHA B. died on 15th ult. at residence of Mrs. E. R.
Tucker near Natchez, Miss. Dau. of Charles Johnston, Esq. of
the Botetourt Springs.
The Lynchburg Virginian, Nov. 14, 1836, p. 3, c. 3.

JOHNSTON, PETER, ESQ. died on 8th inst., age 69, at Ponecillo his late residence in Washington Co., Va. He was Judge of that District; Capt. in Revolutionary Army; member of House of Delegates from Prince Edward Co. for many years.
The Lynchburg Virginian, Dec. 15, 1831, p. 3, c. 3.

JONES, ALEXANDER NELSON died on 9th inst., age 28, at his mother's residence in Amherst Co. He was of Amherst Co. Left mother and brother.
The Lynchburg Virginian, Oct. 19, 1826, p. 3, c. 2.

JONES, MRS. ANN R. died on Dec. 25 ult., aged 17 years, 6 months, 11 days. Wife of Capt. Thomas J. Jones. Dau of Mrs. Eliza C. Calland of Pittsylvania. Also left child.
The Lynchburg Virginian, Dec. 16, 1830, p. 3, c. 2.

JONES, CHARLES died on 2nd inst., age 69, at his residence in Nelson Co. Left a large family.
The Lynchburg Virginian, Aug. 10, 1826, p. 3, c. 3.

JONES, GRIFFIN died July 6, 1833 in Lynchburg. Resident of Elizabeth City, N.C. It is requested that "Norfolk papers will please notice his death."
The Lynchburg Virginian, July 8, 1833, p. 3, c. 5.

JONES, JAMES died Jan. 23, 1819, age 34. Was of Liberty.
The Lynchburg Press & Public Advertiser, Jan. 28, 1819, p. 3, c. 5.

JONES, JAMES C. died on 25th ult., age 31. Was of Bedford Co.
The Lynchburg Virginian, Nov. 5, 1824, p. 3, c. 5.

JONES, MRS. MARTHA died on 12th inst. Consort of Dudley Jones of Campbell Co.
The Lynchburg Virginian, June 22, 1826, p. 3, c. 3.

JONES, MRS. MARTHA died on 1st inst., age 53. Consort of Emanuel Jones of Pittsylvania.
The Lynchburg Virginian, Nov. 24, 1825, p. 3.

JONES, MRS. MARTHA died on 6th inst., age 33. Consort of Jas. S. Jones of Campbell Co. Left husband and several children.
The Lynchburg Virginian, Oct. 20, 1828, p. 3, c. 5.

JONES, MARTHA HUGHES died Aug. 20, 1832, age 20 months. Dau. of Mr. Paul Jones.
The Lynchburg Virginian, Aug. 23, 1832, p. 3, c. 4.

JONES, MRS. MARY J. B. died on the morning of the 4th, age 22 years, at father's residence. Dau. of Col. Stephen Coleman of Pittsylvania Co., Va. Wife of Meredith E. Jones, Esq. Left infant 19 days old. The Randolph (Tenn.) will please publish this.
The Lynchburg Virginian, Sept. 11, 1834, p. 3, c. 4.

JONES, MRS. PATSEY died a few days ago, age 82, at the residence of her daughter in this place.
The Lynchburg Virginian, Jan. 5, 1826, p. 3, c. 3.

JONES, MR. ROBERT died lately in Louisville, Ky. Was for many years a
resident of this place.
The Lynchburg Virginian, July 23, 1832, p. 3, c. 4.

JONES, ROBERT K., ESQ. died on 13th inst., "Hyco" in Halifax Co. at the
residence of Dr. Thomas P. Atkinson. Cashier of Bank of Virginia
at Petersburg.
The Lynchburg Virginian, Sept. 3, 1824, p. 3, c. 3.

JONES, MRS. SARAH ANN died Sept. 23rd last. Age 24. Died in Russellville,
Alabama. Wife of Mr. Manson Jones and youngest dau. of Mr. Henry
Moorman of Campbell Co., Va.
The Lynchburg Virginian, Nov. 7, 1831, p. 3, c. 3.

JONES, CAPT. THOMAS died on 8th inst., age 80, at residence in Nelson Co.
Actively engaged throughout greater portion of the Revolution; was
wounded at battle of Brandywine. Acquired a competency.
The Lynchburg Virginian, July 23, 1835, p. 3, c. 3.

JONES, THOMAS died on 16th inst., age 56, at residence of James P. Martin
in Bedford Co.
The Lynchburg Virginian, Dec. 7, 1835, p. 3, c. 5.

JONES, THOMAS C. died at his father's home in Campbell Co. Was of CampbellCo.
The Lynchburg Virginian, Nov. 17, 1825, p. 3.

JONES, WILLIAM died April 6, 1824, age 64, at his residence in Campbell Co.
The Lynchburg Virginian, April 16, 1824, p. 3.

JONES, WILLIAM, ESQ. died on 6th inst. at Bethlehem, Penn. Late Collector
of the Port of Philadelphia and formerly Secretary of the Navy.
The Lynchburg Virginian, Sept. 15, 1831, p. 3, c. 3.

JONES, WILLIAM S. died on 11th inst. at Louisville, Ky. Was formerly of
Lynchburg and was a Deputy Sheriff.
The Lynchburg Virginian, Aug. 31, 1835, p. 3, c. 5.

JOPLING, MRS. ANN died on 10th inst., age 51. Was consort of James
Jopling of Bedford.
The Lynchburg Virginian, Jan. 18, 1827, p. 3, c. 4.

JOPLING, JESSEE died on 22nd of Jan., 1835 at age 29. Died in Pettis Co.,
Mo. at the house of his uncle, Wm. Jopling. Was of Bedford Co., Va.
The Lynchburg Virginian, Feb. 26, 1835, p. 3, c. 5.

JOPLING, MRS. SUSANNA died June 29, 1833, age 54. Resident of Bedford Co.
Wife of Mr. James Jopling of Bedford Co. and member of Methodist
Church for 34 years.
The Lynchburg Virginian, July 15, 1833, p. 3, c. 6.

K

KABLER, THE REV. NICHOLAS died Sept. 6th at Camp Branch, Missouri. He lived in this vicinity at one time. Minister of M. E. Church.
The Lynchburg Virginian, Sept. 29, 1834, p. 3, c. 5.

KELLY, MICHAEL died Monday morning at Margate in his 64th year. He was a composer of music.
The Lynchburg Virginian, Dec. 7, 1826, p. 1.

KELLY, ROBERT B. died Sat. last, age 15, at residence of Jesse Burton, Esq. in this County. Was of Campbell Co.
The Lynchburg Virginian, April 27, 1826, p. 3, c. 3.

KENT, MARY died on 8th inst., age 84, in Montgomery Co. Also of that Co.
The Lynchburg Virginian, April 17, 1826, p. 3, c. 3.

KENT, MRS. SARAH ANN died April 23, 1828, age 17. Consort of William Kent of Amherst. Member of Methodist Church.
The Lynchburg Virginian, May 1, 1828, p. 3, c. 6.

KILCREASE, MAJ. died of bullet wound. Of Lawrence Co., Tenn.
The Lynchburg Virginian, April 30, 1824, p. 3.

KING, GEORGE PAYNE died on 27th ult., age 58, in this County.
The Lynchburg Virginian, Dec. 11, 1834, p. 1, c. 4.

KING, MARGARET S. died Aug. 13, 1817, age 37. Second daughter of Capt. Sackville King.
The Lynchburg Press, Aug. 22, 1817, p. 3, c. 4.

KING, RUFUS an actor of New York.
The Lynchburg Virginian, May 8, 1827, p. 3.

KING, THOMAS died on Friday, 21st inst., at Martinsville in Henry Co. Mr. King, "a man of property", left a wife and 4 children.
The Lynchburg Virginian, Dec. 15, 1825, p. 3, c. 3.

KING, WILES, THE REV. died on 17th ult. at his residence. Was of Matthews Co. Minister of M. E. Church and formerly an officer in the U.S. Navy.
The Lynchburg Virginian, Oct. 2, 1834, p. 3, c. 4.

KINNEY, CAPT. died at Battle at Bridgewater, near Niagara Falls. (In list of several names in paper).
The Lynchburg Press, Aug. 18, 1814, p. 2, c. 1.

KNIGHT, MRS. MARGARET died on Apr. 22, 1829 at age 58. Was of New Glasgow.
The Lynchburg Virginian, May 1, 1828, p. 3, c. 6.

KRAUTH, CHARLES J. died yesterday in this place. A native of Germany but for some years a resident of this place.
The Lynchburg Virginian, March 9, 1826, p. 3, c. 2.

KRAUTH, ELIZA A. died last Wed., May 11, 1825 in Lynchburg. Age 21.
The Lynchburg Virginian, May 16, 1825, p. 3, c. 6.

L

LACK, ALEXANDER died on 23rd ultimo at residence of Mrs. M. A. Lewis in
Hardeman Co., Tenn. Deceased was late of Bedford Co., Va.
The Lynchburg Virginian, Sept. 17, 1835, p. 3, c. 5.

LACKEY, THOMAS killed in powder mill explosion at age 26. Left mother
and six children. News account Newark.
The Lynchburg Press, May 12, 1814, p. 2.

LAMB, MRS. NANCY died April 20, 1833 in neighborhood of Marysville. Was
consort of Wm. A. Lamb and third dau. of Jonathan Butler. Leaves
husband and two infants.
The Lynchburg Virginian, April 29, 1833, p. 3, c. 5.

LAMB, WALTER RICHARDSON
The Lynchburg Press, Aug. 11, 1814, p. 3, c. 1.

LAMBERT, DANIEL R. killed.
The Lynchburg Virginian, June 1825, p. 2.

LAMBERT, PATRICK died Aug. 12, 1822. Merchant of Lynchburg.
The Lynchburg Virginian, Aug. 19, 1822, p. 3, c. 6.

LAMBETH, MR. GEO. K. died on Saturday last very suddenly.
The Lynchburg Virginian, April 4, 1833, p. 3, c. 3.

LAMBETH, MEREDITH died on 25th ult., age 70, at his residence, Lawpton,
Campbell Co. Left a large family.
The Lynchburg Virginian, April 11, 1836, p. 3, c. 4.

LAMONT, JOHN died Sept. 24, 1823, age 80, in Bedford Co. Was native of
Scotland. Was among first to open store in Lynchburg when known
only as Lynch's Ferry.
The Lynchburg Virginian, Oct. 10, 1823, p. 3.

LAND, GIDEON died, aged 20. See entry for William Godfrey.
The Lynchburg Virginian, Aug. 12, 1827, p. 2, c. 5.

LANGHORNE, ELLIOTT SAMUEL died Dec. 23, age 2. Son of Col. Maurice
Langhorne, Jr.
The Lynchburg Virginian, Dec. 24, 1829, p. 3, c. 5.

LANGHORNE, MRS. FRANCES died on 13th inst., age 34, at the residence of
Col. Maurice H. Langhorne. Consort of Henry S. Langhorne, Esq.
Member of Methodist Episcopal Church and mother of 8 children.
The Lynchburg Virginian, April 19, 1832, p. 3, c. 3.

LANGHORNE, SALLY CARY died March 8, 1833, age 17, at Lynchburg. Second
dau. of Col. Maurice Langhorne.
The Lynchburg Virginian, March 14, 1833, p. 3, c. 4.

LARL, PHOEBE died Nov. 24, 1823, age 40. Native of Alexandria but
resident of Lynchburg for past few years. Survived by 3 children.
The Lynchburg Virginian, Nov. 28, 1823, p. 3.

LATIMORE, WIDOW died on 15th of Sept. near Christiansburg, Va. Born in
Co. of Tyrone, Kingdom of Ireland. Her twin sister, Miss Nancy
Glenn died the same.
The Lynchburg Virginian, Sept. 21, 1835, p. 3, c. 3.

LAVENDER, MR . WILLIAM, SR. died on 17th inst. in Amherst at Ambrose
Burford's. Soldier of Revolution.
The Lynchburg Virginian, Jan. 29, 1835, p. 3, c. 3.

LAZENBY, LUCY consort of Edward Lazenby of Bedford.
The Lynchburg Virginian, July 13, 1826, p. 3.

LEAKE, WALTER died on 17th inst. at his residence in Hinds Co. Governor
of State of Mississippi.
The Lynchburg Virginian, Dec. 22, 1825, p. 3.

LEDBETTER, MRS. HARRIET W. died on 20th of Dec. 1832, age 21. Consort
of Mr. Herbert Ledbetter of Lynchburg.
The Lynchburg Virginian, Jan. 3, 1833, p. 3, c. 4.

LEE, MAJ. BURWELL died Nov. 15, 1825, age 59, at his home in Campbell Co.
Funeral service preached by The Rev. William Leftwich on 3rd Sunday.
The Lynchburg Virginian, Dec. 1, 1825, p. 3, c. 4.

LEE, DANIEL, ESQ. died on April 15, 1833 at Winchester. Was father of
Mrs. P. H. Cabell of Lynchburg. He had been Clerk of the ancient
District Court since 1804 until 1812 when changed. Had held various
court positions and been President of Bank at Winchester.
The Lynchburg Virginian, May 6, 1833, p. 3, c. 5.

LEE, JOHN, died on 6th inst., in the 56th or 57th year of his age.
Deceased was of Campbell Co.
The Lynchburg Virginian, Oct. 13, 1831, p. 3, c. 4.

LEE, JOHN. native of England. Came to this country few years ago. Was
a merchant of this town.
The Lynchburg Virginian, May 22, 1827, p. 3, c. 5.

LEE, MRS. TABITHA died lately, 71 years of age. Relict of Richard Lee.
Died at residence in Bedford.
The Lynchburg Virginian, July 7, 1828, p. 3, c. 6.

LEFTWICH, AMERICA died Nov. 26th, age 19, at residence of General Leftwich.
Consort of J. F. Leftwich, Esq.
The Lynchburg Virginian, Dec. 13, 1827, p. 3, c. 4.

LEFTWICH, MAJ. AUGUSTINE, SR. died on Friday, Oct. 30th, age 91, at his
residence in the Co. of Bedford. Was a Revolutionary soldier.
The Lynchburg Virginian, Nov. 5, 1835, p. 3, c. 3.

LEFTWICH, MRS. FRANCES died Oct. 10, 1825, age 53 years and 4 days. Wife
of The Rev. William Leftwich of Bedford, a Baptist preacher. Died
at home of her son-in-law, Col. Pleasant M. Goggin.
The Lynchburg Virginian, Oct. 20, 1825, p. 3, c. 3.

LEFTWICH, CAPT. GRANVILLE U. S. Army died on 24th inst. Was a native
of Lynchburg, Va.
The Lynchburg Virginian, Nov. 26, 1824, p. 3, c. 5.

LEFTWICH, CAPT. JAMES died Aug. 4, 1825 on road between Lynchburg and
Richmond, Va. Of Powhatan Co. and partner of Leftwich & Claytor
firm in Lynchburg. A leading merchant of Lynchburg. See also
Virginian, Aug. 8, 1825, p. 3.
The Lynchburg Virginian, Aug. 11, 1825, p. 3.

LEFTWICH, MR. W. LILBOURN died Sept. 21, 1823. He was of Lynchburg.
Survived by wife and one child.
The Lynchburg Virginian, Sept. 23, 1823, p. 3, c. 6.

LEFTWICH, MRS. MILDRED A. died on 21st inst., age 23, at resident of
father in Pittsylvania. Wife of Augustine Leftwich, Esq. of
Lynchburg.
The Lynchburg Virginian, May 28, 1829, p. 3, c. 3.

LEFTWICH, MRS. MILLY died on 17th inst., age 60, at the residence of Mr.
Caleb Fuqua in Bedford Co. Consort of Mr. Peyton Leftwich of Campbell Co.
The Lynchburg Virginian, June 28, 1830, p. 3, c. 4.

LEFTWICH, MRS. SARAH died on 21st inst., age 46, in County of Campbell.
Deceased was consort of Capt. Jack Leftwich.
The Lynchburg Virginian, Oct. 1, 1829, p. 3, c. 3.

LEFTWICH, COL. WILLIAM died at age 83. Was of Bedford Co. Survived by
numerous decendants.
The Lynchburg Press & Public Advertiser, June 9, 1820, p. 3, c. 5.

LEFTWICH, DR. WILLIAM died at Pittsylvania Court House, Sept. 13, 1818.
The Lynchburg Press & Public Advertiser, Oct. 15, 1818, p. 3, c. 4.

LEGRAND, MISS LUCY died Aug. 12, 1822 at Montevideo in Buckingham. Was
of Charlotte.
The Lynchburg Virginian, Aug. 10, 1822, p. 3, c. 6.

LENOX, JOHN, ESQ. died on 6th inst., age about 75 years. Died at
Leaksville, N.C. Was a native of Scotland.
The Lynchburg Virginian, Dec. 29, 1825, p. 3, c. 4.

LEUBA, PETER H. died a few weeks since at Lexington, Ky. A native of
Switzerland and recently a resident of Lynchburg.
The Lynchburg Virginian, July 4, 1833, p. 3, c. 5.

LEWELLIN, JAMES (sic) died Aug. 7, 1823. Was of Lynchburg. Survived by
wife and seven children.
The Lynchburg Virginian, Aug. 8, 1823, p. 3, c. 5.

LEWELLIN, MRS. MARY died on 29th ult., age 48, in this place.
The Lynchburg Virginian, Aug. 4, 1831, p. 3, c. 5.

LEWIS, CHARLES died Feb. 2, 1822 at Lynchburg. Was of Spottsylvania Co.
The Lynchburg Press, Feb. 8, 1822, p. 1, c. 2.

LEWIS, HENRY died Nov. 30, 1818 at age 19. Son of William Lewis, Sr. of
Pittsylvania Co.
The Lynchburg Press & Public Advertiser, Dec. 10, 1818, p. 3.

LEWIS, MRS. JANE died July 27th at age 65. She was of Pittsylvania Co.
and is survived by husband, Mr. Wm. Lewis and 12 children.
The Lynchburg Press, Aug. 10, 1821, p. 3, c. 5.

LEWIS, WILLIAM of Halifax County, N.C.
The Lynchburg Virginian, July 16, 1824, p. 3, c. 2.

LEWIS, COL. WILLIAM died on Sunday, last at his residence near this place.
He represented this County in the Virginia Legislature.
The Lynchburg Virginian, Oct. 30, 1828, p. 3, c. 5.

LIGGAT, JOHN died on 24th ultimo, age 63, at the home of his brother,
Alexander Liggat. He was a native of the County of Antrim, Ireland
and resided for many years in Baltimore.
The Lynchburg Virginian, Sept. 14, 1835, p. 3, c. 4.

LIGHTFOOT, JOHN WESSLEY died on the 7th at the residence of Mr. Franklin
in Amherst Co. He was of Amherst Co.
The Lynchburg Press, Jan. 25, 1822, p. 3, c. 4.

LINCOLN, MRS. MARTHA died Friday morning last, age 66, at Worcester, Mass.
Relict of The Hon. Levin Lincoln of Mass. Survived by two sons who
are now Governors of Mass. and Maine.
The Lynchburg Virginian, Thurs., April 17, 1828, p. 3, c. 6.

LINDEN, LT. HENRY ST. JAMES died on 10th ult. at Baltimore, Md. He was
of the 6th regiment U.S. Infantry.
The Lynchburg Virginian, Sept. 5, 1836, p. 3, c. 4.

LINTON, JOHN, ESQ died at Saratoga Springs. Eminent merchant of New
Orleans and President of Canal Bank of that City.
The Lynchburg Virginian, Sept. 11, 1834, p. 3, c. 5.

LIVINGSTON, BROCKHOLST died March 18, 1823, age 66. Was an associate
Justice of the Supreme Court of U.S.
The Lynchburg Virginian, March 25, 1823, p. 3, c. 1.

LLOYD, MR. EDWARD died Sunday evening last at Fincastle. Was of Fincastle,
formerly of Lynchburg.
The Lynchburg Virginian, March 21, 1831, p. 3, c. 5.

LLOYD, THE HON. JAMES died Tuesday evening, age 61 in New York. He was
of State of Boston, Mass. Formerly a distinguished Senator in
Congress from State of Mass.
The Lynchburg Virginian, April 15, 1831, p. 1, c. 5.

LOCKHART, JAMES of Rawdom, died at his home; killed by fallen tree which
crushed his leg. Survived by wife and one child.
The Lynchburg Press & Public Advertiser, Feb. 18, 1820, p. 3.

LOGWOOD, MISS ELIZA died May 31, age 18. Died at residence of her father,
Capt. Burwell Logwood of Bedford.
The Lynchburg Virginian, June 12, 1828, p. 3, c. 4.

LOGWOOD, JOHN C. died on 9th inst. in 26th year. Son of Capt. Burwell
Logwood of Bedford.
The Lynchburg Virginian, Aug. 23, 1827, p. 3, c. 2.

LOGWOOD, MISS NANCY died on 30th inst. Youngest dau. of Catherine and
Thomas Logwood, deceased, of Bedford Co.
The Lynchburg Virginian, Oct. 19, 1826, p. 3, c. 2.

LOGWOOD, MAJOR THOMAS died at age 80 at his residence in Bedford County.
Survived by numerous family. He was a firm Republican, a patriot in
cause of Liberty through the Revolution.
The Lynchburg Press, Sept. 21, 1821, p. 1.

LOLLAR, JOHN R. died on 29th inst. Funeral to be from the Methodist
Church by The Rev. Martin P. Parks.
The Lynchburg Virginian, Aug. 19, 1830, p. 3, c. 4.

LOLAR, JOHN died Sat. last, 31st ult. Formerly of Petersburg, Va.
The Lynchburg Virginian, Aug. 5, 1830, p. 3, c. 5.

LONG, MRS. ELIZABETH died Friday night last at Laneville, near Amherst.
The Lynchburg Virginian, Jan. 5, 1835, p. 3, c. 3.

LOUGHBOROUGH, LIEUT. HARRISON died on 20th ult. at Shelbyville, Ky. Was
Lieut. of 2nd Artillery of U.S. Army.
The Lynchburg Virginian, Sept. 5, 1836, p. 3, c. 4.

LOVE, ROBERT died Jan. 4, 1827 in 73rd year. Of New London, a native of
North Briton. Born in Kynlin, near Campbellton in North Briton.
Emigrated to America soon after close of Revolution.
The Lynchburg Virginian, Jan. 18, 1827, p. 3, c. 4.

LOVE, SAMUEL died last Tues., age 42. Was of this place and left a wife
and small children.
The Lynchburg Virginian, April 21, 1836, p. 3, c. 3.

LOVING, EDWIN P. died on 5th inst., age 21, at his father's residence
near Lovingston. Left parents and brothers.
The Lynchburg Virginian, Jan. 12, 1835, p. 3, c. 5.

LOWRY, MRS. ABIGAIL died June 23, 1833 in 63rd year. Wife of Mr. John
Lowry, Sr. of Bedford Co. Member of Baptist Church for about 40 yrs.
The Lynchburg Virginian, June 29, 1833, p. 3, c. 5.

LUCK, RICHARD died May 26, 1809. Resident of Campbell Co.
The Lynchburg Press, June 3, 1809, p. 3, c. 3.

LUCUS, MRS. POLLY died on 4th inst., age 25, in Amherst Co. She left
husband and two small children. Wife of Winston Lucas of Amherst.
The Lynchburg Virginian, Sept. 25, 1826, p. 3, c. 4.

LYNAR, DAVID died on Aug. 22, 1827 in Edgefield. Copied from Edgefield
Hive.
The Lynchburg Virginian, Sept. 24, 1827, p. 3, c. 2.

LYNCH, ALEXANDER died on July 18th at Velasco, Texas. Was surgeon in
Texan Army, late of Petersburg, Va.
The Lynchburg Virginian, Aug. 21, 1837, p. 3, c. 4.

LYNCH, MRS. ANN died July 15th at residence of Mrs. Henry Clark of
Lynchburg. Husband was Capt. Micajah Lynch. Dau. of James C.
Moorman, Esq.
The Lynchburg Virginian, July 18, 1823, p. 3, c. 5.

LYNCH, ANSELM died Nov. 12, 1814. Youngest son of John Lynch, Sen.
The Lynchburg Press, Nov. 17, 1814, p. 3, c. 3.

LYNCH, CHRISTOPHER died March 14, 1818. Son of John Lynch, Sen. of
Lynchburg.
The Lynchburg Press, March 20, 1818, p. 3, c. 2.

LYNCH, JOHN, JR. died Aug. 20, 1832, age 30. Was of Lynchburg.
The Lynchburg Virginian, Aug. 23, 1832, p. 3, c. 3.

LYNCH, MRS. MARY died on 5th inst., age 77, at residence of Edward Lynch.
Relict of John Lynch, Sen. dec'd., the patentee and former proprietor
of lands upon which stands the Town of Lynchburg.
The Lynchburg Virginian, Aug. 10, 1829, p. 3, c. 4.

LYNCH, CAPT. MICAJAH died on Tuesday. Was of Lynchburg.
The Lynchburg Virginian, May 25, 1826, p. 3, c. 3.

LYNCH, COL. WILLIAM B. died on Monday last. Was of Lynchburg. Son of
John Lynch, Sen.
The Lynchburg Virginian, June 1, 1826, p. 3, c. 3.

LYON, COL. MATTHEWS died at Spadre Bluff, Arkansas. Native of Ireland.
The Lynchburg Virginian, Nov. 5, 1822, p. 3.

MCALEXANDER, WILLIAM died March 8, 1822, age 79. He was of Patrick Co. and is survived by his widow and 8 children.
The Lynchburg Press, April 5, 1821, p. 3.

MCALLISTER, MRS. ELIZABETH died March 2nd last, age 84, at Trigg Co. Formerly of Campbell County.
The Lynchburg Virginian, June 30, 1836, p. 3, c. 3.

MCCABE, MRS. CLEOPATRA ALBERTINE died on 22nd inst., age 42, in Bedford Co. Was the consort of Wm. McCabe.
The Lynchburg Virginian, March 28, 1836, p. 3, c. 3.

M'CLANAHAM, JOHN died Sept. 9, 1814. He was of Botetourt Co., and is survived by his widow and 4 children.
The Lynchburg Press, Sept. 29, 1814, p. 3, c. 2.

MCCLELLAND, THOMAS S. died on 20th of August at Montezuma, his place of residence in Nelson Co. He was a lawyer.
The Lynchburg Virginian, Sept. 7, 1835, p. 3, c. 5.

MCCORKLE, FRANCES MILDRED died on 15th inst., age 2, in this place. She was the dau. of Capt. Samuel McCorkle.
The Lynchburg Virginian, Jan. 23, 1832, p. 3, c. 3.

MCCOY, CORNELIUS shot and died on Tuesday last. He was of Norfolk Co. and residing at North-West River Bridge.
The Lynchburg Virginian, Nov. 12, 1822, p. 3.

MCCOY, GEN. WILLIAM died on 19th ult. at his residence in Pendleton Co. Was formerly a Representative of that District in Congress.
The Lynchburg Virginian, Sept. 3, 1835, p. 3, c. 4.

M'CULLOCH, MRS. MARY W. died on Feb. 5, 1819, age 26, at her home in Amherst Co. She was the wife of Thomas H. McCulloch.
The Lynchburg Press & Public Advertiser, Feb. 11, 1819, p. 3, c. 4.

MCCULLOCK, CAPT. RODERICK died on 31st ult., age 85, at his residence.
The Lynchburg Virginian, Nov. 16, 1826, p. 3, c. 4.

MCDANIEL, EDWARD JACKSON died on Oct. 5, 1832, age about 4 yrs. He was the youngest child of Wm. and Elizabeth McDaniel of Amherst Co.
The Lynchburg Virginian, Oct. 29, 1832, p. 3, c. 3.

MCDANIEL, MRS. FRANCES died Sept. 26, 1822, age 37, at her father's residence in Amherst. She was the wife of George McDaniel and dau. of Joseph Higginbotham. She is survived by her husband and 2 children.
The Lynchburg Virginian, Oct. 18, 1822, p. 3, c. 4.

MCDANIEL, GEORGE, SR. died Nov. 22, 1821 at age 100. Was of Amherst Co. He was born in Richmond Co., Va.
The Lynchburg Press, Dec. 7, 1821, p. 3, c. 4.

MCDANIEL, JOHN died in January 1818.
The Lynchburg Press, May 25, 1821, p. 3, c. 4.

M'DONNOUGH, COMMODORE died on 10th inst. on board the Brig. Edwin. The
interment in Conn.
The Lynchburg Virginian, Dec. 1, 1825, p. 3, c. 3.

MCDONOLD, JOHN died on Thurs. last, age 80. Was an old soldier of the
Revolution and served throughout the war in the Pittsylvania line.
Interred with military and masonic honors.
The Lynchburg Virginian, March 1, 1830, p. 3, c. 3.

MCDUFFIE, MRS. MARY REBECCA died Sept. 14, 1830 at her father's residence
near Manchester, S.C. Consort of the Hon. George McDuffie and dau.
of Richard Singleton.
The Lynchburg Virginian, Sept. 30, 1830, p. 3, c. 3.

M'FARLAND, MAJOR killed in Battle at Bridgewater near Niagara Falls.
The Lynchburg Press, Aug. 18, 1814, p. 2.

MCGREE, BARKLEY, ESQ. died on 17th of this month at his residence in
Maryville. Deceased was a contractor in the U.S. Army.
The Lynchburg Press & Public Advertiser, Sept. 10, 1819, p. 3, c. 4.

MCILVAINE, BLOOMFIELD died in Burlington, N.J. He was of Philadelphia.
The Lynchburg Virginian, Aug. 31, 1826, p. 3.

MCKEE, MRS. P. E. died on 4th inst. in Abingdon, Va. She moved from New
York City to Abingdon. Was consort of William McKee, Esq.
The Lynchburg Virginian, June 16, 1825, p. 3, c. 4.

MCKEE, MRS. WILLIAM died in Abington, Va. at about age 50 at the residence
of Mr. Elias Ogden. He was one of the firm of McKee and Meem and of
McKee, Robinson and Co. of Lynchburg.
The Lynchburg Virginian, May 30, 1833, p. 3, c. 4.

MCKINNEY, WILLIAM, ESQ. died last Friday in this place at age 52. He
was a member of the Bar and of the Court of Campbell which Body
took official note of his passing.
The Lynchburg Virginian, Nov. 19, 1832, p. 3, c. 4.

MCLEAN, MRS. ALEXANDER died May 16, 1827. Wife of Alexander McLean and
dau. of Mr. Thompson. Leaves 1 child. Account dated New York,
May 17, 1827.
The Lynchburg Virginian, May 29, 1827, p. 2, c. 4.

MCMURPHY, DANIEL, SR. died in Georgia on 17th ult., age 89. Was a
native of Antrim Co., Ireland. Served in various military appoint-
ments during Revolutionary struggle. Also Rep. in State Legislature.
Taken from Nat. Intelligencer.
The Lynchburg Press, Nov. 23, 1819, p. 3.

MCREA, LT. COL. WILLIAM died on 3rd inst. on the steamboat Express on his
way from Louisville to St. Louis, age 65. Was of the 2nd Regiment
U.S. Artillery. Upward of 34 years spent in service of his country.
The Lynchburg Virginian, Nov. 29, 1832, p. 3, c. 4.

MCVICKER, JOHN O. died on Tuesday the 14th inst., age 32. Deceased was
of Winchester, Va.
The Lynchburg Virginian, June 16, 1831, p. 3, c. 2.

M

MADISON, MRS. ELIZABETH died July 28, 1825, age 38. She was of
Charlotte Co., Va.
The Lynchburg Virginian, Aug. 4, 1825, p. 3.

MADISON, JOHN, ESQ. died on 27th inst., age 84. Was a native of Louisa
Co. where he spent the greater part of his life. He lived also in
Nelson and was late of Augusta Co.
The Lynchburg Virginian, May 23, 1833, p. 3, c. 3.

MANDARIS, JOHN drowned in Rappahannock River. Was of Nelson Co.
The Lynchburg Press, Nov. 23, 1821, p. 1.

MARR, MRS. SARAH died on Sept. 3rd, age 26. Was consort of Dr. Ambrose
Marr of Pittsylvania Co., Va. Left husband and infant child.
The Lynchburg Virginian, Oct. 13, 1836, p. 1, c. 6.

MARSHALL, MR. JAMES EDGAR died Nov. 3, 1825, age 18, at the University
of Virginia. Was the son of Horace Marshall of Fredericksburg, Va.
A resolution of respect was passed by the University students.
The Lynchburg Virginian, Nov. 14, 1825, p. 3.

MARSHALL, CHIEF JUSTICE JOHN died July 6, 1835, age 80, at the boarding
house of Mrs. Crim on Walnut Street in Philadelphia. Copied from
the Philadelphia Gazette of July 7th which carried a lengthy eulogy.
The Lynchburg Virginian, July 13, 1835, p. 2, c. 6.

MARSHALL, SAMUEL died on 4th inst. in Richmond. Was of Henry Co., Va.
The Lynchburg Virginian, Nov. 20, 1834, p. 3, c. 4.

MARTIN, MRS. ANN A. died on 15th inst., age 29. Was wife of James A.
Martin of Bedford and a dau. of Jacob Feazle.
The Lynchburg Virginian, June 1, 1835, p. 3, c. 4.

MARTIN, CULWELL W. died lately. Was the 3rd son of James Martin. Was
formerly of this place.
The Lynchburg Virginian, March 5, 1829, p. 3, c. 2.

MARTIN, MRS. ELIZABETH died last Friday in this place. She was the
relict of the late Rev. W. P. Martin and dau. of John Pendleton, Esq.
She was in King and Queen County in 1750. Was a member of the Methodist Church.
The Lynchburg Virginian, March 28, 1831, p. 3, c. 4.

MARTIN, MRS. ELIZABETH died Nov. 3, 1832, age 18, at the residence of her
father, Thomas Starling of Henry Co. She was the widow of Capt.
George W. Martin. See also Lybg. Virginian, Nov. 29, 1832.
The Lynchburg Virginian, Nov. 12, 1832, p. 3, c. 5.

MARTIN, HUDSON, SR., ESQ. died on 28th ult., age 79, at his residence on
Rockfish, in Nelson Co. Was a member of the Episcopal Church.
The Lynchburg Virginian, Dec. 13, 1830, p. 3, c. 4.

MARTIN, JESSE died Nov. 28th, age about 53, at his residence in Henry Co.
He left a large family.
The Lynchburg Virginian, Dec. 8, 1836, p. 3, c. 5.

MARTIN, THE REV. WILLIAM PETERS died on Oct. 30, 1829 at the residence
of Mr. Richard Thurman. He was born in King William Co. June 1, 1745.
He was a lawyer and then became a minister of the Methodist Episcopal
Church.
The Lynchburg Virginian, Jan. 9, 1829, p. 3, c. 5.

MASON, ARMISTEAD T. died in a duel in vicinity of Bladenburg, Loudon Co., Va.
The Lynchburg Press, Feb. 15, 1819, p. 3.

MASON, MRS. SIDNEY died March 15, 1815. Was the wife of David F. Mason
of Lynchburg.
The Lynchburg Press, March 23, 1815, p. 3, c. 1.

MASSIE, MRS. MARTHA died a few days since, 20 yrs. of age, at the residence
of her husband in the county of Nelson. Was the wife of William Massie,
Esq. and dau. of the late Thomas Wiatt of Lynchburg.
The Lynchburg Virginian, July 16, 1832, p. 3, c. 5.

MASSIE, MRS. WILLIAM died at residence of her brother, Dr. Wm. Steptoe
in Bedford. Was consort of Mr. Wm. Massie of Nelson.
The Lynchburg Virginian, July 31, 1828, p. 3, c. 6.

MATHEW, SOLOMON died at Tuscumbia, Alabama. Formerly of Lynchburg.
The Lynchburg Virginian, Nov. 23, 1826, p. 3.

MAY, POWHATTAN, ESQ. Was an attorney-at-law and native of Buckingham Co.,
Va. Had moved to Jackson, Tenn. where he died on Monday last. Copied
from Jackson Tenn. Gazette.
The Lynchburg Virginian, Aug. 30, 1830, p. 3, c. 3.

MAYS, JOSEPH died Sept. 11, 1832 in this place. He was a merchant of the
firm of Kyle and Mays.
The Lynchburg Virginian, Sept. 13, 1822, p. 3, c. 4.

MEADE, NICHOLAS died on 2nd inst., age about 84, at his residence in
Bedford Co.
The Lynchburg Virginian, April 7, 1831, p. 3, c. 4.

MEADOWS, OBEDIAH died on 13th inst., age 60, at his residence in Bedford
Co. Was of Bedford and left a wife and 9 children.
The Lynchburg Virginian, July 27, 1826, p. 3, c. 2.

MEGGINSON, MRS. ALMIRA died on 13th inst., age 26, at the residence of
her father, Capt. Jos. Montgomery of Nelson Co. Was the consort of
Jos. Megginson, Esq. Husband and 2 little daughters survive.
The Lynchburg Virginian, April 22, 1830, p. 3, c. 4.

MEIGS, COL. RETURN JONATHAN a native of Connecticut died at the Cherokee
Agency, Jan. 28, 1823.
The Lynchburg Virginian, March 7, 1823, p. 3.

MENNIS, MRS. ANN B. died on 25th ult., age 26. Was the wife of Calohill
Mennis of Bedford. She left two children.
The Lynchburg Virginian, March 5, 1829, p. 3, c. 2.

MENNIS, CALOHILL died on 19th inst., age 33, at the residence of Mrs.
Callaway, in Bedford Co. Former member of the Convention of Va.
The Lynchburg Virginian, Dec. 28, 1829, p. 3, c. 5.

MEREDITH, MRS. JANE died Aug. 11, 1819, age 83. She was consort of the
late Col. Samuel Meredith of Amherst Co. and sister of Patrick Henry.
The Lynchburg Press & Public Advertiser, Aug. 20, 1819, p. 3, c. 6.

MERRITT, MRS. JOHN died Sept. 24, 1825. She was of Amherst and the
consort of John Merritt of Amherst.
The Lynchburg Virginian, Oct. 6, 1825, p. 3, c. 4.

MERRIWETHER, MRS. ELIZABETH died around Feb. 5, 1815. She was about 80
years of age and of Richmond.
The Lynchburg Press, April 27, 1815, p. 3, c. 2.

MERRIWETHER, GEORGE DOUGLAS died Jan. 8, 1825, age 29. Was of Bedford.
The Lynchburg Virginian, Jan. 14, 1825, p. 3.

MICHAUX, MRS. ANN died on 3rd inst. Was consort of Richard W. Michaux
of Pittsylvania Co., Va.
The Lynchburg Virginian, July 21, 1831, p. 3, c. 4.

MILER, MRS. THOMAS died May 7, 1814. Was the wife of Thomas Miler of
Lynchburg.
The Lynchburg Press, May 12, 1814, p. 5, c. 2.

MILES, CAPHAS died Aug. 19, 1824 at the residence of Dr. Taliaferro in
Franklin Co. He was formerly of Hebron, Conn.
The Lynchburg Virginian, Aug. 24, 1824, p. 3.

MILLER, JAMES, ESQ. died on 23rd inst. He was High Sheriff of Campbell Co.
The Lynchburg Virginian, Nov. 26, 1829, p. 3, c. 6.

MILLER, MRS. MARY died Sept. 6, 1814. She was the relict of the late
John Miller of Lynchburg.
The Lynchburg Press, Sept. 8, 1814, p. 3, c. 2.

MILLER, MARY FRANCES died on Wed., Aug. 31st, age 10 mos. and 4 days.
Only dau. of F. S. Miller.
The Lynchburg Virginian, Sept. 5, 1831, p. 3, c. 5.

MINTER, JEREMIAH died on 29th ult., age 64, in Chesterfield Co. He was
a Methodist minister.
The Lynchburg Virginian, Dec. 17, 1829, p. 3, c. 6.

MITCHELL, MRS. APHIA died on 20th inst., age 31. Was wife of Mr. Pleasant
Mitchell. Obituary is dated New Glasgow, May 27.
The Lynchburg Virginian, May 31, 1830, p. 3, c. 5.

MITCHELL, MRS. CHARLES L. died on 7th ultimo. Husband, Dr. Charles L.
Mitchell who died on 6th inst. was of St. Louis, Mo. Formerly of
Lynchburg.
The Lynchburg Virginian, Sept. 12, 1823, p. 3, c. 5.

MITCHELL, DR. CHARLES L. died on 6th ult. He was of St. Louis, Mo.
Formerly of Lynchburg.
The Lynchburg Virginian, Sept. 12, 1823, p. 3, c. 5.

MITCHELL, EDWARD died on 7th inst., age 4. Was son of Robert C. Mitchell,
Esq. of Bedford.
The Lynchburg Virginian, Aug. 11, 1836, p. 3, c. 2.

MITCHELL, ELIZABETH died on May 15th in Charlestown, Mass. Was wife of
Harvey Mitchell of Lynchburg.
The Lynchburg Virginian, June 4, 1829, p. 3, c. 3.

MITCHELL, GEORGE W. died July 2, 1819, age 27. He was of Lynchburg and
left wife and child.
The Lynchburg Press & Public Advertiser, July 5, 1819, p. 3, c. 5.

MITCHELL, MARY died on Aug. 29, 1832, age 2. Was of Lynchburg and the
only dau. of The Rev. Jacob Mitchell of this place.
The Lynchburg Virginian, Sept. 3, 1832, p. 3, c. 5.

MITCHELL, MRS. MARY ANN died on Sept. 28th in her 70th year at her residence in Montgomery Co. She was the consort of Thos. Mitchell, dec'd.
The Lynchburg Virginian, Oct. 5, 1835, p. 2, c. 1.

MITCHELL, MAJOR SAMUEL died on 25th inst., age 70, at his residence in
Bedford Co. He was of Bedford Co. and a member of the Presbyterian
Church. He was a soldier in Revolutionary War and held civil and
military offices.
The Lynchburg Virginian, March 30, 1835, p. 3, c. 6.

MITCHELL, DR. SAMUEL L. died on 7th inst. in New York, age 70. Was a
member of many learned societies both in this country and in Europe.
The Lynchburg Virginian, Sept. 15, 1831, p. 3, c. 3.

MITCHELL, STEPHEN T., ESQ. died yesterday in his 29th year. An attorney-
at-law and formerly Editor of the Morning Bulletin in this Burough.
He was a native of Bedford Co., Va. Lately resident of Giles Co.,
N. C. Copied from Norfolk Beacon, Jan. 18.
The Lynchburg Virginian, Jan. 27, 1831, p. 3, c. 5.

MITCHELL, CAPT. WILLIAM died June 12, 1824 in Amherst Co. He was of
Amherst and formerly a merchant of Lynchburg.
The Lynchburg Virginian, June 18, 1824, p. 3, c. 5.

MITCHELL, WILLIAM, JR. died Sept. 21, 1824, age 29. Merchant of Lynchburg.
The Lynchburg Virginian, Sept. 24, 1824, p. 3.

MONROE, JOSEPH JONES died in Franklin Co., Miss.
The Lynchburg Virginian, Sept. 3, 1824, p. 3.

MONTGOMERY, MRS. MARY W. died Aug. 3, 1814, age 36. Was of Amherst Co., sister of Mr. Richard S. Ellis of Amherst Co.
The Lynchburg Press, Aug. 11, 1814, p. 3, c. 1.

MONTGOMERY, THE HON. THOMAS died April 21, 1828 at residence in Lincoln Co., Kentucky. Was for several years a member of Congress, and a Judge of the Circuit Court.
The Lynchburg Virginian, May 8, 1828, p. 3, c. 5.

MOOR, CAPT. EDWARD died at age 33 on Feb. 15, 1824 at Henry Courthouse. He was of Georgetown, N. C.
The Lynchburg Virginian, March 12, 1824, p. 3.

MOORE, MRS. POLLY P. died on Jan. 31st in her 57th year at the residence of her son-in-law, Doc. J. D. McGee in Crawford Co., Arkansas Territory.
The Lynchburg Virginian, July 2, 1835, p. 3, c. 6.

MOORE, ROBIN died on May 28th in Bedford City, age 85. He was a soldier of the Revolution.
The Lynchburg Virginian, Aug. 24, 1835, p. 3, c. 4.

MOORE, COL. THOMAS died on 31st ult., age 66, at his seat in Bedford.
The Lynchburg Virginian, Aug. 4, 1831, p. 3, c. 5.

MOORE, ZEPHANIAH SWIFT died July 30, 1823. He was of Amherst, New Hampshire and Pres. of the Collegiate Institution of Amherst N. H.
The Lynchburg Virginian, Aug. 1, 1823, p. 3.

MOORMAN, CAPT. ACHILLES died May 25, 1809. Was a resident of Campbell Co., Va. and formerly Representative to General Assembly of Virginia.
The Lynchburg Press, May 27, 1809, p. 4, c. 3.

MOORMAN, MISS ELIZABETH died on 16th inst., age 21, in this Town.
The Lynchburg Virginian, Nov. 24, 1836, p. 3, c. 4.

MOORMAN, HENRY, SR. died on 1st inst., age 74. Was of Campbell Co.
The Lynchburg Virginian, June 20, 1836, p. 3, c. 5.

MOORMAN, JAMES C. died Aug. 18, 1836, age 58, at his residence in the Co. of St. Louis Mo. opposite the town of St. Charles. Was formerly of Campbell Co., Va.
The Lynchburg Virginian, Oct. 24, 1836, p. 3, c. 3.

MOORMAN, LEMUEL, ESQ. died Sept. 13th last in Lincolnton, N.C. Was a native of Bedford Co.
The Lynchburg Virginian, Nov. 3, 1828, p. 3, c. 5.

MOORMAN, MARY CORNELIA died on 15th inst., age 6, at residence of her father at Shady Grove, Henry Co. Was the 2nd dau. of Achilles H. and Eliza S. Moorman.
The Lynchburg Virginian, July 27, 1835, p. 3, c. 5.

MOORMAN, SAMUEL died on July 1, 1835, age 64, at residence on Flat Creek
in Campbell Co., Va. Was of Flat Creek and left a large family.
The Lynchburg Virginian, July 16, 1835, p. 3, c. 5.

MORGAN, MRS. ELIZABETH died on Monday, March 12th, age 28 in Pittsylvania
Co., Va. She was consort of Mr. John Morgan of Amherst.
The Lynchburg Virginian, March 29, 1832, p. 3, c. 5.

MORGAN, ELIZABETH K. died Sept. 2, 1823, age 43. Was consort of William
Morgan of Lynchburg.
The Lynchburg Virginian, Sept. 5, 1823, p. 3.

MORGAN, FRANCES died on 24th ult. in 106th year of age. Was of Nelson Co.
The Lynchburg Virginian, May 4, 1826, p. 3, c. 2.

MORGAN, HAYNES was of Rowan, N.C. but a native of Pittsylvania Co., Va.
The Lynchburg Virginian, Oct. 12, 1826, p. 3.

MORGAN, MORDECAI died Jan. 31, 1828, age 70. Survived by wife. He was
of Bedford.
The Lynchburg Virginian, Feb. 21, 1828, p. 3.

MORING, THE REV. CHRISTOPHER SIMMONS died Sept. 30, 1825, age 36, at home
of The Rev. Edward Cannon. He was a Methodist minister and his
funeral was conducted by The Rev. H. G. Leigh.
The Lynchburg Virginian, Oct. 3, 1825, p. 3.

MORRISS, MRS. ANN JENNIFER died on Tues. the 7th inst. at Port Tabacco,
Maryland. She was the widow and relict of Henry Villiers Morriss;
a native of England and late of Lynchburg, Va. Deceased was dau.
of the late Dr. Thomas Nixon of Delaware. Left 2 males and 2
female children.
The Lynchburg Virginian, Feb. 12, 1829, p. 3, c. 4.

MORRIS, HENRY VILLIERS died Oct. 4, 1824 at Port Tobacco, Maryland. He
was a native of England, but for many years a resident of this Co.
He is survived by a wife and 5 small children.
The Lynchburg Virginian, Oct. 22, 1824, p. 3.

MORRISS, MISS FRANCES ANN died on 23rd Jan., age 27. Was of Amherst.
The Lynchburg Virginian, Feb. 1, 1827, p. 3, c. 4.

MORRISS, GEORGE died Aug. 30th, age about 65, in Amherst Co. He left a
wife and family.
The Lynchburg Virginian, Sept. 14, 1826, p. 3, c. 4.

MORRISS, HENRY S. died on 11th inst. in his 24th year. Was of Amherst.
The Lynchburg Virginian, Feb. 1, 1827, p. 3, c. 4.

MORRISS, MAURICE was son of Thomas Morriss of Amherst but resident of
Indiana.
The Lynchburg Virginian, Sept. 8, 1825, p. 3.

MORRISS, MRS. NANCY died on 9th inst. at residence of Thos. Morris in
Amherst Co.
The Lynchburg Virginian, Feb. 1, 1827, p. 3, c. 4.

MORRISS, PETER died Aug. 14th, age 15, in Amherst Co. He was the son of
George Morriss of Amherst.
The Lynchburg Virginian, Sept. 14, 1826, p. 3, c. 4.

MORRISS, RACHEL died July 10th, age 19, in the Co. of Amherst. Was the
dau. of George Morriss of Amherst.
The Lynchburg Virginian, Sept. 14, 1826, p. 3, c. 4.

MORRISS, MR. THOMAS died on Wed., 10th inst. after an illness of ten days
at age 73.
The Lynchburg Virginian, Feb. 1, 1827, p. 3, c. 4.

MORRISS, THOMAS A. died on 9th inst., age 27.
The Lynchburg Virginian, Nov. 30, 1826, p. 3.

MORRISS, THOMAS G. died on 15th inst., age 26. Was of Amherst.
The Lynchburg Virginian, Feb. 1, 1827, p. 3, c. 4.

MORTON, JOSEPH, ESQ. died Dec. 10, 1817, age 60. Was of Pittsylvania Co.
The Lynchburg Press, Jan. 23, 1818, p. 3, c. 2.

MORTON, JOSIAH died on 11th inst. in Pittsylvania Co., Va.
The Lynchburg Virginian, Sept. 20, 1832, p. 3, c. 3.

MORTON, WILLIAM died on Monday last. Was of Lynchburg.
The Lynchburg Virginian, Feb. 16, 1826, p. 3, c. 5.

MOSBY, ELBERT murdered in Powhatan Co.
The Lynchburg Virginian, Jan. 17, 1828, p. 3, c. 3.

MOSBY, GEORGE died on 22nd. ult., age 31, in Lynchburg. Left a devoted wife.
The Lynchburg Virginian, Aug. 11, 1836, p. 3, c. 2.

MOSBY, GEORGE died on 22nd ult., age 31, in Lynchburg, Va. Was son of
Joseph Mosby. Left a wife.
The Lynchburg Virginian, Aug. 11, 1836, p. 3, c. 2.

MOTLEY, CHRISTOPHER WILLIAM died on 6th inst., age 19, at Mrs. Walker's
in Campbell Co. Deceased left wife and child, father and mother.
The Lynchburg Virginian, Aug. 10, 1835, p. 3, c. 4.

MOUNTCASTLE, JOHN died on 21st ult. at residence near New Glasgow,
Amherst Co. Deceased was husband and father.
The Lynchburg Virginian, Aug. 9, 1830, p. 3, c. 5.

MUNFORD, MRS. SARAH died on Sat. the 26th of May last at Flood's Tavern,
in the county of Buckingham. Was the wife of Captain Edward Munford
and dau. of the late Gen. Mosby of Powhatan.
The Lynchburg Virginian, June 11, 1832, p. 3, c. 4.

MUNFORD, WILLIAM died June 21, 1825, age 52. Was of Lynchburg and Clerk
of the House of Delegates.
The Lynchburg Virginian, June 27, 1825, p. 3.

MURRELL, ELIZABETH, MRS. died on 25th inst., age 37. Consort of Capt.
Thomas Murrell. Left husband and 7 children.
The Lynchburg Virginian, March 30, 1826, p. 3, c. 4.

MURRELL, CAPT. THOMAS died on Tues. last in this place. Formerly of
Amherst Co.
The Lynchburg Virginian, Nov. 16, 1826, p. 3, c. 4.

MUSGROVE, NATHANIEL killed. Was of Montgomery County.
The Lynchburg Virginian, July 29, 1823, p. 3.

MYLER, MISS EMILY C. died on 3rd inst. in 26th year of her age.
The Lynchburg Virginian, Aug. 12, 1827, p. 3, c. 4.

N

NAPIER, MOSES C. died Thurs., Jan. 26th, age 68. Was of Amherst.
The Lynchburg Virginian, March 5, 1832, p. 3, c. 4.

NAPIER, MR. WM. BRYDIE died March 28th in Calloway Co. Missouri. Age 35.
The Lynchburg Virginian, May 14, 1832, p. 3, c. 4.

NASH, ABNER died March 2, 1823, age 64, in Lynchburg. Was of Prince
Edward Co. Survived by wife and 6 children.
The Lynchburg Virginian, March 4, 1823, p. 3.

NASH, MRS. DIANA R. died on Feb. 1st in Hanibal, Missouri. Consort of
Abner O. Nash merchant, formerly of Lynchburg. Mrs. Nash was a
native of Ireland; resided in Lynchburg until 1832.
The Lynchburg Virginian, March 19, 1835, p. 3, c. 5.

NEBLETT, MISS REBECCA died on 8th inst. at the residence of brother-in-law,
Charles Smith, Esq. of Lunenburg Co., Va.
The Lynchburg Virginian, Feb. 25, 1836, p. 3, c. 5.

NEILSON, MRS. EDMONIA LEE died Sun. night, the 21st inst., age 23, in
Richmond, Va. Was the wife of Hall Neilson, Esq. of Richmond; dau.
of Wm. Boyd Page, Esq. deceased of Frederick Co., Va. Left three
infant children.
The Lynchburg Virginian, Dec. 29, 1834, p. 3, c. 3.

NELSON, HUGH died on 18th inst. at Belvoir in this Co. He was son of
Gen. Thomas Nelson and a member of the Legislature of Virginia,
Speaker of the House of Delegates, Judge of the General Court,
Member of House of Representatives of the U.S. and Minister Plen-
ipotentiary near the Court of Spain.
The Lynchburg Virginian, March 28, 1836, p. 3, c. 3.

NEW, JOHN died Monday morning. Was a Lynchburg resident and of the
business firm of New & Ayres, Richmond and Lynchburg.
The Lynchburg Virginian, Dec. 13, 1827, p. 3, c. 4.

NEWBILL, MRS. SARAH died at age 67. Was consort of Nathaniel Newbill of Franklin Co. and left number of children.
The Lynchburg Virginian, March 7, 1823, p. 3.

NEWHALL, MRS. LUCY died on Thurs., Jan. 14th, age 47. Was consort of James Newhall of this place and dau. of Capt. Levi Kemp of Weathersfield, Vermont.
The Lynchburg Virginian, Jan. 18, 1830, p. 3, c. 5.

NICAR, SARAH ANN died on 8th inst., age 11 months. Was dau. of Hugh M. and Eliza H. Nicar.
The Lynchburg Virginian, Aug. 25, 1834, p. 3, c. 5.

NICHOLAS, JOHN, ESQ. died at age 56 in New York. Originally of Virginia.
The Lynchburg Press, Jan. 28, 1820, p. 3.

NICHOLAS, COL. JOHN died on 29th ult., age 79, in Richmond. Was in Revolutionary War, perhaps the last surviving field officer.
The Lynchburg Virginian, May 12, 1836, p. 3, c. 4.

NICHOLSON, THE REV. JESSE died on 26th ult., age 77, at Portsmouth, Va. Soldier of the Revolution and minister of the M. E. Church. He also served as Postmaster.
The Lynchburg Virginian, Oct. 2, 1834, p. 3, c. 4.

NILES, CEPHAS died on 19th inst. at Dr. Taliaferro's in Franklin Co. He was of Hebron, Conn.
The Lynchburg Virginian, Aug. 24, 1824, p. 3, c. 4.

NIMMO, PETER H. died Feb. 19, 1827, age 19, at father's residence. Was attended by physician, Dr. Samuel I. Cabell. Was of Bedford.
The Lynchburg Virginian, March 2, 1827, p. 3, c. 3.

NIMMO, WILLIAM died Feb. 15, 1835 at Velasco, mouth of Brezo, Texas. Son of James Nimmo, Esq. of Charlotte Co., Va.
The Lynchburg Virginian, April 30, 1835, p. 3, c. 5.

NIVISON, JOHN died in Norfolk, Va. He was father-in-law of Littleton Waller Tazewell, Esq.
The Lynchburg Press, May 30, 1820, p. 3.

NIXON, MRS. ELIZA MASON died in New Glasgow, Va., age 66. Relict of Dr. Thomas Nixon of Dover, Delaware.
The Lynchburg Press, Nov. 16, 1821, p. 3, c. 4.

NOEL, MRS. NANCY died on Friday the 20th inst. at her residence in Scottsville, Albemarle Co. She was consort of the late Thompson Noel, Sen.
The Lynchburg Virginian, Nov. 26, 1829, p. 3, c. 6.

NOELL, THOMAS died on 21st inst., age 76, at his residence in Bedford, Va. The Lynchburg Virginian Oct. 20, 1831 gives age 77 and name given as Thomas Noel, Sr.
The Lynchburg Virginian, Sept. 26, 1831, p. 3, c. 5.

NORBURY, LORD died on July 27 in Dublin, Ireland. Was a Judge. His name is identified with the trial of Emmett, the celebrated Irish patriot.
The Lynchburg Virginian, Sept. 15, 1831, p. 3, c. 3.

NORMAN, MRS. ELIZABETH died Sept. 22, 1822. Was wife of William Norman of Henry Co. and dau. of The Rev. Samuel Lane. She left several children.
The Lynchburg Virginian, Oct. 4, 1822, p. 3, c. 3.

NORRIS, ANDREW died in Powder Mill explosion. Single man. News account from Newark, N.J., April 26, 1814.
The Lynchburg Press, May 12, 1814, p. 2.

NORRIS, THE REV. OLIVER died Aug. 19, 1825. Was of Alexandria and of the Protestant Episcopal Church.
The Lynchburg Virginian, Sept. 8, 1825, p. 3, c. 3.

NORTH, OWEN J. died July 21st in Missouri. Formerly of Campbell County.
The Lynchburg Virginian, Nov. 12, 1835, p. 3, c. 3.

NORTH, MR. THOMAS A. died Jan. 12th, age 40. Leaves wife and 6 small children.
The Lynchburg Virginian, Feb. 3, 1831, p. 3, c. 4.

NORTH, THOMAS JEFFERSON died last Friday. Infant son of Major Abram North.
The Lynchburg Virginian, July 21, 1831, p. 3, c. 3.

NORVELL, EDMUND B., ESQ. died in this place last Monday night. "One of our most esteemed fellow citizens."
The Lynchburg Virginian, Nov. 4, 1830, p. 3, c. 5.

NORVELL, GEORGE ROBERT died June 8th in the 32nd year of his age at Liverpool, England. Was a merchant of this place.
The Lynchburg Virginian, July 28, 1828, p. 3, c. 5.

NORVELL, MARIA ANN died last Thursday, age 2 yrs., 1 mo., in this place. Only child of Mr. Samuel G. Norvell of this place.
The Lynchburg Virginian, April 2, 1832, p. 3, c. 4.

NORVELL, MRS. POLLY died Sun., June 19th at residence "Solitude" of Capt. Norvell of Amherst. Funeral sermon preached by The Rev. Wm. S. Reid. Was consort of Capt. Reuben Norvell.
The Lynchburg Press, June 22, 1821, p. 1.

NORVELL, MRS. POLLY died on Thursday, 17th inst., age 70. Consort of Mr. Henry Norvell of this town. Leaves aged husband and children. Member of Methodist Church.
The Lynchburg Virginian, Feb. 24, 1831, p. 3, c. 5.

NORVELL, MR. SPENCER, SR. died on 2nd inst., age 82. Resident of Amherst Co; farmer by occupation and a member of M. E. Church.
The Lynchburg Virginian, Aug. 13, 1829, p. 3, c. 4.

NORVELL, WILLIAM died Oct. 27, 1823, age 53. Was a resident of Lynchburg from the time of its incorporation. Was President of the Office of Discount and Deposit, of Bank of Virginia in Lynchburg.
The Lynchburg Virginian, Oct. 31, 1823, p. 3, c. 2.

NOWELL, MR. killed Aug. 4, 1821 by Mr. Robert Lewis in a quarrel. He was an Inn-keeper at Scottsville, Va.
The Lynchburg Press, Sept. 14, 1821, p. 3.

NOWELL, MARY (Twin of Susannah) died on Aug. 31st, age 66, in Heland, Mass. Twin of Susannah Nowell. They died within 10 hours of one another and buried in same grave.
The Lynchburg Virginian, Sept. 22, 1836, p. 3, c. 4.

NOWELL, SUSANNAH (Twin of Mary) died on Aug. 31st, age 66, in Heland, Mass. Twin of Mary Nowell. Both died within 10 hours of one another, and buried in same grave.
The Lynchburg Virginian, Sept. 22, 1836, p. 3, c. 4.

NOWLIN, MRS. FANNY W. died on 25th inst., age 25. Died at Brookneal, Campbell Co., Va. Consort of Capt. Bryan W. Nowlin. Leaves devoted husband and affectionate brother and sister.
The Lynchburg Virginian, Nov. 29, 1832, p. 3, c. 4.

NOWLIN, MRS. RANEY died Tues. the 15th inst. Was wife of Major James Nowlin of Pittsylvania Co.
The Lynchburg Virginian, March 28, 1831, p. 3, c. 3.

O

O'CONNOR, JAMES died July 3, 1819, age 60, at Norfolk, Va. Editor and Proprietor of the Norfolk Herald. He was a native of Sligo, Ireland.
The Lynchburg Press & Public Advertiser, July 27, 1819, p. 3, c. 5.

OGDEN, MRS. SARAH died on 13th inst., age 36. Was wife of Mr. Henry M. Ogden. She leaves husband and two children.
The Lynchburg Virginian, May 30, 1833, p. 3, c. 4.

OGLESBY, DAVID died July 26, 1821, age 77. He was of Campbell Co. and leaves aged widow and 6 children.
The Lynchburg Press, July 27, 1821, p. 3, c. 3.

OGLESBY, MRS. ELIZABETH died Oct. 12, 1822, age 39. She is survived by husband, Jacob Oglesby and 6 children.
The Lynchburg Virginian, Nov. 1, 1822, p. 3, c. 4.

OGLESBY, MRS. SARAH died last Monday, age 78, at her residence in Campbell Co. Relict of the late Mr. David Oglesby.
The Lynchburg Virginian, Oct. 23, 1828, p. 3, c. 5.

OGLY, WILLIAM killed in an Indian massacre.
The Lynchburg Press, April 24, 1816, p. 2.

OLIVER, CHARLES died Oct. 18, 1832, age 10 months, at Liberty. Only child of Capt. Yelverton N. Oliver.
The Lynchburg Virginian, Oct. 25, 1832, p. 3, c. 4.

OLIVER, ROBERT MORRIS died on 8th inst., age 2 mos. and 12 days. Infant son of Sarah Elizabeth and Isaac H. Oliver.
The Lynchburg Virginian, April 14, 1836, p. 3, c. 4.

OLIVER, MRS. SARAH GLEN died Friday morning, age 56, at the Franklin Hotel in this place. She was a member of the Methodist E. Church.
The Lynchburg Virginian, Nov. 3, 1834, p. 3, c. 5.

O'NEAL, JOHN killed in Powder Mill explosion. Single man. News account from Newark, N.J., April 26, 1814.
The Lynchburg Press, May 12, 1814, p. 2.

ORGAN, MAJ. JOHN died on 13th inst., age 56, at his residence in Campbell Co. Left a wife and 9 children.
The Lynchburg Virginian, Feb. 23, 1826, p. 3, c. 4.

OTEY, MISS ELIZABETH B. died March 18, 1819, age 21. She was the dau. of Capt. Frazer Otey of Bedford Co.
The Lynchburg Press & Public Advertiser, March 25, 1819, p. 3, c. 3.

OTEY, CAPTAIN JOHN H. died Dec. 9, 1830, age 63, at residence in Bedford Co.
The Lynchburg Virginian, Dec. 16, 1830, p. 3, c. 2.

OTEY, MRS. SARAH died Saturday evening, the 13th inst., age 43, in Liberty. Deceased was wife of Col. Armistead Otey.
The Lynchburg Virginian, Aug. 22, 1831, p. 3, c. 4.

OVERTON, JUDGE JOHN died a few days since at his residence near Nashville. He had been a member of the Supreme Court of Tenn. but for some years a private citizen.
The Lynchburg Virginian, May 2, 1833, p. 3, c. 5.

OWENS, DR. BENJAMIN F. died on June 22, 1833, age 28, at Macon Georgia. Formerly of Lynchburg, he settled in Ga. seven or eight years ago. Joined the M. E. Church and became an exhorter. Left wife and 2 children in Ga.; also in Lynchburg mother, brother and sister.
The Lynchburg Virginian, July 8, 1833, p. 3, c. 5.

OWENS, MRS. JANE J. died on 17th inst., age 34, in Lynchburg. Consort of Dr. William Owens.
The Lynchburg Virginian, Nov. 29, 1827, p. 3, c. 4.

OWENS, MISS NANCY died on 9th inst. at residence of Mr. James Fowler of Bedford Co. She was dau. of Mr. Taliaferro Owens of Bedford Co.
The Lynchburg Virginian, Nov. 20, 1834, p. 3, c. 4.

OWENS, OWEN died June 2, 1819, age 67. Was of Lynchburg.
The Lynchburg Press & Public Advertiser, June 7, 1819, p. 3, c. 5.

OWENS, MRS. PARTHENA died Nov. 24, 1823. She was dau. of Wm. Porter of Bedford Co. and consort of Wm. Owens of Botetourt Co. Survived by husband and 2 children.
The Lynchburg Virginian, Jan. 7 or 9, 1824, p. 3.

OWENS, DR. SEPTIMUS D. died at his mother's residence in this place, in his 29th year.
The Lynchburg Virginian, Aug. 6, 1829, p. 3, c. 5.

P

PACKARD, MR. BENJAMIN D. died on 18th inst., age 54, in Albany, N.Y. He was a proprietor of the Albany Evening Journal.
The Lynchburg Virginian, May 30, 1833, p. 3, c. 4.

PACKETT, LIEUT. JOHN died, age 29, at his home in Charlestown, Va. (now West Va.). He was of the U.S. Navy.
The Lynchburg Press & Public Advertiser, May 30, 1820, p. 3, c. 6.

PADGETT, AMANDA JUNE CATHARINE died April 10, 1833, age 2 yrs. and 2 mos., in this place. She was youngest child of Lindsey B. Padgett.
The Lynchburg Virginian, April 15, 1833, p. 3, c. 6.

PADGETT, MISS CATHARINE died Jan. 12, 1833, age 78, in Amherst Co. She and sister Rosa had dwelt together through a long life. She died in the evening of same day as sister.
The Lynchburg Virginian, Jan. 17, 1833, p. 3, c. 5.

PADGETT, EPHRAIM died on Dec. 22nd, age 82, at his residence in Amherst Co. He was a soldier of the Revolution.
The Lynchburg Virginian, Jan. 5, 1835, p. 3, c. 3.

PADGETT, MISS ROSA died Jan. 12, 1833, age 84, in Amherst Co. She and sister Catharine had lived together through a long life. She died in morning of same day as sister.
The Lynchburg Virginian, Jan. 17, 1833, p. 3, c. 5.

PAGE, WILLIAM BYRD, ESQ. died on 2nd inst., age 40, at Pagebrook, Va., the seat of his father, Mr. John Page, Sen.
The Lynchburg Virginian, Sept. 15, 1828, p. 3, c. 5.

PALMER, MRS. MARTHA P. died on Sunday, 18th inst., age 33, at the residence in Campbell Co. She was the consort of Cr. Reuben D. Palmer. Her parents were Henry and Martha Christian. She was a member of the Methodist Episcopal Church.
The Lynchburg Virginian, Jan. 29, 1829, p. 3, c. 4.

PALMORE, JOHN died June 26, 1825, age 36. He was of Bedford Co.
The Lynchburg Virginian, July 21, 1825, p. 3, c. 5.

PANKEY, MRS. KEZIAH died on Sunday evening the 8th inst., age about 70, at her residence in Buckingham Co. She was the relict of John Pankey, dec'd. who was one of the Revolutionary worthies who fought for the liberties of his country.
The Lynchburg Virginian, July 19, 1832, p. 3, c. 4.

PANKEY, PETER died at age 32 at home of his mother in Buckingham Co.
The Lynchburg Virginian, May 11, 1829, p. 3, c. 4.

PANKEY, YOUNG, ESQ. died on 25th inst. in his 54th year in Richmond, Va.
The Lynchburg Virginian, May 30, 1833, p. 3, c. 4.

PARISH, GEN. RICHARD C. died on 12th inst. at Philadelphia. Gen. Parish was of Florida.
The Lynchburg Virginian, Aug. 21, 1837, p. 3, c. 4.

PARTRIDGE, GEORGE died on 7th inst., age 89, at Duxbury, Mass. He was member of the First Congress under the new Constitution.
The Lynchburg Virginian, Aug. 7, 1828, p. 3, c. 5.

PATRICK, JOHN ROBERT ROSE died on 12th inst., age 19, in Amherst at the residence of William N. Price.
The Lynchburg Virginian, April 21, 1831, p. 3, c. 4.

PATTEN, DR. OLIVER died on Dec. 22, 1822 at Columbia, Va. He was a native of Westford, Mass.
The Lynchburg Virginian, Jan. 3, 1822, p. 3.

PATTERSON, WM. B. died on Wednesday last in this place. He was of Bent Creek, Buckingham Co., Va.
The Lynchburg Virginian, Jan. 30, 1826, p. 3.

PATTESON, ALEXANDER, ESQ. died on Friday last at his residence in Prince Edward Co. He was mail contractor between Lynchburg and Richmond. He is survived by a large family.
The Lynchburg Virginian, Jan. 25, 1836, p. 3, c. 4.

PATTESON, MRS. FRANCES died on Tues. night last in this place. She was the consort of Dr. John H. Patteson and a member of the Methodist Episcopal Church.
The Lynchburg Virginian, October 8, 1838, p. 3, c. 3.

PATTESON, LANDIS died on April 8, 1825, age 75, at the home of Mr. Wm. Evans. He was of Campbell Co.
The Lynchburg Virginian, April 28, 1825, p. 3.

PATTESON, MARTHA A. died on April 5th at residence of her uncle, Mr. Alexander Patteson in Prince Edward Co., Va. Dau. of Lilburne Patteson.
The Lynchburg Virginian, May 18, 1835, p. 3, c. 2.

PATTESON, MARY DUIGUID died on Feb. 28th at Clover Hill, Prince Edward Co. She was the dau. of Alexander Patteson, Esq. deceased.
The Lynchburg Virginian, April 28, 1836, p. 3, c. 5.

PATTESON, ROBERT died Nov. 8, 1817. He was of Lynchburg.
The Lynchburg Press, Nov. 1817, p. 3, c. 3.

PATTERSON, WILLIAM, ESQ. died in Baltimore. One of oldest and most
valued citizens of this place.
The Lynchburg Virginian, Feb. 16, 1835, p. 3, c. 5.

PAUL, MRS. HANNAH died on 19th inst. Was wife of The Rev. Isaac Paul
of Albemarle Co., Va. She was a member of the Presbyterian Church.
The Lynchburg Virginian, Jan. 29, 1835, p. 3, c. 5.

PAULETTE, WILLIAM died on Sat. 28th ult., age 5 yrs., 8 mos. in this
place. He was the son of Mr. Anderson B. Paulette. He died from
swallowing bean which lodged in his throat -"baffled skills of
attending physician."
The Lynchburg Virginian, April 9, 1835, p. 3, c. 3.

PAXTON, CAPT. died on 22nd ult. near Buffalo in a duel. He was of the
13th Infantry.
The Lynchburg Press, Dec. 29, 1814, p. 3.

PAYNE, MRS. ELIZABETH died on April 26, 1833, age 69. Was consort of
Philip Payne, Esq. of this county.
The Lynchburg Virginian, May 9, 1833, p. 3, c. 5.

PEARCY, ABNER died on Friday, 21st of July, last in 26th year of age at
his residence in Bedford Co. He left a wife and 2 children. He
was a member of the Baptist Church.
The Lynchburg Virginian, Aug. 3, 1837, p. 3, c. 4.

PEGRAM, GEN. JOHN died on 8th inst., age 59, at Petersburg. He was of
the Eastern District of Va.
The Lynchburg Virginian, April 18, 1831, p. 1, c. 5.

PEGRAM, RICHARD G., ESQ. died on 8th inst., age 29, at his father's
residence in Dinwiddie Co. He was the son of Gen. John Pegram.
The deceased was a Counsellor-At-Law.
The Lynchburg Virginian, Nov. 16, 1829, p. 3, c. 6.

PENDLETON, JAMES died on July 2nd, age 82, in Amherst Co.
The Lynchburg Virginian, July 5, 1832, p. 3, c. 4.

PENDLETON, JOSEPH died on Sept. 27, 1825 in his 26th year. He was of
Nelson Co. and son of Micajah Pendleton.
The Lynchburg Virginian, Sept. 29, 1825, p. 3.

PENDLETON, MRS. MILLICENT died Jan. 30, 1815, age 70. She was the wife
of Col. E. Pendleton of Caroline Co., Va.
The Lynchburg Press, April 27, 1815, p. 3, c. 2.

PENDLETON, RICHARD died May 20th, age 74, at his residence in Amherst Co.
Left wife and large family.
The Lynchburg Virginian, June 4, 1829, p. 3, c. 3.

PENDLETON, MRS. SARAH died Feb. 15, 1815, age about 90. She was the
relict of The Hon. Judge Pendleton of Caroline.
The Lynchburg Press, April 27, 1815, p. 3, c. 2.

PENN, CATHERINE died Dec. 11, 1824, age 25, at the home of Nathaniel
Reid. Was of Bedford and is survived by husband.
The Lynchburg Virginian, Dec. 24, 1824, p. 3.

PENN, MRS. FRANCES died June 24, 1833, age 18, at Col. Penn's, her
husband, in Patrick Co. Col. Penn's first wife had died about
2 years ago.
The Lynchburg Virginian, July 11, 1833, p. 3, c. 4.

PENN, MRS. FRANCES R. died on 24th ult., age 25, in Patrick Co. The
deceased was the wife of Peter P. Penn.
The Lynchburg Virginian, July 11, 1831, p. 3, c. 4.

PENN, COL. GEORGE died in Madisonville, Louisiana. He represented
Patrick Co. many years in Virginia Legislature. Was formerly of
Patrick Co. and now of Madisonville, Louisiana.
The Lynchburg Virginian, March 27, 1828, p. 3, c. 5.

PENN, MRS. MARGARET died Dec. 15, 1832 near Tuscaloosa, Ala. She was
the widow of the late James Penn, formerly of the Grove, Campbell
Co., Va.
The Lynchburg Virginian, Jan. 17, 1833, p. 3, c. 5.

PENN, MRS. MARY died on June 24, 1795 in Amherst, Va. Was the consort of
Mr. George Penn of Amherst Co.
The Lynchburg & Farmer's Gazette, July 4, 1795, p. 3, c. 1.

PENN, DR. PETER L. died on 22nd ultimo, age 29, near the town of Taledago
in State of Alabama. Formerly of Patrick Co., Va.
The Lynchburg Virginian, June 29, 1835, p. 3, c. 5.

PENN, MISS SALLY died at age 15 in the home of Col. S. Staples in Patrick
Co. while on a visit. She was the dau. of the late Gabriel Penn, Esq.
The Lynchburg Press & Public Advertiser, June 8, 1821, p. 3, c. 5.

PENN, MRS. SARAH died on 22 ult. She was the relict of Col. Gabriel Penn
of Amherst, an officer of the Revolution.
The Lynchburg Virginian, Feb. 2, 1826, p. 3.

PERKINS, BENJAMIN died on 8th ult. at Limestone Co., Ala. He was
formerly of Lynchburg.
The Lynchburg Virginian, Sept. 2, 1830, p. 3, c. 2.

PERKINS, MRS. BENJAMIN died on 8th ult. in Limestone, Ala., same day as
her husband.
The Lynchburg Virginian, Sept. 2, 1830, p. 3, c. 2.

PERKINS, MR. GEORGE M. died on 9th inst., age 29, in this place.
The Lynchburg Virginian, Jan. 15, 1827, p. 3, c. 5.

PERKINS, ROBERT died on Thurs., 9th inst., age 4 yrs. and 6 mos., at
Locust Grove near Lynchburg. He was the son of Captain Richard
Perkins.
The Lynchburg Virginian, April 13, 1835, p. 3, c. 3.

PERKINS, MRS. SARAH ANN died July 13, 1833 at Lovingston, Nelson Co. She
was the consort of Mr. Hardin Perkins, merchant of Lovingston and
dau. of Capt. John H. Mosby of Nelson Co. She left 3 children.
The Lynchburg Virginian, July 29, 1833, p. 3, c. 3.

PERROW, MRS. DOLLY died May 29, 1821. She was wife of Stephen Perrow of
this county. She is survived by husband and 10 children.
The Lynchburg Press & Public Advertiser, June 1, 1821, p. 3, c. 3.

PERRY, MR. GEORGE R. died last Sunday in this place, age 28 yrs., 8 days.
The Lynchburg Virginian, Feb. 5, 1835, p. 3, c. 5.

PERRY, COL. JAMES died Feb. 23rd, age 70, in Zanesville, Ohio. "First
white man who made a permanent settlement west of the Alleghany
Mountains and the second who ever trod the soil of Ky."
The Lynchburg Press, March 29, 1822, p. 1, c. 1.

PERRY, CAPT. PETER died at Salem, murdered by Thomas Wells. He is
survived by a family.
The Lynchburg Press, Oct. 3, 1820, p. 3.

PERRY, SAMPSON, ESQ. died in London, age 78.
The Lynchburg Virginian, Sept. 30, 1823, p. 3, c. 4.

PERSON, MRS. ANNA died 28th ult., age 68. She was the mother of
Spotswood Garland of Nelson Co.
The Lynchburg Press & Public Advertiser, Oct. 19, 1818, p. 3, c. 5.

PETERS, MR. MOSES died on Sat., 28th ult., age 56, in Bedford Co. He was
a resident of Bedford Co. and a member of Methodist Episcopal Church.
Left a large and respectable family.
The Lynchburg Virginian, April 9, 1835, p. 3, c. 3.

PETERS, MISS NARCISSA died June 26th, age 19 at her father's.
The Lynchburg Virginian, Aug. 6, 1829, p. 3, c. 5.

PETERS, JUDGE RICHARD died on Friday last at Philadelphia. Was Judge
of District Court of U.S.A. for Eastern District of Pennsylvania.
The Lynchburg Virginian, Sept. 1, 1828, p. 3, c. 6.

PETROSS, JOHN L. died on 13th inst. at his residence in Pittsylvania Co.
The Lynchburg Virginian, Jan. 23, 1832, p. 3, c. 3.

PETTIT, MRS. FRANCES died on Aug. 31st, age 57, in Amherst Co. Left
husband and 8 children. Was consort of James Pettit of Amherst.
The Lynchburg Virginian, Sept. 7, 1826, p. 3, c. 4.

PETTYJOHN, MRS. ELIZABETH died on 26th inst. Consort of Wm. Pettyjohn of
Amherst.
The Lynchburg Virginian, June 29, 1826, p. 3, c. 4.

PEUGH, LOT died on 9th inst., age 43, at his residence in Campbell Co.,Va.
Left wife and 8 children. Was member of Methodist Episcopal Church.
The Lynchburg Virginian, Sept. 20, 1827, p. 3, c. 2.

PHAUP, MRS. ELIZABETH died Oct. 31, 1823. Consort of William Phaup of
Charlotte Co.
The Lynchburg Virginian, Nov. 14, 1823, p. 3.

PHELPHS, CAPT. CHARLES died on 18th inst., age 55, at his residence in
Buckingham Co. Was member of Baptist Church.
The Lynchburg Virginian, Aug. 24, 1829, p. 3, c. 5.

PHELPS, CAPT. RICHARD R. died Oct. 10th, age about 35, at St. Louis,
Missouri. He was formerly of Lynchburg and left a wife and two
children. He died from wound received on hunting excursion.
The Lynchburg Virginian, Nov. 5, 1835, p. 3, c. 3.

PHILIPS, DABNEY T. died Aug. 6, 1833, age 40, at his residence in Amherst Co.
The Lynchburg Virginian, Aug. 8, 1833, p. 3, c. 4.

PICKENS, ISRAEL died on 23rd ult. near Mantanzas, where he had gone for
benefit of his health. He was late Governor of Alabama.
The Lynchburg Virginian, June 15, 1827, p. 3, c. 2.

PIERCE, JACOB died on 27th ult., age 70, at his residence in Amherst Co.
The Lynchburg Virginian, May 7, 1835, p. 3, c. 4.

PILCHARD, DANIEL drowned Sept. 6, 1819, age 60. Was of Stafford Co.
The Lynchburg Press, Sept. 17, 1819, p. 3.

PINKHAM, DAVID COFFIN died April 11, 1833 at Key West. He was Counselor-
At-Law and Deputy Collector of the Port. He was native of Mass.
Death caused by wound received in a duel with Dr. B. B. Strobel,
formerly of Charleston, on 23rd of March.
The Lynchburg Virginian, May 6, 1833, p. 3, c. 5.

PINCKNEY, HON. CHARLES died Oct. 29th, age 66. He was a U.S. Senator and
Ambassador to Spain.
The Lynchburg Virginian, Nov. 26, 1824, p. 3, c. 4.

PINKNEY, CHARLES, ESQ. died on 20th ult., age 39, in Washington City
suddenly. Was Junior Editor of The Sun. He was the son of the
late William Pinkney.
The Lynchburg Virginian, April 2, 1835, p. 3, c. 4.

PINKNEY, GEN. CHAS. COTESWORTH died Aug. 16, 1825 at Charleston, S. C.
He was a soldier of the Revolution.
The Lynchburg Virginian, Sept. 1, 1825, p. 3, c. 5.

PITKIN, THE REV. J. B. died on 9th ult. at St. Augustine. He was the
Pastor of the Fast Independent Christian Church in Richmond.
The Lynchburg Virginian, March 5, 1835, p. 3, c. 4.

PLEASANTS, MRS. ANN died May 3, 1819. Was consort of John H. Pleasants.
(Buried in the Old City Cemetery.)
The Lynchburg Press & Public Advertiser, May 6, 1819, p. 3, c. 5.

PLEASANTS, JAMES died Nov. 9th, age 68, at his residence in Goochland Co.
He was a member of U.S. Senate and Governor of Va.
The Lynchburg Virginian, Nov. 24, 1836, p. 3, c. 4.

PLEASANTS, SAMUEL died Oct. 4, 1814 at Richmond. He was late Proprietor
and Editor of The Virginia Argus.
The Lynchburg Press, Oct. 13, 1814, p. 3, c. 1.

PLUNKETT, MRS. ADELINE M. died Aug. 9th, age 19 at Lagrange, Tenn. She
was late of Bedford Co., Va. and the dau. of Jabez W. White, dec'd.
She was consort of Alexander A. N. Plunkett. Left one child.
The Lynchburg Virginian, Oct. 1, 1835, p. 3, c. 4.

POE, MRS. ANNE died Jan. 17, 1815. Was of Lynchburg and wife of John Poe.
The Lynchburg Press, Jan. 19, 1815, p. 3, c. 2.

POE, BENJAMIN died Sept. 17, 1825, age 29, in Lynchburg. Was late of
Richmond.
The Lynchburg Virginian, Sept. 22, 1825, p. 3, c. 4.

POINDEXTER, MRS. NANCY died Sat., July 25th, age 32. Was of Bedford Co.
Wife of Mr. John Poindexter and member of Methodist Episcopal Church.
The Lynchburg Virginian, Sept. 3, 1829, p. 3, c. 5.

POINTER, JOHN died on morning of 23rd inst. at his residence in St. Louis.
Was late of Lynchburg, Va. Taken from St. Louis Times, Sept. 22.
The Lynchburg Virginian, Oct. 13, 1831, p. 3, c. 4.

POLLARD, JOHN died on latter end of March last, in Texas, age 20. He was
from Virginia. He was a student of West Point Academy and a volunteer
in the Texas Army.
The Lynchburg Virginian, Nov. 7, 1836, p. 3, c. 4.

POLLARD, ROBERT died on 23rd of Aug. 1820. Was the second son of Maj.
Richard Pollard of this place.
The Lynchburg Press & Public Advertiser, Aug. 28, 1820, p. 3, c. 6.

PORTER, MRS. LETITIA died on 27th ult., age 43, at her residence at Black
Rock. Was wife of Gen. Peter B. Porter, formerly Secretary of War.
The Lynchburg Virginian, Aug. 11, 1831, p. 3, c. 4.

PORTER, WILLIAM died Aug. 23rd in Madison Co., Missouri. Was formerly of
Bedford Co., Va.
The Lynchburg Virginian, Nov. 16, 1835, p. 3, c. 4.

POWELL, ALFRED HARRISON, ESQ. died two days after Legislature convened,
age about 50 yrs. Died during session of the Legislature. He was
Delegate from Frederick County.
The Lynchburg Virginian, Aug. 11, 1831, p. 3, c. 4.

POWELL, MRS. ELIZABETH died Dec. 25, 1821, age 88, in Nelson Co. She was
the relict of Lucus Powell and leaves many descendents.
The Lynchburg Press, Jan. 25, 1822, p. 3, c. 4.

POWELL, MRS. ELIZABETH died on 6th inst., age 44. Was consort of
Cornelius Powell of Amherst.
The Lynchburg Virginian, Feb. 16, 1826, p. 3, c. 5.

POWELL, MRS. JANE died Aug. 15, 1832, age 64, at Lovingston, Va. She was
relict of the late Benjamin Powell of Nelson Co. Member of Methodist
Church.
The Lynchburg Virginian, Aug. 30, 1832, p. 3, c. 4.

POWELL, MRS. MILDRED died Oct. 11, 1832, age 49. Was of Amherst Co., and
wife of Dr. James Powell of Amherst.
The Lynchburg Virginian, Nov. 1, 1832, p. 3, c. 3.

POWELL, MISS NANCY W. died in her 22nd year. Dau. of Mr. Powell of Amherst Co.
The Lynchburg Virginian, Jan. 29, 1835, p. 3, c. 5.

PRENTISS, WILLIAM R. died on Thurs. night last. He had been learning his
trade in this newspaper office.
The Lynchburg Virginian, April 13, 1829, p. 3, c. 4.

PRESTON, MISS VIRGINIA ANN died Feb. 18, 1833, age 16, at Smithfield,
Montgomery Co., eldest dau. of Col. James P. Preston.
The Lynchburg Virginian, March 14, 1833, p. 3, c. 4.

PRESTON, WILLIAM S. died on 11th inst. 1828, age 25, at the residence of
his father. Was son of Bowker Preston of Bedford.
The Lynchburg Virginian, June 16, 1828, p. 3, c. 3.

PRICE, CHARLES funeral sermon will be preached at his late residence in
Bedford Co. the first Sunday in April by The Rev. Nicholas Kabler.
The Lynchburg Virginian, March 28, 1833, p. 3, c. 4.

PRICE, MISS CAMELIA J. died at father's residence in Bedford Co., age 22.
Was a member of the Methodist Episcopal Church.
The Lynchburg Virginian, Nov. 21, 1831, p. 3, c. 5.

PRICE, MRS. DOSHY died March 20, 1825. Survived by husband, mother,
sister and brother. Consort of Capt. John A. Price of Bedford.
The Lynchburg Virginian, April 28, 1825, p. 3.

PRICE, ELIZABETH N. died Aug. 11, 1825. Dau. of Patrick Hose and wife of
Dr. Price of Buckingham Co.
The Lynchburg Virginian, Aug. 25, 1825, p. 3.

PRICE, MISS SUSAN W. died Dec. 10, 1831, age 19. She was the eldest dau.
of Capt. Nathaniel H. Price of Bedford Co. and a member of the
Methodist Episcopal Church.
The Lynchburg Virginian, Dec. 19, 1831, p. 3, c. 4.

PRICE, MAJOR WILLIAM died on June 28th at an advanced age in Richmond.
The Lynchburg Virginian, July 12, 1830, p. 3, c. 5.

PURSELL, MRS. ELIZABETH died Oct. 16, 1832, age 40, at Bedford. She
was of Bedford and the wife of Mr. Thomas Pursell and second dau.
of Henry Moorman of Campbell. Leaves large family of daughters.
The Lynchburg Virginian, Oct. 25, 1832, p. 3, c. 4.

Q

QUARLES, JOHN he was of Spottsylvania Co. and member of House of Delegates.
Copied from The Enquirer.
The Lynchburg Press, May 25, 1821, p. 3, c. 5.

R

RANDOLPH, JOHN of Roanoke. "The Amethyst arrived at Boston from Liverpool,
brings a report of the death of John Randolph of Roanoke. The
Amethyst is 2 days later than the N. York Packet - but the report of Mr.
Randolph's death is discountenanced by the Boston Editors seems
improbable." [The actual date of John Randolph's death was 24 May 1833.]
The Lynchburg Virginian, Aug. 14, 1826, p. 3, c. 4.

RANDOLPH, MRS. JANE CARY died on March 2nd at Leon City, Florida at her
residence. Wife of Thomas E. Randolph, Esq., Marshall of the
Middle District.
The Lynchburg Virginian, April 2, 1832, p. 3, c. 4.

RANDOLPH, PETER, ESQ. died lately at his residence, Wilkinson Co., Miss.
He was Judge of the U. S. District Court.
The Lynchburg Virginian, Feb. 23, 1832, p. 3, c. 4.

RANDOLPH, COL. THOMAS M. died on 20th inst. at Monticello. He was
formerly Governor of Virginia.
The Lynchburg Virginian, June 26, 1828, p. 3, c. 5.

RANKIN, ANDREW died on 4th inst. He had been a resident of Lynchburg a
short time and was member of Presbyterian Church where his funeral
will be preached on the 14th instant.
The Lynchburg Virginian, May 8, 1828, p. 3, c. 5.

RAWLINS, WILLIAM, ESQ. died on 2nd inst., age 71, at his residence in
Franklin Co., Tenn. Formerly of Virginia and resided for many
years in Pittsylvania Co.
The Lynchburg Virginian, June 2, 1836, p. 3, c. 3.

RAWSON, EVANDER F. he was an Attorney-At-Law in Richmond and a native
of Paris, Maine.
The Lynchburg Virginian, Aug. 22, 1825, p. 3.

READ, EDMUND died on 2?th ult., age 46, at his residence in Bedford Co.
He left a wife and son.
The Lynchburg Virginian, March 9, 1826, p. 3, c. 2.

READ, MRS. ELIZABETH died Jan. 10, 1833, age 45, at her residence in
Bedford Co. She was the wife of Dr. John T. W. Read.
The Lynchburg Virginian, Jan. 17, 1833, p. 3, c. 4.

READ, ISAAC died at Sweet Springs, July 2, 1823. Was of Charlotte Co., Va.
The Lynchburg Virginian, July 25, 1823, p. 3, c. 5.

REDD, OVERTON died Feb. 7, 1818, age 28. He was of Henry Co.
The Lynchburg Press, Feb. 20, 1818, p. 3, c. 2.

REDD, MR. WALLER died Sept. 22, 1825. Was Clerk of the Court of Henry Co.
The Lynchburg Virginian, Sept. 29, 1825, p. 3, c. 5.

REED, MISS ELIZA died Nov. 23, 1814 at home of The Rev. Joseph Carson.
Was of Winchester.
The Lynchburg Press, Dec. 1, 1814, p. 3, c. 2.

REID, MAJOR NATHAN died Nov. 6, 1830, age 78. "Was a gallant and distinguished officer of our Revolution." Funeral sermon preached at the
New London Academy, near the residence of the deceased. See also
The Lynchburg Virginian, Nov. 15, 1830, p. 3, c. 2., which carries
a very long write-up, with biographical information and an account
of his activities in the American Revolution.
The Lynchburg Virginian, Nov. 8, 1830, p. 3, c. 4.

REID, MRS. SOPHIA died at Liberty; survived by husband and 5 children.
She was the wife of a Revolutionary officer. Died on way to Springs
but had only reached Liberty in Bedford Co.
The Lynchburg Virginian, Aug. 15, 1823, p. 3, c. 4.

RELF, SAM'L died Feb. 14, 1823 at Philadelphia, age 47. He was late
Editor of the Philadelphia Gazette.
The Lynchburg Virginian, March 7, 1823, p. 3.

REVELY, MISS HARRIET died Dec. 7, 1822. She was the dau. of George
Revely of Campbell Co.
The Lynchburg Virginian, Dec. 13, 1822, p. 3, c. 4.

REVELY, MRS. JUDITH died Sept. 8, 1823, age 44, at her residence. She
is survived by husband, Geo. Revely of Campbell Co.
The Lynchburg Virginian, Sept. 12, 1823, p. 3.

REVELY, MARY died Jan. 19, 1821, age 20. She was the dau. of George
Revely of Campbell Co.
The Lynchburg Press, Feb. 1, 1822, p. 3, c. 3.

REVELY, JOHN WILLIAM died June 11, 1833, age 12 mos. and 3 days. Infant
son of John Revely.
The Lynchburg Virginian, June 17, 1833, p. 3, c. 5.

REVELY, WILLIAM, ESQ. died last Sat. He was of Campbell Co. and one of
the members-elect to the next Legislature of Virginia.
The Lynchburg Virginian, May 25, 1826, p. 3, c. 3.

REYNOLDS, MRS. ANN died Jan. 15th, age 23, at Amherst. She was the
consort of Mr. Isaac Reynolds and left 2 small children.
The Lynchburg Virginian, Feb. 16, 1832, p. 3, c. 4.

REYNOLDS, MR. DAIRD H. died on 20th ult., age 25, at residence of Col.
James M. Redd of Patrick Co.
The Lynchburg Virginian, Oct. 13, 1836, p. 1, c. 6.

REYNOLDS, JESSE died last Friday, age 83, at a friend's house. The
deceased was of Bedford Co. and was a soldier of the Revolution.
The Lynchburg Virginian, April 25, 1836, p. 3, c. 3.

REYNOLDS, MRS. MARY died Feb. 2, 1828, age 84. She left a husband and
10 children and was a member of the Baptist Church.
The Lynchburg Virginian, Feb. 14, 1828, p. 3, c. 5.

REYNOLDS, MRS. SARAH ANN died on 7th inst., age 23, at the residence in
Bedford Co. She was wife of Mr. John Alexander Reynolds.
The Lynchburg Virginian, Aug. 25, 1834, p. 3, c. 5.

RHOR, PHILIP died Aug. 10, 1830, age 51, at his home in Lynchburg. A
native of Frederick Co., Md. He left wife and aged mother & father.
The Lynchburg Virginian, Aug. 23, 1830, p. 3, c. 5.

RICE, EPHRAIM H. died at Col. Gray's in Bedford Co. Formerly a resident
of Brighton, Mass. Boston papers asked to copy obituary so relatives
of deceased could know.
The Lynchburg Virginian, Jan. 24, 1833, p. 3, c. 6.

RICE, THE REV. DR. died last Sat. evening in Richmond. Was born Nov. 28,
1777 and not yet 54 years of age.
The Lynchburg Virginian, Sept. 19, 1831, p. 3, c. 5.

RICHARDSON, MRS. ANN died March 7, 1822 in Hanover Co. Wife of Geo. P.
Richardson and dau. of James Govan of Hanover Co.
The Lynchburg Press, March 15, 1822, p. 3, c. 4.

RICHARDSON, GEORGE died Feb. 5, 1823. He was of Goochland Co., and is
survived by a family.
The Lynchburg Virginian, Feb. 11, 1823, p. 3.

RICHARDSON, MARY JANE died July 13th, age 9 mos. Infant dau. of Mr.
Henry Richardson of Pittsylvania Co.
The Lynchburg Virginian, Aug. 2, 1833, p. 3,

RICHARDSON, MRS. SARAH died Sept. 6, 1821.
The Lynchburg Press, Sept. 7, 1821, p. 3, c. 5.

RICHARDSON, WALTER died Aug. 5, 1814. Son of John F. Lamb, Jr. of Lynchburg. (Sic.
The Lynchburg Press, Aug. 11, 1814, p. 3, c. 2.

RICHESON, MR. EDWELL died on 20th inst., age 20 yrs. and 11 days., at his parent's home. He contracted his illness in Louisville, Ky. and is survived by parents and brother and sister.
The Lynchburg Virginian, May 28, 1833, p. 3, c. 3.

RICHESON, JOHN died Aug. 17th, age 55, at Mount Airy, his residence in Amherst Co.
The Lynchburg Virginian, Sept. 7, 1835, p. 3, c. 5.

RICHESON, MRS. SUSAN D. died Oct. 11, 1832, age 28, at "Spring Garden" home of Wm. R. Roane, Esq. Consort of John Richeson. She died a few days after birth of twins. Left 3 children and husband.
The Lynchburg Virginian, Oct. 29, 1832, p. 3, c. 3.

RIDDICK, ROBERT died of bullet wound. Lived on Main Road from Suffolk to Edenton, in Virginia.
The Lynchburg Press, April 4, 1820, p. 3.

RIDER, JACOB M. died Dec. 23, 1819. He was of Littleton, Pa. and is survived by his widow.
The Lynchburg Press, Jan. 28, 1820, p. 3.

RIDGELY, DR. JOSHUA W. died Feb. 23, 1820 at Havanna. He was of Little River, N.C. and his parents live in Ohio.
The Lynchburg Press, March 28, 1820, p. 3, c. 6.

RIPLEY, DOROTHEA died Dec. 23rd at the residence of Wm. Green in Mecklenberg Co., Va. She was of Whitby, England. Born in 1767. Was most religious and a public minister.
The Lynchburg Virginian, Jan. 16, 1832, p. 3, c. 4.

RITCHIE, CAPT. killed in Battle of Bridgewater near Niagara Falls.
The Lynchburg Press, Aug. 18, 1814, p. 2.

RIVERS, THE REV. ROBERT died Sept. 15th, age 66, at his residence near Bolivar, Tenn. Was formerly of Amherst Co., Va.
The Lynchburg Virginian, Nov. 6, 1828, p. 3, c. 5.

RIVES, NATHANIEL, SR., ESQ. died last Friday at his residence near Henry Co. Courthouse. Was formerly a resident of this place.
The Lynchburg Virginian, Oct. 9, 1828, p. 3, c. 5.

ROANE, MARTHA ANN died Oct. 17th last in 17th year of her age. She was of Charles City.
The Lynchburg Virginian, Nov. 23, 1826, p. 3.

ROANE, MRS. MARY E. died on Thurs., 8th inst. at Amherst Co. She was the wife of Capt. Wm. R. Roane. Left 8 children.
The Lynchburg Virginian, Oct. 15, 1829, p. 3, c. 4.

ROANE, SPENCER, ESQ. died on Wed. the 4th at Warm Springs, Va., age 60. Was Judge of the Court of Appeals, and son-in-law of Patrick Henry and a Republican '98 and '99. "Friend of Jefferson, and of Madison and of Monroe."
The Lynchburg Virginian, Sept. 21, 1822, p. 3, c. 4.

ROANE, CAPT. WILLIAM R. died recently in Amherst. He was of that Co.
The Lynchburg Virginian, Aug. 15, 1833, p. 3, c. 3.

ROBERTS, CHRISTOPHER, ESQ. died Thursday A.M. in this place. Had a
seat in Common Council of Lynchburg.
The Lynchburg Virginian, Nov. 7, 1836, p. 3, c. 4.

ROBERTS, ENOCH reference to his being deceased and to the sale of his
estate by his executor, Wm. Davis.
The Lynchburg Press & Public Advertiser, June 7, 1819, p. 3.

ROBERTS, MRS. GEORGE died April 21, 1814. She was of Lynchburg and the
consort of the late George Roberts, Esq.
The Lynchburg Press, April 28, 1814, p. 3, c. 3.

ROBERTS, JOHN L. died on 27th ult., age 10, near father's residence. He
was drowned in a pond.
The Lynchburg Virginian, Sept. 1, 1834, p. 3, c. 5.

ROBERTS, MR. SAMUEL L. died on Monday last near Lynchburg.
The Lynchburg Virginian, Feb. 9, 1835, p. 3, c. 5.

ROBERTS, ZALINDA died Nov. 20, 1814, age 8. She was dau. of Enoch
Roberts of this vicinity and was killed by accidental burning of
her dress.
The Lynchburg Press, Dec. 1, 1814, p. 3, c. 2.

ROBERTSON, ARTHUR died Oct. 22, 1821, age about 70, at Big Lick,[now
Roanoke,] in Botetourt Co. He was a native of Scotland.
The Lynchburg Press, Nov. 9, 1821, p. 3, c. 4.

ROBINSON, THE REV. JOHN died Feb. 26th. He was Clerk of Charlotte Co.
and a Methodist minister for thirty years.
The Lynchburg Press, April 3, 1818, p. 3.

ROBINSON, JOHN died. He was of Campbell Co. and a native of Ireland.
The Lynchburg Virginian, July 3, 1826, p. 3.

ROBINSON, JOHN died last Tues., Dec. 11th, in this place. Was a native
of Ireland, but was for a long time one of our most respectable
inhabitants.
The Lynchburg Virginian, Dec. 13, 1832, p. 3, c. 5.

ROBINSON, MISS REBECCAH died Jan. 14th in 10th year of her age.
The Lynchburg Virginian, Feb. 16, 1827, p. 3, c. 5.

ROBINSON, THE REV. WILLIAM died Mar. 18, 1825, age 67. He was of Amherst
and a soldier of the Revolution.
The Lynchburg Virginian, April 1, 1825, p. 3.

ROBINSON, WILLIAM W. died Dec. 4th, age 29, in Fredericktown, Mo. Was
formerly a resident of Bedford, Va.
The Lynchburg Virginian, Jan. 8, 1835, p. 3, c. 5.

ROHR, JACOB died May 7, 1814. He was of Lynchburg.
The Lynchburg Press, May 12, 1814, p. 5, c. 2.

RORER, ABRAHAM, SEN. died on 20th ult., age 62. He left a wife and
numerous offspring.
The Lynchburg Virginian, July 19, 1830, p. 3, c. 4.

ROSE, MILDRED I. died on morning of the 5th of October, 1831 at the
residence of Sterling Claiborne in Nelson Co.
The Lynchburg Virginian, Oct. 17, 1831, p. 3, c. 4.

ROSE, COL. PATRICK died Dec. 4, 1822, age 78, at the residence of his
son in Amherst Co. Survived by wife and numerous progeny. Of
Fermont."
The Lynchburg Virginian, Dec. 20, 1822, p. 3, c. 4.

ROSE, JUDGE ROBERT S. died on Tues. of last week at Waterlob. He was of
the town of Fayette on the eastern shore of Seneca Lake. Judge Rose
was a Virginian and had long resided in this state. Was a member
of both branches of our Legislature; Representative in Congress.
From the Com. Adv.
The Lynchburg Virginian, Dec. 14, 1835, p. 1, c. 3.

ROSE, MRS. SARAH died June 30, 1833 at Bellevetta her place of residence
in Nelson Co. Was the widow of Col. Charles Rose, deceased.
The Lynchburg Virginian, Aug. 5, 1833, p. 3, c. 4.

ROSIQUE, DON FRANCISCO TACONY died on 23rd ult at Philadelphia. He was
Minister Plenipotentiary and Envoy Extraordinary of her Catholic
Majesty the Queen of Spain, to the Gov't. of the United States.
The Lynchburg Virginian, July 2, 1835, p. 3, c. 6.

ROSS, ALEXANDER native of Scotland, lived to be 120 years of age.
The Lynchburg Press, Sept. 24, 1818, p. 3.

ROSS, DAVID, JR. died of a bullet wound at New Canton, Buckingham Co.
He was from Lynchburg and the son of Mr. David Ross, Sr.
The Lynchburg Press, May 4, 1821, p. 3, c. 3.

ROSSER, MISS ELIZABETH died on 7th inst. Was the dau. of Thomas Rosser
of Lynchburg.
The Lynchburg Virginian, July 20, 1826, p. 3, c. 5.

ROYALL, JOSEPH EDWIN, ESQ. died last Thurs., age 43. Was of the firm of
Royall, Young and Co. He left a wife and 6 children.
The Lynchburg Virginian, June 6, 1836, p. 3, c. 3.

ROYAL, WILLIAM died June 24, 1817, age 37. He was of Lynchburg.
The Lynchburg Press, June 27, 1817, p. 3, c. 3.

ROYALL, MR. WILLIAM R. died Sept. 8th at Brazoria, Texas. Was from
Lynchburg, Va. and served in the Texian Army.
The Lynchburg Virginian, Nov. 14, 1836, p. 3, c. 3.

RUCKER, MRS. MALINDA died on 28th inst. at Williamson Co., Tenn. Was of
Bedford Co., Va. and removed to Tenn. in 1819. Was the consort of
Benjamin Rucker.
The Lynchburg Virginian, Jan. 19, 1832, p. 3, c. 4.

RUCKER, MRS. MARY J. S. died on 23rd ult. at Lynchburg, Va., age 25. Was
consort of Clifton H. Rucker and leaves 2 small children. A member
of Methodist Episcopal Church.
The Lynchburg Virginian, Sept. 28, 1835, p. 3, c. 4.

RUCKER, WILLIAM P. died. His funeral service to be preached at father's
home first Sunday in Oct. in Amherst Co.
The Lynchburg Press, Sept. 28, 1818, p. 3, c. 3.

RUSH, BENJAMIN died on 17th ult., age 24, in New Orleans. He was a
brother of the present Minister to Great Britain, and son of the
late Dr. Benjamin Rush of Philadelphia.
The Lynchburg Virginian, Jan. 28, 1825, p. 3, c. 5.

S

SADLER, MRS. MARY died Sept. 11, 1821 at Bedford County Courthouse.
Consort of Willis Sadler.
The Lynchburg Press, Sept. 14, 1821, p. 3, c. 5.

SAINT LEU, COUNT BARRE DE died at Paris, France. "The old and venerable
Rear-Admiral, late of the French Navy. He was the friend of the
venerated Lafayette." Fought in American Revolution. "Never have
I lamented of having spent one hour in fighting for Washington's
Country."
The Lynchburg Virginian, Oct. 4, 1830, p. 3, c. 5.

SALE, LAURISTON H. died on 13th inst., age 27, in Bedford Co. at the
residence of his father, Mr. Thomas Sale.
The Lynchburg Virginian, July 21, 1831, p. 3, c. 4.

SAMPLE, MR. ANDREW died Nov. 12, 1824, age 21. Son of John Sample of
Franklin Co.
The Lynchburg Virginian, Nov. 26, 1824, p. 3.

SAMPLE, MISS FRANCES S. died Sun. morning, Feb. 8th, age 17 in the Co. of
Franklin. Fourth dau. of Mr. John Sample.
The Lynchburg Virginian, Feb. 16, 1829, p. 3, c. 5.

SANDIDGE, BENJAMIN died on 1st inst., age about 70, in Amherst Co., in
Buffalo River. She was of Amherst Co.
The Lynchburg Virginian, Nov. 5, 1829, p. 3, c. 5.

SANDIDGE, RICHARD A. died at Lexington, Va., age 18. Son of Mr. Rowland
Sandidge of Amherst Co. He had worked at the Virginian Office.
Member of Washington Literary Soc. of Lexington, Va.
The Lynchburg Virginian, March 14, 1833, p. 3, c. 4.

SANDIDGE, W. M. died Wednesday last, age 79, in Amherst Co.
The Lynchburg Virginian, Aug. 26, 1830, p. 3, c. 4.

SAUNDERS, CAPT. ROBERT died on 31st of October, age 45, at his home. Was of Franklin Co.
The Lynchburg Virginian, Nov. 10, 1825, p. 3, c. 3.

SAUNDERS, SARAH WATTS died Nov. 4, 1832, age 16, at residence of Mrs. Mary Watts of Campbell Co. Dau. of Judge Fleming Saunders of Franklin Co., Va.
The Lynchburg Virginian, Nov. 8, 1832, p. 3, c. 5.

SAY, THOMAS died on 10th ult. at New Harmony, State of Indiana. "Distinguished naturalist" From Philadelphia National Gazette.
The Lynchburg Virginian, Nov. 13, 1834, p. 1, c. 4.

SCEA, MRS. JOHN died on 31st ult. Was of Campbell Co. Wife of John Scea.
The Lynchburg Virginian, Aug. 4, 1828, p. 3, c. 4.

SCHOEMAKER, ELIZABETH ANN died on 11th inst., age 7. Dau. of Charles Schoemaker of this place.
The Lynchburg Virginian, Oct. 18, 1832, p. 3, c. 5.

SCHOOLFIELD, MRS. JOHN died Thurs., 8th inst., age 66, in this place. Was native of Maryland. He moved to this town nearly 42 yrs. ago. "At time of death had been here longer than any other person known in place." Parents were Quakers. 27 yrs. ago he joined M. E. Church.
The Lynchburg Virginian, Dec. 12, 1831, p. 3, c. 4.

SCHOOLFIELD, MR. BENJAMIN died at his father's home. Was of Lynchburg and 18 years of age.
The Lynchburg Virginian, Sept. 22, 1825, p. 3, c. 4.

SCHOOLFIELD, WILLIAM DUDLEY died on 11th ult. of scarlet fever. Was only child of John W. Schoolfield, aged one year, 6 months and 12 days.
The Lynchburg Virginian, June 18, 1832, p. 3, c. 3.

SCOTT, GENERAL CHARLES died Oct. 22, 1813, age 74, in Kentucky. He was Gov. of Kentucky and an American Revolutionary war soldier.
The Lynchburg Star, Nov. 18, 1813, p. 3, c. 4.

SCOTT, DR. JOHN died on 14th inst., age 33, in this place. He left aged mother, a wife and 3 children. Copied from Huntsville Advocate.
The Lynchburg Virginian, Sept. 3, 1829, p. 3, c. 5.

SCOTT, CAPT. JOSEPH died at residence, age 69. Was of Campbell Co. and an officer of American Revolution.
The Lynchburg Virginian, May 5, 1828, p. 3, c. 4.

SCOTT, MRS. MARGARET P. died **Dec. 23rd inst. Was of Campbell Co. and consort of Thomas H. Scott who was a Professor of Religion.**
The Lynchburg Virginian, Dec. 1834, p. 3, c. 4.

SCOTT, MRS. MARY died on 17th inst. at her residence. Widow of Thomas
A. Scott of Campbell Co. Referred to children "she left".
The Lynchburg Virginian, Oct. 4, 1827, p. 3, c. 3.

SCOTT, MISS MARY WALLER died on 19th inst. in 18th year. Of Lynchburg
The Lynchburg Virginian, July 26, 1827, p. 3, c. 3.

SCOTT, RICHARD P. died Jan. 23rd, age about 23, at Louisville, Ky. He
was the son of Capt. Robert Scott, late of Lynchburg.
The Lynchburg Virginian, March 3, 1836, p. 3, c. 2.

SCOTT, MAJOR ROBERT C. died Thurs. after a protracted illness. Age 46.
The Lynchburg Virginian, May 13, 1833, p. 3, c. 4.

SCOTT, MRS. SALLY died last Friday, age 40, in this place. Was wife of
Capt. Robert C. Scott. She was a Methodist.
The Lynchburg Virginian, March 7, 1831, p. 3, c. 5.

SCOTT, SALLY PRICE died June 22nd, age 6 mos., 2 days, at Amherst Courthouse. Dau. of Capt. Robert C. Scott.
The Lynchburg Virginian, July 11, 1831, p. 3, c. 4.

SCOTT, THOMAS, ESQ. of Campbell Co. died May 5, 1823. Survived by family.
The Lynchburg Virginian, May 16, 1823, p. 3, c. 4.

SCOTT, CAPT. WILLIAM died Oct. 6, 1817, age 67, at Cherry Grove, his
residence in Campbell Co.
The Lynchburg Press, Oct. 24, 1817, p.3, c. 6.

SCRUGGS, JOHN P. died Wed. the 15th at Amherst Co. He was a resident of
Amherst Co. and survived by widow and several children.
The Lynchburg Virginian, March 23, 1835, p. 3, c. 5.

SCRUGGS, MRS. MARY died Sept. 19th at Red Sulphur Springs, Va. Wife of
Gross Scruggs, Esq. of Madison Co., Ala. Member of Methodist Church.
The Lynchburg Virginian, Oct. 18, 1832, p. 3, c. 3.

SCUIZE, JOSEPH died in Birmingham, England at age 77.
The Lynchburg Virginian, Oct. 31, 1825, p. 3, c. 5.

SEDDON, THOMAS, ESQ. died on 6th inst. in Fredericksburg. Was Cashier
of the Farmer's Bank of Virginia in Fredericksburg.
The Lynchburg Virginian, Oct. 13, 1831, p. 3, c. 4.

SEMPLE, ELDER ROBERT B. died last Sun. morning, age 63 at Fredericksburg,
Va. Was engaged in ministry for 42 yrs. Pastor of Bruington Church
from its first constitution under his labors in 1793 until present time.
The Lynchburg Virginian, Jan. 2, 1832, p. 3, c. 4.

SEMPLE, MISS SARAH died March 22, 1831, age 20 yrs., 1 mo. and 22 days.
Died at her father's residence in Franklin Co.
The Lynchburg Virginian, April 4, 1831, p. 3, c. 4.

SERVANT, RICHARD B., LT. COL. COMT. of the 115th Regt. V.M. died at his
residence in Hampton Feb. 21st. Left wife and 6 small children.
The Lynchburg Press, April 3, 1818, p. 3, c. 1.

SETTLE, JOHN M. died June 29, 1823 in this place. Merchant of Lynchburg.
The Lynchburg Virginian, July 5, 1823, p. 3, c. 4.

SETTLE, SUSAN died on 16th inst. at Lynchburg, Va. Consort of John M.
Settle of Lynchburg.
The Lynchburg Press, June 22, 1821, p. 1, c. 2.

SEYBERT, DR. ADAM died June 2, 1825 in France. Formerly a Representative
in Congress. Was of Philadelphia.
The Lynchburg Virginian, July 21, 1825, p. 3, c. 5.

SHAW, COM., JOHN died lately at Philadelphia. Was of U.S. Navy.
The Lynchburg Virginian, Oct. 3, 1823, p. 3, c. 4.

SHAYS, GEN. DANIEL died at Sparta.
The Lynchburg Virginian, Nov. 7, 1825, p. 3.

SHEARER, WILLIAM died on Tues., the 4th inst. Was of Campbell Co.
The Lynchburg Virginian, July 20, 1826, p. 3, c. 5.

SHEFFY, DANIEL died last Friday evening at Warm Springs at the house of
Mr. John M'Clung. Occupied high standing as practicing attorney in
the courts of Va. and in the Supreme Court of the U.S. Left a
widow and 5 children. From the Stanton Spectator, Dec. 10th.
The Lynchburg Virginian, Dec. 16, 1830, p. 3, c. 2 and 3.

SHELTON, ABNER died between Richmond and Burks Tavern. Killed in accident,
"horse frightened." Survived by wife and 3 children.
The Lynchburg Virginian, Jan. 14, 1836, p. 4, c. 2.

SHELTON, BOOKER died at Natchez, Jan. 7, 1818. Formerly of Lynchburg.
The Lynchburg Press, Feb. 6, 1818, p. 3, c. 3.

SHELTON, CAROLINE MATILDA died Jan. 28th, age 2 years, 7 months, 8 days.
Second dau. of Dr. T.C. Shelton of Pittsylvania Co.
The Lynchburg Virginian, Feb. 8, 1830, p. 3, c. 3.

SHELTON, CAPT. ELIPHEZ died on 16th inst., age 86, at his residence. Was
of Taylorsville, Patrick Co. Was an officer of Revolutionary War.
The Lynchburg Virginian, March 23, 1826, p. 3, c. 4.

SHELTON, ELLEN VIRGINIA died on 21st ult. Infant dau. of Mr. John G.
Shelton, formerly of Lynchburg.
The Lynchburg Virginian, Aug. 2, 1833, p. 3, c. 3.

SHELTON, MRS. FRANCES died Nov. 28, 1824, age 36. Consort of Wm. H. Shelton
of Mount Laurel, Pittsylvania Co.; survived by husband and family.
The Lynchburg Virginian, Dec. 24, 1824, p. 3.

SHELTON, MRS. MARY died April 30, 1821 in Nelson Co. Consort of Maj. Wm.
H. Shelton and dau. of James Stevens of Nelson. Survived by husband
and 4 children.
The Lynchburg Press & Public Advertiser, May 11, 1821, p. 3, c. 4.

SHELTON, MRS. MARY LEIGH died on 7th inst., age 34. Consort of Abram C.
Shelton, Esq. of Pittsylvania.
The Lynchburg Virginian, July 25, 1836, p. 3, c. 3. & Ju., 28, p.3,c.4.

SHELTON, MRS. PHEBE died on Thursday, the 17th inst. at age 52 in Pittsylvania Co. Was consort of Capt. John Shelton. The Lynchburg Virginian April 4, 1831, p. 3, c. 3 says consort of Captain Thomas Shelton.
The Lynchburg Virginian, March 28, 1831, p. 3, c. 3.

SHELTON, WILLIAM died on 4th inst., age 69. Of Pittsylvania Co.
The Lynchburg Virginian, August 23, 1827, p. 3, c. 2.

SHERMAN, MRS. HARRIET died August 18th at her residence in Bedford Co. Was consort of Wm. N. Sherman, Esq.
The Lynchburg Virginian, Sept. 15, 1828, p. 3, c. 5.

SHIPPEN, EDWARD, ESQ. died Dec. 23, 1832 at Louisville. Cashier of Branch Bank in that city.
The Lynchburg Virginian, Jan. 14, 1833, p. 3, c. 5.

SHOEMAKER, EDWARD DOYLE died on 4th inst., age 6 yrs. and two months. Son of Mr. Lindsey Shoemaker of this place.
The Lynchburg Virginian, Feb. 16, 1832, p. 3, c. 4.

SHOEMAKER, FRANCES LUCINDA died on 3rd inst., age 3 yrs., 7 mos. Dau. of Mr. Lindsey Shoemaker.
The Lynchburg Virginian, March 15, 1832, p. 3, c. 3.

SHOEMAKER, MADISON died July 7th at Vicksburg, Miss. Deceased formerly of Lynchburg. Left a wife.
The Lynchburg Virginian, Aug. 18, 1836, p. 3, c. 5.

SHRIVER, JAMES died on 8th inst.
The Lynchburg Virginian, Sept. 7, 1826, p. 3, c. 4.

SIMMS, COLONEL CHARLES died Sept. 6, 1819. Collector of the Port of Alexandria.
The Lynchburg Press & Public Advertiser, Sept. 7, 1819, p. 3, c. 6.

SINCLAIR, COMMODORE ARTHUR of the U.S. Navy died last Monday night. He entered the Naval service as Midshipman Nov. 15, 1798. Rank of Captain July 28, 1813. He leaves several children. Copied from Norfolk Beacon.
The Lynchburg Virginian, Feb. 21, 1831, p. 3, c. 4.

SLAUGHTER, MRS. ELIZABETH died on 1st inst., age 81, at the residence of her son, Dr. John Slaughter. She was the widow of the late Charles Slaughter of Campbell.
The Lynchburg Virginian, Sept. 7, 1835, p. 3, c. 5.

SLAUGHTER, LAWRENCE died Sept. 8, 1823, age about 35, at the house of John Watson in Pittsylvania Co. Was of Fredericksburg.
The Lynchburg Virginian, Sept. 19, 1823, p. 3.

SLAUGHTER, DR. ROBERT H. died on Oct. 24th. Of Pittsylvania Co. Died of
"the prevaling epidemic." Long eulogy - reference to family and friends.
The Lynchburg Virginian, Nov. 19, 1832, p. 3, c. 4.

SMITH, DANIEL P. PERKINS died April 4, 1828. Youngest son of James Smith
of Amherst Co.
The Lynchburg Virginian, April 17, 1828, p. 3, c. 6.

SMITH, HENRY DAVIS died on Friday last. Infant son of The Rev. F.C. Smith.
The Lynchburg Virginian, Nov. 7, 1836, p. 3, c. 4.

SMITH, MISS JANE E. died Sept. 5, 1827, age 17. Eldest Dau. of John and
Martha J. Smith of Lynchburg. Died at home of Mr. Logan near
Lexington, Va.
The Lynchburg Virginian, Sept. 20, 1827, p. 3, c. 2.

SMITH, JOHN died on 30th ult., age 1 yr., 15 days. Son of Jabez Smith,
Esq. of Pittsylvania Co.
The Lynchburg Virginian, June 9, 1831, p. 3, c. 3.

SMITH, JOHN of Rutherford Co., Tenn. Once a sheriff of Goochland and a
merchant of Cumberland.
The Lynchburg Virginian, April 1, 1825, p. 3.

SMITH, COL. JOHN died on 12th ult., age 36, in Pittsylvania Co. Left
wife and 2 small children.
The Lynchburg Virginian, Sept. 8, 1836, p. 3, c. 2.

SMITH, MAJOR JOHN died on 21st inst., age upward of 80, at residence in
Pittsylvania on Pig River. Resident of Pittsylvania.
The Lynchburg Virginian, Jan. 4, 1836, p. 3, c. 4.

SMITH, MRS. JUDITH died Nov. 24, 1819, age 25. Wife of Ralph Smith, Jr.
of Pittsylvania Co. and dau. of Major Benjamin Cook of Franklin Co.
The Lynchburg Press & Public Advertiser, Dec. 3, 1819, p. 3, c. 2.

SMITH, MARCELLUS, ESQ. died on 19th inst. at the residence of James
Pleasants, Esq. of Goochland Co. Late one of the editors and
proprietors of the Richmond Whig and formerly of this paper.
The Lynchburg Virginian, March 5, 1829, p. 3, c. 2.

SMITH, MARY ELIZABETH died July 29, 1831, age 6. Was dau. of Mr. Ralph
Smith of Campbell Co.
The Lynchburg Virginian, Aug. 11, 1831, p. 3, c. 5.

SMITH, MRS. MATILDA ANN died on 18th inst., age 18. Consort of John
Smith of Lynchburg.
The Lynchburg Virginian, Feb. 23, 1826, p. 3, c. 4.

SMITH, PETER **died lately at North Muir of Forfar. In 1745 he assisted in
conveying Prince Edward's baggage from this quarter to the North.**
The Lynchburg Virginian, June 14, 1830, p. 2, c. 4.

SMITH, PHILIP died on 4th inst. around 80 yrs. of age. Was of Amherst Co.
The Lynchburg Virginian, Sept. 11, 1834, p. 3, c. 4.

SMITH, RALPH, SR. died on 28th ult., 1827 in 74th year, at home, "The Pocket", in Pittsylvania.
The Lynchburg Virginian, March 13, 1827, p. 3, c. 5.

SMITH, CAPT. STITH died on 21st inst., age about 50, at his residence in Dinwiddie Co.
The Lynchburg Virginian, July 28, 1831, p. 3, c. 4.

SMYTH, ALEXANDER died Aug. 14, 1817, age 6. Was of Wythe Court House.
The Lynchburg Press, Aug. 22, 1817, p. 3.

SMYTH, MRS. NANCY died on 20th inst., age 62, at residence of her son-in-law, Capt. John P. Mathews, near Wythe Court House. Was widow of General Alexander Smyth.
The Lynchburg Virginian, April 30, 1832, p. 3, c. 3.

SNEAD, JAMES died on 13th inst. at home of his father of this place. Was in his 35th year.
The Lynchburg Virginian, Sept. 27, 1832, p. 3, c. 4.

SNEAD, WILLIAM, JR. died in Nashville, Tenn., age 22. Moved from Lynchburg about 2 years since. Was engaged in mercantile business in Nashville. Copied from Nashville Banner.
The Lynchburg Virginian, Oct. 1, 1827, p. 3, c. 4.

SOMERVILLE, WILLIAM C. died in France; minister to Sweden.
The Lynchburg Virginian, March 23, 1826, p. 3.

SPAIN, CAPT. EPPS died yesterday morning. Was of Dinwiddie Co. Copied from N. Y. Herald, Sept. 27th.
The Lynchburg Virginian, Oct. 2, 1826, p. 3, c. 3.

SPEECE, DR. CHARLES died Jan. 24, 1828. Of Halifax Co.
The Lynchburg Virginian, Feb. 4, 1828, p. 3, c. 4.

SPEECE, CONRAD, SR. died Aug. 19, 1820, age 69, at residence in Campbell Co. Survived by a large family.
The Lynchburg Press & Public Advertiser, Sept. 22, 1820, p. 3, c. 4.

SPEECE, THE REV. CONRAD D.D. died on 15th inst. at house of Dr. Allen Sear near Staunton.
The Lynchburg Virginian, Beb. 25, 1836, p. 3, c. 5.

SPEECE, EDWARD Y. died on 17th inst., age 16, at residence of his father, Peter Speece, Esq.
The Lynchburg Virginian, Feb. 4, 1830, p. 3, c. 3.

SPEECE, EDWIN M. died on 20th inst., age 16, at father's residence, Lynchburg. Son of Mr. Frederick Speece.
The Lynchburg Virginian, Dec. 24, 1829, p. 3, c. 5.

SPENCE, THE REV. WILLIAM died on July 3rd. Was of Franklin Co. and a Methodist preacher.
The Lynchburg Press, April 27, 1821, p. 3, c. 1.

SPINNER, MRS. MARY died on 8th inst. at residence of husband in Bedford
    Co. Wife of Mr. Jesse Spinner.
    The Lynchburg Virginian, May 16, 1831, p. 3, c. 4.

SPOTSWOOD, ALEXANDER died at age 2. He was fourth son of Alexander
    Spotswood of Campbell Co.
    The Lynchburg Virginian, Aug. 26, 1830, p. 3, c. 4.

SPOTSWOOD, ALFRED R. died Feb. 28, 1833, age 8. Son of Norborne Spotswood
    of New Glasgow.
    The Lynchburg Virginian, March 11, 1833, p. 3, c. 4.

STABLER, SARAH ZALINDA died on 3rd inst., age 6, in Baltimore. Dau. of
    Robinson and Mary Annis Stabler of Lynchburg.
    The Lynchburg Virginian, Nov. 13, 1834, p. 3, c. 4.

STANLEY, JOHN, ESQ. died on 3rd inst. in Newbern, N.C. "One of North
    Carolina's most distinguished and useful sons." Served in Congress
    and in North Carolina Legislature.
    The Lynchburg Virginian, p. 3, c. 3.

STANTON, MAJOR killed at Battle of Bridgewater near Niagara Falls. Was
    of New York.
    The Lynchburg Press, Aug. 18, 1814, p. 2.

STAPLES, EDWARD died on 25th ult. 1828, age 83. Youngest son of Wm.
    Staples. Died at residence in Buckingham Co.
    The Lynchburg Virginian, June 5, 1828, p. 3, c. 4.

STAPLES, EDWARD C. died Sept. 11, 1823, age 36. Of Henry Co.
    The Lynchburg Virginian, Sept. 19, 1823, p. 3.

STAPLES, JAMES died on 12th inst., age about 49, at his residence in
    Campbell Co.
    The Lynchburg Virginian, Dec. 21, 1835, p. 3, c. 3.

STAPLES, JOSEPH, ESQ. died April 22nd, age 40 in New Glasgow.
    The Lynchburg Virginian, May 5, 1836, p. 3, c. 3.

STAPLES, COL. SAMUEL died March 23, 1825 at Patrick Courthouse. Died at
    age 65 of paralytic attacks; survived by large family. Of Patrick Co.
    The Lynchburg Virginian, April 21, 1825, p. 3.

STARLING, JANE died June 24, 1824, age 13, at Oak Hill, Henry Co. Dau.
    of Thomas Starling.
    The Lynchburg Virginian, July 16, 1824, p. 3.

STARLING, MARY W. died on 20th inst., age 21, at Oak Hill in Henry Co.,
    her father's home. Dau. of Thomas Starling, Esq.
    The Lynchburg Virginian, June 30, 1825, p. 3, c. 4. & July 14, 1825, p. 3.

STARLING, OVERTON R. died June 8, 1833, age 21, at New Orleans. Late of
    Henry Co., Va.
    The Lynchburg Virginian, Aug. 1, 1833, p. 3, c. 5.

STARR, MRS. SARAH died Tues. 5th inst., age 37, in Bedford Co. Wife of
The Rev. Wm. H. Starr. Dau. of John McCabe of Bedford Co.
The Lynchburg Virginian, July 14, 1831, p. 3, c. 4.

STAUGHTON, THE REV. WILLIAM died on 12th inst. in Washington City. Was
Pres. of Georgetown College in Kentucky and formerly Pres. of the
Columbian College in this District.
The Lynchburg Virginian, Dec. 21, 1829, p. 3, c. 5.

STEEL, JOHN died on 28th inst., age about 60, in Campbell Co. Was of
Campbell Co. Left a family.
The Lynchburg Virginian, Aug. 31, 1826, p. 3, c. 3.

STEPTOE, ELIZABETH DILLON died on 10th inst. Eldest dau. of The Rev.
Wm. Steptoe of Bedford.
The Lynchburg Virginian, March 28, 1833, p. 3, c. 4.

STEPTOE, JAMES died on 9th inst. at his residence near New London. Was
Clerk of the Court of Bedford.
The Lynchburg Virginian, Feb. 16, 1826, p. 3, c. 5.

STEPTOE, JAMES C., ESQ. died at his residence on Oct. 24th in town of
Liberty. Was Clerk of County of Bedford and son of James Steptoe
also Clerk of County of Bedford.
The Lynchburg Virginian, Nov. 8, 1827, p. 3, c. 5.

STEPTOE, RICHARD H. D. died Feb. 3, 1819 at home of Dr. Wm. Steptoe.
Was of Bedford.
The Lynchburg Press & Public Advertiser, Feb. 8, 1819, p. 3, c. 3.

STERRY, ROBERT died in shipwreck of the "Helen". Was 38 years old and
of Providence, R. I. and son of Cypriant Sterry.
The Lynchburg Press & Public Advertiser, Feb. 18, 1820, p. 3.

STEVENSON, JOHN died in Powder Mill explosion. Left wife. News account
from Newark, April 26th.
The Lynchburg Press, May 12, 1814, p. 2.

STEWART, MISS BETSEY died last Sat. evening at residence of her brother,
Captain James Stewart.
The Lynchburg Press & Public Advertiser, Nov. 26, 1818, p. 3, c. 5.

STEWART, CAPT. CHARLES died on 14th inst., age 81, at his residence in
Bedford Co. Was Captain in Revolutionary War.
The Lynchburg Virginian, Aug. 18, 1836, p. 3, c. 5.

STEWART, JAMES died last Tuesday at his residence in Campbell Co. Was a
merchant of this place.
The Lynchburg Virginian, Sept. 8, 1828, p. 3, c. 6.

STETH, JOHN, ESQ. died Oct. 25, 1824 at Mr. Early's in Lynchburg. Was
of Petersburg.
The Lynchburg Virginian, Oct. 29, 1824, p. 3.

STONE, BENAMMI died on Dec. 19, 1831, age 81 at Huntingtower, his late residence near Amherst Court House.
The Lynchburg Virginian, Jan. 23, 1832, p. 3, c. 3.

STONE, MRS. ELIZABETH died Dec. 6, 1830, age 80. Lived at Huntingtower, Amherst Court House. Husband survives.
The Lynchburg Virginian, Dec. 16, 1830, p. 3, c. 2.

STONE, JAMES died at his home in Bedford, age 52. Member of Methodist Episcopal Church.
The Lynchburg Virginian, Nov. 3, 1831, p. 3, c. 3.

STORER, EDWARD died on 17th inst., age 82, at his residence near Marysville, Campbell Co. A soldier of the Revolution and a member of Methodist Episcopal Church.
The Lynchburg Virginian, Aug. 14, 1837, p. 3, c. 4.

STOUGHTON, JAMES killed on Dec. 28, 1819 in New York. Stabbed. Son of Spanish Consul. From the New York Commercial Advertiser.
The Lynchburg Press, Jan. 4, 1820, p. 2, c. 6.

STREET, CAPT. ANTHONY died on 11th inst. at residence in Franklin Co. Age upwards of 50 years. At time of death he was High Sheriff of Franklin Co.
The Lynchburg Virginian, Jan. 23, 1832, p. 3, c. 3.

STRONG, JOHN died at Norfolk lately. Member of Lynchburg Rifle Company.
The Lynchburg Press, Sept. 8, 1814, p. 3, c. 2.

STUART, JUDGE ALEXANDER died Dec. 9, 1832 at Staunton. Was from Missouri.
The Lynchburg Virginian, Dec. 20, 1832, p. 3, c. 5.

STUART, ARCHIBALD, ESQ. died last Wed. morning, age 75. Was volunteer soldier in Revolution. Filled various responsible civil stations. Member of the State Convention for adopting the Federal Constitution. Judge of the General Court. From the Staunton Spectator, July 13.
The Lynchburg Virginian, July 19, 1832, p. 3, c. 4.

SUTPHIN, MRS. CATHARINE died Dec. 2nd, age 38, in Lynchburg. Was member of the Presbyterian Church.
The Lynchburg Virginian, Dec. 11, 1834, p. 1, c. 4.

SWANN, COL. JAMES died on 18th ultimo in Paris. Formerly of Boston.
The Lynchburg Virginian, April 28, 1831, p. 3, c. 4.

SWIFT, MRS. ANN died Jan. 16, 1833, age 65, at Madison C. H., Va. Recently a resident of Lynchburg. Relict of Jonathan Swift, Esq. late of Alexandria.
The Lynchburg Virginian, Feb. 14, 1833, p. 3, c. 4.

SWINNEY, MRS. CATHARINE died June 22, 1825. Consort of Capt. William Swinney of Lynchburg.
The Lynchburg Virginian, June 27, 1825, p. 3, c. 5.

SWINNEY, MR. THOMAS died on 25th ult. in 57th year at his residence in this County. He left wife and large family of children.
The Lynchburg Virginian, Sept. 5, 1836, p. 3, c. 4.

SYMMES, CAPT. JOHN CLEVES died Thursday, 19th ultimo in Hamilton, Butler County, Ohio.
The Lynchburg Virginian, June 18, 1829, p. 3, c. 4.

T

TAIT(TATE),CALEB, SR. died Sept. 2, 1814 at his home. Merchant of Lynchburg.
The Lynchburg Press, Sept. 8, 1814, p. 3, c. 1.

TAIT, CHARLES HENRY died Dec. 5, 1827, age 33. Of Columbia, Tenn. and native of Lynchburg.
The Lynchburg Virginian, Jan. 3, 1828, p. 3, c. 2.

TAIT, MISS ELOISE died Feb. 25th at residence of Mrs. Dabney in Campbell Co.
The Lynchburg Virginian, March 1, 1830, p. 3, c. 3.

TALBOT, MISS ADALINE W. died on 3rd inst., age 18, at her mother's residence in Campbell Co. Youngest dau. of Williston Talbot deceased.
The Lynchburg Virginian, Nov. 26, 1835, p. 3, c. 5.

TALBOT, MR. ALLEN died on 13th inst., age 37. Was of this place.
The Lynchburg Virginian, Sept. 24, 1829, p. 3, c. 4.

TALBOT, MISS ANN ELIZABETH died Aug. 16, 1830, age 16. Dau. of Allen Talbot.
The Lynchburg Virginian, Aug. 23, 1830, p. 3, c. 5.

TALBOT, MISS MARY H. died on 14th inst., age 30, at the residence of her mother, Mrs. Nancy Talbot. Was eldest dau. of John Talbot, dec'd.
The Lynchburg Virginian, Aug. 20, 1835, p. 3, c. 5.

TALBOT, MATTHEW died in 59th year of his age at his residence near this place (Washington, Georgia). "The good man, the patriot and the Statesman, is no more!" In 1785 he emigrated to Georgia from Bedford Co., Va. of which state he is a native. First settled in Weeks Co., Ga. and later moved to Oglethorpe from which Co. he was elected to the Convention which formed the Constitution. Returned to Weeks Co. where he resided prior to his death. 1808 a senator in Ga. Legislature. 1818 Pres. of Senate to 1823. Copied from Washington, Ga. News, Nov. 20.
The Lynchburg Virginian, Oct. 8, 1827, p. 3, c. 4.

TALBOT, WILLIAM HARRISON died on 15th ult., age 25, in Lost Prairie, Arkansas Territory. Was eldest son of John Talbot, dec'd.
The Lynchburg Virginian, Aug. 27, 1835, p. 3, c. 5.

TALIAFERRO, COL. CHARLES died June 29, 1824, age 63, at Amherst Co.
The Lynchburg Virginian, July 9, 1824, p. 3.

TALIAFERRO, MRS. MARTHA died March 25, 1820 at residence of her mother in Henrico Co. Was wife of James Taliaferro.
The Lynchburg Press & Public Advertiser, April 4, 1820, p. 3, c. 5.

TALIAFERRO, MRS. MARY died Aug. 1st, age 43, at Rocky Mount. Consort of Dr. Richard M. Taliaferro. Left also children and aged mother.
The Lynchburg Virginian, Aug. 3, 1837, p. 3, c. 4.

TARDY, A. H. P. died on 4th inst., age 4 yrs., 2 mos., 8 days. Was eldest son of Samuel Tardy, Esq. of this county.
The Lynchburg Virginian, March 16, 1835, p. 3, c. 4.

TARDY, JOHN CYRUS died Aug. 26, 1832, age 7 months, at Amherst. Infant son of Elihu Tardy.
The Lynchburg Virginian, Aug. 30, 1832, p. 3, c. 4.

TARDY, PAUL J. died Feb. 5, 1828, in Lynchburg.
The Lynchburg Virginian, Feb. 7, 1828, p. 3, c. 5.

TARDY, WILLIAM died Friday last in Lynchburg, Va. Left large and numerous family.
The Lynchburg Virginian, Sept. 13, 1830, p. 3, c. 3.

TATE, MRS. CATHARINE died May 21, 1828 at Rocky Mount, Va. Was consort of Col. Edmund Tate.
The Lynchburg Virginian, June 23, 1828, p. 3, c. 5.

TATE, COL. EDMUND died last Wed. at advanced age at his residence in this county. Soldier of the Revolution. He was of Campbell Co.
The Lynchburg Virginian, Oct. 30, 1826, p. 3, c. 4.

TATE, COL. EDMUND died on 9th inst. in Franklin Co.
The Lynchburg Virginian, Feb. 23, 1829, p. 3, c. 5.

TATE, MR. EDMUND W. died on 9th inst. in Columbus, Miss. at age 24. Left last summer, the residence of an aged mother and a large circle of friends in Lynchburg and sought in Mississippi a settlement and home.
The Lynchburg Virginian, Aug. 15, 1833, p. 3, c. 3.

TATE, MR. HENRY died Feb. 13th at Bedford Co. at age 59. Left 5 children. His wife, age 38, died on 22nd of same month.
The Lynchburg Virginian, July 2, 1835, p. 3, c. 6.

TATE, GENERAL WILLIAM died Feb. 11th, age 79. Was of Abington and an officer of Revolutionary War.
The Lynchburg Virginian, April 15, 1830

TAYLOR, ALLEN, ESQ. died a few days ago at his residence. Was one of the Judges of the General Court of Va.
The Lynchburg Virginian, June 9, 1836, p. 3, c. 4.

TAYLOR, MRS. ANNE died Feb. 5, 1815, age about 80. Mother of Col. John Taylor of Caroline Co.
The Lynchburg Press, April 27, 1815, p. 3, c. 2.

TAYLOR, ARCHIBALD RITCHIE died Jan. 23, 1833, age 43, at St. Louis, Missouri at residence of his brother. Born in Fredericksburg Nov. 28, 1790.
The Lynchburg Virginian, Feb. 18, 1833, p. 3, c. 4.

TAYLOR, CREED died on 17th inst., age 70, at Needham, his residence in Cumberland. Late Chancellor of Richmond and Lynchburg District. Long distinguished member of General Assembly; Speaker of Senate; efficient leader of Republican party.
The Lynchburg Virginian, Feb. 1, 1836, p. 3, c. 4.

TAYLOR, GEORGE W. died Sept. 12, 1821 at Bedford Courthouse.
The Lynchburg Press, Sept. 14, 1821, p. 3, c. 5.

TAYLOR, HUGH P., ESQ. died on 1st inst. in town of Covington, Alleghany Co. A distinguished Civil engineer. Left widow and 2 children.
The Lynchburg Virginian, Jan. 17, 1831, p. 3, c. 4.

TAYLOR, JOHN died Aug. 26, 1821. Was of Bedford Courthouse.
The Lynchburg Press, Sept. 14, 1821, p. 3, c. 5.

TAYLOR, JOHN of Caroline. Member of State Legislature & member of U.S. Senate.
The Lynchburg Virginian, Sept. 3, 1824, p. 3, c. 3.

TAYLOR, SAMUEL died on 10th inst., age 39. Of Amherst Co. Left a wife and two children.
The Lynchburg Virginian, Oct. 19, 1826, p. 3, c. 2.

TEAS, MRS. ELIZABETH V. died April 28, 1833, age 47, at New London, Va. Consort of Mr. John Teas. Dau. of The Rev. John Mitchell of Bedford Co.
The Lynchburg Virginian, May 20, 1833, p. 3, c. 5.

TEAS, MRS. MARY died June 22nd, age 42, at her residence in New London, Campbell Co., Va. Consort of John Teas, dau. of Frederick Hass of Winchester, Va.
The Lynchburg Virginian, July 6, 1826, p. 3, c. 4.

TEAS, CAPT. WILLIAM died Feb. 16, 1824, age 74, at his residence. Was of Nelson Co. He came from Donagal, Ireland. Survived by wife and child.
The Lynchburg Virginian, March 19, 1824, p. 3.

TERRY, JANE S. died on 11th inst. Eldest dau. of William Terry of Liberty, Va.
The Lynchburg Virginian, Aug. 23, 1827, p. 3, c. 2.

THOMAS, ISAIAH died on 4th inst., age 82, at Worcester, Mass. Was Patriarch of American Printers and founder of American Antiquarian Soc.
The Lynchburg Virginian, April 18, 1831, p. 1, c. 5.

THOMAS, JOHN died March 3, 1825. Of Rutherford Co., Tenn., formerly of Shenandoah, Va. from which place he moved in 1815.
The Lynchburg Virginian, April 1, 1825, p. 3, c. 5.

THOMAS, JOHN W. died on 4th inst. in Henry Co. Was formerly of Pittsylvania. Was husband and father of five children.
The Lynchburg Virginian, Aug. 22, 1831, p. 3, c. 4.

THOMPSON, MRS. DAVID died Dec. 18, 1819. Relict of Mr. David Thompson of Lynchburg.
The Lynchburg Press & Public Advertiser, Dec. 21, 1819, p. 3, c. 5.

THOMPSON, JAMES, ESQ. died July 24, 1821. Was attorney-at-law in Tazewell Co. and died there. A member of the General Assembly of Virginia.
The Lynchburg Press, Aug. 24, 1821, p. 3, c. 6.

THOMPSON, JOHN died April 8, 1830, age 86, at his residence in Campbell Co. He was a professor of religion for many years.
The Lynchburg Virginian, April 26, 1830, p. 3, c. 5.

THOMPSON, MARY died Aug. 28, 1832, age 2 yrs., 6 mos. Was of Bedford Co. and dau. of Capt. Bartlett Thompson of Bedford Co.
The Lynchburg Virginian, Sept. 3, 1832, p. 3, c. 5.

THOMPSON, PHILIP R., ESQ. died on 22nd ult., age 71, at his residence in Kanawha Co. Was delegate in State Legislature for many years from his native Co. of Culpeper, also a Representative in Congress.
The Lynchburg Virginian, Aug. 3, 1837, p. 3, c. 4.

THOMPSON, SAMUEL of Norfolk died July 29, 1814 in Amelia Co. Son of Washington Thompson of Pittsylvania Co. and grandson of James Scott of Amelia Co.
The Lynchburg Press, Oct. 27, 1814, p. 3, c. 2.

THOMSON, CHARLES Sec. of Congress of Montgomery Co.
The Lynchburg Virginian, Sept. 3, 1824, p. 3, c. 3.

THORNTON, MISS MARY died Sept. 11, 1823. Dau. of Peter P. Thornton of Amherst Co. Survived by her parents.
The Lynchburg Virginian, Sept. 19, 1823, p. 3, c. 5.

THORNTON, MR. STERLING C. died last Tues. morning, age 78. Was a Revolutionary soldier.
The Lynchburg Virginian, Aug. 4, 1831, p. 3, c. 5.

THURMAN, MRS. CAMILLA died at residence of Dr. Geo. W. Clement in Franklin Co. Wife of Dr. Robert Thurman of Pittsylvania Co. Member of Methodist Episcopal Church.
The Lynchburg Virginian, Sept. 10, 1832, p. 3, c. 4.

THURMAN, JOSEPH HENRY died on 21st inst., age 6 mos. and 29 days. Son of William and Eliz Thurman of this place.
The Lynchburg Virginian, Feb. 29, 1836, p. 3, c. 4.

THURMAN, LUCY died July 14th, age 63. She was of Amherst Co. and consort of Mr. Wm. Thurman.
The Lynchburg Virginian, Aug. 11, 1828, p. 3, c. 5.

THURMAN, MARBORNE R. died on 20th ult., age 21, at Natches. Was formerly of Lynchburg.
The Lynchburg Virginian, June 15, 1831, p. 3, c. 3.

THURMAN, RICHARD, SEN. died on 14th inst., age 87. Was husband and father. Also soldier of Revolution. Interred Saturday afternoon with military honors. Buried in old Methodist (City) Cemetery. Had two deceased wives, and third survives. Issue only by first wife. Friend of both Washington and Lafayette.
The Lynchburg Virginian, Aug. 16, 1830, p. 3, c. 5.

TILLMAN, MRS. HANNAH died lately at age 109 at Fluvanna Co.
The Lynchburg Virginian, Oct. 2, 1834, p. 3, c. 4.

TIMBERLAKE, MRS. POLLY died on 10th inst., age 39. Consort of Christopher I. Timberlake. Left 8 children.
The Lynchburg Virginian, Sept. 20, 1827, p. 3, c. 2.

TINSLEY, DAVID, SENR. died April 23, 1828, age 81. Was of Amherst. "Was not a soldier of the Revolution in field of battle, he occupied an important and useful station."
The Lynchburg Virginian, May 12, 1828, p. 3, c. 6.

TINSLEY, GEORGE died Feb. 1, 1828, age 55. He was of Amherst Co.
The Lynchburg Virginian, Feb. 7, 1828, p. 3, c. 5.

TINSLEY, REUBEN died on 3rd ult. at his residence in Franklin Co. He was long a resident of Franklin.
The Lynchburg Virginian, Jan. 5, 1832, p. 3, c. 6.

TINSLEY, MISS SALLY died Jan. 12, 1828, age 27. She was of Amherst Co. and eldest dau. of George M. Tinsley.
The Lynchburg Virginian, Jan. 21, 1828, p. 3, c. 2.

TINSLEY, MRS. SARAH ANN died on 18th inst., age 20 in Danville. Consort of The Rev. Isaac S. Tinsley of that place.
The Lynchburg Virginian, Dec. 1, 1836, p. 3, c. 5.

TOLER, ABSALOM died Aug. 28, 1832 at Jefferson Co., Kentucky. Was formerly of Va. Probably about 22 years old. Son of Lemuel Toler. Member of Methodist Protestant Church in Lynchburg.
The Lynchburg Virginian, Oct. 25, 1832, p. 3, c. 4.

TOLER, MRS. CYNTHIA died on 13th inst. in Richmond. Mother of one of the editors of this paper.
The Lynchburg Virginian, Nov. 19, 1829, p. 3, c. 4.

TOLER, FRANCIS CAMPBELL died on 18th inst., age 1 yr., 2 mos. and 4 days. Son of Richard H. Toler, one of the editors of this paper.
The Lynchburg Virginian, Dec. 23, 1836, p. 3, c. 2.

TOLLY, BARCLEY de died recently in Russia. Renowned in late wars between Russia and France.
The Lynchburg Virginian, April 14, 1828, p. 3, c. 5.

TOMPKINS, DANIEL D. died at Staten Island, age 51. Late Vice-President
of the U.S.
The Lynchburg Virginian, June 20, 1825, p. 3.

TOMPKINS, MRS. ELIZABETH died May 16th, 1824. Survived by numerous family.
The Lynchburg Virginian, May 21, 1824, p. 3, c. 4.

TOMPKINS, MRS. EVELYN died on 8th inst. Was wife of R. Q. Tompkins, Esq.
The Lynchburg Virginian, May 17, 1830, p. 3, c. 5.

TOWLES, COL. OLIVER died Nov. 18, 1821, age 80. Hero of Revolutionary
War and a lawyer of distinction.
The Lynchburg Press, Nov. 23, 1821, p. 1, c. 1.

TOWLES, DR. OLIVER M. died on Nov. 22, 1830, age 31, in the Lake Sabine
on borders of United States. Native of Virginia. Completed medical
education at Univ. of Penn. Moved to State of Louisiana in 1821.
The Lynchburg Virginian, Aug. 4, 1831, p. 3, c. 5.

TOWNES, EDWARD died Jan. 11, 1822 en route from New Orleans. Formerly
of Pittsylvania Co.
The Lynchburg Press, Jan. 25, 1822, p. 3.

TOWNES, GEORGE died lately at age 18 in Norfolk. Late of Pittsylvania Co.
Son of Stephen C. Townes, Esq. of Pittsylvania Co.
The Lynchburg Virginian, April 9, 1835, p. 3, c. 3.

TOWNSEND, GREEN JORDAN died Oct. 13, 1822 at Springfield Co., Ky.
The Lynchburg Virginian, Nov. 19, 1822, p. 3.

TRACEY, MR. WILLIAM died at his residence in Bedford Co. on July 4, 1833
at age 75. Fought in Revolution; taken prisoner by the Indians for
a time. Member of Methodist Episcopal Church. Left wife, Ann
Tracey and 4 children "scattered in different parts of the world."
The Lynchburg Virginian, Aug. 2, 1833, p. 3, c. 3.

TRASK, OLIVER J. died April 20th, age 21 at Galveston Island, Texas when
Col. Shearman attacked the Mexican Army. Youngest son of the Hon.
Israel Trask of Gloucester, Mass.
The Lynchburg Virginian, July 25, 1836, p. 3, c. 4.

TRIPP, SUSAN died last Friday, age 8, in city of New York.
The Lynchburg Virginian, May 30, 1831, p. 3, c. 3.

TRUSLOW, ARMISTEAD died on 27th inst., age 55, in this place. Left a
wife and several children.
The Lynchburg Virginian, March 31, 1836, p. 3, c. 3.

TUCKER, HENRY ST. G. died on 22nd of this month, age 18, at Winchester,
Va. Eldest son of The Hon. St. George Tucker of Winchester, Va.
The Lynchburg Virginian, March 9, 1826, p. 3, c. 2.

TUCKER, DR. HENRY WM. died at house of his brother, Professor Tucker, at
University of Va. Was of Charlotte Co., Va.
The Lynchburg Virginian, Feb. 14, 1828, p. 3, c. 5.

TUCKER, MRS. JUDITH died on July 29th, age 73.
The Lynchburg Virginian, Aug. 4, 1831, p. 3, c. 5.

TUCKER, MRS. MARIA died Jan. 29, 1823. Consort of Geo. Tucker, Representative to Congress. Obituary appeared also in the press, Feb. 11, 1823.
The Lynchburg Virginian, Jan. 31, 1823, p. 3, c. 5.

TUCKER, ROSALIA died Dec. 7, 1818, age 15. Dau. of George Tucker, Esq. of Lynchburg.
The Lynchburg Press & Public Advertiser, Dec. 14, 1818, p. 3.

TUCKER, HONORABLE ST. GEORGE died on 10th inst., age 77, at Warminster.
The Lynchburg Virginian, Nov. 26, 1827, p. 3, c. 5.

TUNSTALL, LUCY CAROLINE died June 10, 1826, age 17, at her father's residence. Dau. of Wm. Tunstall, Esq. of Bell Grove, Pittsylvania.
The Lynchburg Virginian, June 29, 1826, p. 3, c. 4.

TURNBULL, MISS ELIZABETH died on 21st at residence of mother in Franklin Co.
The Lynchburg Virginian, Oct. 31, 1836, p. 3, c. 1.

TURNER, MAJ. HENRY died on 23rd inst., age 78, in Amherst Co. "Another Revolutionary Patriot gone."
The Lynchburg Virginian, Oct. 26, 1829, p. 3, c. 5.

TURNER, THE REV. JAMES died Jan. 8, 1828, age 69. Was of Bedford and member of Presbyterian Church.
The Lynchburg Virginian, Jan. 17, 1828, p. 3.

TURNER, MRS. SAMUEL died lately at residence near Glasgow in Amherst Co.
The Lynchburg Virginian, Aug. 17, 1829, p. 3, c. 4.

TURNER, MRS. SARAH L. died on 11th inst., age 32. Wife of Mr. Lawson Turner and member of M. E. Church. Left 8 children and husband.
The Lynchburg Virginian, Aug. 28, 1834, p. 3, c. 5.

TURNER, WILLIAM T. died on 2nd inst., age 20, at his residence in Amherst Co. Left wife and 4 small children. He was of Amherst Co.
The Lynchburg Virginian, Aug. 10, 1826, p. 3, c. 3.

TURPIN, RACHEL died on 13th inst. Consort of Thomas Turpin of Bedford. Left husband and 5 children.
The Lynchburg Virginian, Dec. 29, 1825, p. 3, c. 4.

TYLER, JOHN died Aug. 19th, age 69, at home of Mrs. Oney Hucksters. Was soldier under Washington in Revolution. (See Amherst Co. Miniatures by Davis).
The Lynchburg Virginian, Aug. 26, 1830, p. 3, c. 4.

TYREE, MARION FISHER died June 27, 1833, age 10 mos., 8 days. Dau. of John H. Tyree of this place.
The Lynchburg Virginian, July 8, 1833, p. 3, c. 5.

V

VADEN, MRS. REBECCA died on April 23rd, age 47. Wife of Wilson Vaden
of Pittsylvania Co.
The Lynchburg Virginian, May 11, 1826, p. 3, c. 4.

VAN NESS, WILLIAM P. died on 7th inst. in New York. Was Judge of the
U.S. District Court for the Southern District of N.Y.
The Lynchburg Virginian, Sept. 18, 1826, p. 3, c. 3.

VANNERSON, MRS. HENRIETTA died July 23rd, age 31, in Natchez, Miss. She
came to this city in 1832. Was consort of William Vannerson, Esq.
of that city, and dau. of the late William S. Crawford of Amherst Co.
The Lynchburg Virginian, Aug. 31, 1835, p. 3, c. 5.

VARNUM, JOHN, ESQ. died July 23rd, age 63, at Niles, Michigan. Was
formerly member of Congress of Massachusetts.
The Lynchburg Virginian, Sept. 5, 1836, p. 3, c. 4.

VAWTER, SILAS died July 31, 1833, age 22.
The Lynchburg Virginian, Aug. 8, 1833, p. 3, c. 4.

VENABLE, MRS. ELIZABETH died Sept. 6, 1822, age 22, at her father's home
in Bedford. Wife of Dr. Paul Venable of Charlotte and dau. of Capt.
Robert L. Coleman of Bedford.
The Lynchburg Virginian, Sept. 13, 1822, p. 3, c. 4.

VENABLE, COL. SAMUEL died on 7th inst. 1821, at Monroe Co. (Sweet Springs).
He was of Prince Edward Co., Va.
The Lynchburg Press, Sept. 14, 1821, p. 3, c. 5.

VEST, JOHN, SR. died June 23rd, age 85, at his residence near Bunker's Hill
in Bedford Co. Served in Revolutionary Army.
The Lynchburg Virginian, July 16, 1835, p. 3, c. 5.

VICK, ELI died July 25th of a bullet wound in Nash Co., N.C. Copied from
Raleigh Register.
The Lynchburg Virginian, Au. 26, 1823, p. 3, c. 3.

VICTOR, TILDEN died on 13th ult., age about 25. Was a native of Lynchburg,
Va. From the Vicksburg Advocate.
The Lynchburg Virginian, Oct. 13, 1836, p. 3, c. 3.

W

WADE, MR. JAMES died on 26th ult. at Rock Landing, N.C. A native of
Ireland and citizen of Lynchburg for several years.
The Lynchburg Virginian, Sept. 5, 1823, p. 3, c. 3.

WADE, MRS. LUCY died on 3rd inst., age 90 yrs. and 3 mos., at the residence
of Zack Field Wade in this county.
The Lynchburg Virginian, June 28, 1830, p. 3, c. 4.

WALKER, THE HON. DAVID of Kentucky. Was Representative of Congress from Ky.
The Lynchburg Press & Public Advertiser, March 7, 1820, p. 3, c. 3 & 4.

WALKER, MRS. ELEANOR died June 27th. Consort of Elder Arnold Walker of
Henry County.
The Lynchburg Virginian, July 13, 1829, p. 3, c. 4.

WALKER, COL. JAMES died on 9th inst., age about 55, at residence in
Buckingham. Father of John Patrick Walker of Buckingham.
The Lynchburg Virginian, July 17, 1828, p. 3.

WALKER, JOHN, ESQ. died on 7th ult., age about 50, at his residence in
Buckingham Co.
The Lynchburg Virginian, Aug. 7, 1828, p. 3, c. 5.

WALKER, JOHN WILLIAM, ESQ. died near Huntsville, Ala., age 40. Late
Senator from that State in the Congress of U.S. Of Huntsville, Ala.
The Lynchburg Virginian, May 2, 1823, p. 3.

WALKER, LUCY LEWIS died Aug. 29, 1832 at Milton, N.C. Youngest dau. of
Dr. Ajax Walker formerly of Amherst Co., Va.
The Lynchburg Virginian, Sept. 10, 1832, p. 3, c. 4.

WALKER, MRS. MARGARET died on 4th inst., age 26. Was of Amherst and
consort of Mr. Thomas Walker of Amherst. Survived by infant son.
The Lynchburg Virginian, Jan. 15, 1829, p. 3, c. 5.

WALKER, ROBERT died June 23, 1824, age 53.
The Lynchburg Virginian, July 16, 1824, p. 3.

WALKER, SUSAN died Oct. 10th, age 62. Wife of Richard Walker, Esq. of
Bedford. She was of Bedford Co.
The Lynchburg Virginian, Oct. 15, 1827, p. 3, c. 4.

WALKER, WILLIAM died Aug. 31, 1825, age 75. Resident of Campbell Co.
The Lynchburg Virginian, Sept. 8, 1825, p. 3.

WALKER, DR. WYATT P. died on 19th ult., age 25, at his residence in
Merridianville, Ala. Was a native of Virginia.
The Lynchburg Virginian, Jan. 15, 1827, p. 3, c. 5.

WARD, HENRY C. died on 20th ult., age 27, at Charleston, S. C. Resident
of Lynchburg, Va. Survived by consort and 3 infant children.
The Lynchburg Virginian, March 23, 1835, p. 3, c. 5.

WARD, PAULA JANE died on 20th ult. "Most lovely and interesting child of
Benjamin and Elizabeth Ward of New London". Age one yr. and 11 mos.
The Lynchburg Virginian, Jan. 7, 1833, p. 3, c. 3.

WARE, NANCY funeral services at Pedlar Mills on 3rd Sunday in October.
The Lynchburg Virginian, Oct. 6, 1825, p. 3, c. 5.

WARWICK, MAJOR WILLIAM died Aug. 19, 1832, age 67 at Salt Sulphur Springs. Was of Amherst Co. and Pres. of Branch Bank of Va. at Lynchburg. Thrice married and reared three families of children.
The Lynchburg Virginian, Aug. 20, 1832, p. 3, c. 5.

WASHINGTON, JOHN A., ESQ. died on 14th inst. at Mount Vernon. Was proprietor of that estate.
The Lynchburg Virginian, June 25, 1832, p. 3, c. 5.

WATKINS, PHILIP, ESQ. died on 20th inst., age 57 at Prince Edward Co.
The Lynchburg Virginian, Oct. 26, 1829, p. 3, c. 5.

WATSON, JAMES died Sept. 25, 1824, age 52, at Maysville, Ky. Survived by wife. He was of Kanawha and Amherst Counties.
The Lynchburg Virginian, Nov. 26, 1824, p. 3.

WATSON, MARY WILKINS died Oct. 30, 1832, age 9. Dau. of Wilkins Watson of Amherst Co.
The Lynchburg Virginian, Nov. 5, 1832, p. 3, c. 5.

WATSON, THE REV. RICHARD died lately in England. Minister of Methodist Episcopal Church. Author of Theological Institutes and Biographical and Theological Dictionary.
The Lynchburg Virginian, March 14, 1833, p. 3, c. 4.

WATSON, RUEL A. died May 7, 1833 at Vicksburg, Miss. Merchant and was to have married one of the Hegeman sisters who died on the same day also of cholera.
The Lynchburg Virginian, June 6, 1833, p. 3, c. 5.

WATTS, DILLARD RODES died on 3rd inst. in 3rd year of age at residence of his parents, Jas. D. and Eliza H. Watts. His mother died on same day and was interred in same grave with her son.
The Lynchburg Virginian, Aug. 21, 1837, p. 3, c. 4.

WATTS, ELIZA HORSLEY died on 3rd inst. in 32nd year of age at her residence in Albemarle Co., Va. Wife of Jas. D. Watts. Member of Methodist Church.
The Lynchburg Virginian, Aug. 21, 1837, p. 3, c. 4.

WATTS, MRS. ELIZABETH died on Oct. 12th, age 64, at her residence in Bedford Co. Was the widow of Col. John Watts.
The Lynchburg Virginian, Oct. 24, 1836, p. 3, c. 3.

WATTS, HENRY H., ESQ. died Dec. 13, 1832 at his residence in Amherst. He was from Amherst.
The Lynchburg Virginian, Dec. 20, 1832, p. 3, c. 5.

WATTS, CAPT. JAMES died Jan. 25, 1828, age 60. Was of Bedford Co.
The Lynchburg Virginian, Feb. 7, 1828, p. 3, c. 5.

WATTS, COL. JOHN died on June 8, 1830, age 75, at his residence at Gravelly Hill in Bedford Co.
The Lynchburg Virginian, June 17, 1830, p. 3, c. 4.

WATTS, MRS. MARY died on 12th inst., age 80, at her residence at Flat
   Creek, Campbell Co.
   The Lynchburg Virginian, Sept. 22, 1836, p. 3, c. 4.

WATTS, CAPT. STEPHEN died on 13th inst. at his residence in Nelson Co.,
   age 83. Soldier of the Revolution. "No man in his circle of his
   acquaintance ever lived more respected or died more sincerely
   lamented." Reference to "his children".
   The Lynchburg Virginian, Oct. 1, 1832, p. 3, c. 3.

WEATHERFORD, THE REV. JOHN died Feb. 23, 1833, age 90, at residence of
   Mr. Price in Pittsylvania. A soldier of the Revolution and a
   minister of the Church of Christ.
   The Lynchburg Virginian, March 11, 1833, p. 3, c. 4.

WEBB, JOE of Pottsville, Mt. Carbon of the Schuylkill Mts.
   The Lynchburg Virginian, March 6, 1827, p. 3.

WEBB, WILLIAM, SENIOR died on 8th inst., age 73, at his residence in
   Buckingham Co. He was a Revolutionary soldier.
   The Lynchburg Virginian, June 21, 1830, p. 3, c. 3.

WEEMS, THE REV. MASON L. died at Beaufort, S. C. He was of Dunfries, Va.
   and author of a life of George Washington.
   The Lynchburg Virginian, July 21, 1825, p. 3.

WEIR, MR. HUGH died on 24th ult., age about 38. Merchant of Pittsylvania
   Court House. Native of Ireland. Left wife and 2 small children.
   The Lynchburg Virginian, Feb. 9, 1835, p. 3, c. 4.

WELCH, JOHN L. died on 4th inst. in Georgetown, S. C. Was a native of
   Buckingham Co., Va., and by profession a boot and shoemaker.
   The Lynchburg Virginian, Sept. 15, 1831, p. 3, c. 3.

WELCH, THOMAS died at his late residence in Allen Co., Ky., age 60. He
   was a native of Loudoun Co.
   The Lynchburg Virginian, Dec. 24, 1824, p. 3.

WELLS, MRS. WILHELMINA L. died Sept. 17, 1821 at White Sulphur Springs.
   Was of Lynchburg and wife of Mr. Thomas Wells of Lynchburg.
   The Lynchburg Press, Sept. 28, 1821, p. 3, c. 6.

WHARTON, JESSE died lately near Nashville, Tenn. Believed to be one of
   the earliest settlers of Tenn. Formerly a member of Congress from
   Nashville District. Believed to have been a native of Bedford Co., Va.
   The Lynchburg Virginian, Aug. 8, 1833, p. 3, c. 4.

WHEELER, MRS. MILDRED died March 5th, age 67. Relict of Mr. John Wheeler.
   Died in Charlotte Co.
   The Lynchburg Virginian, March 15, 1830, p. 3, c. 3.

WHIPPLE, JOHN died Monday evening. Shot while working in room on second
   floor. Of Albany.
   The Lynchburg Virginian, May 22, 1827, p. 2, c. 5.

WHITE, HOWSON S., CAPT. died May 1st at residence of Mrs. Moore, Bedford Co. "Left a wife to weep."
The Lynchburg Virginian, May 16, 1836, p. 3, c. 3.

WHITE, CAPT. JACOB died on 2nd inst. at his residence in Bedford Co.
The Lynchburg Virginian, June 11, 1832, p. 3, c. 4.

WHITE, JOHN died Sept. 15, 1822, age 26. Was of Halifax Co., brother of Capt. Hawson S. White of Lynchburg.
The Lynchburg Virginian, Sept. 17, 1822, p. 3, c. 5.

WHITE, MRS. LORENZO died Aug. 27, 1823, age 18. Son of Joseph White of Nelson Co.
The Lynchburg Virginian, Oct. 3, 1823, p. 3.

WHITE, DR. RALEIGH died on 15th inst., about 90 years old, at his residence. Was of Pittsylvania Co., Rep. in House of Delegates from Pittsylvania Co. and Senator for the District.
The Lynchburg Virginian, Sept. 25, 1831, p. 3, c. 5.

WHITE, THE HON. ROBERT died last Wed., age 72, at Winchester. Placed on General Court of Va. in 1793. Soldier of Revolution, severely wounded in 1777 in New Jersey.
The Lynchburg Virginian, March 21, 1831, p. 3, c. 5.

WHITE, ROBERT S. died May 1st, age 24, in Pittsylvania Co. at home of his father, Maj. J. White.
The Lynchburg Virginian, May 11, 1829, p. 3, c. 4.

WHITE, SAMUEL, ESQ. died on 29th ultimo, age 64, in Botetourt Co.
The Lynchburg Virginian, Dec. 22, 1831, p. 3, c. 5.

WHITE, WILLIAM died on 12th inst. in this place. Was of Lynchburg. Was merchant here last 6 or 7 years, formerly a merchant in Lexington. Was native of Ireland. Had 2 brothers in Rockbridge and Augusta.
The Lynchburg Virginian, July 16, 1835, p. 3, c. 5.

WHITLOCKE, PAULINA R. died on 18th inst. Wife of George Whitlocke, Esq. of this place. Leaves "doating husband" and daughter.
The Lynchburg Virginian, Jan. 25, 1827, p. 3, c. 5.

WHITTEN, LEONARD H. died on 17th inst., age 13, at the residence of Mr. Wm. McCabe of Bedford Co. Only son of Mr. Abner Whitten.
The Lynchburg Virginian, July 26, 1832, p. 3, c. 6.

WHITTEN, WILLIAM died July 21st, age 90, at the residence of Capt. I. Whitten of Botetourt Co. Deceased was of Bedford.
The Lynchburg Virginian, July 25, 1836, p. 3, c. 4.

WHITTENTON, THOMAS died last Wed., age 62, at his residence in Bedford Co.
The Lynchburg Virginian, Feb. 28, 1831, p. 3, c. 5.

WHITTMORE, AMOS died March 27, 1828, age 69. Was of West Cambridge, Mass. "Inventor of machine for sticking cards."
The Lynchburg Virginian, April 17, 1828, p. 3, c. 6.

WHITTON, SHERROD died Sept. 21, 1830, age 34, at Bedford, Va.
The Lynchburg Virginian, Sept. 27, 1830, p. 3, c. 5.

WIATT, DR. EDWARD of Knoxville, Tenn. died in Paris, Maine. Son of
Thomas Wiatt of Lynchburg.
The Lynchburg Virginian, Aug. 10, 1826, p. 3.

WIATT, COL. JOHN died last Sunday in this place, age 77. Revolutionary
soldier.
The Lynchburg Virginian, Feb. 20, 1827, p. 3.

WIATT, JOHN F. a native of Lynchburg, died in Jackson, Mississippi.
Was attorney-at-law.
The Lynchburg Virginian, Nov. 30, 1824 & Feb. 18, 1825, p. 3.

WIATT, JOHN J. died May 24, 1809. Was resident of Richmond and merchant
there. Formerly of Lynchburg.
The Lynchburg Press, June 3, 1809, p. 3, c. 3.

WIATT, MRS. MARY of Amherst died at home of Mr. Edmund Winston. Consort
of Captain Samuel I. Wiatt of Lynchburg.
The Lynchburg Virginian, Sept. 29, 1825, p. 3, c. 5.

WIATT, SAMUEL JORDAN died on 2nd inst., age 1 yr., 2 mos. and 27 days,
at this place. Son of Samuel I. Wiatt.
The Lynchburg Virginian, May 11, 1835, p. 3, c. 3.

WIATT, MRS. SUSAN died Nov. 2, 1810. She was of Lynchburg and far
advanced in years.
The Lynchburg Press, Nov. 5, 1810, p. 3, c. 2.

WIATT, CAPT. THOMAS died last Saturday night in this place. One of the
oldest citizens.
The Lynchburg Virginian, Sept. 18, 1828, p. 3, c. 6.

WIGGINGTON, BENJAMIN died on 1st inst., age 2. Eldest son of Benjamin
and Harriet Wiggington of Bedford Co., Va.
The Lynchburg Virginian, Aug. 2, 1833, p. 3, c. 3.

WIGGS, THOMAS died June 14, 1825. Was of Lexington, Ky. Was murdered.
The Lynchburg Virginian, Sept. 12, 1825, p. 3, c. 1.

WIKEMAN, MATTHEW of Norfolk Va.; murdered at Portsmouth, Va., Dec. 29,
1819. Survived by wife and 2 children. Native of England and a
ship carpenter.
The Lynchburg Press, Jan. 7, 1820, p. 3, c. 3.

WILCOX, FIRST LIEUT. JOSEPH M. U.S. Infantry, native of Conn. but
resident of Ohio.
The Lynchburg Press, May 12, 1814, p. 3, c. 1.

WILEY, JANE S. died on 20th inst., age 23. Consort of George A. Wiley
of Halifax.
The Lynchburg Virginian, Jan. 25, 1827, p. 3, c. 3.

WILEY, MISS POLLY died on May 9th, age 93, at the residence of Walker
   Terry in Amherst Co.
   The Lynchburg Virginian, Aug. 3, 1837, p. 3, c. 4.

WILKERSON, MRS. PARSON died on 20th inst., age 70 Was of Bedford Co.
   The Lynchburg Virginian, April 25, 1836, p. 3, c. 3.

WILKES, MINER died March 3rd, age about 35, at the residence of Mr.
   Lilbourn H. Johnson near Lynchburg. Deceased was of Charlotte Co.
   The Lynchburg Virginian, Feb. 8, 1832, p. 3, c. 3.

WILLIAMS, MRS. ELIZABETH T. died on 18th inst., age 26, at Bedford Co. Was
   wife of Albert G. Williams. Left 1 child.
   The Lynchburg Virginian, July 23, 1835, p. 3, c. 4.

WILLIAMS, MRS. FRANCES died June 29, 1833, age 27. Consort of Fielding
   L. Williams. Member of First Presbyterian Church in Lynchburg.
   The Lynchburg Virginian, July 8, 1833, p. 3, c. 5.

WILLIAMS, GEORGE died on 19th inst. Was recently of this place and long
   a citizen of Richmond.
   The Lynchburg Virginian, June 21, 1832, p. 3, c. 4.

WILLIAMS, MISS MARY ANNE died Nov. 19th, age 19, at the residence of Dr.
   Robert J. Kincaid in Nelson Co. She was of Nelson Co. and dau. of
   Mr. George Williams of Nelson.
   The Lynchburg Virginian, Dec. 1, 1831, p. 3, c. 4.

WILLIAMS, THE HON. NATHANIEL W. died June 10, 1833 at home of Col. John
   Williams of this vicinity (Lynchburg or Campbell Co.). Deceased was
   of Smith Co. and was for many years one of the judges of the Circuit
   Court of Tenn.
   The Lynchburg Virginian, June 20, 1833, p. 3, c. 5.

WILLIAMS, ROBERT D. died Dec. 28, 1818 at residence of Mrs. Jones of
   Campbell Co. Formerly of Lynchburg.
   The Lynchburg Press & Public Advertiser, Dec. 31, 1818, p. 3, c. 3.

WILLIAMS, MR. SAMUEL died on Tues. week at Halifax Courthouse Va. Was
   of Halifax Co. and Clerk of the County Court of that Co.
   The Lynchburg Virginian, Sept. 4, 1834, p. 3, c. 4.

WILLIAMSON, CALWELL died lately of cholera at Fortress Monroe. Was a
   soldier of the U.S. Army and son of Nathan Williamson of Amherst Co.
   The Lynchburg Virginian, Sept. 24, 1832, p. 3, c. 3.

WILLIAMSON, CULWELL died lately in Union Co., Ohio. Formerly of this place.
   The Lynchburg Virginian, March 5, 1829, p. 3, c. 2.

WILLIAMSON, MRS. SARAH G. died Friday morning, age 19, at her father's
   residence. Was consort of Littleberry E. Williamson and dau. of
   Samuel Quarles.
   The Lynchburg Virginian, July 13, 1826, p. 3, c. 4.

WILLIS, MRS. HARRIET died Nov. 28, 1832 in Tallahassee, Florida. Consort of Dr. Lewis Willis and dau. of Thomas Eaton Randolph, Esq. formerly of Lynchburg.
The Lynchburg Virginian, Jan. 7, 1833, p. 3, c. 3.

WILLS, CAPT. ELIAS died on 20th inst., age 57 yrs. and 54 days. Was of Amherst. See also Lynchburg Virginian, June 25, 1829, p. 3, c. 4.
The Lynchburg Virginian, July 2, 1829, p. 3, c. 3.

WILLS, JAMES died on 22nd ult. Was a grocer of Philadelphia.
The Lynchburg Virginian, Feb. 22, 1825, p. 3, c. 1.

WILSON, MRS. ANN died Oct. 17, 1825, age 68 yrs. and 9 mos. Consort of Capt. Richard Wilson of Amherst Co. Left many relatives and friends.
The Lynchburg Virginian, Oct. 27, 1825, p. 3, c. 4.

WILSON, MRS. ELIZABETH (widow) died on 20th inst., age 45.
The Lynchburg Virginian, Aug. 31, 1835, p. 3, c. 5.

WILSON, EUGENIUS M., ESQ. died recently at Morgantown, Monongalia Co., Va.
The Lynchburg Virginian, June 13, 1831, p. 3, c. 2.

WILSON, COL. JOHN died May 21, 1820, age 72, at his home, "Donshell", in Pittsylvania Co. Survived by widow and 6 children.
The Lynchburg Press & Public Advertiser, June 9, 1820, p. 3, c. 5.

WILSON, JOHN died on Tuesday, the 11th inst. Was of Concord.
The Lynchburg Virginian, July 20, 1826, p. 3, c. 5.

WILSON, CAPT. RICHARD died on 5th inst., age 74, at his residence near Amherst Courthouse. Formerly of Caroline Co., Va. but for many years a resident of Amherst.
The Lynchburg Virginian, June 13, 1836, p. 3, c. 3.

WINCHESTER, GEN. JAMES died July 27th in Nashville, Tenn. Officer in the North Western Army during War of 1812.
The Lynchburg Virginian, Aug. 24, 1826, p. 3, c. 4.

WINFREE, MRS. LUCY died on 19th inst. at residence of her son, Christopher Winfree, Esq. near Lynchburg. Relict of late Valentine Winfree, Esq. of Chesterfield.
The Lynchburg Virginian, March 21, 1836, p. 3, c. 2.

WINFREE, MRS. CORNELIA M. died on July 4th, age 41. Consort of Christopher Winfree, Esq. of this place. Dau. of John B. Tilden, M.D. of Frederick County, Va.
The Lynchburg Virginian, July 11, 1836, p. 3, c. 2.

WINGFIELD, MRS. NANCY died Oct. 26, 1832, age 78, at Amherst Co. Deceased was of Amherst Co.
The Lynchburg Virginian, Nov. 8, 1832, p. 3, c. 5.

WINGFIELD, WM. JR., ESQ. died July 2nd at his residence in Franklin Co. Was son of late Dr. John Wingfield.
The Lynchburg Virginian, Oct. 8, 1829, p. 3, c. 4.

WINSTON, CHARLES died Oct. 1, 1821 at residence of Mrs. Dabney of Campbell.
Was of Amherst and son of Edmund Winston, Esq. of Amherst.
The Lynchburg Press & Public Advertiser, Oct. 5, 1821, p. 3, c. 4.

WINSTON, MRS. DOROTHEA died on 16th inst., age 74, in Halifax Co. at her
daughter's, Mrs. Sarah B. Scott. Widow of Judge Edmond Winston and
of Patrick Henry. She was of ancient Dandridge family. She
married Patrick Henry in 1777.
The Lynchburg Virginian, Feb. 28, 1831, p. 3, c. 4.

WINSTON, GEORGE D., ESQ. died July 15th, age 57, at his seat in Rockingham
Co., N.C. Was son of late Judge Winston.
The Lynchburg Virginian, Aug. 15, 1831, p. 3, c. 3.

WINSTON, WILLIAM died March 2, 1815. Was son of George D. Winston and was
of this vicinity. (See entry for Winston, George D., Esq.)
The Lynchburg Press, March 23, 1815, p. 3, c. 1.

WISNER, JOHN died March 26, 1820, age 25. Was of Willistown. Killed by
a pistol in his desk.
The Lynchburg Press & Public Advertiser, April 18, 1820, p. 3, c. 5.

WITHERS, JAMES W. died last Friday, age 21, in this place. Was a native
of Spottsylvania but resided in this place 2 years.
The Lynchburg Virginian, Sept. 1, 1828, p. 3, c. 6.

WITT, MRS. MARY T. died on 12th inst., age 25. Wife of Wm. Witt and eldest
dau. of Hardaway Hatcher, late of Bedford Co. Left husband and infant
daughter.
The Lynchburg Virginian, Dec. 21, 1826, p. 3, c. 3.

WOLCOT, DR. JOHN died Jan. 31, 1819, age 81. Author of Peter Pindar.
The Lynchburg Press & Public Advertiser, April 1, 1819, p. 3.

WOOD, DAVID M., ESQ. died on 14th inst., age 28, in the lower part of
Madison Co., Alabama. Was a native of Virginia and lived in or
near Abingdon where he learned the carpenter's trade. Lived near
Huntsville 8 or 9 years in the capacity of a grocer.
The Lynchburg Virginian, Sept. 17, 1835, p. 3, c. 5.

WOOD, JESSE died on 17th inst., age 77 yrs., 3 days, at his residence in
Campbell Co. Was in the Revolutionary War.
The Lynchburg Virginian, June 23, 1836, p. 3, c. 5.

WOLCOTT, OLIVER died June 1, 1833, age 74, in New York. Was Secretary of
the Treasury under Washington and more recently Gov. of Conn. "He
was deservedly ranked among the distinguished Patriots of his Country."
The Lynchburg Virginian, June 10, 1833, p. 3, c. 5.

WOOD, RICE W., ESQ. died April 12, 1833, age 34, at Charlottesville, Va.
Had been a delegate to Legislature from Albemarle Co.
The Lynchburg Virginian, April 18, 1833, p. 3, c. 4.

WOODING, GEORGE W. died on 14th inst., age 24, at residence of father in
Pittsylvania Co. Deceased worked in Lynchburg.
The Lynchburg Virginian, Aug. 1, 1836, p. 3, c. 4.

WOODING, JAMES C., ENSIGN died April 5, 1814. Was of Pittsylvania Co. and son of Col. Thomas H. Wooding.
The Lynchburg Press, June 2, 1814, p. 3, c. 2.

WOODROOF, MRS. ELIZABETH died Aug. 18, 1824, age 38, at her residence in Amherst Co. Survived by numerous family.
The Lynchburg Virginian, Aug. 24, 1824, p. 3.

WOODROW, HENRIETTA she was late of Lynchburg and sister of Mrs. Tipton B. Harrison. See entry for Tipton G. Harrison and "His Lady".
The Lynchburg Virginian, Nov. 8, 1822, p. 3, c. 6.

WOODRUF, CLARA died on 21st inst., age 87, at her residence in Amherst Co. Deceased was of Amherst.
The Lynchburg Virginian, Feb. 25, 1825, p. 3.

WOODROW, HENRY died July 18, 1810 in Lynchburg.
The Lynchburg Star, July 20, 1810, p. 3, c. 4.

WOODRUF, WILLIAM "died after having been struck in the head by a negro at the farm at Westham."
The Lynchburg Press, Feb. 18, 1820, p. 3.

WOODS, MISS MARTHA died on 20th ult. at residence of Mr. Josiah Dickinson in Franklin Co. She was member of Methodist Church.
The Lynchburg Virginian, Dec. 6, 1830, p. 3, c. 4.

WOODS, MISS SARAH died Oct. 29, 1825, age 38, at the home of John S. Burwell, Esq.
The Lynchburg Virginian, Nov. 10, 1825, p. 3.

WORD, GRANVILLE L. died on 23rd ult., age 22, in Richmond. Formerly worked in this office as printer, moved to Richmond about 2 years ago.
The Lynchburg Virginian, Sept. 1, 1834, p. 3, c. 5.

WREN, WILLIAM C. died at his residence about 9 miles from Charlottesville last Wednesday of hydrophobia. Copied from Charlottesville Advocate. Cause of death from dog bite.
The Lynchburg Virginian, Aug. 30, 1830, p. 3, c. 3 & 4.

WRIGHT, JAMES T. died Feb. 2, 1822, age 34. He was of Bedford and is survived by wife and one child.
The Lynchburg Press, Feb. 8, 1822, p. 1.

WRIGHT, LEWIS A. died July 28, age 28. Was of Pittsylvania Co., Va.
The Lynchburg Virginian, Aug. 12, 1827, p. 3, c. 4.

WRIGHT, MRS. LUCY died April 10, 1821, age 34, at the residence of Mr. Sterling Claiborne in Nelson Co. She was of Nelson Co.
The Lynchburg Press & Public Advertiser, April 20, 1821, p. 3, c. 5.

WRIGHT, MRS. SALLY died Sept. 27, 1821, age 25, at her home in Bedford Co. She was wife of George Wright and dau. of Capt. James Watts.
The Lynchburg Press, Oct. 5, 1821, p. 3, c. 4.

WYTHE, GEORGE, ESQ. died June 15, 1806. Was Judge of the High Court of Chancery for the Richmond District.
The Lynchburg Star, June 19, 1806, p. 3, c. 1.

Y

YANCEY, BARTLETT, ESQ. died Aug. 30th at Oak Grove, his residence in Caswell Co., N.C. He was a native of Va. and Representative in Congress from the Caswell District.
The Lynchburg Virginian, Sept. 15, 1828, p. 3, c. 5.

YANCEY, FRANCIS G. died last Saturday. Was Senior Editor of Petersburg Intelligenser. Taken from Petersburg Intelligenser, July 12th.
The Lynchburg Virginian, July 18, 1833, p. 3, c. 3.

YANCEY, JAMES died Dec. 18, 1817. He was of Campbell Co. and son of Col. Thornton Yancey of Granville Co.
The Lynchburg Press, Dec. 26, 1817, p. 3, c. 2.

YANCEY, WILLIAM H. died Dec. 23rd, age 23, in Lynchburg. Formerly a resident of Oxford, N.C.
The Lynchburg Virginian, Jan. 1, 1835, p. 3, c. 3.

YOUNG, THE REV. ARTHUR died in Russia recently. Was a celebrated English Agriculturalist.
The Lynchburg Virginian, April 17, 1828, p. 3, c. 6.

YOUNG, ELIZABETH M. died on 9th ult., age 26. Wife of Wm. D. Young of Patrick Co. "Affectionate wife; kind mother, dutiful dau." Died of consumption.
The Lynchburg Virginian, Aug. 9, 1832, p. 3, c. 4.

YOUNG, JOSHUA died on 21st ult. in Henrico Co. He and wife and two children, 9 and 12, and wife's niece, age 18, drowned in Mayo River.
The Lynchburg Virginian, March 29, 1825, p. 2, c. 6.

YOUNG, MR. PEYTON, JR. died Jan. 24th, age 24, at residence of his father, Peyton Young, Sr. in Pittsylvania Co. Youngest son of his parents.
The Lynchburg Virginian, March 21, 1833, p. 3, c. 3.

www.ingramcontent.com/pod-product-compliance
Lightning Source LLC
Chambersburg PA
CBHW051632230426
43669CB00013B/2267